The War against Animals

Critical Animal Studies

VOLUME 3

The titles published in this series are listed at *brill.com/cast*

The War against Animals

By

Dinesh Joseph Wadiwel

BRILL
RODOPI

LEIDEN | BOSTON

Cover illustration: Courtesy of Jo-Anne McArthur/We Animals.

Library of Congress Cataloging-in-Publication Data

Wadiwel, Dinesh Joseph.
  The war against animals / by Dinesh Joseph Wadiwel.
    pages cm. -- (Critical animal studies ; volume 3)
  Includes index.
  ISBN 978-90-04-30041-5 (pbk. : alk. paper) -- ISBN 978-90-04-30042-2 (e-book) 1. Human-animal
relationships--Moral and ethical aspects. 2. Speciesism. I. Title.

  QL85.W33 2015
  179'.3--dc23

                    2015019147

This publication has been typeset in the multilingual "Brill" typeface. With over 5,100 characters covering
Latin, IPA, Greek, and Cyrillic, this typeface is especially suitable for use in the humanities.
For more information, please see www.brill.com/brill-typeface.

ISSN 2212-4950
ISBN 978-90-04-30041-5 (paperback)
ISBN 978-90-04-30042-2 (e-book)

Printed by Printforce, the Netherlands

Contents

Acknowledgments   VII
Foreword   IX
   Matthew Calarco
Introduction: The Live Hang   1

PART 1
Biopolitics

1 Bare Life   65
2 Governmentality   97

PART 2
Conquest

3 Immunity   127
4 Property and Commodity   147

PART 3
Private Dominion

5 Privatisation and Containment   177
6 Companionship   202

PART 4
Sovereignty

7 Capability   223
8 The Violence of Stupidity   252

   Conclusion: Truce   273
   Index   297

Acknowledgments

This work is the culmination of a long trajectory of research, beginning initially with an essay entitled "Cows and Sovereignty" in the then new political theory journal *Borderlands e-Journal* in 2002. Along the way there have been too many people who have contributed to the current shape of this work, including many anonymous reviewers who have read my writing over this period; as such, I doubt I could ever produce an exhaustive list here to acknowledge all who contributed. However, and in no particular order, I would like to acknowledge the following scholars for important contributions and conversations at varying stage of this work: Fleur Ramsay, Meta Etcetera, Deirdre Tedmanson, Richard Twine, Jacqueline Dalziell, Matthew Calarco, Tom Tyler, Chloë Taylor, Thomas Viola Rieske, Zoë Sofoulis, Penny Rossiter, Paul Alberts, Brett Neilson, Fiona Nicoll, Gaia Giuliani, Joseph Pugliese, Goldie Osuri, Maria Giannacopoulos, Suvendrini Perera, Fiona Probyn-Rapsey, Jessica Ison, Angela Mitropoulos, Anat Pick, Robert McKay, Krithika Srinivasan, Melanie Rock, Christiane Bailey, Zakiyyah Iman Jackson, Matthew Chrulew, Kiran Grewal, Danielle Celermajer, Jasbir K. Puar, Darius Rejali, Claire Jean Kim, Fahim Amir, Jan Dutkiewicz, Alastair Hunt, Hilal Sezgin, Lara Polombo, Sue Donaldson and Will Kymlicka. I thank Vasile Stanescu and Helena Pedersen for their tireless efforts in supporting the development of this book from initial proposal to completed manuscript, as well as the anonymous reviewers who contributed to shaping this work. I also thank John Mahony for his sharp editing on the final manuscript. I have been particularly gifted to have enjoyed the personal support, friendship and love from many of these intellectuals for many years, and for this I am immensely grateful. All scholars work amidst a personal network of support, acknowledged or otherwise. In this regard I would like to particularly acknowledge and thank Mary Wadiwel, Julianne Elliott, Graham Meintjes, Jessica Robyn Cadwallader and Rhiannon Galla.

There are numerous parts of this book that feature sections which have been published elsewhere and are reproduced here with kind permission: Dinesh Joseph Wadiwel, "Cows and Sovereignty: Biopower and Animal Life," *Borderlands e-Journal,* 1.2, 2002; Dinesh Joseph Wadiwel, "Animal By Any Other Name: Patterson and Agamben Discuss Animal (and Human) Life," *Borderlands e-Journal,* 3.1, 2004; Dinesh Joseph Wadiwel, "Three Fragments from a Biopolitical History of Animals: Questions of Body, Soul, and the Body Politic in Homer, Plato, and Aristotle," *Journal for Critical Animal Studies,* 6.1, 2008, 17–31; Dinesh Joseph Wadiwel, "The War Against Animals: Domination, Law and Sovereignty," *Griffith Law Review,* 18.2, 2009, 283–297; Dinesh Joseph

Wadiwel, "A Human Right To Stupidity," *Borderlands e-Journal*, 9.3, 2010; Dinesh Joseph Wadiwel, "Zoopolis," *Dialogue*, 52.2, 2013; Dinesh Joseph Wadiwel, "Il capro di Guida. Una rilettura governamentalità di Foucault," *Animal Studies: Revista Italiana di Antispecismo*, 2.4, 2013; and Dinesh Joseph Wadiwel, "The Will for Self Preservation: Locke and Derrida on Dominion, Property and Animals," *Substance*, 43.2, 2014.

This work is wholeheartedly dedicated to Jinder Romana Elliott-Wadiwel.

Foreword

Matthew Calarco

The overarching theme of Dinesh Wadiwel's important book is that human-animal relationships and interactions should be understood as taking place in the context of a recurrent and sustained human war against animals. This thesis will no doubt seem counter-intuitive to many readers, as (no doubt some will initially object) most human interactions with animals are arguably peaceful or at the very least neutral and non-instrumental in nature. As Wadiwel demonstrates, however, this appearance of peaceful human-animal interactions—even when true in particular instances—is fundamentally ideological. The war against animals that he describes here goes essentially unnoticed and unremarked inasmuch as it forms the deep background against which human interactions with animals occur. It is an exceedingly violent and remorseless war, one from which members of the dominant culture are largely shielded. The various means that are used to occlude this war from sight—from advertising and media images, to the architecture and geography of industrial animal production, to the laws and discourses that shape our understanding of animals—encourage us to believe that violence toward animals is the exception when, in fact, that exception has become the ubiquitous rule.

Wadiwel explains this violent state of affairs with regard to animals in terms of a politics of *sovereignty*, a concept that refers to a set of practices, institutions, and discourses aimed at preserving human domination and rule over animals. In approaching violence toward animals in explicitly political terms, Wadiwel is effectively seeking to shift pro-animal discourse away from its over-emphasis on explaining animal violence as being primarily a consequence of personal ethical failings and irrational prejudice. While Wadiwel acknowledges the importance of individual ethical transformation in view of human-animal interactions, his approach suggests that the most important avenues for pursuing justice for animals are not to be found in an ethics of personal purity. Instead, his work points us toward trying to understand and contest the structural and institutional means whereby violence toward animals is enacted and maintained.

One of the major advances of Wadiwel's book is his careful unfolding of the precise nature and functioning of human political sovereignty over animals. What he accomplishes along these lines is significant, inasmuch as the vast majority of frameworks we have for understanding violence and war overlook animals altogether and remain inter- and intra-human in scope. Such is the case even with the sophisticated contemporary discourse surrounding Foucauldian biopolitics (one of our most useful frameworks for deciphering the machinations of modern sovereignty), which focuses on the ways in which power functions not just negatively through death and repression but productively through fostering life and shaping conduct in human affairs. Wadiwel intervenes in this biopolitical discourse and argues that, in order to be complete, biopolitics must take account of the ways in which sovereignty is founded on the regulation, control, and shaping of both human *and* non-human/animal life. What is more, he demonstrates convincingly that many of the apparatuses and technologies of governmentality that are used to shape human conduct have their origins in the controlling of animal life.

The chief means whereby the biopolitical war against animals is codified and secured, according to Wadiwel, is by placing animals in the legal and economic category of property. Reduced to the status of property, animals reside in a space that effectively renders them *sacred* (in Giorgio Agamben's sense of the term), that is, subject to being killed with impunity. Whether animals are in fact killed or are welcomed into our homes as pets does not displace the logic of sovereignty; rather, both modes of treatment are simply alternative faces of the same sovereignty. In other words, human sovereignty and property relations frame and structure nearly all of our relations with animals, from the most hostile to the most pacific. If Wadiwel's analysis is correct here—and I would suggest that it is—then those of us who are animal advocates will have to rethink much of the work being done in critical animal studies. We will have to think more carefully about the ways in which relational ontologies based on such concepts as "companion species" unwittingly participate in and reinforce human sovereignty and property relations. And we will also have to think more critically about the ways in which attempts to include certain animals within the moral and political community have been secured through the furthering of human dominion and exclusion of other (marginalized) human and more-than-human beings of various sorts. In brief, then, Wadiwel's argument is asking us to rethink pro-animal discourse from the ground up in view of the ways we might have been unsuspectingly furthering the war against animals.

Wadiwel indicates a path beyond human sovereignty with his insightful reworking of the notions of *counter-conduct* and *truce*. If sovereignty and governmentality are modes of shaping conduct, then counter-conduct and reconstitution of subjectivities become necessary as modes of resistance. In view of animal issues, Wadiwel proposes that veganism can be understood as such a mode of counter-conduct, insofar as it is carried out beyond asceticism and toward an impassioned disruption of the systems of animal violence. Similarly, with the notion of a truce in the war against animals, Wadiwel argues that the point of seeking a temporary disarmament is to call our attention to the systemic violence of this war and to find ways to displace that violence in various ways. When politics is reconceived in this post-sovereign manner, a wide range of possible alliances with other struggles against sovereignty opens up; and one of the most promising aspects of Wadiwel's approach is that it shows us the path along which animal advocacy can move beyond the asceticism of personal purity and toward becoming a mature struggle for justice in solidarity with other radical and transformational movements.

Although, as I mentioned at the outset, the vast majority of Wadiwel's book is dedicated to what might be properly termed political concerns, it is clear that his critical analysis of sovereignty and the war against animals is seeking to provide the opening for another kind of animal ethics as well. If an ethics beyond human sovereignty is to be developed, it must not be pursued starting from premises that seek to demonstrate that "animals are like us." Instead, following Wadiwel's suggestion, we need to think ethics starting from responsiveness to *animals themselves*, to the ways in which animals exceed and contest the machinations of sovereignty to which they have been subjected. Wadiwel here joins other voices in the growing discourse on animal agency, which seeks to show that animals are not merely moral patients on the receiving end of moral consideration. Instead, they should be seen, this emerging discourse argues, as active agents capable of their own modes of resistance and agency. What Wadiwel's text gives us to think is that animal agency and alterity need not be located only in heroic acts of resistance. Instead, traces and reminders of animal agency are to be found everywhere that the war against animals is carried out—for it is the apparatuses of war themselves that testify to the fact that animals *are subjected* to sovereignty and thus exceed its machinations. It is through carefully and responsively attending to these excesses that Wadiwel helps us to catch sight of another animal ethics and the manifold animal sovereignties that lie beyond human sovereignty.

Introduction: The Live Hang

> Though bullets and cannon balls were not whistling here on the road along which he was going, still he saw here on all sides the same sights as on the field of battle. There were everywhere the same suffering, exhausted, and sometimes strangely indifferent faces; everywhere the same blood and soldiers' overcoats, the same sound of firing at a distance, yet still rousing the same horror.
>
> LEO TOLSTOY, *War and Peace*[1]

An essential feature of contemporary industrialised chicken slaughter is the use of a "live hang." Chickens arrive at processing plants, packed tightly into crates. Workers open the crates, seizing the live chickens one by one by their legs, and hanging them upside down on fast moving conveyor hangers. The birds will then proceed swiftly through the next stages of the mechanical process of their transformation from living being into dead meat. The birds will be led through an electrical water bath which is designed to stun them into senselessness, their necks will be cut, they will be bled, and then their bodies will be scalded in defeathering tanks.[2]

The smooth, seamless operation of the conveyor system enables large numbers of live birds to be "processed" quickly. Some systems are capable of killing and transforming more than 1000 birds per hour into food. The speed and precision of death, and the intricate breeding and containment facilities that precede the slaughter machines, guarantee a seemingly limitless supply, feeding a voracious human demand for chicken meat. The speed of industrialised killing helps us to understand how it is possible for chickens within the "animal industrial complex"[3] to be one of the most prolifically slaughtered land species on earth.[4] Technologies in this case have facilitated killing on a scale that defies imagination. The Food and Agriculture Organization of the

---

1   Leo Tolstoy. *War and Peace.* New York: The Modern Library, 1994. 959.

2   See Annie Potts. *Chicken.* London: Reaktion Books, 2012. 166–9.

3   See Barbara Noske. *Beyond Boundaries: Humans and Animals.* Montreal: Black Rose Books, 1997. For a discussion of this phrase, see Richard Twine. "Revealing the 'Animal-Industrial Complex'—A Concept & Method for Critical Animal Studies?" *Journal for Critical Animal Studies.* 10.1 (2012). 12–39. See also Richard Twine. *Animals as Biotechnology: Ethics, Sustainability and Critical Animal Studies.* London: Routledge/Earthscan. 2010.

4   Almost certainly there may be single fish species killed in a more voluminous manner; the lack of data makes this difficult to establish with certainty.

United Nations estimates that approximately 55 billion chickens were slaughtered in 2010 for food.[5]

The "live hang" is far from a painless process for chickens; the velocity of the operation makes the potential for suffering more extreme. Birds will sustain injuries and pain, and because of the speed of the process, many birds will be incorrectly hung (for example, suspended by one rather than two legs). Some birds will not be stunned in the electrical water bath. As a result, they will then either experience neck cutting while conscious or, worse (if their necks are not properly cut and they are not killed), will be boiled alive in the scalding tanks. Annie Potts reminds us that in the UK, "up to 50 birds an hour are conscious when their throats are cut, and up to 9 in 1,000 birds survive the blade and perish in scalding tanks."[6] Regardless of what sort of death the birds face, the machine rolls smoothly on.[7]

Through all of this, the mechanised process of death aims to put down the resistance of birds to their own torment and eventual extermination. The birds struggle, they flap, they bite. The pace of the killing operations will mean that human workers will need to work quickly to keep up, and potential handling related injury is a risk. Slaughter-line chickens inflict damage upon human workers as they "scratch, peck and defecate all over them."[8] Inevitably some birds arrive in crates already dead or seriously injured: these birds will meet their death regardless (many are still hung, to be processed with other "meat"). Some birds are thrown aside to be disposed of later; in some cases, cruel or insensible workers will tread on or beat birds prior to hanging.

The technologies of death are simple, yet diabolical. The live hang is utilised to nullify any possibility of escape for birds who are "correctly" hung. The hangers (or "shackles") are designed to prevent release, by clasping the birds around the hock joint and limiting escape regardless of how vigorously the chickens attempt to work against their capture. The physical dimensions of the birds' own feet will work against them in this regard, since the hangers are designed to use the chickens' own body parts as a means of imprisonment.[9] As Elaine Scarry observes in her famous study of torture, the most effective and simple

---

5   Food and Agriculture Organization of the United Nations, *FAOSTAT*. 2010 data. At: www.faostat.fao.org/.

6   Potts. *Chicken*. 168.

7   From Franz Kafka.: "these days the machine no longer manages to squeeze out of the condemned man a groan stronger than the felt is capable of smothering." See Franz Kafka. "In the Penal Colony." *Metamorphosis, A Hunger Artist, In the Penal Colony and Other Stories*. Arlington: Richer Resources Publications, 2007. 87.

8   Public Justice Centre. *The Disposable Workforce: A Worker's Perspective*. Washington D.C. 1992.

9   Another diabolical piece of equipment used in small scale chicken slaughter is the "kill cone." The bird is dangled upside down into an inverted steel cone. Gravity does the work here: the

torture techniques will use the prisoner's body against themselves.[10] Surely, something similar is occurring here in the design of chicken hanger: the feet of the chickens, which had prior to this point provided elevation, stability and mobility to the bird, become weapons against the self when the birds are wedged into the hangers by their feet, and the dimensions of the chicken's own feet will prevent any escape from the death that is impending.[11] However, perhaps like any life form faced with its end, the entrapped birds will resist the death to come; a desire to preserve the self will remain until the end. The chickens will flap their wings and lift their heads; some will avoid the stunning baths by exerting their strength to elevate themselves above the water, only to be later confronted in full consciousness by the blade or, worse, to experience the scalding bath with full sensibility intact. At all points in this horrific—yet terrifyingly everyday—machinery, an intimate story of conflict and resistance, struggle and restraint, is being told: between the chickens and their forms of containment, the workers in the live hang, and the limits of the chickens' own body, as they are finally propelled towards the inescapable abyss of death.

War against Animals

In this book, I treat our systems of violence towards animals precisely as constituting a war. I am certainly not the first to imagine human violence towards animals as warlike. Animal advocates, for example, have frequently described human violence towards non human life as "a war on animals" as part of their

---

bird's head and neck will protrude downwards from the hole at the base of the cone, allowing the cutter to perform the killing operation.

10   Thus, if we are forced into "standing positions"—for example, when made to stand for hours on end with arms extended—our own body will betray us, as a simple pose becomes, as the minutes extend into hours, excruciating. Scarry states that "this unseen sense of self-betrayal in pain, objectified in forced confession, is also objectified in forced exercises that make the prisoner's body an *active* agent, an actual cause of pain." See Elaine Scarry. *The Body in Pain: The Making and Unmaking of the World.* New York: Oxford University Press, 1985. 47. In this regard, see Darius Rejali's discussion of positional torture, particularly the use and development of the *shabeh* technique. See Darius Rejali. *Torture and Democracy.* Princeton: Princeton University Press, 2007. 354–7.

11   As Noske observes: "its body often is the very cause of the animal's misery. Perhaps we can speak of the body as 'an alien and hostile power confronting the animal'? The body which makes up an important part of the animal 'self' used to be steered largely by the animal itself but now has become like a machine in the hands of management and is actually working against the animal's own interests." Noske. *Beyond Boundaries.* 18.

campaigning.[12] The philosopher Jacques Derrida, in his late work, identified the Western philosophical tradition as tied to a hostility against animals, remarking that the "Cartesianism belongs, beneath its mechanicist indifference, to the Judeo-Christiano-Islamic tradition of a war against the animal, of a sacrificial war that is as old as Genesis."[13] Similarly, Jonathan Safran Foer has framed industrialised meat production as a war: "We have waged war, or rather let a war be waged, against all of the animals we eat. This war is new and has a name: factory farming."[14] This book seeks to extend these intuitions to present a theoretical argument for how we might conceptualise our primary relationship with animals as being a war.

I concede, however, that there are challenges to understanding our relationships with animals as comprising a "war." We might conventionally understand war as involving an armed contest between two opposing sides, aimed at out-damaging an opposition.[15] This view of war would emphasise an active process

---

12   See, for example, People for the Ethical Treatment of Animals. "Oliver Stone Says, 'End the War on Animals.'" URL: www.peta.org/features/oliver-stone-says-end-the-war-on-animals.aspx. Steve Best has also recently associated with the phrase. See Steve Best. "The War Against Animals." *International Animal Rights Conference.* Luxembourg 2012.

13   Derrida. *The Animal That Therefore I Am.* New York: Fordham University Press, 2008. 101. Derrida goes on to state:

> And that war is not just one means of applying technoscience to the animal in the absence of another possible or foreseeable means; no, that violence or war has until now been constitutive of the project or of the very possibility of techno-scientific knowledge within the process of humanization or of the appropriation of man by man, including its most highly developed ethical or religious forms. No ethical or sentimental nobility must be allowed to conceal from us that violence, and acknowledged forms of ecologism or vegetarianism are insufficient to bring it to an end, however more worthy they be than what they oppose" (101). Earlier in the book, Derrida refers to a need to "situate the present" in an "unequal struggle, a war" between "on the one hand those who violate not only animal life but even and also this sentiment of compassion, and, on the other hand, those who appeal for an irrefutable testimony to this pity... War is waged over the matter of pity. This war is probably ageless but, and here is my hypothesis, it is passing through a critical phase... To think the war we find ourselves waging is not only a duty, a responsibility, an obligation, it is also a necessity, a constraint that, like it or not, directly or indirectly, no one can escape (29).

14   Jonathan Safran Foer. *Eating Animals.* New York: Little, Brown and Company, 2009. 33. Foer goes on to state: "If we are not given the option to live without violence, we are given the choice to center our meals around harvest or slaughter, husbandry or war. We have chosen slaughter. We have chosen war. That's the truest version of our story of eating animals."

15   This would certainly conform to the definition that is offered by Elaine Scarry in her *Body in Pain*: war is when two sides seek to out-injure each other.

by oppositional combatants to dominate each other, assuming a reciprocal intentionality to attack an enemy (even if at least one of the combative opponents does not initiate war). Armies, we might imagine, hatefully pick up weapons and, whether by force of circumstance or through desire for conquest, enact a mass form of violence with winner takes all stakes. However, this picture of war is not clear cut nor definitive of all combat. If anything, the twentieth century has demonstrated the difficulty of clearly defining war in terms of imagined opposing combatants. At least on one level, from the twentieth century onwards, war was increasingly waged against *non* combatants; that is, civilians. Not only were civilians more and more the targets of armed force, whether in international or civil conflicts, but there was also an increasingly blurred set of thresholds between civilian and combatant, as the guerrilla, insurgent and terrorist bore the marks of indistinguishability from the citizen. We might also note that war in the twentieth century and beyond underwent a number of innovations in form, so that we can no longer clearly conjure an image of war as comprising two armies facing each other in a field of battle. Rather, it is not clear where the battlefield starts and where it ends, when war is declared, and when peace is declared to end hostilities. Guerrilla warfare and State terrorism seamlessly blended the war zone and civil political space. War by "remote" is increasingly commonplace, as missile and drone warfare replaces frontline armed combat between opposing forces. War can be "hot" or "cold" (and every variation in between), and States can be in an ever present readiness for war, even if formal conflict with an identified enemy has not, or may never, begin. So much so that, for many parts of the world, war and States of emergency are a seemingly endless main event within civil and political affairs.[16] These endless variations in what war looks like provide an opportunity to re-understand how war as a concept might be redeployed in different contexts, particularly beyond the human theatre. That is, in the case of this book, how war might provide an illustrative and productive description of our relationship with animals.

There is material evidence that we might use to construct this case for understanding our relationship with animals as primarily hostile. The scale by which we kill and harm animals would seem to confirm that our mainstay

---

16   Referring to post World War One Europe, Hannah Arendt comments: "Nothing perhaps illustrates the general disintegration of political life better than this vague, pervasive hatred of everybody and everything, without a focus for its passionate attention, with nobody to make responsible for the state of affairs—neither the government nor the bourgeoisie nor an outside power." Hannah Arendt. *The Origins of Totalitarianism.* Orlando: Harvest, 1976. 268.

relationship with animals is combative or at least focused upon producing harm and death. Factory farming and industrialised slaughter technologies, for example, enable a monstrous deployment of violence and extermination. The scale of death defies imagination. One conservative estimate is that worldwide over 60 billion land animals are killed annually for food.[17] Since these figures do not include sea animals killed for human use, they do not illustrate the full scale of death.[18] Aside from food production and experimentation, animals are subject to torment and death in order to satisfy human recreational pursuits, in hunting, sport fishing, circuses, racing, bullfighting and rodeos. A United States based NGO estimates that approximately 200 million animals are killed every year through hunting in the United States alone.[19] Other animals are subject to experimentation for medical research, product trials, psychological study or military testing, and subject to intensive forms of confinement, chemical exposure, physical trauma and death within experimentation facilities.[20]

---

17   Sourced from the Food and Agriculture Organization of the United Nations. 2010 data, see Food and Agriculture Organisation of the United Nations, FAOSTAT. This informs us that more than 63 billion (63,303,649,624) land animals were killed in 2010, including 55,334,057,000 chickens, 425,947,124 goats, 1,375,216,728 pigs and 537,791,052 sheep. These figures do not include sea animals killed for food during this period, nor animals who die as a result of human utilisation for food (such as eggs or dairy) or recreation. The UN figures are necessarily conservative.

18   There remains a lack of data to accurately estimate the number of marine animals killed for human consumption. The United States non government organisation, ADAPTT, estimates that 90 billion marine animals are killed each year, based on US consumption rate estimates. See ADAPTT. "More than 150 Billion Animals Slaughtered Every Year." ADAPTT website. At: www.adaptt.org/killcounter.html. However the numbers are potentially substantially higher: one report estimates that over 1 trillion (up to 2.7 trillion) fish are caught annually. See Alison Mood. *Worse Things Happen at Sea: The Welfare of Wild-Caught Fish.* fishcount.org.uk. 2010. At: www.fishcount.org.uk/published/standard/fishcountfullrptSR.pdf.

19   In Defence of Animals. "Hunting: Facts." *In Defense of Animals* Website. At: http://www. idausa.org/campaigns/wild-free2/habitats-campaign/anti-hunting/. Hunting is perhaps the most openly "pleasurable" expression of joy in killing animals: Garry Marvin states that:
      the hunter commits himself or herself intensely and fully to the visceral and emotional pleasures of hunting. This is not utilitarian work but a passionate pursuit in which the animal is sacrificed to the pleasure of that passion.
      See Garry Marvin. "Wild Killing: Contesting the Animal in Hunting." The Animal Studies Group. *Killing Animals.* Urbana and Chicago: University of Illinois Press, 2006. 25.

20   Although some forms of cruelty to some animals are forbidden by law, other forms of violence are tolerated; indeed openly permitted. In Australia, for example, the *New South Wales Crimes Act 1900,* provides an offence for a person who "tortures," "beats" or "kills" an animal (Section 530(1)), yet provides an exception for animals used in research, "routine

We should not forget that human encroachment of non human habitats, through the spread of industrialisation and global human economies, has meant and continues to mean suffering and death for many animals. The effect of pollution and loss of food supplies have seen species extinction and immeasurable injury and death for non human life. Human activities have an impact on all life: for non human animal life this impact has been devastating. Certainly, taking this grim picture into account, it seems reasonable to suggest that if this mass-scale injury and death is systematic and directed, then perhaps it conforms to an understanding of "war."

Objections might be anticipated at this point. Perhaps foremost here is the objection that describing our relationship with animals as fundamentally about war runs against the grain of emerging theory in animal studies which stresses a "relational" rather than "conflictual" approach to analysing human relationships with animals. Donna Haraway, for example, as I shall discuss in Chapter 6, argues against a "radical language of animal rights" and its universal problematisation of slaughter, in favour of an approach that recognises that humans and animals engage in relations that involve "coshaping one another in layers of reciprocating complexity all the way down."[21] I do recognise that totalising categories, perhaps as found in traditional animal rights theory, do nobody any favours in attempting to detail intricate multidirectional power relationships or challenge simplistic constructions of agency. I don't believe, however, that a relational perspective need be incompatible with a contextual argument that applies a normative view to human utilisation and slaughter. Relational approaches can be adapted to take into account systems of violence and the way in which ethics might be formed by context and situation. Clare Palmer, for example, uses a relational approach to argue that moral duties are generated through proximity, interaction and spheres of human contact and intervention, offering an argument for why we might have differing moral obligations between domestic animals, wild animals, and animals we have historical and/or present interaction with.[22] Importantly Palmer offers a nuanced

---

agricultural or animal husbandry activities, recognised religious practices, the extermination of pest animals or veterinary practice" (Section 530(2)(b)). In other words, it would appear that cruelty is permitted treatment for most animals in regular contact with humans.

21 Donna J. Haraway. *When Species Meet*. Minneapolis: University of Minnesota Press, 2008. 42.

22 Clare Palmer. *Animal Ethics in Context*. Columbia: Columbia University Press, 2010. 7. Palmer states her approach might explain why we might have "no moral obligation to prevent the migrating wildebeest from drowning in the Mara River, even if that would bring about a better state of affairs in the world, but that those who allowed the Amersham horses to suffer and starve were indeed behaving in a way that was morally reprehensible."

and careful account which problematises industrialised forms of slaughter and violence, while suggesting that some practices, including hunting for food, may not represent the same level of harm.[23]

Understanding fundamental conflict and the role of violence in shaping relationships is also important in comprehending the way in which power interacts with hierarchised difference and systems of truth. Perhaps of relevance here is Kelly Oliver's discussion of human/animal difference in *Animal Lessons*.[24] Drawing connections between feminist discussion of sexual difference and animal studies articulations between human and animal, and pointing out Derrida's problematisation of conceiving difference as a binary rather than multiplicity, Oliver asks:

> Why is sexual difference marked and then reduced to a binary or primary difference between two? How is the distinction between two conceived as opposition or even war? Finally how can we open the field to multiple unaccountable differences and unlock the stranglehold of two warring opponents?[25]

At first take, Oliver's observations would appear to go against the grain of the argument I present in Chapter 5: namely, that the radical feminist discussion of sexual violence as functioning within the context of patriarchy as a "war against women" might very well—at least in my view—be a useful way to conceptualise our war against animals. I believe, however, the approach I describe in this book is not antagonistic to the relational approach put forward by Oliver. As I argue in the Conclusion, the spaces of "truce" that we must construct are necessarily relational; moving beyond the war on animals surely means developing new forms of connection, friendship, topography, love and living-together that have been previously unimaginable, and, as a result, lead to reconstruction of the human/animal binary in ways which might recognise

---

For a Foucaldian/relational analysis, see also Clare A. Palmer. "'Taming the Wild Profusion of Existing Things?': A Study of Foucault" *Environmental Ethics*. 23.494, 2001. 339–58.

23   See Palmer. *Animal Ethics in Context*. 117–19.

24   See Kelly Oliver. *Animal Lessons: How They Teach Us to Be Human*. New York: Columbia University Press, 2009, particularly 131–51. See also Kelly Oliver. "Sexual Difference, Animal Difference: Derrida and Difference 'Worthy of its Name.'" *Hypatia*. 24.2, 2009.

25   Oliver. *Animal Lessons*. 134. Oliver discusses Derrida's observations on the German word *Geschlecht* pointing out the way in which it accounts for both animal human difference and sexual difference: "it names a splitting in two that sets two sides apart and figures them as opposites or one as the negation of the other, making the duality essentially dissension, war and violence" (134).

multiple non hierarchised difference.[26] However, my sense is that there remains the difficult task of attending to the violence that is present today, and understanding how this violence constructs the terms of our relations and, simultaneously, the way we understand and position the "opponents" that are assembled by this binary themselves. As I discuss in Chapter 5, sexual violence—as a taken for granted everyday form of hostility—both maintains patriarchal relations and constructs gender roles. In this sense it appears reasonable to understand sexual violence against women as a war, a war that maintains male domination against women, and simultaneously articulates a binary between "man" and "woman" as normative gender constructions. Sexual violence does *not* explain everything about gender role construction or gender power relations (for example, the effects that normative gender construction, tied to interpersonal, legal and social violence, have for trans people); however, persistent violence, supported and allied by State power which reproduces systems of subordination and domination—a war—must be accounted for in any description of the way in which gender interacts with subjectivity and social position. There is an equally persuasive argument for understanding the way in which mass orchestrated violence against animals both maintains systems of human domination and, simultaneously, constructs epistemologically how we understand the "animal" as a discursive category that is opposed and subordinated to the "human." In this sense, as I argue in Chapter 6 with reference to Haraway's *When Species Meets*, acknowledging the way in which humans and animals "co-shape" each other, even in "significantly unfree" relationships, does not mean we can easily side-step the question of violence, and the way in which large scale forms of violence create and reproduce systems of domination and enable constructions of truth. As I discuss below, there is a challenge in dealing with the *epistemic violence* of the construction of human superiority, and this task should seek to address the binary constructions of human/animal, reason/nature, knowledge/instinct, superior/inferior and other hierarchical forms of differentiation. This task must be situated within the battlefield of the ever present, everyday

---

26   Karl Steel states:

>   the human tries to distinguish itself from other animals by laying claim to the sole possession of reflective language, reason, culture, and above all an immortal soul and resurrectable body; it lays claim to these qualities for itself, and itself only, through acts of violence against others that, by routinely suffering this violence, are designated 'animal'; because the category of the human is a retroactive and relative effect of the action of domination, no such human can do without the domination of animals without abandoning itself.

See Karl Steel. *How to Make a Human: Animals and Violence in the Middle Ages*. Columbus: Ohio State University Press, 2011. 21.

violence that characterises many of our relations with animals; a war with measurable effects in suffering and death for billions.

Some may also object that violence against animals, particularly in the case of industrialised slaughter or animal experimentation, does not conform to war in the usual sense, since animals cannot be reasonably said to "resist" their domination. It might be argued that since these forms of domination seem overwhelmingly one-sided and oriented to nullify escape, then there is no possibility of interaction, response or "politics." This is the view put forward by Palmer in an example of a cat that has been strapped and bound so that movement is impossible. Palmer, following a Foucauldian approach, argues that there is no means for the cat to react or respond to human interaction (including acts of violence such as a kick): "There is no relationship; no possibility for it to be a being who reacts. All spontaneity and almost all communication is removed from our brutal encounter. Thus it cannot be a power *relationship*."[27] I would suggest, on the contrary, that the question of resistance seems complex and worth reconsidering here. In the example I presented above of chicken slaughter, it seems difficult to avoid the way in which animal resistance (even if this resistance is "futile") plays a part in the process of slaughter. This whole process is one of struggle; a struggle between life forms, which seeks to bend the lives (and deaths) of chickens to human utility. Although it might be easy to imagine animals as passive in this process—as restrained bodies hung on processing lines to be fabricated into meat—the reality involves a more intense and intimate engagement in a violent power relation, in which humans and machines "struggle" against chickens who would prefer not to die. This is a two-way process in which animals are instrumentalised, but are not passive. Tim Ingold reminds us that violence always aims to put down resistance; technologies of violence would not be used if the objects of violence were not sentient, autonomous and evaded capture and utilisation in the first place:

> Consider the slave-driver, whip in hand, compelling his slave to toil through the brute infliction of severe pain. Clearly the autonomy of the slave in this situation to act according to his own volition is very serious curtailed. Does this mean that the slave responds in a purely mechanical way to the stroke of the whip? Far from it. For when we speak of the

---

27   Palmer. "Taming the Wild Profusion of Existing Things?" 354. See also Jonathan L. Clark on animal resistance in Jonathan L. Clark. "Labourers or Lab Tools? Rethinking the Role of Lab Animals in Clinical Trials." Nik Taylor and Richard Twine Eds. *The Rise of Critical Animal Studies: From Margins to Centre*. London and New York: Routledge, 2014. 139–164.

application of force in this kind of situation, we impute to the recipient powers of resistance—powers which the infliction of pain is specifically intended to break down. That is to say, the use of force is predicated on the assumption that the slave is a being with the capacity to act and suffer, and in that sense a person. And when we say that the master *causes* the slave to work, the causation is personal, not mechanical: it lies in the social relation between master and slave, which is clearly one of domination. In fact, the original connotation of 'force' was precisely that of action intentionally directed against the resistance of another sentient being.[28]

This reading of resistance treats technologies and agent interaction as formed and designed to counter and put down resistance of opponents, human or otherwise. This allows us to read even seemingly benign agent interaction and apparatuses as designed precisely to counter resistance. For example, in chicken slaughter, low light serves numerous functions, including stymieing resistance: "if chickens cannot easily see their flock mates being stunned they are less likely to struggle and incur an injury that would downgrade the carcass."[29] We find a similar situation in the corrals used to lead bovine to slaughter. Temple Grandin is famous for her animal corral designs with curved races.[30] The introduction of curves into the chutes that led cattle towards death minimised the possibility of an animal responding to the chute by balking and backing up.[31] These curved corrals should be understood precisely as

---

28 Tim Ingold. *The Perception of the Environment: Essays on Livelihood, Dwelling and Skill.* London and New York: Routledge, 2006. 73. Note the subtle shift between Gary Francione's baseline for moral community membership (that is, sentience) and Ingold's observation that sentience plus resistance to violence demonstrates a form of agency.

29 Potts. *Chicken.* 166.

30 See, for example, Temple Grandin. "Race System for Cattle Slaughter Plants with 1.5 m Radius Curves." *Applied Animal Behaviour Science.* 13, 1984/85. 295–99.

31 Grandin. "Race System for Cattle Slaughter Plants with 1.5 m Radius Curves." 295. For this reason, I would subtly disagree with the perspective put forward by Palmer in her essay, "Taming the Wild Profusion of Existing Things?", where she describes an absence of power in situations where there is no opportunity to resist. Naturally, if we follow a Foucauldian schema of force / resistance (at least in Foucault's earlier sense), then power is not present where there is no resistance. Palmer identifies:
    ...practices of such extreme violence/domination that animals have no opportunity to resist at all: where they are in the situation equivalent to Foucault's shackled slave. This includes direct violence to animal bodies where escape or resistance is not possible. Clearly such situations are commonplace for animals. Further, much of the time animals, not sharing human language, will not recognise that they are being threatened, or in what precise way they are being threatened, which may prevent

means of containing and dealing with resistances. The curves, which obscure from the sight of animals the impending death that awaits, operate simultaneously as a means of welfare and a means to lubricate resistance.[32] In the first sense, the curves protect animals from a vision of what is to come, and thus arguably reduce suffering. However, in the second interconnected sense, the curves are also there to subdue resistance and enable the effective and smooth process of slaughter, maximising human utilisation (and profit) value. In this regard, the approach taken in this book builds and enhances on emerging work in animal studies that seeks to identify and understand animal resistance, such as the work of Jason Hribal, which examines containment strategies, pain inducing devices such as whips, bodily modification and training as means to subdue resistance.[33] That humans need to constantly innovate to find ways to make the slaughter of animals smoother, more efficient and less "fricative," already suggests that the process of the instrumentalisation of animals for human use must squarely deal with the resistance of animals to that same use, often in such a way as to use animals and their own bodies against

---

them from exhibiting resistance, even if they were in principle able to respond in such a way.

See Palmer. "Taming the Wild Profusion of Existing Things?" 353.

I would note however, even in extreme cases of violence, there is a form of resistance, as sentient creatures are dragged kicking and screaming to their ends. The problem, as I discuss below, is partly epistemic. The knowledge/power relationship codes this violence as non political and devoid of resistance; as such, resistance is always epistemologically rendered as not violence. As a related, albeit separate observation, note Catharine MacKinnon's observations on the possibility of rendering the "truth" of women's resistance to male subordination:

> Both sexists and feminists have difficulty explaining women who resist, but for different reasons: the first because nonsubmission is so unnatural, the second because resistance is so expensive. Both solve this difficulty by envisioning women as victims. But where sexism sees woman and victim as tautologous, feminism conceives of woman and victim as contingent-upon enforced social subordination to men. Feminism relies upon the ultimate possibility of resistance, even though the feminist analysis of the crushing totality of subordination has difficulty accounting for it. Sexism relies upon its ultimate impossibility.

See Catharine A. MacKinnon. "Toward Feminist Jurisprudence." *Stanford Law Review.* 34.3, 1982. 703–37. 720.

32   In relation to lubrication, resistance and power, see my earlier essay: Dinesh Joseph Wadiwel. "Lubricative Power." *Theory and Event.* 12.4, 2009.

33   See Jason Hribal. "Animals Are Part of the Working Class": A Challenge to Labor History." *Labor History.* 44.4, 2003. 435–53. 448–50. And Jason Hribal. *Fear of the Animal Planet: The Hidden History of Animal Resistance.* Oakland: AK Press/Counter Punch Books, 2010.

themselves (as in the "shackle" used in industrialised chicken slaughter).[34] The final element of this process is *epistemic*. If violence can be smoothed in such a way that it does not appear as violence, then the process of converting an animate sentient being into a "thing"[35] is complete, and resistance and war become hidden under a veneer of peaceability; as Carol J. Adams has noted, meat in this process becomes separated from the living animal that was its original referent.[36] (Surely the tendency of industrialised slaughter to opacity, speed and apparent bloodlessness points to a desire for killing to happen without any trace of resistance?[37])

This view of resistance as generated, and working intimately against, systems of production is intended to tie closely with a conceptualisation of labour which sees "autonomous" resistance as central to systems of production.[38] In this view, systems of production and exchange, such as capitalism,

---

34   Upton Sinclair states:

> In these chutes the stream of animals was continuous; it was quite uncanny to watch them, pressing on to their fate, all unsuspicious a very river of death. Our friends were not poetical, and the sight suggested to them no metaphors of human destiny; they thought only of the wonderful efficiency of it all. The chutes into which the hogs went climbed high up—to the very top of the distant buildings; and Jokubas explained that the hogs went up by the power of their own legs, and then their weight carried them back through all the processes necessary to make them into pork.

    Upton Sinclair. *The Jungle*. Pennsylvania: The Pennsylvania State University, 2008. 37.

35   See discussion of "thingification" in Palmer. "Taming the Wild Profusion of Existing Things?" 358.

36   Carol J. Adams. *The Sexual Politics of Meat: A Feminist-Vegetarian Critical Theory*. New York: Continuum, 1990. 40.

37   With regard to this desire for a bloodless violence, see Jacques Derrida. "Force of Law. 'The Mystical Foundation of Authority.'" *Cardozo Law Review*. 11 (1990). 919–1045. 1044–45.

38   In my understanding of autonomism I am influenced by "operaist" applications of Marxist thought. For one summary of the operaist tendency, see Sandro Mezzadra. "Italy, Operaism and Post-Operaism." Immanuel Ness Ed. *International Encyclopedia of Revolution and Protest*. Oxford: Blackwell Publishing, 2009. 1841–45. I have been strongly influenced here by the work of Fahim Amir, who explores operaism as way to explain animal subordination in systems of production. See, for example, Fahim Amir. "Zooperaismus: 'Über den Tod hinaus leisteten die Schweine Widerstand...'" Presentation at *Critique of Political Zoology Conference*. Hamburg, June 14–15, 2013. For a discussion of the relationship of pigeons to the city, see also Fahim Amir. "1000 Tauben: Vom Folgen und Fliehen, Aneignen, Stören und Besetzen." *Eurozine*. May 2013. First published in *dérive* 51 (2013). The final lines read: "Wo es Stadt gibt, da gibt es auch Stadttauben. Und wo es Stadttauben gibt, da gibt es auch Widerstand." Where pigeons are present where cities are present, and where this interaction occurs, there is resistance to the actions by cities to quell the presence of pigeons. See also Agnieszka Kowalczyk. "Mapping Non-Human Resistance in the Age of

parasitically[39] feed upon the productive capacities and creativity of the bodies that labour within these systems. Capitalism thus always moves to capture the productivity of those bodies through modes of disciplinarity and subordination. In this reading, extreme forms of domination that appear to lack resistance are in fact the product of active forms of creative resistance by those who are subordinated, a resistance that is subsequently coopted by capitalism as a new mode of production. Thus, for example, as Michael Hardt and Antonio Negri argue, new flexibilities in workplace arrangements that characterise post-Fordist production (flexible work hours, work from home arrangements, teleworking etc.) are the result of capitalism adapting to the resistance of workers to Fordist modes of disciplined production: it is because workers actively dropped out of labour through absenteeism, through cultural experimentation against the imposition of work, through everyday resistances and sabotage, that capitalism needed to adapt and re-mould work itself in order to maintain productivity.[40]

We might equally apply this view to understanding the technology of animal containment, breeding and slaughter. Consider again the curved corral. This architectural solution adapts itself to the autonomy of animals themselves, working with the decisions made by animals within a horizonal narrowing space (the chute leading to slaughter), rather than against. Bodies are moulded by production, and production moulded almost symbiotically by bodies into exchange.[41] As such, at each moment at which friction threatens to slow the process of killing, when forms of animal agency might reveal resistance to the process of slaughter, industrialised production systems shift to

---

Biocapital." Nik Taylor and Richard Twine Eds. *The Rise of Critical Animal Studies: From Margins to Centre*. London and New York: Routledge, 2014. 183–200.

39   See Noske's discussion of human domestication as a case of social parasitism. See Noske. *Beyond Boundaries*. 4–5. See also Michel Serres. *The Parasite*. Baltimore: John Hopkins University Press, 1982.

40   See Michael Hardt and Antoni Negri. *Empire*, Cambridge: Harvard University Press, 2000. 272–6.

41   Hardt and Negri state:

> The great industrial and financial powers thus produce not only commodities but also subjectivities. They produce agentic subjectivities within the biopolitical context: they produce needs, social relations, bodies, and minds-which is to say, they produce producers. In the biopolitical sphere, life is made to work for production and production is made to work for life. It is a great hive in which the queen bee continuously oversees production and reproduction. The deeper the analysis goes, the more it finds at increasing levels of intensity the interlinking assemblages of interactive relationships.

Hardt and Negri. *Empire*. 32.

enable enhanced productivity, simultaneously creating the illusion that animals are helping themselves to die. The parasitism of industrialised slaughter does not restrict itself merely to animal movement in the face of increasingly impermeable containment systems. The creativity of animals is exploited right down to the metabolic and generative capacities of the living organism. On one hand, as I will discuss below and in Chapter 1, the reproductive capacities of animals are central to the biopolitics of the whole animal industrial complex, since large scale killing requires equally large scale breeding. On the other hand, production processes will work with the vitality and processes of the living organism to capture every ounce of the creativity and energy produced in order to maximise profit. This capture might even work against the body in such a way as to lead to auto-destruction: Lori Gruen, for example, points out that "intensively reared dairy cows are so overworked that they begin to metabolize their own muscle in order to continue to produce milk."[42]

Production systems seek always to capture and utilise any productivity and creativity; bodies seek to evade capture and generate productivity that is surplus to production. In this sense, as I discuss in Chapter 4, my perspective here subtly reworks Barbara Noske's view that:

> the animals' natural capacity for movement, play, preening, social interaction and contact with the natural environment is almost felt to be subversive... Like the human worker's creativity it has to be kept under control, or better still, done away with.[43]

It is true that industrialised slaughter, containment and breeding systems must continually respond to animal resistance. But animal creativity is a source of profit; the drive for production systems will be to capture creative activity, including overt acts of resistance, in order to generate continually increased productivity.[44] To refer again to the curved coral leading animals to slaughter, its development relies upon animal intersubjectivity, coproductivity and agency; as Anna Williams observes, "these manufacturing devices all proceed

---

42   Lori Gruen. "The Faces of Animal Oppression." Ann Ferguson and Mechthild Nagel Eds. *Dancing with Iris: Between Phenomenology and the Body Politic in the Political Philosophy of Iris Marion Young.* Oxford: Oxford University Press, 2009. 161–72. 162.

43   Noske. *Beyond Boundaries.* 15.

44   Indeed, as Noske notes, domestication of animals such as sheep, goats and bovine precisely relied upon the creativity of these animals to generate social connectivity: "the reason why humans could domesticate them in the first place has got a great deal to do with their high degree of sociality." Noske. *Beyond Boundaries.* 17–18.

from an understanding of the animal as a subject whose sentient engagement with the world can be recruited to assist production by manipulating the environment."[45] The genealogy of the war against animals is one of continual adaption and reworking of systems of domination to most effectively capture the agency, escape and vitality of animals and simultaneously maximise human use value. The façade this process projects is one of seamlessness; absence of hostility; no friction.

In this book I have been attracted by the characterisation of war that is offered by the military theorist, Carl von Clausewitz. Early in his treatise *On War*, Clausewitz provides the simple prescription that war is *"an act of violence to compel our opponent to fulfil our will."*[46] Clausewitz's description facilitates an understanding of war as a phenomenon of mass or corporate organised violence that aims at total domination.[47] This view *avoids* limiting the concept

---

45   Anna Williams. "Disciplining Animals: Sentience, Production, and Critique." *International Journal of Sociology and Social Policy*. 24.9, 2004. 45–57. 52.

46   Carl Von Clausewitz. *On War*. In public domain. Project Gutenberg. 15.

47   A definition such as this is not without difference of opinion. Some may object that war requires at least two collectives, and preferably two nation States, who are involved in some form of conflict. Certainly Brian Orend's entry in the *Stanford Encyclopedia of Philosophy* seems to conform to this:

> War should be understood as an actual, intentional and widespread armed conflict between political communities. Thus, fisticuffs between individual persons do not count as a war, nor does a gang fight, nor does a feud on the order of the Hatfields versus the McCoys. War is a phenomenon which occurs only between political communities, defined as those entities which either are states or intend to become states (in order to allow for civil war).

See Brian Orend. "War." *Stanford Encyclopedia of Philosophy*. At: www.plato.stanford.edu/entries/war/.

Roger Scruton has advanced a view that seems less prescriptive: "war is centrally a state of affairs in which two or more corporate entities, at least one of them politically organized, are disposed to fight collectively, and where the decision to fight arises, at least on one side, through the process of government, and not from some private faction or feud." See Roger Scruton. "Notes on the Sociology of War." *The British Journal of Sociology*. 38.3, 1987. 295–309. 301. Although Scruton's definition lacks a political and social context, and unnecessarily constructs a private/public distinction in the decisionality around war, it does not contain any necessary prescription on what combatants to war look like, nor how war should be conducted. Although Scruton intends "government" to be in some way reflective of a collective process for political decision making, we might equally treat this in a Foucauldian sense, as a rationality for organising conduct. Scruton's argument should be read in context with Martin Shaw's response, and Scruton's subsequent reply. See Martin Shaw "The Real Sociology of War: A Reply to Roger Scruton." *The British Journal of Sociology*. 39.4, 1988. 615–618; and Roger Scruton. "Reply to Martin Shaw." *The British Journal of Sociology*. 39.4, 1988. 619–623.

of war to an engagement that is intentionally fought between two armed combative (human) opponents.[48] What is also useful about this prescription is that it is not contaminated by a conflation between *object* and *means*. When we concentrate on the object of war—violence aimed at compelling an opponent to fulfill our will—then the means (armies, weapons, declarations etc.) are secondary. Understanding the object of war as domination—a way in which to bend an opponent's will in conformity to one's own—offers us a way to frame our instrumental relations with animals in the context of a wider, more systemic, violent relationality.[49]

---

48   Regardless, it would seem that the need for a broader definition of war—one that goes beyond simply defining war as a contest between two armies—itself highlights the poverty of available language, at least in English, for describing large scale organised violence that has the all intensity of war, yet lacks clearly demarcated combatants.

49   This certainly does not mean that the *means* for war are not relevant, rather that we must always seek to capture how means and ends engage with each other. An important element in Clausewitz's definition is precisely this interaction of the object of war—that is, to compel an opponent to be bound to our will—and the means used to attain this object (namely, violence). Indeed the nature of this interaction is that means and ends oscillate between each other: means will take the place of ends, while the primary object—submission of an enemy to our will—will be lost. Thus Clausewitz observes:

Violence arms itself with the inventions of Art and Science in order to contend against violence. Self-imposed restrictions, almost imperceptible and hardly worth mentioning, termed usages of International Law, accompany it without essentially impairing its power. Violence, that is to say physical force (for there is no moral force without the conception of states and law), is therefore the *means*; the compulsory submission of the enemy to our will is the ultimate *object*. In order to attain this object fully, the enemy must be disarmed; and this is, correctly speaking, the real aim of hostilities in theory. It takes the place of the final object, and puts it aside in a manner as something not properly belonging to war.

Clausewitz. *On War*.15.

This dynamic of the exchanges between means and ends is worth taking note of. While war seeks as its object submission of an opponent to a combatant's will, the action of war is about a violent means that *disarm* an enemy. The means to achieve this end are an ever-present distraction. The technology of violence, and the law surrounding its conduct, in the midst of this interplay, will appear itself to be tied to the exercise of violence, affecting its characteristics, and obscuring the object. As a result, discussion of war will centre upon questions in relation to means: What level of violence is appropriate and proportionate? What technologies of violence will be agreed upon? How will non combatants be treated? And are non violent means possible to achieve the same end? All these features are present in contemporary human-to-human conflicts, where technology, resource demands, law and international moral force interact to determine what sort of violence or intervention will occur, their timing and intensity. However, as Clausewitz

War was clearly influential during a period of transition in Michel Foucault's thinking between the publication of *Discipline and Punish*, and his later works on sexuality and government. These thoughts are made available in a 1975–6 series of lectures, published in English under the title *Society Must Be Defended*.[50] Here Foucault's starting point is Clausewitz's aphorism "war is

---

observes, the primary aim of war—that is submission of an opponent to our will—remains intact, even if it is an apparently hidden dimension.

The applicability of this understanding of war, as a mobile interaction between the "purity" of ends and the "reality" of means is immediately applicable to violence against animals. We live in a world where violence towards animals is configured as non violence, and where forms of violence are rendered as *beneficent*. It is certainly notable that animal welfare discussions frequently enact this sort of distraction, where the means of violence, organised around an economy of determining lines between necessary and unnecessary suffering, obfuscate from view a primary object, namely, domination of non human animals in the name of human utility. Thus discussions on cage dimensions for battery hens, "environmental enrichment" for laboratory rats, and even stunning techniques prior to slaughter, will take precedence within animal welfare discussions, leaving to the side the pressing question of why we are at war in the first place, and is it justifiable. War and politics have an intimate relationship with each other: one substitutes for the other, and each hides the other's objectives. The challenge for analysis is locating the primary objective in our relationships. This means when we consider something like the industrialised slaughter of chickens, we must consider each processing plant as just one battlefield within a wider war; each chicken hung a minor skirmish. That is, we must look for war precisely where it is discursively coded as "peace."

50   Michel Foucault. *Society Must Be Defended: Lectures at the College de France*, 1975–76. London: Penguin Books, 2004. See also Michel Foucault. "Two Lectures." Colin Gordon Ed. *Power / Knowledge: Selected Interviews & Other Writings 1972–1977*. New York: Pantheon Books, 1980 and Michel Foucault. *The Will to Knowledge: The History of Sexuality: 1.* London: Penguin Books, 1998. I note that this book sits within an emerging field of Foucault scholarship, interrogating the philosopher's work and its potential application to thinking about animals. Notable (but non exhaustive) works within this field include: Richard Twine. *Animals as Biotechnology*; Matthew Cole. "From 'Animal Machines' to 'Happy Meat'? Foucault's Ideas of Disciplinary and Pastoral Power Applied to 'Animal-Centred' Welfare Discourse." *Animals*. 1.1, 2011.83–101; Lewis Holloway and Carol Morris. "Exploring biopower in the regulation of farm animal bodies: genetic policy interventions in UK livestock." *Genomics, Society and Policy*. 3.2, 2007. 82–98; Clare Palmer. "Taming the wild profusion of existing things?"; Chloë Taylor. "Foucault and the Ethics of Eating." *Foucault Studies*. 9, 2010. 71–88; and Matthew Chrulew. "Managing Love and Death at the Zoo: The Biopolitics of Endangered Species Preservation," *Australian Humanities Review*. 50, May 2011. At: www.australianhumanitiesreview.org/archive/Issue-May-2011/chrulew. html. An example summary of this emerging critical field of scholarship is Chloë Taylor. "Foucault and Critical Animal Studies: Genealogies of Agricultural Power." *Philosophy Compass*. 8.6, 2013. 539–51.

policy pursued by other means." Foucault inverts Clausewitz in his own rendering of the statement as: "politics is war pursued by other means." This forces an understanding of politics as war under a different guise, and simultaneously offers a challenge to a tradition of political theory—such as that presented by social contract perspectives—that would see the civil political space as offering a salvation from the ravages of open hostility between warring parties:

> War is the motor behind institutions and order. In the smallest of its cogs, peace is waging a secret war. To put it another way, we have to interpret the war that is going on beneath peace; peace itself is a coded war. We are therefore at war with one another; a battlefront runs through the whole of society, continuously and permanently, and it is this battlefront that puts us all on one side or the other. There is no such thing as a neutral subject. We are all inevitably someone's adversary.[51]

If civil peaceable relations are the means by which war is enfolded within a new set of relations, then sovereign law becomes a means by which continuing domination is encoded: the methodology by which it is possible to continue forms of domination that would otherwise be openly expressed in war. Foucault notes that sovereignty is founded upon a continuing victory in war, and an accompanying right to inflict death that follows this victory. If a sovereign nation is defeated by another, Foucault observes:

> The vanquished are at the disposal of the victors. In other words the victors can kill them. If they kill them, the problem obviously goes away: the

---

51   Foucault. *Society Must Be Defended.* 50–1. In an interview Foucault clarifies the problematic:

> This is the problem I now find myself confronting. As soon as one endeavours to detach power with its techniques and procedures from the form of law within which it has been theoretically confined up until now, one is driven to ask this basic question: isn't power simply a form of warlike domination? Shouldn't one therefore conceive all problems of power in terms of relations of war? Isn't power a sort of generalised war which assumes at particular moments the forms of peace and the State? Peace would then be a form of war, and the State a means of waging it.

See Michel Foucault. "Truth and Power." Colin Gordon Ed. *Power / Knowledge: Selected Interviews & Other Writings 1972–1977.* New York: Pantheon Books, 1980. 109–33. 123. Note that here Foucault repeats in a different guise Clausewitz's demarcation between ends and means in war; once we separate ends from means in war, a different problematic opens up, where means must be interpreted towards a set end, namely, domination.

Sovereignty of the State disappears simply because the individuals who make up that State are dead. But what happens if the victors spare the lives of the vanquished? If they spare their lives...are granted the temporary privilege of life... [they] ...agree to work for and obey the others, to surrender their land to the victors, to pay them taxes. It is therefore not the defeat that leads to the brutal establishment of a society based upon domination, slavery, and servitude; ... It is fear, the renunciation of fear, and the renunciation of the risk of death. The will to prefer life to death; that is what founds sovereignty.[52]

Sovereignty from this perspective becomes a means to enforce forms of domination that emanates from the right of death held by the sovereign, and the avoidance of death by those who submit to the violence of law: "the will to prefer life to death; that is what founds sovereignty."

The term *sovereignty* usually implies a mandated system of authority, rule or control that provides a nodal point for the organisation of political and social relations. Contemporary understandings of sovereignty are in many ways coloured by the Western—distinctly Hobbesian—conception: namely, the perceived right of a monarch or delegated authority to make a singular, unifying claim to territory and life within a particular domain, and to both organise and exercise legitimised violence. This framework for sovereign power casts a shadow over other possible forms of geo-political organisation, and increasingly we observe that variations of this model of sovereignty are extending their reach into every territorial and biological region of this planet.[53] The contemporary nation State—which is legitimised through the sovereign right—embodies many of the generic principles which defined the rule of the Western sovereigns of old: centralised decision making; a prerogative to lay claim to resources within borders; the fixture (or conversely removal) of populations within territorial domains of power; a monopoly exercised over the mechanisms of violence; and the power to legitimise its own violent acts. However, there is certainly a large degree of scholarly discussion that suggests that sovereignty is evolving from this traditional conceptualisation. For example, it has been noted that "globalisation"—the process by which capital, markets, governments and authorities, and particular peoples have re-situated themselves within an emerging international perspective[54]—raises questions for how we

---

52   Foucault. *Society Must Be Defended*. 95.

53   See Hardt, and Negri. *Empire*.

54   Or to borrow from Jacques Derrida, "a geopolitical process of a becoming-worldwide." See Jacques Derrida. *Politics of Friendship*. London: Verso, 2000. 302.

think about sovereign power. As Hardt and Negri emphasise, the restructuring of nation States which has accompanied this process of globalisation has not spelled the end of sovereignty, but, on the contrary, has forced a re-negotiation of the terms of its power.[55] In a different vein, scholars articulating Indigenous sovereignty, have argued not only for recognition of sovereignty claims within settler colonial societies, but left open the question of what this sovereignty might look like, suggesting indeed that there is a significant capacity to re-imagine sovereignties, including through forms of co-existence and an ample ability to imagine sovereign pluralities.[56]

In this book, I offer a reconceptualisation of sovereignty, arguing that it might be understood as a mode of human domination of animals. In the Judeo-Christian religious tradition, there is a *Genesis* narrative of God granting dominion to "man" over the other animals. Certainly, as I shall discuss in Chapter 4, this is a central and important facet for how John Locke develops his theory of property (at least, as I shall argue, in Locke's innovative reworking of what this dominion may look like). It is also no accident that thinkers interested in animal welfare put store in an assumption that humans have some sort of right of dominion over "creation," whether as guardians of animals, evolutionary "high cards" which have earned the right to dominate through biological superiority,[57] self-appointed custodians over territory, or simply the ones who must decide in a situation of exception. John Webster sums this attitude up perfectly in his *Animal Welfare* when he states succinctly: "Man has

---

55   See Hardt and Negri. *Empire*.

56   In Australia, for example, Irene Watson has suggested:

> against the view that Aboriginal sovereignty is no more than a 'wet dream' is one of an Aboriginal law which lives, and one which cannot be extinguished, for the law lives in this land—a fact, a belief, a way of knowing the world that is still alive and waiting that 'impossible' moment of recognition and activation.

See Irene Watson. "Aboriginal Sovereignties: Past, Present and Future (Im)Possibilities." Suvendrini Perera Ed. *Our Patch: Enacting Australian Sovereignty Post-2001*. Perth: Network Books, 2007, 23–43. 28. See also Irene Watson, "Aboriginal Laws and the Sovereignty of Terra Nullius" *Borderlands e-Journal*. 1:2, 2002. At: http://www.borderlands.net.au/vol1no2_2002/watson_laws.html.

See also Paul Keal. "Indigenous Sovereignty." Trudy Jacobsen, Charles Sampford and Ramesh Thakur Eds. *Re-Envisioning Sovereignty: The End of Westphalia?* Aldershot: Ashgate, 2008. 315–30.

57   Lewis Petrinovich puts forward an evolutionary argument for human utilisation of animals, arguing that "when push comes to shove, the interests of members of our species should triumph over comparable interests of members of other species." See Lewis Petrinovich. *Darwinian Dominion: Animal Welfare and Human Interests*. Cambridge: The MIT Press, 1999. 3.

dominion over the animals whether we like it or not."[58] Leaving aside for the moment whether this presumed inherited sovereignty over animals—"whether we like it or not"—is self evident or is justifiable (indeed, as ecofeminist scholars such as Val Plumwood have noted, our assumed mastery must be challenged[59]) we might note this standpoint has a powerful effect in determining the ethics of our relationship with animals. Once we assume we have a right of dominion, then it would seem that ethics is forced to attend to questions of how we use this dominion; that is, how we use animals, rather than whether we should use them in the first place. In other words, ethics becomes a question of how to manage or regulate the effects of our own self proclaimed dominion. It is thus no accident that Webster begins with the "problem" of dominion as a means to construct a case for welfare; dominion is assumed to be an inescapable fact, and our only course of action, "whether we like it or not," is to moderate the effect of our position. As a result, as I shall outline below, this creates a problem that when we consider our relationship to animals, sovereignty appears to *precede* ethics. It is a problem because ethics constructed after sovereignty works only to regulate or mitigate the violent effects of that sovereignty, while leaving the basic structure of domination intact. This result, in other words, is *welfare*. We might then understand welfare as precisely an "ethical" action that is limited or governed by a sovereign prerogative for continuing utilisation. We offer welfare to those we have dominion over, and wish to continue to dominate for our own benefit, but have the freedom to provide forms of limited consideration that do not temper our dominion right (captured perfectly in that diabolical phrase "unnecessary suffering"[60]).

Gary Francione has provided a useful analysis of the way in which welfare considerations spring from human use value for animals as property.[61] However, I would extend Francione further here, to argue that we need to interrogate the way in which *sovereignty* is anchored to human positionality, not through just a property right, but through an overarching system of domination that both encompasses and exceeds animals as property. This does not mean that property is unimportant. As I discuss in Chapters 3 and 4, property

58   John Webster. *Animal Welfare: A Cool Eye Towards Eden*. Oxford: Blackwell, 1994. 3.

59   See Val Plumwood. *Feminism and the Mastery of Nature*. London and New York: Routledge, 1993. See particularly "Conclusion: Changing the Master Story," 190–6. See also Val Plumwood. *Environmental Culture: The Ecological Crisis of Reason*. London and New York: Routledge, 2002, particularly 97–122.

60   In this context, see Stephen R.L. Clark On "necessary suffering" in Stephen R.L. Clark. *The Moral Status of Animals*. Oxford: Clarendon Press, 1977, 42–45.

61   Gary Francione, *Animals, Property and the Law*. Philadelphia: Temple University Press, 2007.

in animals is an articulation for a human victory in appropriation that establishes sovereign rights. In this sense, we need to understand a claimed human sovereign right of dominion over animals as setting in train a set of relationships. These relationalities articulate over and over again human freedoms that rely upon the continuing *unfreedom* of animals. These freedoms are *securitised* through institutional and epistemic forces, including legalised violence. Thus, the property rights established in animals merely "insure" or underwrite a human claim of freedom which requires the unfreedom of animals as its guarantee. Freedom in this sense is not connected to equality; on the contrary, it conveys the opposite sense; in Foucault's words "freedom is the ability to deprive others of their freedom."[62] This in turn enshrines a chain of legitimation that guarantees a continual pleasure for the victors in war; a freedom of unending satisfaction, pleasure for some won through the suffering of others:

> the freedom enjoyed...was essentially the freedom of egoism, of greed—a taste for battle, conquest and plunder. The freedom of these warriors is not the freedom of tolerance and equality for all; it is the freedom that can be exercised only through domination.[63]

In other words, sovereignty, at least in the form I am identifying here, guarantees an unending flow of pleasures, laying in place an almost absurd economy of greed that can only be secured through the life and death domination of total defeat. It is no coincidence, as I shall discuss in Chapter 8, that Derrida also takes note of this tendency for hyperbole and excess within sovereignty: "the majesty of the absurd in so far as it bears witness to the human."[64] Human sovereignty over animals is characterised by excess beyond proportionality.

Foucault's conceptualisation of war and sovereignty offers us a way to understand how it is that mass orchestrated violence is seamlessly integrated within civil political spaces in an imperceptible way, and the inherent resistance of institutions of violence to change, since change potentially threatens a rupture to the continual excess of human claimed rights and pleasures (the spoils of war). This mass violence exerted towards animals is frequently shielded in such a way as to not disrupt our apparent peaceable relations: large scale slaughter, experimentation and grand and petty apartheids all occur as daily events, yet appear as indistinguishable from the background noise of

62   Foucault. *Society Must Be Defended*. 157.
63   Foucault. *Society Must Be Defended*. 148.
64   Jacques Derrida. *The Beast and the Sovereign Vol. 1*. Chicago: University of Chicago Press, 2009. 230, [D307].

everyday life. As Timothy Pachirat points out in his brilliant *Every Twelve Seconds*, this is in part a question of topographical organisation, with violence against animals contained to zones of exception and segmented in such a way to conceal its operations, even from workers themselves who are intimately involved in the slaughter process.[65] As I have argued in Chapter 5, the organisation of this "gulag archipelago" might be conceptualised as comprising an interconnected set of containers of violence, with stratified modes of delegated sovereignty regulating micro spheres that stretch across almost all modes of human existence, encompassing heterogeneous scenes of domination, from animals in the dock in a slaughterhouse, rats in cages in experimental labs, to dogs at the ends of leashes in suburban backyards. War, in this case, operates as a coordinated and legitimised web of contained violences, which linked with a massive organisation of death and reproduction, enables a continuous, precise and unrelenting effort to quell resistance. War is thus almost perfectly internalised as a mode of sovereignty which bends the will of animals to our own.

Biopolitics

I argue in this book that the nature of our war against animals is distinctly *biopolitical*. Michel Foucault described biopolitics as a shift away from a directly coercive model of power focused upon the acquisition of territory and resources, towards a rationality that attends to populations and life. Foucault marks this shift in the *History of Sexuality* with the now famous summary that "the ancient right to *take* life or *let* live was replaced by a power to *foster* life or *disallow* it to the point of death."[66] Here Foucault suggests that political discourse is increasingly directed towards a concern for the nature of *life*, its vicissitudes, its requirements, its essence: "For millennia, man remained what he was for Aristotle: a living animal, with the additional capacity for a political existence; modern man is an animal whose politics places his existence as a living being in question."[67] Perhaps the easiest way to think about biopolitics is by understanding the way in which sovereign power—that is, in this instance, sovereign rule by humans over other humans—has evolved in the modern period. Where sovereignty was traditionally understood as a brute exercise in domination by the sword, often with the aim of accumulating resources and

---

65   Timothy Pachirat. *Every Twelve Seconds: Industrialized Slaughter and the Politics of Sight.* New Haven: Yale University Press, 2011.

66   Michel Foucault. *The Will to Knowledge: The History of Sexuality: 1.* 138.

67   Foucault. *The Will to Knowledge: The History of Sexuality: 1.* 143.

capturing territory, Foucault would suggest that increasingly modern sovereignty is shaped by biopolitical rationalities that direct attention towards managing the biological life of (human) populations who had previously only been
a secondary concern. Government fosters the lives of populations through the
deployment of resources for education and training, public health, the facilitation of relationships and organisations, fertility and "family" planning, the
management of the economy, and generalised financial wellbeing. As such
politics itself is attentive to the functioning of the human as an organism on an
individual and collective level. Foucault states:

> Western man was gradually learning what it meant to be a living species
> in a living world, to have a body, conditions of existence, probabilities of
> life, and individual and collective welfare, forces that could be modified,
> and a space in which they could be distributed in an optimal manner.[68]

Whilst many of these programs and initiatives may actually benefit, and
enhance, the existence of particular populations, we cannot assume that sovereign biopolitics is merely concerned with what has been called the "fostering
of life." For, as Foucault suggests, the power to foster life is connected to a more
insidious arm of sovereign power: namely, the power to "disallow it [life] to the
point of death."[69] In other words, we must keep in mind that biopolitical sovereignty is about *both* life and death. This has been highlighted by a number of
recent thinkers on sovereignty including Giorgio Agamben, Roberto Esposito
and Achille Mbembe (all three of whom I examine in this book). Agamben in
his now famous study *Homo Sacer*, draws attention to the *foundational* relationship between the Foucauldian concept of biopolitics and political sovereignty, and its implicit link to violence and exclusion. Agamben differs from
Foucault on biopolitics in two identifiable ways. Firstly, Agamben treats biopolitics as a concept fundamental to the whole Western political tradition
(rather than as a recent development): in Agamben's words, "Western politics
is a biopolitics from the very beginning."[70] Secondly, as I shall discuss in detail
in Chapter 1, Agamben understands biopolitics explicitly as an ongoing form
of differentiation between human and animal. This continual re-expression of
the fuzzy human animal distinction defines biopower, in so far as biopolitics is
not merely politics attuned to questions of life and population, but in essence,

---

68   Foucault. *The Will to Knowledge: The History of Sexuality: 1*. 142.
69   Foucault. *The Will to Knowledge: The History of Sexuality: 1*. 138.
70   Giorgio Agamben. *Homo Sacer: Sovereign Power and Bare Life*. Stanford: Stanford
      University Press. 1998. 181.

at least in Agamben's reading, politics itself becomes concerned with the violent articulation of the borders between the human and the animal. In Agamben's words, "the decisive political conflict, which governs every other conflict, is that between the animality and the humanity of man. That is to say, in its origin Western politics is also biopolitics."[71] We can certainly summarise here that biopolitics according to both Agamben and Foucault is precisely located at the point or threshold between human and animal; biopolitics is almost, as it were, "the productive" effect of the tension between human and animal. If we take seriously the manifest and extraordinary forms of violence that institutionally rearticulate the differentiation between human and animal, Western politics, in other words, expresses the fact of war between human and animal life.

Sovereignty remains important within this understanding of biopolitics. As I have stated above, sovereignty is tied to the biopolitical *caesura*—a pause or a break—that divides between populations on species, race, gender, ability or other grounds. Following Foucault, sovereignty is a means to internalise war within social relations; biopolitics a description for the dividing lines that are drawn between populations. Law, institutions and knowledges reproduce these dividing lines, by fostering lives while simultaneously allowing others to diminish, and deploying technologies of care and violence. In this sense, I do not wholly agree with the view put forward by Cary Wolfe that biopolitics involves a distancing from sovereignty towards a politics of biological bodies.[72] This view might accord if we treat sovereignty as merely implying the (human) State, with demarcated territories of control and a codified legal order. However, as I discuss in Chapter 8, with reference to Derrida's *The Beast and the Sovereign* lectures, sovereignty need not be confined to the State and a

---

71   Giorgio Agamben. *The Open: Man and Animal.* Stanford: Stanford University Press, 2004. 80.

72   Wolfe distinguishes between the biopolitics of Agamben and that of Foucault, arguing that the latter argues for a shift away from the "domain of legal codes and sanctions" towards a power addressed at the body, with a "growing need, in an increasingly complex and differentiated field of operation, for the various techniques of management, surveillance, and so on." See Cary Wolfe. *Before the Law: Human and Other Animals in a Biopolitical Frame.* Chicago: Chicago University Press, 2012. 31. Wolfe thus argues against Agamben's reading of biopolitics as essentially tied to and, determined by, sovereignty (see 24). Wolfe states:

> This compels us, then, to firmly distinguish between biopolitics in its declension towards sovereignty as constitutive and biopolitics as a relation of bodies, forces, technologies, and *dispositifs* which, *by definition*, could entail no such formal symmetry between sovereignty and bare life of the sort we find in Agamben (and, as it turns out, in Badiou and Žižek) (33).

codified legal order. Sovereignty can be characterised as a mode of domination that auto-legitimises not only its own force but its own rationality. Sovereignty in this understanding is neither distinctly something humans alone are capable of, nor does it necessarily or essentially hold particular attachments to the State, or territory. It is for this reason that we can apply sovereignty aptly to understand human domination of animals, since under this sovereign order rationality follows violence as a form of claimed superiority. Humans declare themselves exceptionally intelligent, but only after they have prevailed over other animals with violence. As such, biopolitics, sovereignty and knowledge are linked. If biopolitics expresses a contestation between human and animal, this war can only take place within the context of a sovereign order that seeks to reproduce this conflict, and an authorising system of rationality and truth that tells us that violence against animals is either justifiable or, at its most diabolical, a knowledge system that denies that this violence is occurring. In this sense, sovereignty seems far from occupying a "subordinated" position with respect to biopolitics[73]; on the contrary, sovereignty is tied to the production of biopolitical contestation, and as I shall discuss below, the production of knowledge and epistemic violence are also equal participants in this power relay.

Beyond this conceptual framing of biopolitics, war sovereignty and truth, we might take note of the very clear articulation of human violence towards animals as a biopolitical violence *par excellence*. Our relations with animals appear as biopolitical in an almost archetypal way, in so far as they perfectly and efficiently use violence to locate an exact line between life and death. To take just one example here, it seems clear that industrialised slaughter (making death) is interdependent upon industrialised reproduction (making life). The more animals we kill for food, the more we need to breed; the faster we kill animals, the faster we need to breed them. In Australia the 5 million pigs that are killed annually for human consumption are the product of approximately 320,000 perpetually pregnant sows, who spend their lives within a small enclosure not much bigger than themselves, giving birth to piglets who are only destined for the chopping block.[74] In other words, industrialised slaughter—the power to make die—also relies on an attendant ability to bring to life—a power to make live.[75] Life and death on this scale requires advanced techniques of

---

73 See Wolfe. *Before the Law*. 24.

74 Malcolm Caulfield. "The Law and Pig Farming." *Reform*. 91, 2007–08. 25. See also Noske. *Beyond Boundaries*. 17.

75 See Dinesh Joseph Wadiwel. "Cows and Sovereignty: Biopower and Animal Life." *Borderlands e-Journal*, 1.2 (2002).

   At: www.borderlands.net.au/vol1no2_2002/wadiwel_cows.html.

biological control to enable a gargantuan slaughter machine to function. Animal industries need to scrupulously monitor and regulate nutrition, movement, sociality, sexuality, location and reproductive capacity in order to efficiently produce meat: life itself, the vicissitudes of life in the biological organism, the creativity and productivity of life, become the focus of parasitic control mechanisms. As I discuss in Chapter 1, the techniques of animal control and utilisation that are everyday in industrialised farming and slaughter conform absolutely to how we might conceptualise a violent biopolitics. Indeed, as I discuss with respect to "governmentality" (Chapter 2), and as Wolfe has emphasised in his *Before the Law*, biopolitical human violence towards animals tells us something about human violence towards other humans: biopolitical techniques of control and violence towards animals seem likely to have informed, and continue to be intertwined with, human practices of violence towards other humans.

Pulling together the threads that Foucault and Agamben have provided, we might begin to construct a framework with which to comprehend the war against animals. Firstly, we might note that if the civil political space is founded upon the exclusion of the animal, this same space is a historical reminder of the continuing victory of an ongoing and perhaps originary conflict between humans and animals; the war from which our conceptualisation of the political sphere may be said to have originated; a conflict that correlates with the distinction between civilisation and nature, culture and biology; a war that is also foundationally rooted in the mythology of Western sovereignty; the war which, to take from Plumwood, "has been the master story of Western culture."[76] The civil political sphere is founded upon a primary exclusion of non human life, which in turn continually generates violent divisions between human and animal both within and without the political sphere.

Secondly, the civil political space requires the sublimation of hostility and aggression into forms of apparent civil peace-ability, where war is carried out by other means. The civil political space thus hides forms of intense domination of animal life, through apparatuses that do not, at least on the outside, betray the form of war. As I discuss in Chapter 6, we might find evidence for this, for example, in the legalised controls that are inherent to dog ownership in the West, with expansive powers of regulation available to the State and pet owners on how domestic animals are to be kept, attendant with a range of legal measures, from the compulsory implantation of surveillance technologies, to controls over movement, to the categorisation and segregation of certain classified dogs, to reproductive controls and death for other dogs. In this form, the

---

76   Plumwood. *Feminism and the Mastery of Nature.* 196.

law functions to enable violent forms of subjection and control under the guise of "companionship"; violence and death quite literally enacted in the name of friendship.

Thirdly, we might observe that the law aims to establish a covenant of continuing freedom and plunder for the victors of war: an unending flow of pleasures, an economy of greed. We eat, hunt, torture, incarcerate and kill animals because it is our sovereign right won from total victory; our sovereign pleasure. This perspective on the relationship of domination, politics and freedom to sovereignty might be a way to explain the blatant and horrific excesses of our war with animals. This is perhaps most viscerally evident in factory farm and industrialised slaughter processes, which have enabled death on a scale that has hitherto been completely unimaginable, so much so that the dull drone of incessant slaughter and injury appear as commonplace and almost impervious to critical attention. This might also be a way to explain the complete impotence of ethics, "humane" thinking, and the rights framework before these horrors. Victory in war leads to an intoxication of power that guarantees a total and unending defeat that is so complete that the fact of war becomes utterly imperceptible; a victory so absolute that it appears merely banal, lacking resistance, without politics.

Inter-subjective, Institutional and Epistemic Violence

The main challenges that have arrived to human violence towards animals have been articulated by moral philosophers who, using a range of different frameworks, have pointed out the ways in which our relationship with animals presents a logical inconsistency in relation to contemporary norms of ethical treatment and justice. However, as Sue Donaldson and Will Kymlicka have pointed out, and despite the efforts of the moral philosophers, opponents of animal use and killing remain confronted by a "political impasse," with little evidence of structural reform capable of fundamentally changing our pattern of human exploitation and violence towards animals: "for the foreseeable future, we can expect more and more animals every year to be bred, confined, tortured, exploited, and killed to satisfy human desires."[77] This is in part at least a result of the limits of addressing violence towards animals as a matter for

---

77   Sue Donaldson and Will Kymlicka. *Zoopolis: A Political Theory of Animal Rights*. Oxford: Oxford University Press, 2011. 2. I note three other recent publications within liberal political theory dealing with animals: Alasdair Cochrane. *An Introduction to Animals and Political Theory*. Houndsmills: Palgrave Macmillan, 2010; Siobhan O'Sullivan. *Animals,*

individual ethical choice. Our treatment of animals has often been understood as a moral/philosophical problem, rather than as a political problem which requires strategies to challenge the "institution of speciesism" as Wolfe identifies it.[78] This has arguably lead to tactical errors in responding to the magnitude of human violence towards animals. A frustrating element of this is the over-emphasis of individual actions as a strategy.[79] This has created a perception that the solution to widespread mass orchestrated violence against animals is for individuals to agree to individually withdraw themselves from this violence and act in morally consistent ways, as if *solely* individual decisions (for example to pursue a vegetarian or vegan lifestyle) have a significant impact upon large scale systems of domination. It is clear when we consider other forms of manifest, everyday, encompassing violences, for example patriarchy, that individual actions are only one element within a more deeply entrenched framework of power that continually positions bodies, their movement, and their access to resources. Asking men to desist from sexist behaviour certainly is an important element in dismantling patriarchy. But alone, this is not sufficient for addressing all the forms of violence that patriarchy enacts against women, forms of violence that operate across diverse fields including work, family, movement, space, sexuality and language. Asking men to desist from sexist behavior will not achieve a restructuring of family and home; it won't alone address the intense gender norms that govern movement, dress, utilisation of space; it won't gain equivalent wages for equal or similar work, it won't re-situate sexuality from a violent, normative and phallocentric constitution. Similarly, large scale acts of violence—such as war, terror, and genocide—clearly cannot be addressed solely upon the basis of individual ethics. Of course, it is true that personal decisions made in the context of large scale atrocity are important (the decision to or not to participate, for example). However it seems problematic to assert that preventing these forms of violence is simply down to changing lifestyles or attitudes. Rather, and as has been

---

       Equality and Democracy. Houndsmills: Palgrave Macmillan, 2011; and Robert Garner. *A Theory of Justice for Animals.* Oxford: Oxford UP, 2013.

78   Cary Wolfe. *Animal Rites: American Culture, the Discourse of Species, and Posthumanist Theory.* Chicago and London: The University of Chicago Press, 2003. See 6–7.

79   Donaldson and Kymlicka plainly comment: "Any theory that asks people to become moral saints is doomed to be politically ineffective, and it would be naïve to expect otherwise." See Donaldson and Kymlicka. *Zoopolis: A Political Theory of Animal Rights.* 253. Plumwood observes that "an over-emphasis on person conversion and vegetarian action resulting from neo-Cartesianism and rights theory means that other forms of popular political action, for example alliance politics, remain relatively under-developed and undertheorised." See Plumwood. *Environmental Culture.* 154.

the case when trying to understand large scale violence or atrocity, a stronger perception of the role of individual actions within the context of broad social and political factors—racism, economic distinction, history etc—is required.

The violence of the war against animals operates on an inter-subjective, institutional and epistemic level. We might make sense of this by drawing on the typology of violence that Johan Galtung provides in his influential "Violence, Peace and Peace Research."[80] Galtung divides between personal (I will term this "inter-subjective") violence and structural (I will term this "institutional") violence. Galtung divides between the two on the basis of agency and actors:

> We shall refer to the type of violence where there is an actor that commits the violence as personal or direct, and to violence where there is no such actor as structural or indirect. In both cases individuals may be killed or mutilated, hit or hurt in both senses of these words, and manipulated by means of stick or carrot strategies. But whereas in the first case these consequences can be traced back to concrete persons as actors, in the second case this is no longer meaningful. There may not be any person who directly harms another person in the structure. The violence is built into the structure and shows up as unequal power and consequently as unequal life chances.[81]

For our purposes, the division between violences is important in so far as it enables the possibility of understanding our treatment of animals within a society-wide context, where agency and action occur within intricate networks, and responsibility for violence is diffused, hidden and delegated. Within this view, responsibility for violence is manifold rather than individual. Humans can take responsibility in terms of their individual ethics to remove themselves from this violence; for example by adopting changed diets or changing their consumer preferences for animal based textiles. However, once we acknowledge the institutional or structural characteristic of our treatment of animals, it seems to be a self-deception to imagine that these same individuals do not continue to be beneficiaries of this violence, even where they desist from personally using animal products. To use myself as an example here, I practice veganism, however, I live in a nation (Australia) whose wealth and relative high per capita living standards have been won by force, not only

---

80   Johan Galtung. "Violence, Peace and Peace Research." *Journal of Peace Research* 6: 1969. 167–91. I thank Salvatore Balbones for drawing my attention to this essay.

81   Galtung. "Violence, Peace and Peace Research." 170–71.

through a history of colonialism and continuing economic imperialism (and
the racialised geopolitics that attends this), but also through extraordinary and
intense forms of animal exploitation and violence, which generate continuing
surpluses for killing "industries" in the production of beef, lamb, seafood, dairy
products and wool. My role as a contributor to the war against animals doesn't
end simply because I choose to remove myself directly from use of animal
products. I continue to enjoy the spoils of this ongoing plunder, regardless of
what food I choose to put in my mouth, or what shoes I choose to wear.[82]

Galtung also points out the way in which the division that he draws between
"personal" and "structural" violence corresponds to a politics of "visibility." The
nature of this split is that personal violence is seen, while structural violence is
hidden:

> it is not strange that attention has been focussed more on personal than
> on structural violence. Personal violence *shows*. The object of personal
> violence perceives the violence, usually, and may complain—the object
> of structural violence may be persuaded not to perceive this at all.
> Personal violence represents change and dynamism—not only ripples
> on waves, but waves on otherwise tranquil waters. Structural violence is
> silent, it does not show—it is essentially static, it is the tranquil waters. In
> a *static* society, personal violence will be registered, whereas structural
> violence may be seen as about as natural as the air around us.[83]

The visibility of personal or inter-subjective violence need not be normatively
defined as violence that is "seen" in a "material" sense, at least in my understanding. A strategy of "seeing" violence in a "material" sense (that is, by exposing structural violence as personal violence) appears to me to miss the nature
of institutional violence, which is hidden not because it isn't in sight, but

---

82   See Matthew Calarco's enlightening (albeit all too brief) discussion of vegetarianism and
      its limits as an ethical practice in contemporary industrialised societies in Matthew
      Calarco. *Zoographies: The Question of the Animal from Heidegger to Derrida*. New York:
      Columbia University Press, 2008. 133–6.

83   Galtung. "Violence, Peace and Peace Research." 173. Galtung observes that the stability of
      cessation of formal conflict creates the "dynamic" conditions for shifting focus from per-
      sonal violence to structural violence:

      > For this reason we would expect a focus on personal violence in after-war periods lest
      > they should become between war periods; and if the periods protracts sufficiently for
      > the major outburst of personal violence to be partly forgotten, we would expect a con-
      > centration on structural violence, provided the societies are dynamic enough to make
      > any stability stand out as somehow unnatural (174).

because our knowledge systems do not allow us to see this as violence. It is for this reason, that the proposals made by some animal advocates to expose the inner workings of slaughterhouses to the public (the assumption operating here is that individuals will be revolted by the sights of death and change their dietary preferences overnight) may miss the point on the nature of this violence. This seems to sidestep the very real possibility that humans may look on this violence and not see it as violence, in much the same way that many humans watch other forms of animal exploitation and violence, such as horse racing, without feelings of moral revulsion; indeed Pachirat discusses this very issue in the conclusion to *Every Twelve Seconds*.[84] The question here is *epistemic*, in so far as the act of violence, its recognition by perpetrator, recipient and witness is rendered visible by signification within the context of available knowledge systems. Simply put, we can only see violence towards animals when we can imagine and think this possible (both as violence and animals as authentic victims of violence).

Gayatri Chakravorty Spivak offers a way to conceptualise this epistemic violence in her essay "Can the Subaltern Speak?" Drawing from both Foucault and Edward Said, Spivak renders a concept of epistemic violence, referring to the role of intellectuals in crafting the Other discursively, and simultaneously creating the terms by which the Other can and cannot speak:

> in the constitution of that Other of Europe, great care was taken to obliterate the textual ingredients with which such a subject could cathect, could occupy (invest?) its itinerary—not only by ideological and scientific production, but also by the institution of law.[85]

While—at least within the terms laid out by Galtung—*inter-subjective* violence attacks the entity directly, while *institutional* violence determines the opportunities and outcomes for that same entity, *epistemic* violence determines the terms by which the subject (or its Other) can "know" itself, and speak about its own position, and determine its own possibilities through the domination and

---

84   See Pachirat. *Every Twelve Seconds*. 233–56. As such, I would question the firm link drawn between protections to animal welfare and visibility, as argued by scholars such as Siobhan O'Sullivan. Visibility is an important element to consider, but it must be considered in light of an understanding of the epistemological construction of violence as violence to be seen. See O'Sullivan. *Animals Equality and Democracy*.

85   Gayatri Chakravorty Spivak. "Can the Subaltern Speak?" C. Nelson and L. Grossberg Eds. *Marxism and the Interpretation of Culture*. Basingstoke: Macmillan Education, 1988. 271–313. 75.

rearticulation of knowledge systems.[86] And while Spivak insists that "the clear-est example of such epistemic violence is the remotely orchestrated, far flung and heterogeneous project to constitute the colonial subject as Other,"[87] it might be clear that the whole project of constituting "the animal" as the Other might serve as a clearer example. The epistemic violence of producing "the animal" as an inferior entity, and therefore susceptible to all guises of human utility—reproduced, extinguished, made captive, hunted, companionised, tor-tured and experimented upon—already indicates a monstrous endeavour of limiting any possibility of animal response and resistance to the process of domination. Perhaps a clear example of the epistemic violence that is part and parcel of the informational-knowledge component of our war on animals are the numerous words in English that transform animals into food—"beef," "pork," "veal," "seafood" etc.[88]—which completely hide from view the personal and structural violence that attends both material and symbolic production.[89] It is true that war against animals remains connected in some guises with the

---

86   See Said's discussion in *Orientalism*:

> The Oriental is irrational, depraved (fallen), childlike, 'different'; thus the European is rational, virtuous, mature, 'normal.' But the way of enlivening the relationship was everywhere to stress the fact that the Oriental lived in a different but thoroughly organized world of his own, a world with its own national, cultural and epistemologi-cal boundaries and principles of internal coherence. Yet what gave the Oriental's world its intelligibility and identity was not the result of his own efforts but rather the whole complex series of knowledge manipulations by which the Orient was identified by the West... Knowledge of the Orient, because generated out of strength, in a sense creates the Orient, the Oriental, and his world.

> Edward Said. *Orientalism*. London: Penguin, 2003. 40.

87   Spivak. "Can the Subaltern Speak?" 76.

88   In this regard, see Adams' construction of the "absent referent" in *The Sexual Politics of Meat*. Adams states

> Through butchering, animals become absent referents. Animals in name and body are made absent as animals for meat to exist. Animals' lives precede and enable the exist-ence of meat. If animals are alive they cannot be meat. Thus a dead body replaces the live animal. Without animals there can be no meat eating, yet they are absent from the act of eating meat because they have been transformed into food.

> See Adams. *The Sexual Politics of Meat*. 40.

89   And of course that broadly generic category, which seals the absolute horizon and destiny for so many non human animals on earth, that single word that silences any discursive space for response: namely, "meat" (in this regard, see Plumwood. *Environmental Culture*. 159–66). However, we cannot assume that this is merely about naming, since even the name in its signification and resignifiction already acts as a container that resists the pos-sibility of reinterpretation. We only need think about the word "chicken," which is the same word for both living and dead [meat], plainly and directly describes that entity that

production of the human colonial subject, very clearly seen in the forms of "animalisation" that have attended colonial violence and continue to discursively enable neo-colonialism as a geopolitical facet of our world: it is for this reason that Achille Mbembe comments that "discourse on Africa is almost always deployed in the framework (or in the fringes) of a meta-text about the *animal.*"[90] However, it is this "meta-text" that must be explored: its totality must be unpicked. Tom Tyler names this text "epistemological anthropocentrism," a knowledge assumption that the human comes first and crafts the world through, and only through, human experience:

> the epistemological claim that all knowledge will inevitably be determined by the human nature of the knower and that any attempt to explain experience, understanding, or knowledge of the world, of Being, of others—must inevitably start from a human perspective.[91]

Challenging the epistemic violence of the war against animals necessarily implies de-centring a human perspective.[92]

These levels of violence, *inter-subjective*, *institutional* and *epistemic* are useful for describing the totality of our war against animals. There are individual acts against animals that we might openly describe as "violent," which include human contact in containment, slaughter, experimentation and "sport." There

---

is subject to intense modes of violent biopolitical use, reproduction and death, yet it would seem never seems to qualify as a subject of violence.

90   Achille Mbembe. *On the Postcolony.* Berkeley and Los Angeles: University of California Press, 2001. 1. In relationship to colonisation and animality see also Noske. *Beyond Boundaries,* and Plumwood. *Feminism and the Mastery of Nature.* See also Joseph Pugliese's meditation on the role of speciesism in informing the violence and technologies of violence in the United States war against terror in Joseph Pugliese. *State Violence and the Execution of Law: Biopolitical Caesurae of Torture, Black Sites, Drones.* Abingdon: Routledge, 2013. Note also Spivak's attraction to Sigmund Freud's phrase "A child is being beaten" as the model for her construction "White men saving brown women from brown men." She points out that Freud's sentence conceals within it a history of repression; this is its promise for analysis:

> I am fascinated, rather, by how Freud predicates a history of repression that produces the final sentence. It is a history with a double origin, one hidden within the amnesia of the infant, the other lodged in our archaic past, assuming by implication a preoriginary space where human and animal were not yet differentiated.

Spivak. "Can the Subaltern Speak?" 92.

91   Tom Tyler. *CIFERAE: A Bestiary in Five Fingers.* Minneapolis, London: University of Minnesota Press, 2012. 21.

92   See Plumwood. *Environmental Culture.* For example, 121–2.

are institutional elements of this violence, that involve all humans and the way in which our lives have been structured to maintain a continuing flow of pleasures, either direct or indirect, through violence towards animals. Finally, there is an epistemic level, at which the categories of human and animal, superior and inferior, are constantly rearticulated, silencing the possibility of any response from "the animal" to our onslaught, and systematically rendering the event of violence as natural, friendly, humane or as a non event. Epistemic violence participates in the sublimation of violence as non violence; as such it produces the possibility of a "structural violence." Epistemic violence frames personal and structural violence in such a way as to naturalise our war as a form of legitimised sovereignty, through the hierarchisation of difference. We believe it is our right, "whether we like it or not," to decide whether to kill and to make suffer. And through these knowledge systems animals are framed, they can only be understood, as willing participants in this violence; it is as if, to paraphrase Spivak, "the animals actually want to die."[93]

Sovereignty Precedes Ethics

If war forms the substructure of relationality between human and non human entities, then how might we use this understanding to appraise *animal welfare* and *animal rights* approaches to the question of domination? It is certainly beyond question that over the last three decades there has been a growing recognition of the problem of animal suffering and death; and, in accord with this recognition, continued attempts to improve welfare and minimise suffering through legislation and regulation, as well as an increasingly sophisticated interest in legal protections and rights recognition for animals. However, and despite these efforts, we can persuasively argue that the quantum of animal suffering continues to increase, particularly with respect to the growth of

---

93   Spivak explores the British colonial response to *sati*, which she suggests effectively silences the voice of subaltern women in an epistemic trap:

> The Hindu widow ascends the pyre of the dead husband and immolates herself upon it. This is widow sacrifice. (The conventional transcription of the Sanskrit word for the widow would be *sati*. The early colonial British transcribed it *suttee*). The rite was not practiced universally and was not caste- or class-fixed. The abolition of this rite by the British has been generally understood as a case of 'White men saving brown women from brown men.' White women—from the nineteenth-century British Missionary Registers to Mary Daly—have not produced an alternative understanding. Against this is the Indian nativist argument, a parody of nostalgia for lost origins: 'The women actually wanted to die.' Spivak. "Can the Subaltern Speak?" 93.

factory farming and the use of animals for experimentation. And this increase has occurred in spite of increasing recognition that animals do indeed suffer. This need not be a paradox. As I have argued, if a feature of the war against animals is that forms of violent relationality are coded in the guise of peace, then apparent mitigations of the violence against animals, such as through seeking welfare, might simultaneously function as a fractal of continuing war-like domination.

This concern has been present in critiques of animal welfare which suggest that attempts to reduce the harm and suffering do not fundamentally challenge human domination of non human animal life, but, on the contrary, enable a continuing domination:[94] as Deirdre Bourke suggests, "animal welfare legislation is often used not just to protect animals but also to regulate, and indeed facilitate, the ongoing use of animals."[95] It certainly seems significant that while the focus of animal welfare legislation is to reduce suffering, we rarely find evidence within welfare legislation of a challenge to fundamental practices of domination, including—of course—the right to kill: "killing an animal is not *per se* a cruel act."[96] This is perhaps best illustrated by Webster's "Five Freedoms,"[97] adopted by the United Kingdom Farm Animal Welfare Council: namely, "freedom from thirst, hunger and malnutrition"; "freedom from discomfort"; "freedom from pain, injury and disease"; "freedom to express normal behaviour"; "freedom from fear and distress."[98] The freedom from death (and its correlate, a right to live), and freedom from human interference (which might perhaps be considered as the archetypal "human right" to bodily integrity and/or an individual right to self determination), are curiously absent from these protections: the diabolical promise of a protection for animals from pain and discomfort only highlights that a human right to violent domination—containment, slaughter, experimentation, regulation—remains beyond challenge, since maintaining the continuing use value of animal life for human consumption is the prerogative. Or as Francione terms "legal welfareism":

---

94   See, for example, Francione. *Animals, Property and the Law*.

95   Deirdre Bourke. "The Use and Misuse of 'Rights Talk' by the Animal Rights Movement." Peter Sankoff and Steven White Eds. *Animal Law in Australasia: A New Dialogue*. The Federation Press, 2009. 133.

96   Malcolm Caulfield. *Handbook of Australian Animal Cruelty Law*. Animals Australia, 2008. 139.

97   John Webster. "Farm Animal Welfare: The Five Freedoms and the Free Market." *Veterinary Journal*. 161.3, 2004. 229–37.

98   A similar, albeit less comprehensive, commitment is made in Australian legislation, such as in the *Export Control (Orders) Regulations 1982* (Cth) which stipulates "the minimisation of the risk of injury, pain and suffering and the least practical disturbance to animals."

"the strong presumption in favour of letting animal owners determine what uses of animals best maximize the value of animal property. The presumption is that a benefit exists unless a use can be shown to be gratuitous."[99]

Welfare operates, at least in this reading, as a way to blunt the full force of violence (to remove apparent pain and distress, to enable continuing nutrition, to enable a degree of physical movement) even if a right to a domination until death remains a continuing prerogative. As Peter Sankoff summarises:

> Instead of a neutral balance, whereby human need weighs more than animal suffering, we are presented with a balance tilted heavily from the outset in favour of justification of harm. In effect, human need weighs more than animal suffering, in that it is valued in a much more significant way. Humans sit in a privileged position, and thus the starting point is not a presumption that harm is generally wrong, and must be justified, but that it is humanity's privilege to inflict it.[100]

Welfare mitigates the harm of uncontested and violent domination. It checks against gratuity. In other words, welfare might be regarded, as I note in Chapter 2, as the "governmentality" of the violence of sovereignty.

As I have discussed above, following Foucault, rights might be considered as the product of conquest, as the protections offered to those who capitulate in war as a form of reparation. In this sense rights, although formally offering protection, can also be considered as a tactic of war by other means; that is, as the way in which continuing forms of domination extend into the civil political space, enacting forms of violent relationality that preserve the spoils of victory.[101] It is no accident that Wendy Brown, for example, has pointed out that rights for women are similarly of potentially limited value in achieving substantive change: "rights almost always serve as a mitigation—but not a

---

99   Francione. *Animals, Property and the Law*. 6.

100   Peter Sankoff. "The Welfare Paradigm: Making the World a Better Place for Animals?" Peter Sankoff and Steven White Eds. *Animal Law in Australasia: A New Dialogue*. Annandale: The Federation Press, 2009. 21.

101   Aileen Moreton Robinson says as much in her own reading of Foucault's *Society Must Be Defended* lectures in the context of critical whiteness studies, asking "do rights function as tactics and strategies of race war?" Aileen Moreton-Robinson. "Towards a New Research Agenda: Foucault, Whiteness and Indigenous Sovereignty." *Journal of Sociology*. 42.4, 2006. 398. Further, Moreton Robinson asks: "Did the eruption of 'rights', in its many forms, produce new procedures of Indigenous subjugation? Do these procedures continue today in the remaking of Australian national identity evident in neo-conservative politics, the history wars and High Court decisions on Mabo and Indigenous native title?" (391).

resolution—of subordinating powers."[102] In this guise we might ask the same questions of some animal rights approaches as we might of welfare approaches. In particular, we should be wary of the stratifications of rights, status and value between human and non human, and the way in which differential rights might produce inequalities in opportunities and power, and hence re-inscribe the essential right of human domination of animal life; human dignity only experienced through the indignity of other creatures.

We find rights differentiation and stratification in Tom Regan's *The Case for Animal Rights*, which highlights the challenge of attending to ethics without considering the problem of sovereignty. Regan puts forward a theory of inherent value, arguing that "certain individuals have the basic right to respectful treatment because of the kind of value they have (inherent value), a kind of value that is itself independent of human utility."[103] Those who have inherent value are ascribed as possessing a kind of interest or investment in their own life. Regan establishes the criterion of a "subject-of-a-life":

> ...individuals are subjects-of-a-life if they have beliefs and desires, perception, memory and a sense of future, including their own future; an emotional life together with feelings of pleasure and pain; preference- and welfare-interests; the ability to initiate action in pursuit of their desires and goals; a psychophysical identity over time; and an individual welfare in the sense that their experiential life fares well or ill for them, logically independently of their utility for others and logically independently of their being the object of anyone else's interests.[104]

Regan's rights view then rests upon providing an equal right of respectful treatment to those individuals who have inherent value; that is, those who "satisfy

---

102   Brown goes on:

> Although rights may attenuate the subordination and violation to which women are vulnerable in a masculinist social, political, and economic regime, they vanquish neither the regime nor its mechanisms of reproduction. They do not eliminate male dominance even as they soften some of its effects. Such softening is not itself a problem: if violence is upon you, almost any means of reducing it is of value. The problem surfaces in the question of when and whether rights for women are formulated in such a way as to enable the escape of the subordinated from the site of that violation, and when and whether they build a fence around us at that site, regulating rather than challenging the conditions within.

See Wendy Brown. "Suffering Rights as Paradoxes." *Constellations*. 7.2, 2000. 230–241. 231. I thank Jessica Robyn CadwalIader for bringing this text to my attention.

103   Tom Regan. *The Case for Animal Rights*. Berkley: University of California Press, 1983.

104   Regan. *The Case for Animal Rights*. 243

the subject-of-a-life criterion."[105] In so far as a "subject-of-a-life" criterion might extend to animals, Regan's approach thus offers a foundation for extending moral worth to entities beyond the human.

However, and despite the promise of Regan's framework, there are nagging forms of differentiation that reinforce human supremacy over non human animals. For example, the distinction that is drawn between "moral patients" and "moral agents"—which delineates between "those individuals who are conscious and sentient" and those "who are conscious, sentient, and possess... other cognitive and volitional abilities"[106]—serves a fundamental element in Regan's framework, in demonstrating that those who might not be thought of as moral agents may still possess rights to respectful treatment. But, as I shall discuss below with reference to disability, it is not clear whether the distinction between moral agents and patients—that is the distinction between the "rational," "able" and "autonomous" human, and those who are treated as others (the child, the person with disability, the animal)—is a factual claim made on the basis of an external truth, or a political claim that reflects a hierarchy of differences that has placed a socially and discursively constructed "rational able bodied" human at the top of the "cognitive" heap.

While differences between entities exist, the challenge is how these differences are politically hierarchised, and the material effects of this stratification. We see the possible effects of rights differentiation in Regan's discussion of the "lifeboat case." If in an exceptional circumstance of survival there is a requirement that a choice between human and non human is to be made, then Regan argues that the human would be the inevitable choice: "to save the dog and to throw away any one of the humans overboard would be to give the dog more than his due."[107] Regan extends this further:

> The lifeboat case would not be morally any different if we supposed that the choice had to be made, not between a single dog and the four humans, but between these humans and any number of dogs. Let the number of dogs be as large as one likes; suppose they number a million; and suppose the lifeboat will support only four survivors. Then the rights view still implies that, special considerations apart, the million dogs should be thrown overboard and the four humans saved.[108]

---

105   Regan. *The Case for Animal Rights.* 276.
106   Regan. *The Case for Animal Rights.* 153.
107   Regan. *The Case for Animal Rights.* 324.
108   Regan. *The Case for Animal Rights.* 324–5. See also Gary L. Francione. *Introduction to Animal Rights: Your Child or the Dog?* Philadelphia: Temple University Press. xxxiii.

Regan is clear that actual 'life boat' cases are rare. However, this does necessarily provide comfort, as the material effects of this differentiation in moral status and value are ominous. Certainly, as I will discuss in Chapter 3, the mass exterminations of livestock that have occurred internationally as a result of Bovine Spongiform Encephalopathy (BSE)—where animals were sent to an early death *en masse* to prevent human sickness and safeguard a future food supply—suggest that the blurry lines between exception and norm, and more importantly the sovereign right to declare the exception, contain the perpetual power to erode non human consideration under the ever-present human prerogative.[109] Humans have the security of their own survival as an enduring goal. However, this human desire toward self-preservation is no different from any other creature[110]; what is different, as the discussion of Derrida in Chapter 8 indicates, is that when humans prevail over other animals through violence—such as the act of throwing one (or a million) dogs overboard—we claim this violence as an act that is grounded in, and justified by, our own superiority. In other words, as discussed above, sovereignty arrives with an authorisation structure that epistemologically establishes a human right to decide, because we believe our selves (and our violence) to be superior, to be necessary, to be giving other entities "their due" and therefore justifiable. And in this cycle of committing justifiable violence against entities that we have decided do not have the capabilities that "we" possess, it is somewhat unclear whether a true capability difference underpins our claim of superiority, or whether it is merely the process of violence that crafts other entities as lacking capability and therefore as justifiable targets of domination.

In all of this, I certainly do not mean to suggest that the rights project should be abandoned. It should be stressed that there is no reason to imagine that rights themselves might not provide a way forward in ending human domination of non human life. For example, Francione's approach suggests a rights framework that focuses not simply on the task of extending "human" rights to non human animals, but also on simultaneously denying rights to humans:

---

109   As John Sanbonmatsu points out, these brief spaces of exception—when animals are killed *en masse* to prevent disease outbreak—occur against a backdrop of a continual killing that goes unnoticed: "so normalized and naturalized has this violence become that we only become aware of its existence when the apparatus goes awry, threatening either public health or an industry's bottom line" See John Sanbonmatsu. "Introduction." John Sanbonmatsu Ed. *Critical Theory and Animal Liberation.* Lanham: Rowman and Littlefield Publishers, 2011. 3.

110   Certainly this appears to be Locke's view of the foundation of property rights—as a contestation between competing demands for self-preservation. I discuss this further in Chapters 3 and 4 of this book.

in Francione's framework equal consideration begins through the abolition of the human right to own animals as property.[111] Francione thus recognises that any concept of animal rights must begin with a deterioration of human right, through challenging the sovereign prerogative of the human, which underpins the violent domination of animals and its far ranging effects. Rights themselves are potentially important: but only where they can be tactically used to mount a counter claim against a sovereign order; the absolute right of the human. In other words, as I discuss in the Conclusion of this book, "rights" for animals must begin through an act which disrupts and disarms human sovereignty, since it is only within this space that a "practice of equality" might begin. Both welfare and rights approaches risk entrenching human domination as a starting point, where they do not open human sovereignty over animals itself to ethical interrogation, and allow for the possibility of animal sovereignties.

Without addressing human sovereignty, the ground for enacting an individual ethics is limited, since it appears to always begin with the assumption of our own sovereignty as both a starting point and cause of the ethical dilemma ("whether we like it or not"). One area where we might see this ethical dilemma play out is around the problem of animal suffering. Bentham's question—"Can they suffer?"—seems to dominate so much ethical engagement with our relationship with animals, including for example, Peter Singer, in his *Animal Liberation*.[112] In some respects, the question of suffering already structures

---

111   Francione. *Animals Property and the Law.* 253–61. Francione states:

> We treat animals as the moral equivalent of inanimate objects with no morally signifi-
> cant interests or rights. We bring billions of animals into existence annually simply for
> the purpose of killing them. Animals have market prices. Dogs and cats are sold in pet
> stores like compact discs; financial markets trade in futures for pork bellies and cattle.
> Any interest that an animal has is nothing more than an economic commodity that
> may be bought and sold when it is in the economic interest of the property owner.
> That is what it means to be property.

See Francione *Introduction to Animal Rights.* 79.

112   See Jeremy Bentham. *An Introduction to the Principles of Morals and Legislation.* Chapter
XIX, Note §. The full note is worth exploring in so far as Bentham makes explicit that
continuing use of animals for food is taken for granted; indeed has the potential to offer a
less painful death to animals:

> Under the Gentoo and Mahometan religions, the interests of the rest of the animal crea-
> tion seem to have met with some attention. Why have they not universally, with as
> much as those of human creatures, allowance made for the difference in point of sensi-
> bility? Because the laws that are have been the work of mutual fear; a sentiment which
> the less rational animals have not had the same means as man has of turning to account.
> Why ought they not? No reason can be given. If the being eaten were all, there is very
> good reason why we should be suffered to eat such of them as we like to eat: we are the

both a human subject who has the prerogative to inquire into the reality of the suffering of another being, and the non human subject whose ability to suffer is placed into question. Today, the philosophical questions around animal suffering interact with the scientific: hence the political gravity of contemporary scientific investigations into whether, for example, fish feel pain, or whether they feel pain as humans do.[113] These inquiries are already structured by the assumption that this suffering is open to question, and simultaneously only answerable upon a human prerogative to inquire into the status of this suffering and determine its existence. The answer to these questions will have an enormous impact upon the welfare of billions of animals that humans use, and as such the ethics of this utilisation. However, it seems fair to ask why it is we

---

better for it, and they are never the worse. They have none of those long-protracted anticipations of future misery which we have. The death they suffer in our hands commonly is, and always may be, a speedier, and by that means a less painful one, than that which would await them in the inevitable course of nature. If the being killed were all, there is very good reason why we should be suffered to kill such as molest us: we should be the worse for their living, and they are never the worse for being dead. But is there any reason why we should be suffered to torment them? Not any that I can see. Are there any why we should not be suffered to torment them? Yes, several... The day has been, I grieve to say in many places it is not yet past, in which the greater part of the species, under the denomination of slaves, have been treated by the law exactly upon the same footing as, in England for example, the inferior races of animals are still. The day may come, when the rest of the animal creation may acquire those rights which never could have been withholden from them but by the hand of tyranny. The French have already discovered that the blackness of the skin is no reason why a human being should be abandoned without redress to the caprice of a tormentor. It may come one day to be recognized, that the number of the legs, the villosity of the skin, or the termination of the os sacrum, are reasons equally insufficient for abandoning a sensitive being to the same fate. What else is it that should trace the insuperable line? Is it the faculty of reason, or, perhaps, the faculty of discourse? But a full-grown horse or dog is beyond comparison a more rational, as well as a more conversable animal, than an infant of a day, or a week, or even a month, old. But suppose the case were otherwise, what would it avail? the question is not, Can they reason? nor, Can they talk? but, Can they suffer?

In Bentham's account, ethical consideration for suffering comes after sovereignty: a human right of domination remains absolutely intact, and informs the nature of the ethical question which follows. In this context it is interesting to note that Paola Cavalieri cites the same quotation at length in *The Animal Question*, however, excludes crucial elements, particularly the overt sense in which Bentham believes human utilisation may possibly involve less suffering. See Paola Cavalieri. *The Animal Question: Why Non Human Animals Deserve Human Rights*. Oxford: Oxford University Press, 2001. 60.

113   J.D. Rose, R. Arlinghaus, S.J. Cooke, B.K. Diggles, W. Sawynok, E.D. Stevens and C.D.L. Wynne. "Can fish really feel pain?" *Fish and Fisheries*, 15.1, 2014. 97–133.

have the right to put this suffering into question in the first place, and whether this right to question whether a living being suffers, or not, as a result of our use, is itself an effect of our utilisation. In these cases, ethics *proceeds* or *follows* domination; it reverberates after it almost as an echo through a canyon. Ethics that begins with assumed sovereignty is likely to only lead to what I have described above as epistemological violence.

In order to illustrate this problem further, I wish to pause here to discuss the troubling way disability, and particularly distinctions in "cognitive ability," have been utilised and reproduced uncritically by both Singer and Regan as a means to put forward a case for non human justice. This provides an example of the way in which some liberal humanist conceptualisations of ethics end up simply reinscribing arbitrary forms of human exceptionalism that do violence even as they seek to rescue entities from the violence of humanism (as Wolfe notes, "the discourse and practice of speciesism in the name of liberal human-ism have historically been turned on other *humans* as well"[114]). As I shall out-line, a construction of ethics that comes after sovereignty will only regulate the effects of that sovereignty, rather than challenge the violent terms of that rela-tionship of domination itself.

Peter Singer is perhaps most notorious for his construction of disability in relation to animality, not only in the argument he puts forward in *Animal Liberation*, but in his latter ethical arguments which aim to challenge a view that "species membership is crucial to moral status, and that all human life is of equal value."[115] The crux of Singer's argument is that it is speciesist to protect a right to life on the basis of species membership: "we must allow that beings which are similar in all relevant respects have a similar right to life—and mere membership in our own biological species cannot be a morally relevant crite-rion for this right."[116]

How "similar in all relevant respects" might be defined in this context is poten-tially problematic, at least in so far as it relies on a production of disability as the

---

114   Wolfe. *Animal Rites.* 37. See also, in this regard, Wolfe's discussion of the intersection between animal studies and disability studies. See Cary Wolfe. *What is Posthumanism?* Minneapolis: University of Minnesota Press, 2010. 127–42.

115   Peter Singer. "Speciesism and Moral Status." *Metaphilosophy.* 40.3–4, 2009. 567–81. For examples of critiques of Singer's position, see Per Sundström, "Peter Singer and 'Lives Not Worth Living': Comments on a Flawed Argument from Analogy." *Journal of Medical Ethics*, 21.1, 1995. 35–8; Nora Ellen Groce and Jonathan Marks. "The Great Ape Project and Disability Rights: Ominous Undercurrents of Eugenics in Action." *American Anthropologist.* 102.4, 2000. 818–22; and Harriet McBryde Johnson. "Unspeakable Conversations." *The New York Times.* February 16, 2003.

116   Peter Singer. *Animal Liberation.* London: Jonathan Cape, 1975. 21.

threshold between the "normal" human lives and other lives. Referring to a hypo-thetical example of a child "born with massive and irreparable brain damage" who is "unable to talk, recognise other people, act independently of others, or develop a sense of self awareness," Singer suggests that the child's parents may "ask the doctor to kill the infant painlessly" to avoid unnecessary costs for the parents or the State. How should the doctor respond? Here, Singer points out that the belief in the sanctity of human life—which is placed in contrast to non human life—generates an arbitrary inconsistency in treatment:

> Should the doctor do what the parents ask? Legally, he should not, and in this respect the law reflects the sanctity of life view. The life of every human being is sacred. Yet people who would say this about the infant do not object to the killing of nonhuman animals. How can they justify their different judgements? Adult chimpanzees, dogs, pigs, and many other species far surpass the brain-damaged infant in their ability to relate to others, act independently, be self aware, and any other capacity that could reasonably be said to give value to life. With the most intensive care possible, there are retarded infants who can never achieve the intelli-gence level of a dog.[117]

These views on the inherent value of lives and how this hierarchisation might inform a decision to take life are refined in the views Singer has later expressed on the right of parents to take the life of their "mentally retarded child."[118] Responding to the argument that differentiating in the value status of humans is a "slippery slope" (towards the sorts of eugenicist arguments that enable geno-cide), Singer points out that maintaining a fiction of the sanctity of all human life comes at two costs. *Firstly*, there is a cost for non human animals, who would be offered due protection if the sanctity of the lives of some non human animals were recognised through consistent application of value across species lines:

> For example, the breeding sows that produce almost all of the pork, bacon, and ham sold in this country are so tightly confined in metal

---

117   Singer. *Animal Liberation.* 20. Notice the almost unmistakable resonance here with the final lines of Kafka's *The Trial*: "'Like a dog!' he said, it was as if the shame of it should outlive him." See Franz Kafka. *The Trial*. Geneva: Herron Books, 1968. 251.

118   Peter Singer. "Speciesism and Moral Status." 579. Singer points out that he agrees "that there has been a long history of oppression and callous disregard for the lives of individu-als with mental retardation. I also agree that we should do our best to avoid such oppres-sion and callous disregard."

crates that they cannot walk a single step or turn around. And yet, pigs are animals who compare quite well in terms of cognitive abilities with human beings who are profoundly mentally retarded. I doubt that it would be possible for people to treat pigs in this way, if they did not put them in a moral category that is far inferior to that in which they would place any human being.[119]

Secondly, a cost is imposed upon parents who decide "it is in the best interests of their profoundly mentally retarded child and of their family that their child should not live." In Singer's argument, for these parents, the fiction of equal value ascribed to human life exacts an extraordinary burden in terms of care responsibility:

> To force the parents to bring up the child, neither for their own benefit nor for the benefit of the child but so that we do not slide down an allegedly possible slippery slope into a repetition of the Holocaust, is, ironically, to do just what Kantians normally object to doing: treating the child (and the parents) as merely a means to an end. The cost, financial, physical, and emotional, of bringing up a profoundly mentally retarded child is great even when parents positively want to bring up their child. It will clearly be much harder to bear if the parents never wanted to bring up the child but were not able to make that choice.[120]

Here Singer normalises assumptions that underpin a production of disability. *Firstly*, disability is configured as a "cost" to be carried—by the person with disability, by parents, by the State, by society as a whole—in such a way that there is apparently no benefit, or possibility of "return on investment." Here, disability is always configured as a burden on all involved, including for the person with disability, who it is supposed would be better off without life than to live with disability. *Secondly*, the socio-political context of disability is normalised so that what might be considered as variable economic, social, political and cultural factors—such as the caring roles taken on by parents, views on normal and abnormal bodies, regimes of stigma and violence, economic and work arrangements etc.—are assumed to be "natural." That in many societies people with disability are neither provided supports or recognition, and that parents and carers may be isolated and offered little support (financial or

---

119   Peter Singer. "Speciesism and Moral Status." 579.
120   Peter Singer. "Speciesism and Moral Status." 580.

otherwise) does not appear to figure in Singer's calculation of costs. Vast cultural differences in family structure and caring roles across different societies will also mean that these costs are relative to a specific geopolitical set of circumstances. Nor does Singer acknowledge the way in which socio-political structures enable particular individuals and not others to participate in society: the active provision of resources and value to those who are normatively defined as "able" (for example, the "normal" care and support provided by parents and communities to raise children are not treated as costs). Perhaps most telling, and disturbing, is that this ethics creates a justification for who gets a right to decide: Singer assumes that parents should be able to decide to take the lives of their children in certain circumstances (presumably because they will "bear the costs"), thus normalising an assumption that the parents of a child with certain disabilities always have a right to exercise life and death powers over their child, in exception to what would be, in this case, murder under a non exceptional application of law. As Mbembe deftly remarks: "sovereignty means the capacity to define who matters and who does not, who is *disposable* and who is not."[121]

As I have discussed above, Regan differs from Singer in so far as he argues for inherent value underpinning rights obligations. This would suggest that Regan's framework might be more promising in terms of how it produces and understands disability. Unfortunately, this promise is not realised. While it is true that Regan's argument uses a slightly different route from Singer, Regan still relies upon a conceptualisation of moral and intellectual capacity that reproduces a potentially hierarchical norm of disability. As I have discussed above, Regan differentiates between "moral agents" and "moral patients." Moral agents are defined as:

> Individuals who have a variety of sophisticated abilities, including in particular the ability to bring impartial moral principles to bear on the determination of what, all considered, morally ought to be done and, having made this determination, to freely choose or fail to choose to act as morality, as they achieve it, requires.[122]

On the other hand, moral patients are defined as follows:

> In contrast to moral agents, moral patients lack the prerequisites that would enable them to control their own behaviour in ways that would

---

121   Achille Mbembe. "Necropolitics." *Public Culture*. 15.1, 2003. 11–40. 27.
122   Regan. *The Case for Animal Rights*. 151.

make them morally accountable for what they do. A moral patient lacks the ability to formulate, let alone bring to bear, moral principles in deliberating about which one among a number of possible acts it would be right or proper to perform.[123]

Regan's categories of "agent" and "patient" are used to create a distinction between humans, which can then be used to ground inherent rights for non human animals. Regan states that "normal adult human beings are the paradigm individuals believed to be moral agents."[124] Although Regan acknowledges that this is a "large assumption to make," he allows this normalisation to stand.[125] The definition of moral patient is already given as the Other of the moral agent: "Human infants, young children, and the mentally deranged or enfeebled of all ages are paradigm cases of human moral patients."[126] The distinctions don't end here. Moral patients are divided themselves between those which only possess consciousness and sentience, and those that possess additional "cognitive and volitional abilities" including "those who have desires and beliefs, who perceive, and can act intentionally, who have a sense of the future, including their own future (i.e., who are self aware or self conscious), who have an emotional life, who have a psychosocial identity over time, who have a kind of autonomy (namely, preference autonomy), and who have an experiential welfare."[127] In other words, moral patients themselves are stratified between those who have a weak resemblance to the kind of "normal" subjectivity ascribed to moral agents, and those who bear no similarity to those who are associated with full moral agency. Regan argues that both humans and animals may fulfill the criteria for additional "cognitive and volitional abilities," including

---

123   Regan. *The Case for Animal Rights*. 152.

124   Regan. *The Case for Animal Rights*. 152.

125   Regan states:

> To defend this belief would take us far afield from the present inquiry, involving us in debates dealing both with the existence of free will, for example, and with the extent to which we are able to influence how we act by bringing reason to bear on our decision-making. Though it is a large assumption to make, the assumption will be made that normal adult humans are moral agents. To make this assumption in the present case plays no theoretical favourites, since all theories examined in this and the following chapter share this assumption.

> See Regan. *The Case for Animal Rights*. 152.

126   Regan. *The Case for Animal Rights*. 153. Regan continues: "More controversial is whether fetuses and future generations of human beings qualify as moral patients. It is enough for our purposes, however, that some humans are reasonably viewed in this way."

127   Regan. *The Case for Animal Rights*. 153.

some humans who "suffer from a variety of mental handicaps,"[128] but some humans and animals do not.

In all these modes of categorisation and stratification, decisions upon exceptional cases, humans and animals are brought together, with disability constituted upon the threshold between human and animal. Regan observes:

> Given any human being, what we shall want to know is whether his/her behaviour can be accurately described and parsimoniously explained by making reference to the range of abilities that characterizes animals (desires, beliefs, preferences etc.). To the extent that the case can be made for describing and explaining the behaviour of a human being in these terms, to the extent, assuming that we have further reasons for denying that the human in question has the abilities necessary for moral agency, we have reason to regard that human as a moral patient on all fours, so to speak, with animals.[129]

The approach is not without merit. As discussed above, Regan grants inherent value to all individuals who are "subjects-of-a-life"; that is, individuals who possess some of the additional "cognitive and volitional" abilities that Regan lists above as necessary for demonstrating "inherent value." In this sense there is more scope in Regan's framework—at least in comparison to Singer's—to recognise a broader range of entities as being owed inherent value, by extending the line of distinction from mere recognition of moral agency as the minimal threshold, to inclusion of some individuals, human or animals, who possess particular characteristics that look somewhat like moral agency, in at least a "weak form." From Regan's standpoint, there are benefits for both animals and humans with this approach, since a framework has been developed that can take into account duties to human non moral agents, such as children and people with "mental retardation."[130]

However, Regan's approach generates epistemic violence, in so far as one arbitrary hierarchy is replaced by another. Here, disability is treated as an intractable and naturalised "fact" about certain humans, rather than as a norm that is shaped within a social and political institutional context. It is certainly not clear why it is that inherent value should be assumed to be attributed to

---

128 Regan states: "some human moral patients satisfy these criteria—for example, young children and those humans who, though they suffer from a variety of mental handicaps and thus fail to qualify as moral agents, possess the abilities just enumerated."

129 Regan. *The Case for Animal Rights*. 153–4.

130 See Regan. *The Case for Animal Rights*. 156.

"normal adult human beings," while the inherent value of those who do not resemble this normality should be placed in jeopardy. Indeed Regan's own hesitancy on the clarity of his demarcations, indicated both in his acknowledgement that attributing moral agency to "normal adult human beings" relies on an assumption,[131] and his "moral caution" on the dividing line between those who are the subjects-of-a-life and those who are not,[132] already indicates that we are on unstable ground here in relation to definitions. The "normal" reflects a set of contingent social, cultural and political factors within individual, family and institutional structures, which are not a "natural" set of givens on ability or disability. Rather normality is produced through relationships of power across legal, political and social relationships: as Foucault states "the monster falls under what in general terms could be called the framework of politico-judicial powers."[133]

Certainly, as social model disability theorists will point out, disability is a structural form of oppression, rather than solely an impairment characteristic of the individual which can only be responded to through welfare or health interventions.[134] More recent critical disability theorists would extend this problematic further, pointing out that disability is formulated discursively as a

---

131   Regan. *The Case for Animal Rights*. 152.

132   See, for example, Regan. *The Case for Animal Rights*. 245–6, 366–9, and 391. See particularly Regan's discussion of "where one draws the line" in relation to determining whether a person is tall or old (366). Here Regan fails to acknowledge that both these categories—"tall" and "old"—are socially, politically and culturally constructed and belong to specific geopolitical and temporary locations.

133   Michel Foucault. *Abnormal: Lectures at the Collège de France 1974–1975*. London and New York: Verso, 2004. 61. Recent work by Donaldson and Kymlicka have gone some way in critically addressing the norms that have underpinned some animal rights and citizenship theory, by arguing for citizenship upon different bases than the "neurotypical human adult.". Donaldson and Kymlicka state: "our argument is not that 'marginal cases' should be treated alike, but that there are no marginal cases, because neurotypical human adults should never have been defined as the norm from which others are measured." See Sue Donaldson and Will Kymlicka. "Rethinking Membership and Participation in an Inclusive Democracy: Cognitive Disability, Children, Animals." Barbara Arneil and Nancy Hirschmann Eds. *Disability and Political Theory*. University of Pennsylvania Press. *Forthcoming*. I thank Will Kymlicka for making available this forthcoming essay.

134   See Paul Abberley. "The Concept of Oppression and the Development of a Social Theory of Disability." *Disability, Handicap and Society*. 2.1, 1987. 5–19; Mike Oliver. *The Politics of Disablement*. Houndsmills: The Macmillan Press, 1990; Jane Campbell and Mike Oliver. *Disability Politics: Understanding Our Past, Changing Our Future*. London and New York: Routledge, 1996: and Tom Shakespeare. "Disabled People's Self-Organisation: A New Social Movement?" *Disability and Society*. 8.3, 2003. 249–64.

category in relation to regimes of normalisation, and that the construction of disability intersects with other forms of social stratification such as race, gender and sexuality.[135] In both social model and critical disability approaches, disability and ability are productions of society and culture, which mark bodies as normal/abnormal, healthy/sick, productive/unproductive. Indeed, as more recent theorists will point out, these categorisations are precisely a product of political contestation. Thus, Shelley Tremain observes: "it would seem that the identity of the subject of the social model ("people with impairments") is actually formed in large measure by the political arrangements that the model was designed to contest."[136] Distinctions in value here are not generated by essential or natural difference but through political contestation: they are produced by political and social structures that stratify bodies and selves, determining destinies between entities that might otherwise be non-differentiated.

Both Singer and Regan treat people with disability as if they were actually "inferior," rather than treating disability as a production of social and political processes. As such, they cooperate in the construction of ability and disability as apparently given and stable categories, enacting epistemic violence even as these philosophers are attempting to dismantle the arbitrary rationalities that construct "the animal." There *is* indeed a connection between disability and non human animals; however, this connection is not a "resemblance" between people with disability and animals, where disability is configured as an "animalised" or "more animal" version of the human. Rather, the connection lies in the social, political and epistemic production of species difference, which in so far as it generates a normalised human, and privileges this subject within social and political structure, fabricates symbolic and material categories of animality and disability, crafted through arbitrary status differentiation, segregation and violence. As Sunaura Taylor observes, the shared relation between disability and animality conforms to regimes of normalisation which sculpt materiality and value:

---

135 See, for example, Robert McRuer. *Crip Theory: Cultural Signs of Queerness and Disability.* New York and London: New York University Press, 2006; Helen Meekosha and Russell Shuttleworth. "What's So 'Critical' About Critical Disability Studies?" *Australian Journal of Human Rights.* 15.1, 2009. 47–75; Margrit Shildrick. *Dangerous Discourses of Disability, Subjectivity and Sexuality.* Houndsmills: Palgrave Macmillan, 2009; and Fiona Kumari Campbell. *Contours of Ableism: The Production of Disability and Ableness.* New York: Palgrave Macmillan, 2009.

136 Shelley Tremain. "Foucault, Governmentality and Critical Disability Theory: An Introduction." *Foucault and the Government of Disability.* University of Michigan: University of Michigan Press, 2008. 1–24. 10.

...this connection did not lie, as many people suggested, in my being confined to my disabled body, like an animal in a cage. Far from this, the connection I found centered on an oppressive value system that declares some bodies normal, some bodies broken, and some bodies food.[137]

Foucault's account of the development of State racism in the *Society Must Be Defended* lectures is immediately relevant here for thinking about both disability and animality politico-judicial productions.[138] As discussed above, in this account war functions in a biopolitical sense to divide between populations on species grounds. Foucault describes racism as serving the purpose of "subdividing the species it controls."[139] The divisions aim to create hierarchies of "normalness," reinforcing sovereign power and coercing conformity while re-inscribing sovereign disciplinary control. As per above, racialised difference and racism that follows from this is described as a "war"—not just "a military confrontation" in and of itself—but a perpetual biological hierarchisation that configures and deports species life in general. This hierarchisation aims to foster and disallow: Foucault suggests that this racialised logic implies that the so-called "more inferior" sub-species—that is, those who deviate from the regimes of normality, the "abnormal" and the "degenerate"—will slowly disappear or be eliminated:

> the more, 'I—as species not individual—can live, the stronger I will be, the more vigorous I will be. I can proliferate' ... The death of the other, the death of the bad race, of the inferior race (or the degenerate or the abnormal) is something that will make life in general healthier: healthier and purer.[140]

Race is only one vector of this normalisation. The connection of "normality" with perceived health and productivity already signals that perfecting the species not only involves an invention of racialised categories to be eliminated, but also conceptions of able and disabled bodies that pose a similar threat to the floating category of the "normal human." Thus, while we might associate species construction as closely connected to race and animality, we might also

---

137   Sunaura Taylor. "Beasts of Burden: Disability Studies and Animal Rights." *Qui Parle: Critical Humanities and Social Sciences.* 19.2, 2011. 191–222. 191.

138   See Deirdre Tedmanson and Dinesh Wadiwel. "Neoptolemus: the Governmentality of New Race Wars?" *Culture and Organization.* 16.1, 2010. 7–22.

139   Foucault. *Society Must be Defended.* 255.

140   Foucault. *Society Must be Defended.* 255

understand this stratification of distinctions as productive of the "disabled" body as well.[141] It is no accident in this regard that Fiona Kumari Campbell defines *ableism* as "a network of beliefs processes and practices that produces a particular kind of self and body (the corporeal standard) that is projected as the perfect, species-typical and therefore essential and fully human."[142] Campbell observes that:

> The processes of ableism sees the corporeal imagination in terms of compulsory ableness, i.e. certain forms of 'perfected' materiality are posited as preferable. A chief feature of an ableist viewpoint is a belief that impairment (irrespective of 'type') is inherently negative which should, if the opportunity presents itself, be ameliorated, cured or indeed eliminated.[143]

The process is tied directly to perceived modes of "productivity," working and reworking a belief that there are indeed select bodies that are capable of productivity and contribution to social and economic life, and these individuals should be made to thrive, while at the same time there are groups who do not "produce," sap productivity, are a "cost," lack meaningful or signifiable "cognitive ability" and should be made to diminish.[144] If we hold that these processes of

---

141 Ladelle McWhorter states:

> The practices and institutions that divide, for example, the "able-bodied," "sane," and "whole" from the "impaired," "mentally ill," and "deficient" create the conditions under which all of us live, they structure the situation in which each of us comes to terms with ourselves and creates a way of life. Normality has a history, a set of investments, an entire array of supports and investments that bring it into being, sustain it, and alter it when conditions so demand.

See Ladelle McWhorter. "Forward." Shelley Tremain Ed. *Foucault and the Government of Disability*. Ann Arbor: University of Michigan Press, 2005. xiii-xvii.

142 Fiona Kumari Campbell. "Inciting Legal Fictions: Disability's Date with Ontology and the Ableist Body of the Law." *Griffith Law Review*. 10, 2001. 42–62, n44.

143 Fiona Kumari Campbell. "Exploring Internalized Ableism Using Critical Race Theory." *Disability & Society*. 23.2, 2008. 151–62. In terms of the intersection between Foucault's account and race theory, see, for example, Ladelle McWhorter. "Where Do White People Come From? A Foucaultian Critique of Whiteness Studies." *Philosophy and Social Criticism*. 31.5–6, 2005. 533–56; and Moreton-Robinson. "Towards a New Research Agenda?"

144 Thus, as Foucault identifies, the aspect of population health that becomes tied to modern biopower isn't so much the management of sudden epidemics, but the ongoing management of long term health conditions that are perceived to effect the broadly economic functioning of the nation:

biological/species division within population can be characterised as a war—quite literally constituting dividing lines between friend and enemy—then might we also construct that line between able /disabled as another fault line in this war? The biological thresholds that Foucault outlines work to arbitrarily divide between able and disabled along lines of population health, productivity, security and survival. The resultant disabled body is produced as that which will be made to diminish: as an apparently "genuine" inferior model human and as subject to extraordinary and violent regimes of stigmatisiation, social and political isolation, forced treatment, restraint and incarceration, forced sterilisation and, as Singer's discussion illustrates, potentially subject to extermination. Species stratification—producing race, disability, animality, sexuality and other "biological" differences—seeks to exclude constructed populations that do not conform to, or are perceived to have a pernicious effect upon, the social body. This is a circular relationship between truth, power and violence, that in effect authorises and naturalises a system of domination. As Tremain observes: "the category of impairment emerged and, in many respects persists, in order to legitimise the governmental practices that generated it in the first place."[145]

Singer and Regan's use and categorisation of disability highlights a problem with an *ethics that comes after sovereignty*. If sovereignty sets in train both regimes of violence and regimes of truth, then an ethics that begins only after sovereignty will merely be complicit with the violence of the existing order.[146]

At the end of the eighteenth century, it was not epidemics that were the issue, but something else—what might broadly be called endemics, or in other words, the form, nature, extension, duration, and intensity of the illnesses prevalent in a population. These were illnesses that were difficult to eradicate and that were not regarded as epidemics that caused more frequent deaths, but as permanent factors which—and that is how they were dealt with—sapped the population's strength, shortened the working week, wasted energy and cost money, both because they led to a fall in production and because treating them was expensive.

See Foucault. *Society Must be Defended.* 244.

145   Tremain. "Foucault, Governmentality and Critical Disability Theory." 11.
146   Chloë Taylor remarks:

I would suggest that we censor the sight and sounds of animal deaths because we need to keep animal lives and deaths derealized in order to continue with our plans. In Levinasian terms, we wish to avoid having a face-to-face relationship with animals because we want to avoid our ethical responsibility. We censor the truth about the lives and deaths of animals because we want to keep animals outside of the frame of what we consider "real lives," lives worthy of moral consideration, grievable lives.

See Chloë Taylor. "The Precarious Lives of Animals: Butler, Coetzee, and Animal Ethics," *Philosophy Today.* 1.52, 2008. 60–72. 64.

The inter-subjective, institutional and epistemic violence of sovereignty construes and limits ethical possibility. It makes us actually believe that there are "dumb animals" and "inferior humans" to consider in an ethical framework, displacing the urgent need to address and challenge manifest forms of power and violence, and attendant systems of truth, that produce arbitrary hierarchised distinctions between otherwise like entities. It makes us believe that ("fully formed") humans get the right to decide. The challenge, the ethical challenge no less, is to identify and unpick sovereignty in the first instance, rather than attempt to construct an ethics after sovereignty has organised hierarchical divisions.

War and Truth

Putting forward a view that we are at war with animals suggests we must challenge how we conceptualise the political sphere, not only who participates in the political sphere, but the constitution and functioning of institutions within that sphere. There would appear to be at least two paths that inform the orientation of thinkers and their approach to the political sphere. The first, which I would broadly associate with liberalism, assumes justice and rationality behind political institutions, and therefore externalises violence, atrocity and war as exceptional rather than intrinsic to the political sphere. The second path, which I would associate with the "critical tradition," views this same situation with more skepticism, arguing that violence is inherent to the functioning of political institutions, and that asymmetries in power must always be treated as the norm, and therefore a reality of systemic arrangements. In using war as a starting point for understanding our relationship with animals, this book takes this second path. Rather than take violence towards animals as exceptional, I start with the assumption that this is the norm. As far as our intentions go, I have assumed that our intention is almost always the continued instrumental use of animals towards our own ends; we are invested in our own continuing domination of non human life and it continues to provide us "benefits."

One of the challenges with this position is that many people experience relationships with animals that would, on the face of it, appear to be peaceful and friendly, and run against the grain of a presumption that our mainstay relation is one of domination and instrumentalisation. Consider pet ownership, where the lived experience of some pet owners is of companionship, communication and love. Pet owners often lavish deep care on the animals they spend their lives with, and care and affection clearly shape exchanges between humans and animals in these situations. As Haraway suggests, and I discuss in Chapter 6, there is a degree of "co-shaping" in these relationships which makes it difficult to assume a one-way domination, or suggest that instumentalisation is always "problematic."[147] However, these everyday experiences must always be contextualised, even our relationships with pets. Where peaceable coexistence between humans and animals creates possibilities for friendship, such as with companion animals, this bond is placed in question by the modes of disciple, surveillance, containment and control that attend and are inherent to the practice of "pet ownership" and "domestication."[148] The millions of pets "euthanised" in animal shelters annually[149] highlight that even examples of seemingly happy cohabitation between humans and animals are framed within an "adopt, foster, euthanize"[150] context of over-arching, and deadly, violence. If we take this frame into account, as I have suggested we must do in my discussion of privatised government and companionship in Chapters 5 and 6, then it becomes difficult to imagine what friendship might look like within this context. My position, rather, is to suggest that even if friendships with animals are possible today, they must be considered with respect to the violent practices that frame them (surveillance, containment, reproductive control etc.); violence and domination remain the mainstay everyday practice of our relationship with other animals.[151]

---

147   See Haraway. *When Species Meet.*

148   See discussion in Chapter 6 on the *Companion Animals Act 1998.*

149   See, for example, Elizabeth A. Clancy and Andrew N. Rowan. "Companion Animal Demographics in the United States: A Historical Perspective." D.J. Salem, and A.N. Rowan Eds. *The State of the Animals* II: *2003.* Washington D.C.: Humane Society Press, 2003.

150   Bernard E. Rollin and Michael D.H. Rollin. "Dogmatism and Catechisms: Ethics and Companion Animals." Susan J. Armstrong and Richard G. Botzler Eds. *The Animal Ethics Reader* 2nd *Edition Ed.* London: Routledge, 2008. 547.

151   Taking this position has particular effects. We must necessarily suspend any idea that our treatment of animals is due to a misunderstanding by most people—a misunderstanding about the capabilities of animals or the suffering they have experienced—and that rectification of our current situation will come when we make most people understand that animals have equivalent capacities or that they suffer. Singer, for example, famously uses a utilitarian approach to show that our treatment of animals is morally inconsistent. The trajectory of the argument is, at least in some respects, brilliantly logical. However, it is not clear that acknowledging the mere fact of this inconsistency—between how we treat humans and how we treat animals—should be a trigger for reform of our actions. Similarly, Regan demonstrates that sentience implies rights, and again uses an argumentative train that implies knowledge of our own failure to respect rights should lead to just action in favour of ending violence towards animals. Both Singer and Regan's viewpoints would significantly alter the worlds we live in, provided we lived in a world where rational

One of the challenges of this hostile terrain, as I have suggested, is that we don't believe we are at war with animals. Indeed a range of symbolic and material resources are deployed to deny that in fact a war is ongoing. The image that one finds on some butcher shop signs, or on the sides of refrigerated trucks, featuring a smiling cartoonised cow or pig slicing at their own bodies with a knife, attests to the casual way in which everyday violence is discursively hidden from view. Indeed, as in this case, the reality of violence is covered over by the discursive effect that animals actually enjoy suffering and being killed for human palettes, and they would gladly participate in this self execution. As Cathy B. Glenn has observed with regard to the use of animal caricatures in advertising promotion, there is a "painful paradox" here: "nonhuman animals finally can speak to us and reason with us, but only from the perspective of an industry selling them to us, the consuming public. They are virtually gagged— they cannot language their actual pain or protest."[152]

There is a question here of "truth" and its relationship to power. Sovereignty as an internalised war generates "truth effects" which construct subjectivities and knowledges in relation to power. Foucault links truth and power in a

---

argumentation convinced actors to change their worldviews, and then precipitated change. If we lived in such a world, then it would appear that the reason we haven't stopped killing or hurting animals is that we need to do a better job of convincing people that the ethical course of action is to do otherwise. However, as I have described above, the problem is not so much about ethics as about sovereignty. We do not need more argumentation showing us what animals are "capable of." Nor do we need more argument showing us that our treatment of animals is morally or rationally in error. It is not evidence or moral inconsistency that is the problem. Rather the question that seems pressing is why we act, almost "stupidly," in spite of the evidence that suggests we should not act in the way in which we do. Why it is we should make animals suffer when we know they suffer? Why is it that we should continue to kill and deny animals agency and politics when we know they are very much likely to be political and social beings much like ourselves? Note that this is a problem that differs from the ethical problem Aristotle posed with his concept of *akrasia* (that is, choosing a course of action that one knows is not "right" due to a failure of will). This problem is, on the contrary, characterised by a willfulness; that is a choice of action in spite of known facts; as I argue later in this book, this might be called "stupidity." We make animals suffer even though we know they suffer, in spite of their known suffering. This is, I believe, a political rather than ethical problem. The political question seems to me to be about trying to understand how human institutional arrangements should come to be assembled to allow for us to justify the continuation of a violence we are invested in despite known facts or, perhaps worse, deny that war is underway, even as the corpses pile up around us.

152 Cathy B. Glenn. "Constructing Consumables and Consent: A Critical Analysis of Factory Farm Industry Discourse." *Journal of Communication Inquiry*. 28:1, 2004. 63–81. 76.

circular relation, where knowledge and political relationships, authorisations to speak, and subjectivities are inter-related. Foucault states:

> The important thing here, I believe, is that truth isn't outside power, or lacking in power: contrary to a myth whose history and functions would repay further study, truth isn't the reward of free spirits, the child of protracted solitude, nor the privilege of those who have succeeded in liberating themselves. Truth is a thing of this world: it is produced only by virtue of multiple forms of constraint. And it induces regular effects of power. Each society has its régime of truth, its 'general politics' of truth: that is, the types of discourse which it accepts and makes function as true; the mechanisms and instances which enable one to distinguish true and false statements, the means by which each is sanctioned; the techniques and procedures accorded value in the acquisition of truth; the status of those who are charged with saying what counts as true.[153]

In this characterisation, what counts as true is inherent rather than external to a system.[154] I believe this picture Foucault provides of the relationship between truth and power becomes more nuanced in his later work, where a clearer understanding of a "circulatory" relationship emerges between *subjectivity*, *knowledge* and *government*[155] (a relation I shall discuss in the Conclusion of this book), three terms that happen to align with the three forms of violence I have suggested comprise our war on animals (namely, inter-subjective, institutional and epistemic). Understanding our own relationship to this war means deciphering the connections between different strands in this interplay, and understanding how shifts between each of these elements re-mould our

---

153   Michel Foucault. "Truth and Power." 131.
154   Foucault goes on to say:
        In societies like ours, the 'political economy' of truth is characterised by five important traits.
        Truth is centred on the form of scientific discourse and the institutions which produce it; it is
        subject to constant economic and political incitement (the demand for truth, as much for
        economic production as for political power); it is the object, under diverse forms, of immense
        diffusion and consumption (circulating through apparatuses of education and information
        whose extent is relatively broad in the social body, not withstanding certain strict limita-
        tions); it is produced and transmitted under the control, dominant if not exclusive, of a few
        great political and economic apparatuses (university, army, writing, media); lastly, it is the
        issue of a whole political debate and social confrontation ('ideological' struggles).
        See Foucault, "Truth and Power." 131–2.
155   See Michel Foucault. *The Courage of Truth: Lectures at the Collège de France 1983–1984.*
        New York: Palgrave MacMillan, 2011. 8–9.

own relationships to power. Importantly, we must seek to understand how our ability to speak against domination is enabled within particular modes of truth telling—or veridiction—and the way in which "resistance" to wartime truths—such as a belief that animals enjoy suffering for human use—requires us to shift whole knowledge systems in order to challenge human sovereignty over other animals. As I shall suggest in the Conclusion of this book, we need to investigate the possibility of a "counter-conduct" in the way Foucault described, in order to resist these truths produced through a governmental project: "We do not want this truth. We do not want to be held in this system of truth."[156]

This book is divided into four parts. Part One ("Biopolitics") comprises a discussion of Foucault's conceptualisation of biopolitics, its relationship to animality, sovereign exception and governmentality. In Chapter 1 ("Bare Life") I examine biopolitics through Agamben, via Aristotle. A particular interest here is the notion of "bare life" that Agamben constructs from a Foucauldian biopolitics; this term is eminently useful, precisely because it captures the positionality of animals, particularly within the context of industrialised farming, as inhabiting a zone of indistinction between life and death. There is a symmetry and interconnection between the world of human politics and human domination of non human animals, as Wolfe has observed, where our decision to put humans into concentration camps, or torture facilities obeys a similar biopolitical logic to our decisions to subject animals to horrors of industrialised slaughter: "they're animals anyway, so let them lose their souls."[157] Indeed, as I argue, the profitability of industrialised farming, the quest to capture and capitalise at every moment within the process of transformation of animal into meat, a process that encompasses life, death and reproduction, tends precisely towards the production of lives on the threshold of death, since any surplus—a cage that is too large, nutrition beyond strict requirements, flesh, blood, bone or sinew that is not put to sale—is necessarily "waste." In this sense the terms "livestock" should be understood strictly as animals who have life and nothing else. I use Mbembe's exploration of "necropolitics" to think further how it is that biopolitics may establish regimes committed to death, and how war can be structured and "compartmentalised" to achieve these ongoing hostilities.

In Chapter 2 ("Governmentality") I examine Foucault's genealogy of *pastoral* forms of power as a "prelude to governmentality." I propose a rereading of

156   Michel Foucault, *Security, Territory, Population: Lectures at the Collège de France*, 1977–78. London: Palgrave Macmillan, 2007. 201.

157   "Don" Zaluchi, the fictional head of the Zaluchi family in Francis Coppola's *The Godfather* makes this reference to drug use amongst "coloured" people. See Francis Ford Coppola. *The Godfather.* Screenplay by Mario Puzo and Francis Ford Coppola. Paramount Pictures, 1972.

Foucault's model history of the emergence of governmentality, arguing that pastoral power should not be treated as a reaction to sovereignty, but precisely as a modality of sovereignty that reorganises forces of life and death through refined techniques of control. As a result, governmentality might be understood as the progressive extension to human subjects of technologies of pastoral power, including techniques of violence and death, learnt for centuries through human management of non human animals.

Part Two ("Conquest") examines the dynamics of the appropriation of non human animals by humans through biopolitics, property, containment and "friendship." Chapter 3 ("Immunity") interrogates Roberto Esposito's discussion of biopolitics and sovereignty as a guarantor of *immunity*. What interests me here in Esposito's account is the possibility of understanding the dynamics of human violence towards animals as a form of immunity; quite literally, we kill and make animals suffer to immunise (or securitise) a conceptualisation of the human. Chapter 4 ("Property and Excess") extends this further, examining John Locke's configuration of the human property right (a conceptualisation that Esposito suggests is central to the biopolitical process of sovereign immunisation). What I note here is that appropriation of animals appears in Locke's account to be the defining example for how property is acquired; importantly this mode of acquisition does not occur because humans are "superior" to animals, but rather because humans happen to prevail over other animals where competing drives to self-preservation are at stake. My interest here, through a reading of Karl Marx, is to try and identify the way in which this process of appropriation is both prior to the commodification, and obeys a form of commodification that is not present in the exchange of human labour. As I argue, when Marx exclaims in *Capital* that there can be "no boots without leather," he is veiling the forms of war that produce leather as a "simple" commodity for consumption within a process of exchange.

The war against animals operates across multiple levels stretching from macropolitical battles to infinitely segmented micropolitical modes of control. A challenge remains in understanding how individual human action operates in this field, and the authorisations and delegations of sovereignty that accompany this process. Part Three ("Private Dominion") examines the process by which war is conducted utilising individual humans as agents within a broader conflict. In Chapter 5 ("Privatisation and Containment") I turn to radical feminist discussions of rape, particularly that of Susan Brownmiller and Catharine MacKinnon, to understand the way in which we might conceptualise the actions of individuals within a broader systemic form of violence. I note that a feature of radical feminist discussions of rape is an understanding of sexual assault as a "war against women," which places privatised forms of violence in

the hands of individual men, and produces a system of violence that underpins a systemic male dominance in the form of patriarchy. Extending this further, I look at Mbembe's examination of "privatised" forms of government, and
the way in which sovereignty might be defracted and operate through multiple
agents and heterogonous authorisations to violence. Finally, I examine containment as a strategy of war, with a focus on the way in which privatised,
individualised containment authorisations produce a systemic schema of control, from factory farm to experimental lab to suburban back yard, enabling a
type of "gulag archipelago."

The issue I raised above—on how we might conceptualise a war against
animals while many humans enjoy relationships of apparent friendship with
companion animals—is examined in Chapter 6 ("Companionship"). I focus in
this Chapter on Haraway's rejection of an animal rights focus on domination in
favour of an understanding of human/animal relationships as a process of "co-
shaping." Whilst I acknowledge here that indeed humans and animals do
shape each other's actions, the danger of Haraway's approach is to side-step
the question of violence, particularly manifold forms of violent domination
that are the mainstay of our relations with animals and form the context for
companion animal relations. "Friendship" with animals is certainly possible;
however, these friendships must be understood in context of the wider war,
cognisant of the forms of violence that accompany and frame these friendships.

In Part Four of this book ("Sovereignty"), I examine some recent accounts of
animal sovereignties. If our relationships with animals might be understood as
a form of sovereign dominion, it is imaginable that animals might exert their
own sovereignty, and/or humans might recognise the sovereign claims of animals. In Chapter 7 ("Capability") I look at two proposals that emerge from liberal political theory: "Simian Sovereignty" as discussed by Robert E. Goodin,
Carole Pateman and Roy Pateman, and "Wild Animal Sovereignty" as proposed
by Donaldson and Kymlicka. I point out that these liberal visions for sovereignty are constrained in numerous ways. Firstly, as in the Goodin, Pateman
and Pateman's proposal, sovereignty is granted to animals who can demonstrate a "capacity" for sovereignty (in this case great apes), thus distinctions are
introduced as to who can access sovereignty rights, and the terms for establishing a "capability" involve a resemblance to humans. We see this secondly in the
attachment that Goodin, Pateman and Pateman, and Donaldson and Kymlicka
maintain with respect to territory, where sovereignty claims are articulated—
as they are under the Westphalian system—by a claim of a "people" to a relationship
to territory. As I argue, this creates an unnecessarily deterministic affiliation
between sovereignty and territory, where it is assumed that sovereignty can
only exist where a group can assert a claim to territory. This is, in essence, a

"capability" assumption that is arbitrary, and rests upon a human prerogative to decide. Indeed, I note that a key problem with these accounts *is* that the right of humans to decide remains fervently intact. We see this human sovereign prerogative play out to disturbing effect in Donaldson and Kymlicka's account, where, in the case of domestic animals, an argument is made for human control over sexuality and reproduction "for the good" of these animals.

I argue that rather than assume sovereignty rests upon a capability, or is attached to territory, or relies upon a governing authority to award sovereign rights (that is, humans), we must instead treat sovereignty as a groundless claim: in the words of Jens Bartelson, "sovereignty has no essence."[158] In Chapter 8 ("The Violence of Stupidity"), I explore the idea of sovereignty as a groundless claim through Derrida's discussion of sovereignty in *The Beast and the Sovereign* lectures. I note here two distinctive tendencies in Derrida's identification of sovereignty. Firstly, in so far as sovereignty is the assertion of a right irrelevant of a factual grounding, it does not reflect a rational "just" intention, but instead represents a kind of "stupidity." Secondly, sovereignty involves the violence of overcoming and appropriating another entity, which in this process declares a superiority over this same entity. In other words, as Derrida notes, there is nothing superior about the sovereign; only a claim made through violence authorises this superiority. Here we find Derrida in strange agreement with Locke, at least in the sense that human dominion over animals does not necessarily come through any inherent superiority, but through a violent quest for self-preservation which happens to prevail over other animals, and their own push for self-preservation. Force in this case precedes the epistemic claim of superiority, and not the other way around. Human "superiority" is nothing more that the artifice of our own practices of violent domination over other animals.

I conclude this book by speculating on how we might move forward. I explore the possibility of disarmament of human sovereignty through forms of "counterconduct." In particular my challenge here is to think through how to address violence at inter-subjective, institutional and epistemic levels, and not merely reinstate forms of human domination. I finally examine the concept of "truce." My interest here is the idea of a suspension in armed hostilities that might create a space for renegotiating human and animal relationships, realising what Andrea Dworkin had phrased in the context of truce as a beginning "to the real practice of equality."[159]

---

158   Jens Bartelson. *A Genealogy of Sovereignty.* Cambridge and New York: Cambridge University Press, 1995. 51

159   Andrea Dworkin. "Take Back the Day: I Want a Twenty Four Hour Truce During Which There is No Rape." Andrea Dworkin Online Library. At: www.nostatusquo.com/ACLU/dworkin/WarZoneChaptIIIE.html.

PART 1

Biopolitics

∴

Bare Life

> Smithfield's pigs live by the hundreds or thousands in warehouse-like barns, in rows of wall-to-wall pens. Sows are artificially inseminated and fed and delivered of their piglets in cages so small they cannot turn around. Forty fully grown 250-pound male hogs often occupy a pen the size of a tiny apartment. They trample each other to death. There is no sunlight, straw, fresh air or earth. The floors are slatted to allow excrement to fall into a catchment pit under the pens, but many things besides excrement can wind up in the pits: afterbirths, piglets accidentally crushed by their mothers, old batteries, broken bottles of insecticide, antibiotic syringes, stillborn pigs—anything small enough to fit through the foot-wide pipes that drain the pits. The pipes remain closed until enough sewage accumulates in the pits to create good expulsion pressure; then the pipes are opened and everything bursts out into a large holding pond.
>
> JEFF TIETZ. *"Boss Hog: The Rapid Rise of Industrialised Swine."*[1]

How does the question of *life* itself relate to the life of the (non human) animal? And how might including the animal within the sphere of politics reshape how we understand biopolitics? In this chapter I examine biopolitics as a descriptor for human violence towards non human animals. I begin this discussion with Aristotle, who I believe sets the grounds for the contest between humans and animals that is characteristic of politics itself. I then turn to Agamben's influential account of biopolitics and its relation to sovereignty. This account can be adapted to describe human relations with animals, which place animals in industrialised slaughter on the veritable threshold between life and death. I explore this further using Mbembe's concept of "necropower," which allows us to understand the war against animals as comprising interconnected sites or hotspots of intense violence and death, which operate almost imperceptibly within everyday peaceable human relations.

---

1 Jeff Tietz. "Boss Hog: The Rapid Rise of Industrialized Swine." Daniel Imhoff Ed. *The CAFO Reader: The Tragedy of Industrial Animal Factories.* Berkeley and Los Angeles: University of California Press. 109–24. 110.

Aristotle's Biopolitics

That non human animals are not clearly eligible for consideration within a discussion of biopolitics is not due to any essential poverty in the scope of Foucault's term. Indeed, as I have discussed in the Introduction, the *species* context of Foucault's definition of biopolitics provides many avenues for understanding biopolitics as precisely concerning the relation between human and animal. Why it is that Foucault did not consider human treatment of animals as constituting a primary site of biopolitics seems to relate to a deficiency within the tradition of politics itself, at least in the West, which has, by and large, exempted the non human animal from agency as a political being. For, according to this perspective, even if there were to be a non human animal who, through a vocalisation, could make itself understood, that being would still lack the ability to comprehend justice; Aristotle characterises "man" as *the* political animal *par excellence.*[2] The assertion, that there is something essential that separates humans from the rest of the animals, is hardly limited to Aristotle, and has remained in various forms within Western philosophy, whether in the belief that "man" possesses an immortal soul which animals lack, or that "man" possesses a sort of exemplary consciousness which other living matter has no access to. However, Aristotle's pronouncement that "man" distinguishes himself from other animals through the perfection of his status as a "political animal" provides a neat way to conceptualise the problem we have before us: namely, how it is that humans, as just another species of animal, should come to dominate other animals and simultaneously proclaim an intellectual superiority to found this act of sovereignty. For Aristotle, "man" is not a transcendent being who is unrelated to the animal life; rather, "man" is defined as an animal with a surplus ability over and above other animal life. Upon this reckoning, the *gap* between non human and human animals is the ability to vocalise principles related to expediency (or rationality) and justice, a gap which, for all intents, defines the meaning of politics itself, at least in so far as it is perfected by "man."

It would not be unfair to say that Aristotle is almost perversely interested in animals and their relationship to the human. Aristotle, after all, contributed a five volume biological treatise on animal life—*History of Animals, On the Parts of Animals, On the Motion of Animals, On the Gait of Animals* and *On the Generation of Animals*—which variously offer detailed examinations on the anatomy, movement and reproduction of animal life. Importantly, within

---

2   Aristotle. *Politics.* Robert M. Hutchins Ed. *The Works of Aristotle.* Vol. 2. Chicago: Encyclopaedia Britannica. 445–548. 446.

these works, human life was not treated separately, but regarded as one of the many species under Aristotle's magnifying glass, and thus there is an implicit understanding of the interconnection between human and animal life. Aristotle's aim here is to situate the human within the field of animal life by providing a sense as to what human life shares, and does not share, with other animals.

But it is not merely in Aristotle's biological studies that we find a connection drawn between human and animal, but, it would seem, this connection may be found at various important threshold points within the body of Aristotle's work. Consider Aristotle's volume on *Logic*. Here, on page after page, indeed from the first page of the first book, the example of the distinction and non-distinction between animal and human life is used to illustrate the nature of logical argument. For example, in Book 1, Chapter 2 of "Prior Analytics," Aristotle proclaims:

> ...if some B is A, then some of the As must be B. For if none were, then no B would be A. But if some B is not A, there is no necessity that some of the As should not be B; e.g. let B stand for animal and A for man. Not every animal is a man; but every man is an animal.[3]

This distinction, that the human belongs to animals, but not all animals are human, is of course pivotal to Aristotle's definition of the human, and that special quality that is inherent to the human yet not generalisable to other animals. Indeed it is worth emphasising that in the citation above, this particular relationship is not merely "in theory" but elevated to a matter of logic: "Not every animal is a man; but every man is an animal." This is the same "logic" that grounds Aristotle's proclamation in *Politics* on the relationship between humans, animals and politics:

> ...it is evident that the state is a creation of nature, and that man is by nature a political animal. And he who by nature and not by mere accident is without state, is either a bad man or above humanity; he is like the
> *Tribeless, lawless, hearthless one,*
> Whom Homer denounces–the natural outcast is forthwith a lover of war; he may be compared to an isolated piece at draughts.
> Now that man is more of a political animal than bees or other gregarious animals is evident. Nature, as we say, makes nothing in vain, and man is the only animal who she has endowed with the gift of speech. And whereas mere voice is but an indication of pleasure or pain, and is therefore

---

3   Aristotle. *Logic*. Robert M. Hutchins Ed. *The Works of Aristotle*. Vol. 1. Chicago: Encyclopaedia Britannica. 3–253.

found in other animals (for their nature attains to the perception of pleasure and pain and the intimation of them to one another, and no further),
the power of speech is intended to set forth the expedient and inexpedi-
ent, and therefore likewise the just and unjust. And it is a characteristic of
man that he alone has any sense of good and evil, of just and unjust, and
the like, and the association of living beings who have this sense makes a
family and a state.[4]

In this section of *Politics*, Aristotle makes a decisive pronouncement that captures the logic of biopolitics, its necessary connection to politics in the West,
and the extent and limits of its jurisdiction. Indeed I think this section of
Politics provides a template for understanding the mode of the arbitrary distinction between human and animals that crowns the human declaration of
our own sovereignty. The section is interesting for a number of reasons. *Firstly*,
the logical distinction outlined above ("Not every animal is a man; but every
man is an animal") is founded through a differentiation in relation to the
human propensity for political community that apparently exceeds other
comparable species (certainly, more clearly than "bees or other gregarious animals"). Note here that although "man" possesses a quality that is not shared by
other animals, the structure of this same logic dictates that "man" remains at
base an animal. The human is both beyond the animal, yet absolutely captured
by the animal: the human is an entity that extends beyond what it is, yet at the
same time is what it is.

Secondly, Aristotle describes the graduated scheme by which human animals may be distributed across varying positions along the long trajectory
between the animal and the idealised human subject. This entity, "the bad
man" or the one "above humanity," is unable to perfect "his" nature: "For man,
when perfected, is the best of the animals, but when separated from law and
justice, he is the worst of all...he is the most unholy and the most savage of
animals, and the most full of lust and gluttony."[5] This particular bond between
the human who has lost its relation to justice and non human animal life is all
too apparent in Aristotle's discussion of slavery, where the slave is understood
as the human who is closer to the animals, as the human animal who has not
developed that quality that marks it out as a more perfect animal:

> When there is such a difference as that between soul and body, or between
> men and animals...the lower sort are by nature slaves, and it is better for

---

4   Aristotle. *Politics*. 446 [1253a].
5   Aristotle, *Politics*. 446 [1253a].

them as for all inferiors that they should be under the rule of a master...
indeed the use made of slaves and of tame animals is not very different;
for both with their bodies minister to the needs of life.[6]

It seems necessary here to emphasise the importance of the *soul* through
Aristotle's understanding of politics, an importance that is arguably illustrative
of the political sphere in the classical tradition, and its peculiar relationship to
animal life. It is within this tradition that discussions on the nature of the soul
are necessarily wed to an understanding of how the political sphere is constructed. This lies behind so much of the reasoning within Plato's *Republic*; for
example, in so far as the alleged beauty of the political system Plato proposes
is tied intimately to the sense of justice it offers in aligning the political sphere
to the souls of its citizens[7] (in this sense, justice is produced by a harmonisa-
tion of social relations with the souls of its constituents). Yet where Aristotle
differs significantly from Plato is in his resolute understanding of the connection between the human soul and the animal soul. Indeed in his work entitled
On the Soul (De Anima), Aristotle explicitly draws a point of difference between
his own work and that of previous thinkers, by accusing these philosophers of
erroneously only concerning themselves with investigating the "human soul"
rather than the souls of animals in the first instance.[8] According to Aristotle,
the soul is not an essence or spirit that is distinct from, and may survive the
extinguishment of, the biological body. Instead, the soul is presented as the living
presence of the biological organism: in Aristotle's words, "the soul is the cause
or source of the living body."[9] Aristotle states that there are three properties
that may belong to a fully formed soul: thinking; perception; and generation/
nutrition.[10] It is the latter property that refers to the minimal condition of
functioning for any biological organism, and acts as its baseline principle for
living in its barest sense.

It is possible here to see the connection that is drawn between human and
animal life, and the importance of the animal soul as a baseline for the human soul.

---

6   Aristotle. *Politics*. 448 [1254b]. Once again, we find the inescapability of the animal
     essence within the definition of the human essence: the slave is the human animal who
     has failed to demonstrate that he is human, and thus is at base a mere animal.
7   From *The Republic*: "when God fashioned you he added gold in the composition of those of
     you who are qualified to be Rulers...he put silver in the Auxiliaries, and iron and bronze in
     the farmers and other workers." Plato. *The Republic*. London: Penguin, 2003: 116–7, [415a-b].
8   Aristotle. *On The Soul (de Anima)*. Robert M. Hutchins Ed. *The Works of Aristotle*. Vol.
     1.Chicago: Encyclopaedia Britannica, 1952. 631–68. 631 [402b].
9   Aristotle. *On the Soul*. 645 [415b].
10   Aristotle. *On the Soul*. 645 [414b].

The human must be thought of firstly as an ensouled body: in Aristotle's words, "the soul plus the body constitutes the animal."[11] And thus the human is not the only organism owed a soul—rather the human is an animal with a soul which happens to also possess properties that may extend beyond the merely living animal. Although humans are granted a thinking faculty beyond other animals, the human is still at base an animal, and, as Aristotle's discussion of slaves demonstrates, some humans may never be accorded a "fully formed soul," and thus always may be condemned to be closer to the animal.[12] What Aristotle provides here, in other words, is a schema by which organisms are attributed political capacity and authority based upon a biologically prescribed status. Principles of inclusion, exclusion and partial inclusion into political community are determined through a biological schema of classification; this is, as we shall discuss below, a potential preliminary template for a biopolitics.

Agamben's Bare Life

Agamben's concept of "bare life" does not explicitly include animal life, although, as discussed below, it threatens to return human life to a point where it becomes *indistinct* from that of (non human) animals. Agamben's designation of bare life originates in Walter Benjamin's work "Critique of Violence,"

---

11   Aristotle. *On the Soul.* 643 [413a].

12   Foucault makes an important observation in *Discipline and Punish* that modern punishment affected a shift of focus from "the body to the soul" (see Michel Foucault. *Discipline and Punish: The Birth of the Prison.* London: Penguin Books, 1991). In this regard, it is interesting to note Judith Butler's response to Luce Irigaray in *Bodies That Matter* here, and its relevance to how a political technology of the soul might relate to forms of exclusion. Butler states:

> Plato's scenography of intelligibility depends on the exclusion of women, slaves, children and animals, where slaves are characterized as those who do not speak his language, and who, not speaking his language, are considered diminished in their capacity for reason. This xenophobic exclusion operates through the production of racialised Others, and those whose "natures" are considered less rational by virtue of their appointed task in the process of laboring to reproduce the conditions of private life. This domain of the less than rational human bounds the figure of human reason, producing that "man" as one who is without childhood; is not a primate and so is relieved of the necessity of eating, defecating, living and dying; one who is not a slave, but always a property holder; one whose language remains originary and untranslatable.

> See Judith Butler. *Bodies That Matter.* London and New York: Routledge, 2011. 21.

where the term used by Benjamin—*bloße Leben*[13]—signifies "bare life," "naked life," "uncovered life," or, as in the Edmund Jephcott translation of the piece, "mere life." For Benjamin, "mere life" is life that is the subject of "mythical" violence. This is violence which Benjamin suggests founds law, mirroring that of the gods of Greek mythology; a violence which does not merely punish (or maintain law), but at the moment at which it strikes, creates law itself.[14] Benjamin states that all violence as a means is either lawmaking or law-preserving.[15] *Lawmaking* violence refers to an extraordinary violence which is wielded without strict precedent, which subsequently ushers in new law: the violence of colonisation, including dispossession, murder and outright geno-cide, in so far as it inaugurates continuing domination, might serve as an example of this sort of violence. *Law-preserving* violence, on the other hand, is that force which the sovereign wields within the bounds of already existing law (for example, the routine prosecution of those convicted of breaches of regula-tions). For Benjamin, law is caught oscillating between these two exercises of violence as a means.[16]

Agamben's reworking of bare life is located at that space of movement between lawmaking and law-preserving violence. Agamben suggests that the bare or "sacred" life may be distinguished as that "life that may be killed but not sacrificed":

> The most ancient recorded forms of capital punishment (the terrible *poena cullei*, in which the condemned man, with his head covered in wolf-skin, was put in a sack with serpents, a dog and a rooster, and then thrown into water, or defenestration from the Tarpean rock) are actually purification rites and not death penalties in the modern sense: the *neque fas est eum immolari* served precisely to distinguish the killing of *homo sacer* from ritual purifications, and decisively excluded *sacratio* from the religious sphere in the strict sense.[17]

That the law reserves the right to take life is something that has tradition-ally been associated with the prerogative of the sovereign, although in the

---

13   Walter Benjamin. "Critique of Violence." Walter Benjamin. *Selected Writings Volume 1, 1913–1926*. M. Bullock and M.W. Jennings Eds. Cambridge: The Belknap Press of Harvard University Press, 1996. 236–52.

14   Benjamin. "Critique of Violence." 248.

15   Benjamin. "Critique of Violence." 243.

16   Benjamin. "Critique of Violence." 251.

17   Benjamin. "Critique of Violence." 81.

contemporary context, as noted above in relation to Foucault's observations on modern sovereignty, this right may be exercised with differing tactics (e.g., mass war) and towards a different end (that is, life) than that exercised by the kings of old (indeed, as I shall discuss in Chapter 5, this right to kill can be privatised and disseminated when it comes to the life and death powers exercised by humans over animals). But what is distinctive for Agamben about sovereign power is the attempt to wrest life, both from the rule of law ("to kill without constituting homicide") and from the divine ("to kill without sacrifice"). Sovereignty, in the act of condemnation, may both *commit the act which it itself forbids* (thus the State reserves the right to "murder without apparent contradiction in law and exempt the condemned from any trace of the divine in his or her punishment"). If, as Benjamin states, the threat of a divine or "pure" violence (that is, a violence not exercised as means, rather as an expiatory force) is that it deposes sovereign power–"on the abolition of state power, a new historical epoch is founded"[18]–then earthly State making is bound in the exorcism of the threat of the divine from within the sphere of its violence. The bodies of the condemned are not presented up as an offering to the gods, but instead as boundary posts, marked by the violence of the law.

It is this power of the sovereign, to create a space where life is neither subject to law, nor to divine sacrifice, that Agamben links to Carl Schmitt's argument that sovereignty's definitive power lies in its ability to constitute *exception*.[19] The moment where the sovereign decides upon the exception is the moment when the law is apparently suspended. The "state of emergency," declared in the moment of "crisis," is evoked in order for the sovereign to exercise a power which temporarily puts out of operation the laws and rights which are otherwise enforced. The martial law declared in Beijing in 1989, for example, which eventuated in the death of up to 4000 people, created the opportunity for a violence which did not clearly make the law, nor maintain law, but moved indeterminately between these two forms of violence (the military were both "maintaining order" and "taking extra-ordinary measures"). Yet whilst for Schmitt the essence of the power of exception is encapsulated in the decision the sovereign casts in the state of emergency—"an absolute decision created out of nothingness"[20]—for Agamben the exception is treated as a "sphere" within which the exceptional decision may be made, and where the life that is captured within this sphere becomes the focus of exception. To refer

---

18   Benjamin. "Critique of Violence." 252.

19   Carl Schmitt. *Political Theology: Four Chapters on the Concept of Sovereignty*. Cambridge: The MIT Press, 1988.

20   Schmitt. *Political Theology*. 66.

once more to the example of the Beijing massacre, at 1.30am on June 4th government loudspeakers around Tiananmen Square broadcast a warning that the army "would no longer exercise restraint" and that the "personal safety of those who disregarded this warning 'could no longer be guaranteed.'"[21]

Agamben's notion of bare life is the synthesis of at least three theoretical reflections upon sovereignty; firstly, Benjamin's "bare life," which for Agamben, is the "bearer of the link between violence and law;"[22] secondly, Schmitt's concept of exception; and finally Foucault's reflections upon the relation of sovereignty to bio-power.[23] Agamben's bare life is not only the subject of the violence of the law, but also specifically the life that occupies the space that is vulnerable to the exceptional violence of the sovereign. The power of the sovereign is founded upon the right to declare an exception with regard to life, and rule indeterminately over that life which is subject to this ban. It is this very focus of the sovereign upon the life that is held within the sphere of exception that also transforms the sphere of exception into a biopolitical space: Agamben comments, therefore, that "Western politics is a biopolitics from the very beginning."[24] If the distinctive power of the sovereign is to name the exception, and this power is founded upon life itself, then the political question, in so far politics remains articulated through the State, has never been able to escape from the constitution of life.

It is in this sense that Agamben can proclaim that today "it is not the city but rather the camp that is the fundamental biopolitical paradigm of the west."[25] The city, which stands as the symbol of the civil politic and the sign of the "covenant" through which citizens join together and invest their authority in the sovereign,[26] does not for Agamben represent the founding impulse of the modern State; rather this impulse is to be found in exception. If Western sovereignty is characterised by exception, then it cannot be founded fundamentally upon inclusion, rather an *inclusive exclusion,* the creation of a space within the realm of sovereign power which is nevertheless exempted from both law and rights: "Sovereign violence is in truth founded not on a pact but on the exclusive

---

21   Timothy Brook, *Quelling the People: The Military Suppression of the Beijing Democracy Movement.* New York: Oxford University Press, 1992. 135.

22   Agamben. *Homo Sacer.* 65.

23   Additionally, Hannah Arendt's reading of statelessness in *The Origins of Totalitarianism* is arguably formative for Agamben in arriving at a conceptualisation of exception as a space which is capable of capturing life. See particularly Arendt. *The Origins of Totalitarianism.* 267–302.

24   Agamben. *Homo Sacer.* 181.

25   Agamben. *Homo Sacer.* 181.

26   Thomas Hobbes. *Leviathan.* London: Everyman, 1994. 100.

inclusion of bare life in the state."[27] The camp, as the physical space where life is held within a zone of sovereign exception, is not regarded by Agamben as an historical "anomaly," but rather as the "hidden matrix and nomos of the political space in which we are still living."[28] The relation of the camp to sovereignty is one where the powers exercised routinely by the sovereign are present within the space of the camp in a refined and intensified form. If one considers, for example, the law of the camp, it is difficult to locate its governing rules, since within the space, as is infamously recorded in the history of concentration camps in the twentieth century, anything is painfully possible. The law appears as suspended, because the camp is a physical space of pure exception, where decisions over the life of its inmates may be made quickly, without reference to regular legal convention (courts, defence, evidence etc.) Yet this same space is legitimised by the sovereign as "within the law." The camp is also a space for the exercise of a concentrated biopolitics. Not only is this a space where nutrition, sleep, movement, sexuality and work may be ruthlessly surveyed, but the character of every decision is one that inevitably refers to the mere fact of living. (In the Nazi extermination camps, prisoners either joined the queue for the gas chamber or, if fit enough, joined the ranks of prisoners forced to assist in the exterminations). In this sense, the politics of the camp is purely of "life and death."

It is not difficult to see here the possibility for applying Foucault and Agamben to understanding the "animal industrial complex." As I shall discuss below, Agamben's formulations in particular allow us to theorise the factory farm as a zone of juridical exception. However, it is clear that in their construction of biopolitics, Foucault and Agamben are *not* interested in understanding violence towards animals. This is odd, since animality lies at the very centre of biopower. Certainly—in so far as Foucault identifies biopolitics with the "animalisation of man"—the relationship between humans and animals is fundamental to understanding biopolitics as a concept. This is highlighted in Agamben's more focused engagement with the "question of the animal" in his later work, *The Open*.

Agamben begins *The Open* with an inquiry into the separation between human and animal as posited within scripture on the divine. He turns to an image from a Hebrew Bible from the thirteenth century that depicts "the messianic banquet of the righteous on the last day."[29] The image is compelling, since the righteous are depicted "not with human faces, but with unmistakably

27   Agamben. *Homo Sacer.* 107.
28   Agamben. *Homo Sacer.* 166.
29   Agamben. *The Open.* 1.

animal heads."[30] For Agamben this is representative of a connection between the human and the animal within the auspice of the divine. This theme—that the human will eventually be "reconciled with his animal nature"—is pursued in a reading of a series of exchanges between Georges Bataille and Alexandre Kojève around the theorised "end of history," and the subsequent end of "man." In the late 1930s, Kojève's understanding of the "end of history"—a concept that finds its origins in the Hegelian link between time and negativity[31]— pointed to a meeting of the human and animal that mirrors the scene depicted by Agamben in the messianic banquet. Bataille objects to this, pointing to a distinct form of humanity which will survive even "the end of history." Perhaps as a result of Bataille's intervention, Kojève adjusts this position in his later writings, pointing to "snobbery" as a distinctive form of being that is used by humanity to transcend its human nature. What is crucial for Agamben, in this admittedly curious exchange, is that it reveals an instability in the category of human itself:

> ...in Kojève's reading of Hegel, man is not a biologically defined species, nor is he substance given once and for all; he is, rather, a field of dialectical tensions always already cut open by internal caesurae that every time separate—at least virtually—"anthropophorous" animality and the humanity which takes bodily form in it.[32]

For Agamben this is more fundamental than the "dehumanisation" that occurs when a human is vilified as an animal. For Agamben the animal is found within the very core of humanity, and thus the human subject is only achieved through the continual rearticulation of a space beyond animal.

As discussed above, this movement is contained within the Aristotelean conception of "man as a political animal," a statement that propels us simultaneously both towards the grounding of the human in the animal, and towards the form of transcendence that gives definition to "humanity" itself. Accordingly, Agamben draws the reader's attention to Aristotle's conception of the soul, which divides the essence of all living beings into components parts, and identifies "nutritive life" as the core component fundamental to all organic life, human, animal or plant.[33] These divisions run through humanity, and as Agamben infers with his discussion of the *Musselmann* (which I will outline

---

30   Agamben. *The Open.* 2.

31   G.W.F. Hegel. *Phenomenology of Spirit.* Oxford University Press: Oxford, 1977. 486–8.

32   Agamben. *The Open.* 12.

33   Agamben. *The Open.* 14; see also Aristotle. *On the Soul.* 416b.

further below) are encountered wherever life itself is accounted for, evaluated, decided upon. Perceptively, Agamben precisely accounts for the predicament that finds the human continually bleeding into the animal:

> it is possible to oppose man to other living things, and at the same time to organise the complex—and not always edifying—economy of relations between men and animals, only because something like an animal life has been separated within man, only because his distance and proximity to the animal have been measured and recognised first of all in the closest and most intimate place.[34]

We can track humanity's internal "caesura" through developments in the biological and evolutionary sciences, and successive attempts to locate the exact distinction between the human and the animal. For example, Agamben turns to Carolus Linneaus who, writing in the 1700s, can only chart marginal differences between the human and the ape and consequently assigns to human the genus "primate," a category shared with other animals. Agamben pertinently observes that even the categorisation *sapiens* (defined as "wise" or "possessing knowledge") that distinguishes the human from the "mere" ape is a "taxonomic anomaly, which assigns not a given, but rather an imperative as a specific difference."[35] Agamben finds resonances in the wolf-children (or "*enfants sauvages*") that would come to captivate popular sciences in this period, as well as in the "missing link," both figures that mark the immutable intersection of human and animal. Even language, which is frequently cited as that distinctly "human" capacity that distinguishes *Homo sapiens* from other animals, proves fragile, since as Agamben points out it is "a historical production which, as such, can be assigned neither to man nor to animal."[36]

Here Agamben establishes what must be considered as a nodal allusion within his political work, which not only provides further depth to our understanding of the enigmatic figure *bare life*, but also provides a point of connection that leads from the soul of the animal to the heart of the (human) camp. Where in the past there was a movement in which the animal was humanised—in the figure of the "man-ape, the *enfant sauvage*...and above all the slave, the barbarian, and the barbarian"—the modern "anthropological machine" has sought to isolate the in-human from amidst the human: "the Jew, that is the non-man produced within the man, or the *néomort* and the overcomatose

---

34   Agamben. *The Open*. 16.

35   Agamben. *The Open*. 25.

36   Agamben. *The Open*. 36.

person, that is, the animal separated within the human body itself."[37] Both formations represent the same thing, and both signal bare life, since they possess within them the sphere of indistinction that, as suggested above, characterise the *homo sacer* that Agamben argues is the subject of politics. This intersection infers biopolitics, in so far as it seeks to locate the essential animality within the human subject: "the decisive political conflict, which governs every other conflict, is that between the animality and the humanity of man. That is to say, in its origin Western politics is also biopolitics."[38]

Having argued for a fundamental connection between the animal and the human, within politics, science and the divine, Agamben turns attention to another dimension of the relation, which in turn reveals a distinction between the being in the world of the animal and that of the human. Zoologist Jakob von Uexküll describes an intimate relation between the animal and its environment or *Umwelt*, defined as the bare elements constituting the living sphere of any organism. Agamben draws our attention to Uexküll's observations on the life of the tick, which the zoologist uses as an exemplary case to demonstrate that the animal maintains a relationship to only a few specific elements of the environment (for example, the heat produced by the body of the mammal, the smell produced by butyric acid etc.). The tick lives out a short life cycle that comprises almost wholly an intimate relationship with these simple elements: "The tick *is* this relationship; she lives only in it and for it."[39]

Agamben uses this environmental grounding of being to illustrate, via Martin Heidegger, the way in which animal life and humanity are constituted in their communion with the "concealedness" or "non-concealedness" of the world. Heidegger argues that an animal maintains a relationship of "captivation" with its discrete environmental elements or "disinhibitors." In this relationship of captivation, the animal cannot *apprehend or reveal* being—this potentiality is reserved in Heidegger's thought for the distinctly human *Dasein*—instead the animal is caught in a relation of both being openly drawn to elements in the world, yet simultaneously not exposed to the openness of being itself. In Agamben's words, "the ontological status of the animal environment... is *offen* (open) but not *offenbar* (disconcealed; lit., openable)."[40] Human activity is distinct in its capacity to open being itself, to find itself within a world without any specific or essential relation to the environment around it. In other words, where the animal opens itself to a world in which it can never

---

37   Agamben. *The Open.* 37.
38   Agamben. *The Open.* 80.
39   Agamben. *The Open.* 47.
40   Agamben. *The Open.* 55.

move beyond a captivation with its specific dishibitors or environmental elements, the human finds abundant potentiality in its own being that forces the
opposite: a closure of being to this very potentiality for freedom.

There is an intersection between the relation of the human to its environment and the relation of the animal to its own environment in boredom.
According to Heidegger, boredom reveals a human capacity for the depthless
captivation with one's environment that is ascribed to the animal, through a
detached, non-engaged connection to the world around us. Agamben's citation from Heidegger illustrates this well.[41] A long wait for a train may lead us to
check our watch, flip vacantly thorough magazines, draw figures in the sand
and so on. We are not particularly engaged with these activities, in fact they
reveal a disconnection with our environment, a refusal to become entangled.
In these moments, while the human *Dasein* approaches the *"open to a nondis-
concealed"* that characterises the Heideggarian animal, *Dasein* also radically
differentiates itself from animal being at this point, precisely because it is
revealed in its own capacity to unhinge itself from its environment through the
experience of boredom. To quote Agamben, *"Dasein* is simply an animal that
has learned to become bored; it has awakened from its captivation to its own
captivation."[42]

These sections of *The Open* are useful because although they appear to
found a "real" distinction between the human and the animal, they do so while,
almost simultaneously, closing this same gap finding the human once again in
close proximity with the animal. For if boredom only reveals a human ability
to decaptivate itself with its world, then the foundations of humanity must
contain a continual oscillation between animal captivation, and a human
capacity for distraction. Indeed Agamben asks, "in what sense does Heidegger's
attempt to grasp the 'existing essence of man' escape the metaphysical pri-
macy of *animalitas*?"[43] The failure to find any clear points of distinction
between human and animal end in *indistinction*. Thus, *The Open* eventually
poses the same fundamental issue that is raised in *Homo Sacer*, namely, the
extent to which biopolitics—reconfigured by Agamben as the conflict between
animality and humanity—has delimited, and ultimately defined, the horizon
of human politics. This is where the Kojèvian/Hegelian "end of history" becomes
pertinent to the analysis: Agamben speculates whether humanity's quest to
find the animal within the human subject ("genome, global economy, and
humanitarian ideology are the three united faces of this process") can be

---

41   Agamben. *The Open.* 63–4.
42   Agamben. *The Open.* 70.
43   Agamben. *The Open.* 73.

considered humanity's last task.[44] According to Agamben this would be an alarming end for humanity:

> To be sure, such a humanity, from Heidegger's perspective, no longer has the form of keeping itself open to the undisconcealed of the animal, but seeks rather to open and secure the not-open in every domain, and thus closes itself to its own openness, forgets its *humanitas*, and makes being its specific disinhibitor. The total humanization of the animal coincides with a total animalisation of man.[45]

If Agamben were to end his account here, I would be concerned that his intention in *The Open* is simply to restore "dignity" to humanity: to fortify the gap between the human and animal, and live in eternal hope that the animal and the human will never again meet. This would align Agamben's thinking in some respects with humanistic accounts without seeking a more radical way to overturn the human/animal machine. It is thankful therefore that Agamben considers another alternative, although it must be said that on first reading the explication that concludes *The Open* appears to pursue a somewhat "mystical" trajectory. Drawing inspiration from two paintings by Titian, Agamben conjectures the existence of a space beyond both the figure of the human and the animal, in which neither openness or concealedness are constitutive of being. Within this state, being is not driven towards the revelation of being, there is only a "lost mystery" and a suspension of the desire to look further behind the facade of just being.[46] This same movement allows the human to reconfigure its relationship with the animal within itself. As Agamben observes, if humanity defines itself by its capacity to disconnect itself from its animal connection to its disinhibitors, then it should also possess the capacity to allow the animal to exist outside of the sphere of being, to "let the animal be."[47] To allow the animal to exist outside of being is precisely to remove it from the inquiry of human subjectivity, and thus call an end to the continued determination of life that characterises the conflict between human and animal.

However, Agamben's attempt to reconcile human and animal in *The Open* appears as a weak response to the caesura created by biopower. In part this is because Agamben is quite explicitly more concerned with the problem of how to prevent the "animalization of man" than a project to erase the hostility

---

44   Agamben. *The Open.* 77.

45   Agamben. *The Open.* 77.

46   Agamben. *The Open.* 87.

47   Agamben. *The Open.* 91.

between human and animal that gives rise to politics.[48] This is perhaps most clearly evidenced by the absence within Agamben's discussion of attention to systems of violence directed towards animals as a problem that is thrown up by the "anthropological machine." However, while Agamben does not attend to the "animal camp," we might offer a corrective of this perspective. In the next section I focus specifically on how Agamben's model might be usefully applied to understanding animal utilisation in the scene of the factory farm.

A Concentrated Biopolitics

While we might point to resemblances between examples of human violence towards other humans—such as in concentration camps—and draw parallels to human violence towards animals in industrialised slaughter and experimentation,[49]

---

48   In this light, see both Matthew Calarco's discussion of Agamben, and also Kelly Oliver's discussion. See Calarco. *Zoographies.* 79–102; and Kelly Oliver. *Animal Lessons.* 229–44.

49   Charles Paterson's book, *Eternal Treblinka: Our Treatment of Animals and the Holocaust* specifically turns attention to the relation between human violence against humans and that against animals, through exploration of the historical links between the slaughter-house and the extermination camp, and through the testimony of survivors and activists who have been made more aware of animal suffering through their experience of human suffering in the Holocaust (see Charles Patterson. *Eternal Treblinka: Our Treatment of Animals and the Holocaust*. Lantern Books: New York, 2002). Patterson provides an arresting account of the historical links between the forms of human violence practiced by Nazi Germany during the middle of the twentieth century and forms of torture and death developed in the animal slaughterhouse violence. Patterson's technique here is similar to Edmund Russell's very impressive *War and Nature* (see Edmund Russell. *War and Nature: Fighting Insects and Humans with Chemicals from World War I to Silent Spring*, Cambridge University Press: Cambridge, 2001) another work that uses detailed comparisons between the technologies developed to eradicate and control animals and those used for the same purposes against humans. Patterson draws on two important developments in the United States that facilitated the technology of Nazi genocide. Firstly, he suggests that it was the United States that made the most significant contribution to the development of methods of industrial slaughter used to "process" animal life. Patterson points, for example, to the construction of the Union Stock Yards in Chicago in 1865, a slaughterhouse facility with 2300 connected livestock pens, occupying over a square mile of land (Patterson. *Eternal Treblinka.* 57). Technologies that facilitated the movement of animal bodies, whether alive or dead, enabled an increased potential for the process of animal flesh. Rail connections, for example, would prove indispensible as a means to accelerate animal slaughter. Patterson notes further that the introduction of a conveyor belt in 1886 increased this capacity, with line speeds enhanced (71). Today, these developments have been improved upon to a startling degree, to the point where industrialised processes

there are of course limitations.[50] Indeed a focus on these comparisons not only reveals our poverty of language in describing the horrors that are imposed upon animals, but misses the fact that our use of animals contains specific modalities of violence that cannot be compared, in any way, to contemporary instances of violence towards humans. In the most direct sense, we breed animals on an industrial scale to be killed and eaten, something that cannot be compared to any contemporary forms of human violence towards other

---

have enabled slaughter on an almost incomprehensible scale. The numbers killed provide a sense of the scale of these operations.

Secondly, Patterson argues that the growth of the eugenics movement had its roots within the US, where some of the initial "successes" where first reported. Patterson observes that eugenics emerged at the point where the techniques of biological selection and intervention that were commonplace in the management of animal populations were turned towards the manipulation of human populations. The first steps forwards were taken by the United States, which endorsed enthusiastically the sterilisation of people convicted of crimes, people with mental illness and people with disability (87–9). Although by 1933 Germany had taken its own measures along eugenicist principles, Patterson wryly notes: "the Nazis had a good deal of catching up to do. When they embarked on their sterilization program in 1933, the United States already had sterilized more than 15,000 people, most of them while they were incarcerated in prisons or homes for the mentally ill" (92).

Patterson observes that eugenics and industrialised slaughter converge radically in the Nazi extermination camps. Within the camp human death and animal slaughter become indistinguishable. Patterson observes, for example, that the passage leading animals to their deaths is colloquially referred to as a "chute" or "kill alley" or "tube." Uncannily, the barbed wire enshrouded alleyway at Treblinka, through which starved human bodies were hurtled to their deaths, was also referred to as the "tube" (111).

50   These comparisons between violence towards animals and the Holocaust have of course been the subject of contention; see, for example, Roberta Kalechofsky. *Animal Suffering and the Holocaust: The Problem with Comparisons*. Marblehead: Micah Publications, 2003. My view is that we must understand the co-evolution of techniques of violence used by humans against humans and those used against animals. This involves understanding the way in which developments in means for killing and containing animals flow to the human sphere, and vice versa. However, describing human violence towards animals as a "holocaust," "genocide," "slavery" or "colonisation" not only risks emptying examples of mass human violence towards humans of their descriptional specificity and characteristic memory, but simultaneously pretends that what we do to animals can actually be described using existing metaphors of human to human violence. In my view, we have an absolute poverty of language here in the terms we might use to describe this violence. My only attraction to "war" as a descriptor is its lack of inherent specificity over the means and opponents that might comprise war, and the capacity for the descriptor to evolve once we assume the intent of war remains the same (that is, as an intention to bend the will of the other into submission).

humans.[51] A biopolitical perspective offers us a way to deepen our understanding of the links between the human camps and human industrialised breeding, containment and slaughter, but also explore the way in which what we do to animals exceeds and goes beyond human violence towards other humans.

Exception, and a sovereign power to declare exception, clearly operates with regard to our use of animals. Indeed, exception is an increasingly general principle for the organisation of vast sections of animal life across the planet as a whole. Animal life, even when not held in captivity and governed by specific regulations relating to the use of animals for food or research, is nevertheless contained by the powers of the sovereign. Oceans and rivers, forests and deserts, are not only physical territories held within the domain of sovereignty, but increasingly sites for the investment of resources and technologies towards the management of non human animal life. Vast socio-technical networks may be mobilised for such operations, which combine techno-scientific knowledge with capitalist markets to facilitate large scale reproduction, utilisation and death: Richard Twine's reframing of Noske's concept of "the animal industrial complex" seems entirely appropriate here.[52] Yet such management does not operate through some uniformly applied principle relating to all biological life (e.g., all life has a "right to live"): rather, to spaces of exception where each respective bio-population is given consideration, value and a tailored strategy. The extension of law over particular aspects of non human animal life, which in some cases has arguably allowed particular populations of species to enjoy the protection of the law, has also enabled the extension of sovereign managerial powers over an increasingly large section of both human and non human life on the planet.

In the cases of factory farming, and animal experimentation, the lives of the animals involved in these industries are always caught in an exceptionary space. We see this explicitly in the discriminatory exercise of law: anti-cruelty legislation has always provided an exception for animals used for science, and animals used for food.[53] Hence the apparent contradiction, that it is illegal to

---

51   Indeed, as I discuss in Chapter 4, value is realised through the slaughter process. This is
      something Jan Dutkiewicz has recognised: namely, that industrialised breeding containment and slaughter seeks to realise value through working on the body of the animal in
      order to maximise profit at death (and after). Thus, Dutkiewicz states: "The 'living death'
      of animal subjects is not a state akin to a concentration camp or colony, but one of constant biopolitical intervention aimed at the achievement of a specific type of body." See
      Jan Dutkiewicz. "'Postmodernism,' Politics, and Pigs." *PhaenEx*. 8.2, 2013. 296–307.

52   See Twine. "Revealing the 'Animal-Industrial Complex'–A Concept & Method for Critical
      Animal Studies?". See also Twine, *Animals as Biotechnology*.

53   See O'Sullivan. *Animals, Equality and Democracy*.

act violently towards a dog on a public street, yet, this same dog, within a laboratory, may be used in a variety of painful experiments without attracting legal
attention. Further, in so far as it is licit to inflict violence upon a non human
animal in particular situations (e.g. for research or for food), the test for animal
cruelty, that non human animals are not to *unnecessarily* suffer, also contains
within it an implicit exception, that non human animal suffering deemed necessary is acceptable by law.[54]

The capacity of the law to deem suffering necessary in particular circumstances is not a power that is limited in scope to non human animals, but
includes humans themselves, since this is the prerogative the sovereign exercises in the use of legitimised violence: the ability of the sovereign to make
suffer, or "disallow to the point of death," is one that is inescapably part of the
power to punish. The only discernible difference between the suffering
imposed upon the human and that of the non human animal, is that humans,
in so far as they have attributed to themselves freedom of will, are also liable to
suffer the weight of "guilt" before the law, something non human animals are
usually exempt from since they are, at least in the modern era,[55] always "inno-
cent." If consideration over the innocence or guilt of non human animal life is
left aside, then any obscurity around the nature of all animal life (human
included) in the state of exception vanishes. For it may be observed that the
control of life, the power to allow and disallow life, extends to all living beings
within the space of exception: in this sense, Agamben's analysis of the relation
of life to sovereign power may be extended to incorporate the life belonging to
the non human.

The concept of bare life, which refers to life that is held within the grasp of
the legitimised violence of the sovereign, is directly applicable to the life of the
animal, particularly that life which is subject to a biological control which is
directed towards power. Consider the following passage from Peter Singer's
Animal Liberation on the life of calves raised for veal production:

---

54 Mike Radford, writing on the relation of animal welfare to law, states:
    ... the notion of unnecessary suffering means not only that the law contemplates there to
    be situations in which suffering can be regarded as necessary, and therefore lawful, but
    also treatment that might be regarded as unlawful in one context—on the basis that it
    causes unnecessary suffering—can be considered lawful in another because the court
    takes the view that suffering is necessary.
        See Mike Radford. "Partial Protection: Animal Welfare and the Law." Robert Garner Ed.
    Animal Rights: The Changing Debate. Houndmills: Macmillan Press, 1996. 67–91. 69.
55 See Hampton L. Carson. "The Trial of Animals and Insects. A Little Known Chapter of
    Mediæval Jurisprudence." *Proceedings of the American Philosophical Society.* 56.5, 1917. 410–
    15. See also George Ryley Scott. *A History of Torture.* Twickenham: Senate Press, 1995. 278.

Without any iron at all the calves would drop dead. With a normal intake their flesh will not fetch as much per pound. So a balance is struck which keeps the flesh pale and the calves or most of them on their feet long enough for them to reach their market weight.[56]

The short life of the veal calf is one which is determined strictly within the coordinates of domination. Calculations made around nutritional and fluid intake, lighting levels, stall size and flooring are directed towards the maximisation of market profit from the production of the correctly coloured and textured flesh of the animal.[57] But the priority of the life of the veal calf, no matter how short or painful, is apparent in this process. The life of the calf, maintained in a bare, weak state, is monitored scrupulously to prevent a premature death; a death that threatens the profitability of that life for the livestock complex. Thus a "balance" is struck, where life is held at a point that borders upon death itself. We find the same relationship between life and death in the management of battery hens, where maximal profit is achieved through the imposition of the most minimal conditions for life: "on a sloping wire floor (sloping so the eggs roll down, wire so the dung drops through) the birds live for a year or 18 months while artificial lighting and temperature conditions combine with drugs in their food to squeeze the maximum number of eggs out of them."[58]

Agamben suggests that bare life is not only a site of *indistinction* between lawmaking and law-preserving violence, but also the point where a number of other fundamental distinctions are blurred, including that between nature and society, and the animal and the human:

Accordingly, when Hobbes founds sovereignty by means of a reference to the state in which "man is a wolf to men," *homo hominis lupis,* in the word "wolf" (lupus) we ought to hear the echo of the *wargus* and the *caput lupinem* of the laws of Edward the Confessor: at issue is not simply *fera bestia* and natural life but rather a zone of indistinction between the human and the animal, a werewolf, a man who is transformed into a wolf and a wolf who is transformed into a man—in other words a bandit, a *homo sacer*...This threshold alone, which is neither simple natural life

56   Peter Singer. *Animal Liberation*. 132.
57   In this context, see Lewis Holloway, Carol Morris, Ben Gilna and David Gibbs. "Biopower, Genetics and Livestock Breeding: (Re)Constituting Animal Populations and Heterogeneous Biosocial Collectivities." *Transactions, Institute of British Geographers*. 34, 2009. 394–407.
58   Peter Singer. *Animal Liberation*. 16.

nor social life but rather bare life or sacred life, is the always present and always operative presupposition of sovereignty.[59]

The Hobbesian sovereign delivers human life from the chaos of nature through the promise of a legitimised violence, in lieu of "natural" violence wielded by life in the state of nature: a war, "as is of every man against every man."[60] The investment of the civil populace in the sword of the sovereign is the divestment of nature into the sovereign power. But this is not a divestment that promises the extinguishment of violence, only the illegitimisation of violence not wielded at the sovereign's blessing, and thus the internalisation of the "violence of nature" into the hands of the State. Consequently the life which is caught in the ban of the sovereign is not a life that is exempted from the law (and thus surrendered completely to nature), but life that is both held within and without the sovereign. The power of exception is a power to reduce the human to the animal, yet, in this same movement, animal life is not provided a freedom or redemption from law, rather a life caught between law and "nature." This life is "a threshold of indistinction and of passage between animal and man, *physis* and *nomos,* exclusion and inclusion: the life of the bandit is the life of the *loup garou,* the werewolf, who is precisely neither man nor beast, and who dwells paradoxically within both while belonging to neither."[61]

Further, it is upon consideration of the terrifying reality of the biopolitical regime in the camp that one can recognise clearly the insoluble resemblance between the bare life of humanity and that shared by the non human life caught in the sphere of the animal industrial complex. In *Remnants of Auschwitz,* Agamben discusses in detail the *Muselmänner* (or "Muslims"), the term given to the "walking dead" of the camps, who due to the infliction of continued violence—malnutrition, sleep deprivation, extended work, psychological trauma etc.—are reduced to a state of fragile indifference to their immediate conditions.[62] The insensibility of the *Muselmann* to the world, and his or her disjunction from the social interactions of the prisoners and guards around, is also the process by which the *Muselmänner* are apprehended as living beings who have in some way lost their humanity. Agamben states that the "*Muselmann* is not

---

59   Agamben, *Homo Sacer.* 105–6.

60   Hobbes. *Leviathan.* 71.

61   Agamben. *Homo Sacer.* 105.

62   Giorgio Agamben. *Remnants of Auschwitz: The Witness and The Archive.* New York: Zone Books, 1999.

only or not so much a limit between life and death; rather, he marks the threshold between the human and the inhuman."[63] It is in this sense that one cannot fully understand the life held within the camp without understanding the possibilities for non human life, upon which human life itself is wrought:

> The decisive activity of biopower in our time consists not of life or death, but rather of a mutable and virtually infinite survival. In every case, it is a matter of dividing animal life from organic life, the human from the inhuman, the witness from the *Muselmann*, conscious life from vegetative life maintained functional through resuscitation techniques, until a threshold is reached; an essentially mobile threshold that like the borders of geo-politics, moves along according to the progress of scientific and political technologies. Biopower's supreme ambition is to produce, in a human body, the absolute separation of the living being and the speaking being, *zoé* and *bios*, the inhuman and the human—survival.[64]

In the extreme situation of the camp, the "gap" which is assumed to exist between the animal and the human—that between the living being and that between a speaking being, or that which merely has life (*zoé*) and that which also has a cultural or political life (*bios*)—soon eclipses. It is not surprising, then, that in such situations human life takes on the characteristic of that of livestock (people are transported "like cattle," or humans are forced to "live like swine"). *Livestock* represent that which only possess life itself: beings for whom survival may entail a few short months spent in a cramped, dark, and painful factory feedlot. In these senses, the treatment of animals within intensive forms of utilisation—such as factory farming or experimentation—resembles the excesses of human violence towards other humans found in camps and detention centres. However, there are important differences, including, as I have mentioned above, the specific role of death with respects to the animal production system. Death is an event that achieves value within markets and in bodies consumed as food. As I argue in Chapter 4, death marks the point at which a specific use value for humans in the dead body is imposed upon the living animal. This reality forces us to more specifically understand the role of death within the biopolitical production of animals.

---

63   Agamben. *Remnants of Auschwitz*. 55.

64   Agamben. *Remnants of Auschwitz*. 155–6.

Necropolitics

While maintaining life is central to the animal industrial complex, death, orchestrated upon a massive scale, is simultaneously a central element. Bio-politics in this context cannot merely be considered as a beneficent power designed to "foster life," but as a politics that seeks to produce both life and death, simultaneously. In an essay entitled "Necropolitics," Mbembe[65] offers an extension of Foucault's analysis, focusing on the powers of death that are a necessary aspect of biopolitical sovereignty. Like Foucault, Mbembe is drawn to the analogy of war, and the relationship between war and politics. by imag-ining "politics as a form of war" and defining political sovereignty as a project designed to "exercise control over mortality and to define life as the deploy-ment and manifestation of power."[66] It is from this power that Mbembe identi-fies *necropolitics*, the "subjugation of life to the power of death" that enables a reconfiguration of "relations among resistance, sacrifice, and terror."[67]

As I have already discussed, sovereignty, in so far as it concerns itself with life and death, emanates from and seeks to continue hostility to maintain its advantage. This view of political sovereignty would suggest that there is no complete civil political space that is in essence "peaceful." There is only an enduring war, fought in multiple theatres. This war operates through intercon-nected spaces of exception; hotspots within a protracted and violent engage-ment of bodies. This war creates arbitrary forms of distinction, between winners and losers, creating rights to access and pleasure for the victors, and condemn-ing opponents to enduring suffering and loss. Many enjoy a life of peaceful civility, indeed they may have the luxury of never hearing the canons of war; but these spaces of reprieve are quite literally bordered by zones of absolute terror.

Mbembe argues that frequently contemporary political philosophy seeks to define the political space in *opposition* to war and hostility. "Politics," Mbembe states, "is defined as twofold: a project of autonomy and the achieving of agree-ment among a collectivity through communication and recognition. This, we are told, is what differentiates it from war."[68] Mbembe distances himself from this tradition, arguing instead for a focus on:

---

65   Mbembe. "Necropolitics."
66   Mbembe. "Necropolitics." 12. Note the unmistakable resonance with Clausewitz's identifi-
      cation of the object of war as "*an act of violence to compel our opponent to fulfil our will.*"
67   Mbembe. "Necropolitics." 39.
68   Mbembe. "Necropolitics." 13.

…those figures of sovereignty whose central project is not the struggle for autonomy but *the generalized instrumentalization of human existence and the material destruction of human bodies and populations.* Such figures of sovereignty are far from a piece of prodigious insanity or an expression of a rupture between the impulses and interests of the body and those of the mind. Indeed, they, like the death camps, are what constitute the *nomos* of the political space in which we still live. Furthermore, contemporary experiences of human destruction suggest that it is possible to develop a reading of politics, sovereignty, and the subject different from the one we inherited from the philosophical discourse of modernity. Instead of considering reason as the truth of the subject, we can look to other foundational categories that are less abstract and more tactile, such as life and death.[69]

The history of oppression, terror and genocide in the twentieth century would obviously provide much material for this sort of analysis, which might include, as a core aspect of sovereignty, an understanding of *"the generalized instrumentalization of human existence and the material destruction of human bodies and populations."* Certainly, as we have seen, for Agamben the Nazi death camps provide the most telling example of the operation of biopolitical sovereignty, and the experience of exceptional power is tied to the refinement of the concentration/death camp as an apparatus during twentieth century Europe.[70] In contrast, Mbembe points out that this conceptualisation misses the relationship of slavery and the colony in enabling the development of the European camp, and refining the means by which humans may be kept on the threshold of life and death. Mbembe observes that the slave occupies a particular position in the labour process, where his or her life sits at the very intersection between life and death:

---

69   Mbembe. "Necropolitics." 14.

70   Indeed Agamben's discussion of the emergence of the concentration camp is tied closely by the philosopher to the development of the state of exception and "protective custody" by Prussian law. See Agamben, *Homo Sacer*. 166–70. Agamben states (at 167):

   The camps are thus born, not out of ordinary law (even less, as one might have supposed, from a transformation and development of criminal law) but out of a state of exception and martial law. This is even clearer in the Nazi *Lager*, concerning whose origin and juridical regime we are well informed. It has been noted that the juridical basis for internment was not common law but *Schutzhaft* (literally, protective custody), a juridical institution of Prussian origin that the Nazi jurors sometimes classified as a preventative police measure insofar as it allowed individuals to be "taken into custody" independently of any criminal behavior, solely to avoid danger to the security of the state.

As an instrument of labor, the slave has a price. As a property, he or she has a value. His or her labor is needed and used. The slave is therefore kept alive but in a state of injury, in a phantomlike world of horrors and intense cruelty and profanity. The violent tenor of the slave's life is manifested through the overseer's disposition to behave in a cruel and intemperate manner and in the spectacle of pain inflicted on the slave's body. Violence, here, becomes an element in manners, like whipping or taking of the slave's life itself: an act of caprice and pure destruction aimed at instilling terror. Slave life, in many ways, is a form of death-in-life.[71]

Similarly, the colony provides a space for working out the characteristic racialised violence that was to strike Europe in the twentieth century. As such, colonisation, and the violence inherent in its exercise, acts as the test site for the European camp:

> ...in most instances, the selection of races, the prohibition of mixed marriages, forced sterilization, even the extermination of vanquished peoples are to find their first testing ground in the colonial world. Here we see the first syntheses between massacre and bureaucracy, that incarnation of Western rationality. Arendt develops the thesis that there is a link between national-socialism and traditional imperialism. According to her, the colonial conquest revealed a potential for violence previously unknown. What one witnesses in World War II is the extension to the "civilized" peoples of Europe of the methods previously reserved for the "savages."[72]

For Mbembe, recognising the relationship of slavery and the colony to the construction of contemporary biopolitical sovereignty is fundamental to both properly understanding the genealogy of the European camp, and situating the continuing relationship of sovereignty to life and death, including through neo-colonial forms of violence which continue unabated, despite a European sensibility of continuing a newly found, peaceful civility: "all manifestations of war and hostility that had been marginalized by a European legal imaginary had a place to re-emerge in the colonies."[73] As such, Mbembe establishes a political order where norm and exception, war and peace, are set side by side, intertwined with each others' operations, but apparently worlds apart.

---

71   Mbembe. "Necropolitics." 22.

72   Mbembe, "Necropolitics." 23.

73   Mbembe. "Necropolitics." 25.

The applicability of Mbembe's analysis for thinking about the animal industrial complex may be clear. In the Introduction to this book I have asked how it
is that it may be possible for humans to extinguish so much life on this planet,
but not perceive this impact as a systemic form of mass orchestrated violence;
that is, as a form of war. Mbembe demonstrates that the logic of biopower is to
generate simultaneous and complex interlinked zones where life is fostered
and simultaneously made to suffer and die, often through discrete and strategically located forms of containment which hide from view the operation of
extreme forms of violence. The topography of this space defies easy imagination. Like the relationship of the West to those human communities which are
still subject to forms of continuing sovereign, political, economic and cultural
occupation, our relationship with animals allows us to believe fervently that
there is no war, no difference of interest, despite ever-present forms of violence
and oppression which produce and reproduce terror, suffering, and death.[74]
This does not mean, however, that Mbembe recognises the importance of violence towards animals in constructing biopolitics or sovereign violence in the
contemporary period. On the contrary, like both Foucault and Agamben, he
only comes tantalisingly close. However, Mbembe provides the elements of
such a critique in "Necropolitics," but drawing attention to the role of animalisation in providing the logic for structuring forms of violence:

> That colonies might be ruled over in absolute lawlessness stems from the
> racial denial of any common bond between the conqueror and the native.
> In the eyes of the conqueror, *savage life* is just another form of *animal life*,
> a horrifying experience, something alien beyond imagination or compre-
> hension. In fact, according to Arendt, what makes the savages different
> from other human beings is less the color of their skin than the fear that

---

74   In relation to human poverty, even using a liberal Kantian/Rawlsian standpoint (without
        necessarily needing to resort to a more radical neo-Marxist perspective), it is difficult to
        deny the way in which this structural violence of the global economic system reproduces
        poverty. For example, Thomas Pogge has highlighted that these disparities are difficult to
        ignore; see Thomas W. Pogge. "Justice Across Borders: Brief for a Global Resources
        Dividend." Matthew Clayton and Andrew Williams Eds. *Social Justice*. Malden: Blackwell,
        2004. 264–85. Addressing global poverty, Pogge observes that "The worse-off are not
        merely poor and often starving, but are being impoverished and starved under our shared
        institutional arrangements, which inescabably shape their lives" (268). Further, "The
        present circumstances of the global poor are significantly shaped by a dramatic period of
        conquest and colonization, with severe oppression, enslavement, even genocide, through
        which the native institutions and cultures of four continents were destroyed or severely
        traumatized" (270).

they behave like a part of nature, that they treat nature as their undis-
puted master.[75]

But, Membe's critique is unfinished, and like the argument Mbembe puts forward in *On the Postcolony*—where he states in an unabashed fashion that "discourse on Africa is almost always deployed in the framework (or on the fringes)
of a meta-text about the *animal*"[76]—the opportunity for linking violence
towards animals with the colonial experience, or with the experience of slavery, appears missed. Again, I do not argue here that slavery or colonisation
represent the same form of violence that is waged against animals. However,
techniques and logics are shared, despite different forms and modalities; histories are intertwined.

One clear way we might draw connections between the colonial project and
violence against animals is through an understanding of the way in which sites
of intense violence may be separated and contained from spaces of apparent
undisturbed peacability; and how it is that these two forms of radically distinct
existence—war and peace—should sit side by side and thrive off each other
without apparent contradiction. Examining the functioning of segregated
townships and *homelands* under apartheid in South Africa, Mbembe observes
that the regulations on movement (through migration) and property ownership created a way to demarcate between populations and allocate rights:

> ...the functioning of the homelands and townships entailed severe
> restrictions on production for the market by blacks in white areas, the
> terminating of land ownership by blacks except in reserved areas, the
> illegalization of black residence on white farms (except as servants in the
> employ of whites), the control of urban influx, and later, the denial of
> citizenship to Africans.[77]

The effects of these controls, modulated through movement and citizenship
rights, was to separate between populations, and actualise distinction between
population groups that might otherwise be undifferentiated. White economies
thrived and depended upon the subjugated labour of those who were excluded;
however, the peaceful operation of white economies required the removal
from sight of black townships and homelands.

---

75   Mbembe. "Necropolitics." 24.
76   Mbembe. *On the Postcolony*. 1.
77   Mbembe. "Necropolitics." 26.

Consider the connection between the apartheid regime and the modern slaughterhouse, which is the meeting point for both massive extinguishment of animal life, and an exceptional zone for race and low wage work to collide, generating a series of violences that cut across both human and non human. The world's biggest slaughterhouse located in Tar Heel, United States, might count as an example of such a site of exceptionality:

> With a population of 65 and an area of 147 acres, the entire town of Tar Heel is slightly smaller than the slaughterhouse complex; its population dwarfed by the number of slaughterhouse employees. The high wide boxes of the slaughterhouse stretch half a mile and sit directly across the street from the Smithfield medical and employment centres. Every day 38,000 pigs are trucked into these giant, whitewashed, windowless caskets, where they are killed, then cut into pieces–9 million a year. Bladen County is thinly settled; its entire human population is just 33,000. The quiet parking lots of the slaughterhouse complex are filled with battered, ageing American automobiles. When shifts change, their owners, a couple of thousand mostly brown and black faces, pour from the boxes–the knockers, stickers, shacklers, tub dumpers, knuckle droppers, caul pullers, fell cutters, rumpers, splitters, vat dippers, skinners, gutters and others who spend their days disassembling freshly killed pigs. Cars line the single exit from the slaughterhouse complex to Route 87, ferrying hundreds out, passing identical cars carrying hundreds more in.[78]

War in this context, as I shall discuss in Chapter 5, requires extraordinary forms of containment, and the mass organisation of systems of resource supply and human transport to enable death upon a large scale. A zone of absolute exception is required; a small provincial town provides the perfect site for this (though it must be acknowledged that despite the dispersement of these centres as part and parcel of industrialised killing, urban slaughterhouses still exist; indeed local food movements—under the banner of "locavorism"[79]— have progressively pushed for the re-urbanisation of slaughter, sometimes on welfare grounds[80]). The massive technologies for killing are separated out,

---

78   Steven M. Wise. *An American Trilogy: Death, Slavery & Dominion on the Banks of the Cape Fear River*. Boston and New York: Da Capo Press, 2009. 3.

79   See Vasile Stanescu. "'Green' Eggs and Ham? The Myth of Sustainable Meat and the Danger of the Local." *Journal for Critical Animal Studies*. 8.1/2, 2010.

80   See, for example, Erik Hoffner. "Heritage Foods' Patrick Martins Wants to Put Slaughterhouses Back in the City [Q&A]." Grist. 17 June 2010. At: www.grist.org/article/patrickmartins-wants-to-put-slaughterhouses-back-in-the-city/.

and closed off from sight; all that is visible is the coming and going of resources and labour, livestock and dead meat, and even these movements seem to be barely perceptible. Within this zone of exception, the containment and topographical separation of the slaughter and process of bodies means that every stage of the process would appear hermetically sealed from view. Pachirat, in his investigation of industrialised slaughter, highlights this aspect of the production of meat, where human workers themselves are segregated within the production lines of killing and death, and the processing of bodies shifts between extreme compartmentalisations of light and dark, hot and cool, bloody and clean:

> In the separation between life and death, the majority of slaughterhouse workers operate in the zone of death. Only a few see the cattle while they are alive or are in the process of being killed, an even smaller number are actively involved in the killing. Furthermore, the act of killing itself is divided into more stages, which are out of sight of each other.[81]

The compartmentalisation and containment of discrete micro zones of killing and bodily disassembly generates multiple discontinuities in time and space—before/after, upstairs/downstairs—that tightly controls the conduct of war operations through numerous fronts of activity:

> What does the animal look like to the individual worker as it passes? The "sticker"...for example sees something radically different from what is seen by the "spinal cord removers"...and this is yet again completely distinct from what is seen by the "omasum and tripe washers and refiners"... There are 121 job functions, 121 perspectives, 121 experiences of industrialized killing.[82]

We find again that Mbembe's characterisation of the operation of necropolitics provides a way to understand the topographical layering and compartmentalisation of this violence. Examining the Israeli occupation in Gaza and the West Bank, and drawing attention to the "politics of verticality" described by Eyal Weizmann, Mbembe observes the infrastructural dimensions of occupation, which separate out the movements of Israeli traffic from Palestinian through a "network of fast bypass roads, bridges, and tunnels that weave over

---

81   Pachirat. *Every Twelve Seconds*. 61.
82   Pachirat. *Every Twelve Seconds*. 47.

and under one another."[83] Thus two worlds can co-exist, separated by space and time:

> Under conditions of vertical sovereignty and splintering colonial occupa-
> tion, communities are separated across a y-axis. This leads to a prolifera-
> tion of the sites of violence. The battlegrounds are not located solely at
> the surface of the earth. The underground as well as the airspace are
> transformed into conflict zones.[84]

I shall return in Chapter 5 to consider the question of how containment might function in concert with privatised forms of sovereignty to enable a systemic control and violent domination of animals. However, we might note here, drawing on both Mbembe and Pachirat, that the conditions for war require a segmentation that creates a spatial and chronological imperceptibility. The war against animals is below and above us; it happens both too slowly and too quickly to be caught by our senses. The function of the war is to smooth paths for some humans, perhaps most humans, to be always separated by highways, above and below, from the hotspots of violence that hum all around yet are rendered imperceptible.

Beyond Biopower?

Foucault, Agamben and Mbembe appear to miss an opportunity to situate bio-politics within a broader field, recognising the way in which this form of power is founded upon the experience of violent domination of non human animal life. If one considers this aspect of the human/animal divide, it is apparent that the spiritual home of biopolitics is not the concentration camp, nor the colony, but in the technologies of domestication, regulation, control and killing that are the mainstays of our relationships with animals, including the slaughter-house. Today it is within the latter facility that life is measured, contained and extinguished with a monstrous potentiality that defies belief; where the slaughter of billions occurs within spheres of exception that are incorporated within the very heart of the civil space. It is here in the slaughterhouse that the most troubling questions must be asked about the human capacity for the management of life, and the mammoth potential for a seeming infinity of daily torments and mass exterminations to occur. The challenge of contemporary

---

83   Mbembe. "Necropolitics." 28.
84   Mbembe. "Necropolitics." 29.

biopolitics is the challenge of a politics which persistently moves to strike from the political that which does not relate to life itself, a politics that is intrinsically tied to the operation of modern sovereignty. And the consequence of this politics which operates in an exemplary fashion in modern sovereignty is that humanity is returned to the animal. The erasure of that *gap* (the gap through which humanity posited the distance between itself and animal) finds humanity on level with the non human which it had previously condemned to the necessary suffering of the factory farm enclosure, of the slaughter *en masse*, or the vivisector's knife.[85]

These observations should not be read as a demand for the reinstatement of the gap between human and non human animals, for the gap itself inevitably returns to the point of its erasure. The reason for this lies in exception, and the exercise of violence which is intrinsic to sovereignty. The right to constitute an exception, to exercise a violence which is otherwise forbidden, a process which Benjamin refers to as an objective contradiction in the legal situation, but not a logical contradiction in the law,[86] is also the decisive point where any gap that is posited between the human and the non human animal may be eroded. It is exception which makes it possible for a seemingly peaceful society of humans to exercise violence on a massive scale upon non human animal life. And the gap between the human and non human is constituted purely by exception in the belief that humans are deserving of something more than that of the animal, or alternatively, that the animal may be subject to that which human life should never be subjected. Yet in so far as human society actively constitutes the limit for bare life within factory farms and experimental laboratories, the life of the non human animal captured within this sphere of exception represents the limit possibility for human life. And this human life may, by the hand of the sovereign, be banished to this same sphere which non human life is condemned. The problem remains then, that as we attempt to reconstitute the space between humanity and the animal, it inevitably is returned to the animal once again, since the meeting of the human and the animal can only be postponed, and never indefinitely. This is perhaps why Emile Zola comments that the "fate of animals is of greater importance to me

---

85   Cary Wolfe's recent exploration of biopolitics and animality offers further consideration of the relation between human violence towards humans and human violence toward animals, towards a "biopolitics that cuts across species lines and knit together bodies of whatever kind." Leaning on Esposito, Wolfe observes that the process of biopolitical distinction allows "us to explain the differences between how the Nazis treated their pets, their meat, and their Holocaust victims." See Wolfe. *Before The Law.* 102.

86   Benjamin. "Critique of Violence." 240.

than the fear of appearing ridiculous: it is indissolubly connected with the fate of men."[87]

The living population of the earth has inherited a vision of sovereign power, which has spread cancerously into even the most seemingly inaccessible aspects of everyday life. This vision commands all, claims legitimacy for all, and determines the conduct of living for all within its domain. Politics as we know it is caught inextricably in the web of sovereign power, in such a way that it seems that modern political debate cannot help but circulate around the same, routine issues: What is the appropriate legislative response? Is it within the State's powers to intervene in this particular conflict? How can we ensure the citizen's rights are maintained in the face of the State? To challenge such an encompassing and peremptory political discourse where every question implies the sovereign absolutely, and every decision made refers to life itself, would require the most intensive rethinking of the way in which territory, governance and economy are imagined. In this sense, whilst Agamben's analyses of bare life, and Foucault's theory of biopolitics, provide a means by which to assess the condition of non human life with respect to sovereign power, the political project must reach beyond these terms. In so far as biopolitics represents the conflict between human and animal—the war against animals— then perhaps what we are seeking here is a way to end this war.

---

87   Emile Zola quoted in Jon Wynne-Tyson Ed. *The Extended Circle: A Dictionary of Humane Thought.* Sussex: Centaur Press, 1985. 432.

CHAPTER 2

Governmentality

> ...every form of production creates its own legal relations, forms of government, etc. The crudity and lack of comprehension consist in bringing things organically belonging together into a haphazard relation, into a mere reflex connection. The bourgeois economists only see that production is carried on better with modern police than, e.g., under the law of the cudgel. They only forget that the law of the cudgel too is law, and the right of the stronger still survives in a different form even in their "constitutional state."
>
> KARL MARX. *A Contribution to the Critique of Political Economy.*[1]

In Plato's *The Republic* there is an early, albeit crucial, moment, where a somewhat impetuous Thrasymachus challenges Socrates:

> Socrates, have you a nurse?
> Why do you ask such a question as that? I said. Wouldn't it be better to answer mine?
> Because she lets you go about sniffling like a child whose nose wants wiping. She hasn't even taught you to know a shepherd when you see one, or his sheep either.
> What makes you say that?
> Why, you imagine that a herdsman studies the interests of his flocks or cattle, tending and fattening them up with some other end in view than his master's profit or his own; and so you don't see that, in politics, the genuine ruler regards his subjects exactly like sheep, and thinks of nothing else, night and day, but the good he can get out of them for himself. You are so far out in your notions of right and wrong, justice and injustice, as to not know that 'right' actually means what is good for someone else, and to be 'just' means serving the interest of the stronger who rule, at the cost of the subject who obeys; whereas injustice is just the reverse, asserting its authority over those innocents who are called just, so that they minister solely towards their master's advantage and happiness, and not in the least degree to their own[2]

---

1 Karl Marx. *Preface and Introduction to A Contribution to the Critique of Political Economy.* Peking: Foreign Language Press, 1976. 14–15.

2 Plato. *Republic.* I343. 25. Compare to Paul Veyne, quoted by Nikolas Rose, on the way in which utilisation of gladiators for enjoyment might be compared to the utilisation of sheep:

© KONINKLIJKE BRILL NV, LEIDEN, 2015 | DOI 10.1163/9789004300422_004

The section is intriguing for a number of reasons. One of these at least is the gendered nature of Thrasymachus' attack on Socrates. Criticism requires a degree of impudence; a disrespect for the authority of an established argument. In this case Thrasymachus' impudence is expressed though an "emasculation," where a snotty nose and the apparently ever waiting hand of a woman, serves as a prop to undermine the great Socrates. Thrasymachus' act of insolence is to say that Socrates is a child, and that he is in the care of a woman. The insult is sharpened by the suggestion that it is the neglect of this woman who cares for him that leads to Socrates' own self deception. *She* both prevents the child from seeing the truth of the situation, and simultaneously neglects the child, or in this case the child's nose: "like a child whose nose wants wiping." Thrasymachus' attempted "emasculation" of Socrates must be contrasted with Thrasymachus' eventual capitulation to the master later in *The Republic*. It may be recalled that the ensuing dialogue closes with another emasculation towards the end of *The Republic*: this time Socrates outwits Thrasymachus, causing him to blush:

> Thrasymachus' assent was dragged out of him with a reluctance of which my account gives no idea. He was sweating at every pore, for the weather was hot; and I saw then what I had never seen before—Thrasymachus blushing.[3]

On one angle the blush should provoke critical attention, as it is yet another site of claimed human differentiation from non human animals, since it is assumed that shame is a distinctly human attribute.[4] Shame in this case is experienced as a form of emasculation, where woman is positioned in relation

---

Our politics is limited to keeping the flock together as it moves along its historical trajectory; for the rest, we are well aware that animals are animals. We try not to abandon too many hungry ones along the way, for that would reduce the population of the flock; we feed them if we have to...We are no more concerned about denying gladiators' blood to the Roman people than a herder of sheep or cattle would be concerned about watching over his animals' mating behavior in order to prevent incestuous unions. We are intransigent on just one point, which is not the animals' morality but their energy: we do not want the flock to weaken, for that would be its loss and ours.

Paul Veyne, quoted in Nikolas Rose. *Powers of Freedom: Reframing Political Thought*. Port Chester: Cambridge University Press, 1999. 40.

3   Plato. *Republic*. 33. I350.

4   See John Heath. *The Talking Greeks: Speech, Animals, and the Other in Homer, Aeschylus, and Plato*. Cambridge: Cambridge University Press, 2005. 296–8. See also Agamben. *Remnants from Auschwitz*. 103.

to man not as a source of truth itself (as "nature")[5] but as neglectfully (or perhaps stupidly) veiling a source of truth that should be apparent. On another axis, there is a sense in which the play between Thrasymachus and Socrates is essentially one of domestication: that is, of seeking a form of domination which attempts to fold the other into one's own life world without recognition of a difference of interest. This is perhaps evidenced by the statement Socrates advances later in *The Republic*: "Don't try to make a quarrel between Thrasymachus and me, when we have just become friends—not that we were enemies before."[6] This is clearly "companionship" on Socrates terms: that is, through the experience of having Thrasymachus capitulate to his view.

In this chapter, I focus on the question of how we might conceptualise the development of human domination over animals, and the relationship of these techniques of control to human sovereign violence over other humans. The exploration in this chapter takes Foucault's discussion of the genealogy of governmentality, and in particular pastoral power, as its frame, pointing to the failure in Foucault's account to "take stock" of animal domestication and its relationship to the development of government as a means to organise biopolitical violence. As such, in this chapter I seek to extend my intuition which was presented in chapter 1, that suggested a similarity and intertwining of histories of human violence towards humans and human violence towards animals, but, despite this *interdependence*, recognises a need to simultaneously track *independent* histories in understanding these regimes of violence. I do this by framing pastoral power. Like Thrasymachus, our central question here is whether the shepherd can indeed be thought of as "good," and how challenging the purported beneficence of the pastor in turn offers us a way to imagine a reconstruction of the narrative for the genealogy of governmentality.

Governmental Warfare

The organisation of industrialised slaughter and animal utilisation requires the precise management of control apparatuses at different levels of scale, which attribute and delegate responsibility across different actors: States and legitimised authorities, large scale multinational private companies, individual

---

5 Irigaray states: "… since there is also no way of ignoring it/her, *then she/it will be extrapolated into the infinity of the Idea*. Not that the Idea is visible or representable either but *it conjures up a blindness over origin.*" Luce Irigaray. *Speculum of the Other Woman.* Ithaca: Cornell University Press, 1985. 294.

6 Plato. *Republic.* 207. I498.

contractors including farmers and workers who may or may not claim property rights over animals, and animal populations themselves who are resistive agents situated within a topography that precisely dictates movement, nutrition, reproduction and death. Industrial breeding, containment and slaughter provide a useful example for how it is that different delegations of power might operate within a precisely organised framework. Consider the increasing shift towards "vertical integration" in industrialised factory farming of animals.[7] Production is carefully segmented to control every aspect of the "supply chain" from life to death. An emerging feature is the control exerted by meat packing companies, who take responsibility for slaughter, production of meat and distribution, relocating this element of the supply chain away from the lived lives of the animals destined for slaughter, yet simultaneously exerting controls through contractual arrangements on how animals are kept and fed:

> The diversified, independent, family-owned farms of 40 years ago that produced a variety of crops and a few animals are disappearing as an economic entity, replaced by much larger, and often highly leveraged, farm factories. The animals that many of these farms produce are owned by the meat packing companies from the time they are born or hatched right through their arrival at the processing plant and from there to market. The packaged food products are marketed far from the farm itself.[8]

These trends have been accompanied by significant changes in the role of the farmer. More and more animal farmers have contracts with "vertically integrated" meat packing companies to provide housing and facilities to raise the animals from infancy to the time they go to the slaughterhouse. The grower does not own the animals and frequently does not grow the crops to feed them. The integrator (company) controls all phases of production, including what and when the animals are fed.[9]

Unpicking how domination works within this complex field of action involves understanding how techniques might be organised, including through

7   See Noske. *Beyond Boundaries.* 23–7.
8   Pew Commission. *Putting Meat on the Table: Industrial Farm Animal Production*, Report of Pew Commission on Industrial Farm Animal Production. 2008. 5.
9   Pew Commission. *Putting Meat on the Table.* 5–6. The Pew Commission goes on:
    Under the modern-day contracts between integrators and growers, the latter are usually responsible for disposition of the animal waste and the carcasses of animals that die before shipment to the processor. The costs of pollution and waste management are also the grower's responsibility. Rules governing waste handling and disposal methods are defined by federal and state agencies.

autonomous systems that do not rely on a centralised control apparatus. War, in this case, operates through diffused systems of government that sequence and scale technologies of violence and control to achieve a comprehensive life and death management of non human animals, securing maximal human utility. The organisation of complexity, where the right to dominate is claimed as a tool, is essentially a matter of governance. Sovereignty, as I shall discuss, describes a particular radical right or prerogative which has the capacity to establish relations of domination which are *a priori* non contestable. That is, sovereignty is marked by its capacity for a "stupidity" in putting itself beyond all questioning. Government—that is, the question of what rationality or rationalities guides and informs a grid of interconnected sites of action—is a way of describing how this prerogative is put into practice.

As discussed in Chapter 1, the war against animals must be understood as distinctly biopolitical: that is, our relationship to animals is characterised by a balance struck between life and death, where the minute and organised manangement of the life of populations is key to understanding the dynamic of this relation. Foucault's understanding of "governmentality" offers a path by which to further refine this understanding of the way in which war, biopolitics and animal domination inter-relate.[10] For Foucault, governmental rationalities mark a significant shift in the operations of State power, one that by necessity forces a move away from the maintenance of territory (as the mere physical possession of the sovereign) to biopolitical intervention at the level of population, as an end in itself. In contrast to a view that sovereignty is concerned merely with the maintenance of its own means of power, government has as its purpose not the act of government itself, but the welfare of the population, the improvement of its condition, the increase of its wealth, longevity, health and broad "wellbeing." It is the population itself on which government will act directly through large scale campaigns, or indirectly through techniques that will make possible the stimulation of birth rates, the harnessing or creative energies, the directing of the flow of population into certain regions or activities. The population now represents more the end of government than the power of the sovereign.[11] Whilst the core foundations of

---

10   Referring to war in a conventional sense (that is, as conflict between sovereign nations) Nikolas Rose and Peter Miller state that war "is itself dependent upon certain practices of government." See Nikolas Rose and Peter Miller. "Political Power beyond the State: Problematics of Government." *The British Journal of Sociology.* 43.2, 1992. 173–205. 178.

11   Michel Foucault. "Governmentality." *The Foucault Effect: Studies in Governmentality, with Two Lectures and an Interview with Michel Foucault.* Graham Burchell, Colin Gordon and Peter Miller Eds. London: Harvester Wheatsheaf, 1991. 87–104. 100.

sovereign power remain intact, governmental discourses point sovereign energies towards a broad management of life within its domain. Thus Foucault arrives at a "trinity" of relations that organise contemporary power and security: "sovereignty—discipline—government."[12]

The shift from sovereignty to government also represents a shift in strategy. Sovereign power, following the Hobbesian model, was distinctly mechanical in its operations. The sovereign was perceived as deploying force in a directional manner to achieve particular effects which reinforced its own power. The sovereign used the sword bluntly to pursue and punish treason within the sovereign domain. Military forces literally "pushed back" invaders, and power was distributed through "chains" linking sovereign and delegate. Territory was captured through periodic bouts of violence which won resources and new domains of power. Governance, on the other hand, involves a strategy which Foucault suggests is "economic" in nature:[13] rather than exerting force through spectacular bouts of violence which aim to inscribe and win power, government is a rationality of management that seeks, by discreet interventions, to order the behaviour of populations in a relational field. Governmentality thus represents what has been described as "the conduct of conduct."[14] Foucault, for example, offers the metaphor of a ship to describe the way in which a governmental rationality might operate:

> What does it mean to govern a ship? It means to take charge of the sailors, but also of the boat and its cargo; to take care of the ship means also to reckon with winds, rocks and storms; and it consists in that activity of establishing a relation between sailors who are to be taken care of and the ship which is to be taken care of, and the cargo which is to be brought to port, and all those eventualities like winds, rocks, storms and so on; this is what characterises the government of a ship.[15]

---

12   Foucault. "Governmentality." 102.

13   Foucault, "Governmentality." 92–3. See also Colin Gordon, "Governmental Rationality: An Introduction." Graham Burchell, Colin Gordon and Peter Miller Eds. *The Foucault Effect: Studies in Governmentality with Two Lectures by and an Interview with Michel Foucault.* London: Harvester Wheatsheaf, London, 1991. 1–51. 11–12.

14   See Gordon. "Governmental Rationality: An Introduction." See also Mitchell Dean. *Governmentality: Power and Rule in Modern Society.* London: Sage Publications, 1999. 10–16.

15   Foucault. "Governmentality." 93–4. Note that Foucault's choice of the ship as a metaphor is interesting here, as it also correlates with a model of power described briefly in *The Republic*: "and the ship's captain, again, considered strictly as no mere sailor, but in command of the crew, will study and enjoin the interests of his subordinates, not his own." Plato. *Republic*. 24, I343.

The fact that one owns a ship is secondary to the business of its governance: "property and territory are merely one of its variables."[16] As Nikolas Rose summarises: "to rule properly, it is necessary to rule in light of a knowledge of the particular and specific characteristics that are taken to be imminent to that over which rule is to be exercised: the characteristics of a land with its peculiar geography, fertility, climate; of a population with its rates of birth, illness, death; of a society with its classes, interests, conflicts; of an economy with its laws of circulation, of supply and demand; of individuals with their passions, interests and propensities to good and evil."[17] In this sense, Foucault will suggest that governmentality has a distinctly "pastoral" element, something we shall discuss in detail further below. Government attempts to organise a flock, and has a scope that is scalable down to individual elements within a multiciplicity. As such, territory is not an end in itself. Government is a responsibility to ensure the smooth cohabitation of a range of diverse and autonomous agents, and not the maintenance of territory for its own benefit.

Governmental rationalities correlate with Foucault's other work on biopolitical and disciplinary power, particularly with regard to the way in which one comes to manage the *self*. Foucault argues that the focus of disciplinary power is the "soul" of the individual.[18] The disciplines aim at correcting behaviour through the provision of the normalising tools by which one may govern the self. The compulsion to govern oneself, to manage the self for the benefit of the soul, leads to the requirement that one "bares one's soul." The self is opened for interrogation by rationalised expertise. Thus, as Foucault argues in *The History of Sexuality*, the modern individual "confesses" to the other, and opens to discourse an increasing number of aspects of the self.[19] Discourse creates the conditions by which the decisions one makes about one's life, one's inclinations and peculiarities, and one's physical and genetic make-up, become subject to a normalisation which pressures the individual to vigilantly monitor the self, and strictly control behaviour, expression, appearance and deportment. The self becomes split: an assembly of a diverse set of elements which must be brought together with coherence in order to present the self. Governance then, may be understood as the means by which we correlate the self as a bundle of desires, dispositions, physical characteristics, intelligences etc.: the self as an

---

16   Foucault. "Governmentality." 94.

17   Rose. *Powers of Freedom.* 7.

18   Foucault. *Discipline and Punish.* 19.

19   Foucault. *The Will to Knowledge: The History of Sexuality: 1.* 53–73. In this regard see Chloë Taylor. *The Culture of Confession from Augustine to Foucault: A Genealogy of the 'Confessing Animal'.* New York: Routledge, 2009.

entity which is to be managed constantly, as an economy of factors within which discreet interventions may be made.[20]

The seemingly endless discourses available on "fat" and weight control are an example of such governmental models translated to the individual. Those identified with weight "problems" are assessed over their individual physical characteristics, their genetic and hereditary dispositions, their desires and their inclinations and abilities with regard to physical activity; this information is used to develop strategies based upon available food and medication regimes, forms of body drilling, exercise and motivational training to propel the body into modalities of action aimed at managing and curtailing weight gain.[21] Individuals learn to scrupulously monitor movement, appearance, mass, diet, an eternal self-discipline that is reinforced by a surveillance society ready to reinforce a normalised body image. Governance extends the disciplinary model of power by presenting the body as a complex mix of fixed characteristics, passions and desires, dispositions and inclinations, which must be managed by planning, strategic deployment, drilling, and ongoing strategy, towards the achievement of normalised outcomes. These intricate modes of power, which entangle individual bodies, mesh with a broader objective to manage populations. The minute organisation of conduct at an individual level has a broader capacity to complement strategies for organisation of larger multiciplicities at the population level. Inculcating dietary and training regimes amongst individuals for example, is perceived to serve a broader function of reducing the health costs and mortality rate of populations as a result of "obesity." Organisation of the conduct of the individual thus integrates with the organisation of the conduct of the flock.

Governmentality is not, in the Foucaldian model, restricted to the operations of the governmentality of the State. Indeed, Foucault remarks that the

---

20   Thus Mitchell Dean argues that:
           ...if the self is conceived of as a spiralling ribbon which folds over and over itself defining a space of interior being without essential substance, then in contemporary political culture, the self is composed of the different cloths, weaves, colours, and patterns of the various programs of government, techniques of self, and the work of the human sciences.
      See Mitchell Dean. *Critical and Effective Histories: Foucault's Methods and Historical Sociology*. London and New York: Routledge, 1994. 211. See also Michael Clifford. *Political Geneology after Foucault: Savage Identities*. New York and London: Routledge, 2001. 65.
21   Samantha Murray states: "The 'fat' body is maddening: it will not fit, and yet the disciplining imperatives of pathological discourses constantly reign the 'fat' body in, and scrutinise its being-in-the-world." See Samantha Murray. *The 'Fat' Female Body*. New York: Palgrave Macmillan, 2008.

"state is only an episode in government."[22] Governmentality is a "rationality."[23] It comes to instruct ways of dealing with entities ranging in size from the State (and we can infer in the contemporary context, the "international governance" and the "global economy"), to the household, to the individual (the soul).[24] Thus whilst governmental models of power are characteristic of a particular trajectory of State power, they are not limited to this sphere. Other organisations take up principles of governance as a means to manage the interactions of the actors within their particular domains of influence. For example, local organs of government such as councils become concerned about managing the behaviour of residents and visitors within their municipalities. Councils may launch crime prevention strategies, which attempt to supplement the coercive activities of the police force, by providing safe houses within a community, or lighting in dark parks, or consulting with different communities within the municipality, or utilising electronic surveillance in public spaces, or funding youth centres. In this example, the pursuit of crime, which was always a responsibility of sovereign power, also becomes a "community problem" under governmental rationality, one which a diverse range of groups, from councils to churches, schools to parent groups, youth workers to senior citizens associations, become involved in the management of.[25]

---

22   Foucault. *Security, Territory, Population.* 248. Foucault goes on: "What we would have to show would be how, from the sixteenth century, a civil society, or rather, quite simply a governmentalized society organized something both fragile and obsessive that is called the state. But the state is only an episode in government, and it is not government that is an instrument of the state. Or at any rate, the state is an episode in governmentality."

23   Foucault. "Governmentality." 89. See also Gordon. "Governmental Rationality: An Introduction."

24   Foucault. "Governmentality." 90.

25   Similar strategies are discussed by Pat O'Malley with regard to the governance of indigenous communities. See Pat O'Malley. "Indigenous Governance." Mitchell Dean and Barry Hindess Eds. *Governing Australia: Studies in Contemporary Rationalities of Government.* Cambridge: Cambridge University Press, 1988. 156–72. O'Malley also explicitly discusses "community crime prevention" strategies (see 158–9). O' Malley describes a particular intervention which commenced in 1990, when the Department of Community Services in Western Australia approached representatives from the Ngaanyatjarra people to negotiate a cooperative strategy to address petrol sniffing within the Ngaanyatjarra community (163–4). This intervention supplements existing State powers to pursue petrol sniffers through the criminal justice system, and represents a shift from—a more traditional— tactic of the deployment of sovereign force, to an attempt to "manage" the behaviour of communities through the deployment of diverse agencies.

Of relevance to my discussion in this book, it is important to note that rationalities of government can organise violence.[26] Mitchell Dean argues that government may take on modes that do not, at least outwardly, resemble those of liberal democratic States, suggesting that such regimes may be described as examples of "Authoritarian Governmentality."[27] Within liberal States, Dean argues, there are frequent justifications for the exercise of authoritarian forms of rule. Liberalism relies upon a presupposition of free agents who both allow themselves to be governed and provide legitimation for the "training" of subjects who are "suitable" for governance. Liberal discourses often emphasise the need to cultivate the appropriate knowledges within the citizenry, in order that civil subjects may then be able to participate within the formal political process. Thus there is an endorsement for disciplinary pedagogical networks (schools, education campaigns etc.) that are deployed for the benefit of particular populations that "are yet to attain the maturity required of the liberal subject."[28] It is this same logic that may also provide authorisation for the systemic exclusion of those groups deemed unsuitable participants within the civil political space. Justification is found for the use of authoritarian measures

---

26   Aside from Mitchell Dean's discussion of authoritarian governmentalities (discussed below) see also Judith Butler. *Precarious Life: The Powers of Mourning and Violence*. London: Verso, 2004. Butler argues that governmentality provides a point of disruption to the regular juridical order through which a "rogue" sovereignty can emerge (56), "one with no structures of accountability built in" (66). Butler states that "the suspension of the rule of law allows for the convergence of governmentality and sovereignty; sovereignty is exercised in the act of suspension, but also in the self allocation of legal prerogative: governmentality denotes an operation of administration power that is extra-legal, even as it can and does return to law as a field of tactical operations" (55). Butler's perspective is useful in so far as it provides a way to link governmentality to examples of sovereign violence like torture and camps. But the concept of a "legitimate" versus "illegitimate sovereignty" is at odds with the analysis I present here: namely, because examples of torture and camps (and slaughterhouses) must be regarded as inherent components of biopolitical sovereignty that authorises itself and not deviations from "legitimate" rule. In the context of human domination of animals, this sovereignty is always assumed to be "legitimate." For a discussion of Butler's work on precarity and its possible usefulness for considering animals, see Taylor. "The Precarious Lives of Animals: Butler, Coetzee, and Animal Ethics"; James Stanescu. "Species Trouble: Judith Butler, Mourning, and the Precarious Lives of Animals." *Hypatia*. 27, 2012. 567–82; and on vulnerability, see Anat Pick. *Creaturely Poetics: Animality and Vulnerability in Literature and Film*. New York: Columbia University Press, 2011.

27   See Dean. *Governmentality*. 131–48.

28   Dean. *Governmentality*. 133.

against those populations determined as consisting of "poorly developed" political subjects.

In a post-colonial context, pertinent examples of the use of authoritarian—indeed genocidal—forms of governmentality can be found in the systematic acts of violence, domination and annihilation utilised against indigenous peoples. As Fiona Nicoll observes, in the context of white invasion of Australia, this history emphasises the warlike capacity of governmental strategy:

> Following waves of dispossession throughout the continent that saw Aborigines removed and land subdivided and sold to settlers, the colonial authorities were faced with the problem of a dispossessed Indigenous population. 'Settlements' were established to which Aborigines and Torres Strait Islanders were confined. Enforced regimes of labour, prohibitions on particular forms of sociality, such as drinking, and a system of passports which restricted movement from one settlement to another, were elements of this 'carceral regime' well into the twentieth century. The important point here is that *terra nullius* authorised a particularly *governmental* form of warfare.[29]

Thus, even violent forms of biopolitical intervention, such as acts of dispossession or genocide, may be inherent within the sphere of liberal governance: "while the bio-political imperative does not account for all that bedevils liberal-democratic states, it is remarkable how much of what is done of an illiberal character is done with the best of biopolitical intentions."[30] This view of governmentality aligns with Mbembe's conceptualisation, as discussed in Chapter 1, of necropolitical spheres sitting side by side with spheres devoted to fostering lives. Life and death are mapped topographically; they are delineated and separated, but feed off each other.

The violent governmentality of human populations provides an opportunity to understand how governmentality might be applied to non human populations. As discussed, the organisation of large scale modes of domination of non human life, such as those found in industrialised animal farming processes, necessarily involves precise modes of governmental organisation which organise diverse elements within a totalising system. Methodologically, however, I do not seek here to simply suggest that authoritarian modes of governmentality over human populations might aptly describe our relations with

---

29   Fiona Nicoll. *From Diggers to Drag Queens: Configurations of Australian Identity.* Annandale: Pluto Press, 2001. 163–4.

30   Dean. *Governmentality.* 132.

non human animals. On the contrary, my task here is to conceptualise how it is that our treatment of animals may have informed the rationality for our treatment of humans: how it is that a governmentality of non human life might have been transferred systematically as a rationality of organisation to govern human populations.

Pastoral Power

Foucault draws a distinction between governmentality and sovereignty, two concepts that I believe are more difficult to disentangle. The distinction for Foucault is at least in part temporal. The genealogical trail Foucault identifies at some length in the 1977–78 lectures has its starting point in the pastorate; that is, in the modelling of a relationship of control, foremost within the tradition of the Christian church, upon the metaphorical relationship between a shepherd and livestock. Pastoral power is understood to precede governmentality, with the art of government developing out of a combination of concerns—security and population being key drivers—that shift the register for the exercise of sovereignty: pastoral power is, as Foucault notes, a "prelude to governmentality."[31]

The pastorate is seen as a distinct form of power, with its own identifiable characteristics. Firstly the pastorate is concerned with a population and its change: "the shepherd's power is not exercised over a territory but, by definition, over a flock, and more exactly, over the flock in its movement from one place to another."[32] Thus the focus of pastoral power shifts from inanimate property (territory) to animate property (the animal, the slave, the body), with all the vicissitudes of this flock becoming an object of knowledge for the shepherd. Secondly, Foucault argues that pastoral power is seen as a power to "do good," to be "beneficent."[33] Where power is usually identified through a rush of force, "its ability to triumph over enemies, defeat them, reduce them to slavery...by the possibility of conquest and the by the territories, the wealth and so on,"[34] pastoral power is defined by the ability to advantage or provide benefit: "its only *raison d'être* is doing good."[35] Here doing good is, as Foucault points out, aimed at *salut* (salvation or safety), through securing subsistence in a broad sense:

---

31   Foucault. *Security, Territory, Population.* 184.

32   Foucault. *Security, Territory, Population.* 125.

33   Foucault. *Security, Territory, Population.* 126.

34   Foucault. *Security, Territory, Population.* 126.

35   Foucault. *Security, Territory, Population.* 126.

Pastoral power is a power of care. It looks after the flock, it looks after the individuals of the flock, it sees to it that the sheep do not suffer, it goes in search of those that have strayed off course, and it treats those that are injured.[36]

Thus the power of the shepherd is perceived not as a right, exercised for its own end, but on the contrary as a duty to serve, for benefit of the flock. This folds into the third feature of the pastoral model of power: the shepherd's role is to sacrifice him/herself for the wellbeing of the flock. The "good shepherd" is ethically removed from any suggestion that the management of the flock is instrumental in nature: it is, on the other hand, an example of a modest, consuming sacrifice for the welfare of the livestock under his/her guidance:

> The shepherd (*pasteur*) directs all his care towards others and not towards himself. This is precisely the difference between the good and the bad shepherd. The bad shepherd only thinks of good pasture for his own profit, for fattening the flock that he will be able to sell and scatter, whereas the good shepherd thinks only of his flock and of nothing else. He does not even consider his own advantage in the well-being of his flock. I think we see here the appearance, the outline, of a power with an essentially selfless and, as it were, transitional character. The shepherd (*pasteur*) serves the flock and must be an intermediary between the flock and pasture, food, and salvation, which implies that pastoral power is always a good in itself. All the dimensions of terror and of force or fearful violence, all these disturbing powers that make men tremble before the power of kings and gods, disappear in the case of the shepherd (*pasteur*), whether it is the king-shepherd or the god-shepherd.[37]

Foucault adds a fourth feature to his broad identification of the characteristics of pastoral power; namely, the capacity of the shepherd both to individualise and aggregate the flock: "the shepherd directs the whole flock, but he can only really direct it insofar as not a single sheep escapes him."[38] Thus the shepherd has the capacity to adjust the scale of relations, from molar to molecular levels of organisation.[39]

---

36   Foucault. *Security, Territory, Population.* 127.
37   Foucault. *Security, Territory, Population.* 128.
38   Foucault. *Security, Territory, Population.* 128.
39   I use "molar" and "molecular" here based upon Gilles Deleuze and Félix Guattari use of these terms as metaphors for describing micropolitical organisation in *A Thousand*

There are four characteristics of pastoral power then: a power focused on the animate population (as opposed to territory); a power that is beneficent rather than instrumental; a power that transforms a right of domination into a duty to serve; and finally, a power that must adjust its scale in order to attend simultaneously to the individual and to its aggregate. I don't want to challenge here Foucault's conceptualisation of the pastorate; on the contrary, his articulation of the powers of the pastorate remain relevant for thinking through the evolution to governmentality. However, here I wish to address a conceptual gap that informs the assumptions behind Foucault's model; namely, the unspoken role of animals within the model of pastoral power.[40] As Matthew Cole summarises: "Foucault's discussion of pastoral power evidences species-blindness."[41] It strikes me as odd that, through Foucault's analysis of the pastorate, the question of the role of the pastorate as a model for animal control, instrumentalisation and death is not considered a factor in how it is that we might understand the romantic metaphor of the pastorate. For while there is a brief acknowledgment of Thrasymachus' skeptical objection to the concept of pastoral power in Plato's *Republic*[42]—that is, that the shepherd acts towards his own end in harvesting the fleece of the flock and fattening livestock for slaughter–there is little in Foucault's discussion of pastoral power to indicate

---

Plateaus, through the concept of *segmentarity* (see Gilles Deleuze and Félix Guattari. *A Thousand Plateaus: Capitalism and Schizophrenia*. Minneapolis: University of Minnesota Press, 1998. 208–31). The segment is defined by Deleuze and Guattari as the base unit of organisation: "Segmentarity is inherent to all the strata composing us. Dwelling, getting around, working, playing, life is spatially and socially segmented" (208). The differences between forms of segmentation depend on the scale of analysis: that is, as Deleuze and Guattari point out, there is always a plurality of modes of political organisation, composed on both *molar* (macropolitical) and *molecular* (micropolitical) levels (213).

40   A range of scholars have observed the "species" blindness of Foucault in the construction of pastoral power, including Cole. "From 'Animal Machines' to 'Happy Meat'?"; Anand Pandian. "Pastoral Power in the Postcolony: On the Biopolitics of the Criminal Animal in South India." *Cultural Anthropology*. 23.1, 2008: 85–117; and Nicole Shukin. "Tense Animals: On Other Species of Pastoral Power." CR: *The New Centennial Review*. 11.2, 2011. 143–67.

41   Cole. "From 'Animal Machines' to 'Happy Meat'?" 90. Cole's article provides a useful summary of the application of pastoral power to modern animal containment and slaughter, particularly the individuating capacity of contemporary techniques. However, I would disagree with Cole's perspective that "pastoralism differs from discipline in operating as a metaphorical description of power relations" (90). As I argue in this chapter there is no metaphor here; we must understand pastoral power as a form of violent sovereignty, with techniques that differ from that applied in traditional sovereignty "by the sword."

42   Foucault. *Security, Territory, Population*. 140.

an awareness of the brutality that may lie behind the mythology of the peace loving shepherd.

In a re-reading of Foucault's narrative of pastoral power, Christopher Meyes draws attention to this unaccounted for violent relationality that accompanies the pastor's relationship with flock (both animal and human).[43] Meyes argues that a clearer separation is required by Foucault in his analysis of the pastor; in particular, a need to highlight the role of violence as a component of pastoral power in the Hebrew tradition: "despite Foucault's close analysis of the early development of the Hebrew pastor, he overlooks the role of violence and instead focuses on sacrifice."[44] Meyes retells the battle between David and Goliath, highlighting the instrumental role of the "shepherd's slingshot" wielded by David, and David's eventual decapitation of Goliath which precedes his elevation to king: "rather than separating the shepherd from the sovereign, the two are entwined."[45] As such, violence plays a crucial role in the shepherd's management and securitisation of the flock. Meyes states:

> What difference does this ancient Hebrew history make to Foucault's analysis of the pastor? Primarily it adds violence. As noted, Foucault considers the key features of the Hebrew pastor to be a power exercised on a people, for the care and benefit of the people, and that the pastor is willing to sacrifice for the one and the many. However through the inclusion of the Davidic pastor to Foucault's analysis of the shepherd an emphasis on the ability to kill threats becomes an important theme. It is David's experience of caring for the flock that taught and required him to kill for the flock.[46]

Thus beneficence becomes enfolded with violence in a particular way within pastoral power. As Meyes suggests: "the care of the flock rests on an intermingling of love and violence. It is the tension, not opposition, between love and violence in the role of the pastor that is the hidden foundation of biopower."[47]

Extending Meyes' analysis, we might draw attention, not only to the role of violence in the exercise of pastoral power with respect to the human flock, but

---

43   Christopher Meyes. "The Violence of Care: An Analysis of Foucault's Pastor." *Journal for Cultural and Religious Theory*. 11.1, 2010. 111–26. I thank Matthew Chrulew in particular for drawing my attention to this piece.

44   Meyes. "The Violence of Care." 111.

45   Meyes. "The Violence of Care." 116.

46   Meyes. "The Violence of Care." 117.

47   Meyes. "The Violence of Care." 122.

the informative role of violence and its use against the animal flock. For what of course lies hidden within the metaphor (or reality) of the pastorate is the inherent violence that encloses and demarcates the relationship between shepherd and animal, a relationship of domination. The human shepherd of an animal flock seeks a relationship of instrumentalisation that maintains as its goal the harvesting of those animals for human benefit: for wool, for milk, for meat and for leather. Even the kindest shepherd, the most beneficent shepherd, maintains some form of instrumentalisation that guides this practice of pastoral power. In this sense, Thrasymachus was correct to be cynical about the goodness of the shepherd. It is true that the relationship between shepherd and animals may be rendered benign through a metaphor that assumes a mode of care exists with respect to shepherd and the flock. And certainly it is true, that in order for the shepherd to use his or her sheep, then a care must be inculcated in order to maintain the lives of the flock for that use. However, care here is twisted with violence in a particular way to maintain life up until the threshold of slaughter. Care is inscribed in the methods of slaughter and control themselves: thus, as the animal welfare mantra would tell us, humane killing is indeed possible where it limits "unnecessary suffering." This is, after all, a violence that claims to care.

What this means for Foucault's framework is that we can disrupt the distinctions that he draws between sovereignty, pastoral power and governmentality. Importantly, we might offer a different way to understand the emergence of pastoral power and its significance for contemporary governmentality of both human and non human souls. For Foucault, the pastorate is distinguished from sovereignty as essentially a different modality of power. This, in part, emerges as a result of Foucault's conceptualisation of sovereignty as connected to space: in Foucault's words, "sovereignty is first of all exercised within a territory."[48] I do not mean to suggest here that Foucault established a non-communicative disjunction between sovereignty and the individualising power of the pastorate. Indeed, he acknowledges in the 1977–78 lectures that sovereignty, disciplinarity and security all function with respect to a multiplicity or population. However, what is key here is that in Foucault's view a "care" for a population only emerges as an auxiliary feature of sovereignty, and it is placed in an almost dialectical opposition to sovereignty's traditional focus on territory. Thus, when Foucault identifies the emergence of biopolitics, he argues that this shifts the operation of sovereignty from its more familiar concern with territory to an attentiveness to population and the life of the species:

---

48   Foucault. *Security, Territory, Population.* 12.

...the sovereign is no longer someone who exercised his power over a territory on the basis of a geographical localization of his political sovereignty. The sovereign deals with a nature, or rather with the perpetual conjunction, the perpetual intrication of a geographic, climatic and physical milieu with the human species insofar as it has a body and a soul, a physical and moral existence; and the sovereign will be someone who will have to exercise power at the point of connection where nature, in the sense of the physical elements, interferes with nature in the sense of the nature of the human species, at that point of articulation where the milieu becomes the determining factor of nature.[49]

This fundamental distinction between sovereign and pastoral power marks their separation. Foucault's distinction treats pastoral power as a reaction to sovereignty; a whole different mode of organisation which relies on individuation, minute control of conduct, and an ethos of relationships that shifts the gaze of power from self aggrandizement to care, benefit and fostering of life. In this genealogy, pastoral power prepares the ground for governmentality, and it is through eventual challenges to the pastoral model that "the pastorate opened up...burst open, broke up, and assumed the dimension of governmentality." However, in this narrative, governmentality arises from the antagonism between pastoral modes of power and traditional sovereign modes of rule; governmentality was only "able to arise on the basis of the pastorate."[50] Governmentality then resolves the tension that is generated by the emergence of pastoral power; it brings together disparate strands: "the sovereign who rules and exercises his sovereignty now finds himself responsible for, entrusted with, and assigned new tasks of conducting souls."[51] Thus, there is a perception that sovereignty takes a

---

49   Foucault. *Security, Territory, Population.* 23.

50   Foucault. *Security, Territory, Population.*193.

51   Foucault. *Security, Territory, Population.* 231. This seems to be a point of tension in Foucault's account, where since sovereignty is treated as substantially different from pastoral power, it would seem violence becomes an outcome of sovereignty within governmentality rather than a product of governmental rationality itself. We see this distancing between sovereignty and governmentality, for example, in Rose's explanation for Nazi Germany, where liberalism and freedom are aligned to governmentality against the inherent violence of sovereign power:

> And if, in Nazi Germany, the freedom to act, indeed the very existence, of some subjects had to be erased, this was in the name of a greater freedom of the Aryan people and their destiny. Here, without the controls exercised by liberal concerns with limited government and individual freedoms, the despotism of the state that is always an immanent presence in all governmentalities is manifest in all its bloody rationality.

"back seat" when governmentality emerges as a rationality of rule; Rose, for example, states unequivocally: "For all systems of rule in the west since about the eighteenth century, the population has appeared as the terrain of government *par excellence*. Not the exercise of sovereignty—though this plays a part."[52]

As I have stated, the opportunity is here to re-imagine the significance of the pastorate. What if we challenge the assumption that pastoral power is not about the sword; object to the assumption that the pastor does not aim towards death? What if we say from the outset that the pastorate is a different modality of sovereign power that seeks to enclose the operation of sovereignty within a cloak of care? What if, following Thrasymachus' objection, the pastoral model of power is essentially about deception; that is, a technology of careful violence that hides a brutal instrumentality within a logic of beneficence? A means of covering war with peace?

If this is the case, we might propose a different model for understanding sovereignty, pastoral power and governmentality. First, let us dispense with the notion that sovereignty has anything essential to do with territory. Sovereignty describes a mode of relationality that sets forth an array of technologies of domination that work across a whole field of operations, of which territory is only *one* focus. As I shall discuss in Chapter 8, sovereignty is in essence defined by its essential groundlessness as a form of right: it lacks character, nature, divinity. It is, in essence a claim made without basis. While it is true that sovereignty in the West has a history of association with territory, this is neither a defining characteristic of sovereignty, nor the only modality of its operation. We must also stress here any assumption that sovereignty is the sole domain of the human must be suspended.[53] As I have advanced in this book, sovereignty can describe the relationship of dominion claimed by humans over other animals. Likewise we might recognise non human animal sovereignty (indeed this is something to which I will return to in the Conclusion).

Secondly, we might identify pastoral power not as a form of organisation that originates as a different modality of power from sovereignty, but as a form

Rose. *Powers of Freedom*. 23. See also Rose and Peter Miller. "Political Power Beyond the State": "government addresses a realm of processes that it cannot govern by the exercise of sovereign will because it lacks the requisite knowledge and capacities" (180).

52   Nikolas Rose. *Governing the Soul: The Shaping of the Private Self*. London and New York: Routledge, 1990. 5. Rose's discussion on the psychology of war and its relationship to conduct seems an interesting trajectory to explore in relation to the argument I have advanced in this book.

53   Indeed it is interesting that Rose explicitly refers to governmentality as a set of "human technologies," effectively sidestepping the use of governmental rationalities to conduct the conduct of non human animals. See Rose. *Powers of Freedom*. 54.

of sovereignty itself. That is, we must understand pastoral power as precisely a modality of sovereignty. The pastorate describes one specific relationality of human sovereign domination over other animals. This modality has specific characteristics, including the capacity for a minute organisation of techniques in order to foster an efficient instrumentality of power which will stretch from birth to slaughter, and a capacity to almost steplessly adjust the scale of conduct from individual to molar levels of organisation. Let us not forget the history that might inform this genealogy of the pastorate. As Noske observes, "domestication"—which she defines as the process of humans forcing "changes on the animal's seasonal subsistence cycle in order to make it coincide with particular needs"[54]—has had a profound effect on shaping most human relationships with animals, and simultaneously has shaped human societies themselves.[55] Sheep and goats were regarded to have been some of the first animals organised, contained and regulated for human use.[56] Human utilisation is marked by a historical process of parasitically capturing the autonomous sociality and creativity of these animals, and bending this towards human needs:[57] a veritable history of the evolution of "the conduct of conduct." This longstanding relationship allowed for the refinement of human techniques for human control, including, importantly, the development of biopolitical controls over reproduction, which facilitated human utilisation through progressive morphological changes (reduction in horn size, change in wool thickness, reduction in bone size etc.) that have adapted animal populations to human use.[58] The capacity to infinitely adjust the scale of power—from individual units to whole populations, from amoeba to ecosystem, reflects a peculiarly

---

54   Noske. *Beyond Boundaries*. 3.

55   See Noske. *Beyond Boundaries*. 10.

56   Helmut Hemmer. *Domestication: the Decline of Environmental Appreciation*. Cambridge, Cambridge University Press, 1990. 74. See also Juliet Clutton-Brock. *A Natural History of Domesticated Mammals*. Cambridge University Press, Cambridge, 1999; and see also Noske. *Beyond Boundaries*. 5. In relation to the racialised connection between human violence towards animals and that towards other humans, particularly in light of the history of slavery, see Pugliese. *State Violence and the Execution of Law*. 34–44.

57   Noske remarks: "Generally speaking, the two species involved need to be social animals in order for domestication to go ahead, at least in the past. Animals living in a society are more prepared to enter into a social relationship with members of another species than solitary ones." Noske. *Beyond Boundaries*. 3.

58   Robert Nozick perceptively asks: "Would it be all right to use genetic-engineering techniques to breed natural slaves who would be contented with their lots? Natural animal slaves? Was that the domestication of animals?" Robert Nozick. *Anarchy, State and Utopia*. United States of America: Basic Books, 1974. 42.

refined set of tools that when concentrated enables a precise and careful control of life. The shepherd utilises technologies of control that are so minute, careful, vigilant and persistent that they would appear to reflect a deep "care" for the body of both the individual animal and the aggregated flock. The paradox here is that this same care is a care towards instrumentalisation and death. This view would suggest that pastoral power doesn't begin with the idea of a beneficient power as Foucault claims; nor in the twisting of violence and care in the Hebrew tradition as Meyes claims, but begins with the long human history of animal capture, enclosure, domestication, husbandry, utilisation and slaughter. The shepherd stands as a technical inheritor of these combined learned processes, capturing within this enveloping system of domination practices a capacity for a minute vigilance over the flock aimed at maximal utilisation of the animate body; a process so refined and concentrated that we call it "beneficent."[59]

Where does this leave governmentality then? Certainly we cannot say that governmentality is a product of a historical interplay between sovereignty and pastoral power that eventually turns the attention of the sovereign away from territory toward population. If we describe pastoral power as a modality of sovereignty—a modality that has its origins in domination of non human animals—then we arrive at a different genealogy. Governmentality does not describe the extension of concern for population across sovereignty, but instead describes the entry of pastoral power to the field of human sovereignty over other humans, encapsulated in the governmentality of the State. In other words, governmentality is the extension to human subjects of technologies of pastoral power, learnt for centuries through human management of non human animals. This process in the West begins in earnest through the extension of Christianity, which gradually supplants dominant Greek and Roman forms of State sovereignty with forms of power that are informed directly through the experience of the domination of non human animals. Governmentality, its slow encroachment over every aspect of human politics, merely describes this history. In an admittedly provisional way, I have attempted to map this in Figure 1 below. Techniques of pastoral power are refined in an early sense through domination of animals and the production—over millennia—of "livestock."[60] These techniques of control—perhaps "technologies of

---

59   See Cole's discussion of the capacity to individuate within contemporary containment and slaughter. See Cole. "From 'Animal Machines' to 'Happy Meat'?" 91.

60   We might usefully refer to scholars such as Ingold, Noske and Hribal to map this genealogy. See Ingold. *The Perception of the Environment.*; Noske. *Beyond Boundaries*; and Hribal. *Fear of the Animal Planet.*

government" to borrow from Rose[61]—are not initially connected to human domination of other humans, which is a field in which a "rule by the sword" prevails. This situation shifts with the infusion of pastoral modes of domination within Hebrew and Christian traditions, which blend beneficence and force, care and violence, in innovative new ways, and seek simultaneously to securitise the flock. As Figure 1 shows, the two forms of sovereignty–state sovereignty of humans over other humans, and pastoral sovereignty of humans over animals—finally find their meeting point in governmentality, where they bleed into each other and inform each other. We find these elements in a remarkable 1780 oil painting, Angelica Kauffman's *A Sleeping Nymph Watched by a Shepherd*. The work shows the shepherd transferring his gaze from his flock to a sleeping woman in a pasture; cupid is illustrated hovering above the woman, arrow in hand. The shepherd gestures to Cupid with his finger to be quiet. A benign interpretation would say that this is the good shepherd, offering a benevolent power of safety to the sleeping beauty. A different interpretation might tell us that this is a symbol of the transfer of technologies of sovereign power inherent in the shepherd from animal to human populations: a power to survey, to securitise, to reproduce. In this regard it does not seem to be an accident that it is the body of a woman that becomes the site of scrutiny, in much the same way in which the bodies of women are inseparably bound in particular ways with the project of the biopolitical State; all under the watchful gaze of Cupid. Perhaps we might speculate here that the gendered dimension of Thrasymachus' objection to Socrates ("Socrates, do you have a nurse?") is in some ways an accusation that Socrates is indulging in a care *without* violence; the idealised and normalised care of a woman, a mother, as opposed to the "hard reality" of a care that is accompanied by violence, as is wielded by the cunning State. Certainly one reading of Kauffman's *A Sleeping Nymph Watched by a Shepherd* is that the attentions of the shepherd, wanted or not, consented to or not, are essentially violently securitising, since the shepherd offers security to a property right in the flock of animals—human or non human—that are deemed to be protected by his gaze.[62]

---

61   See Rose. *Powers of Freedom*. 52.

62   There is scope here for a more detailed understanding of how pastoral management of animals might intersect with governmental regulation of women. I note that one synergy here is the range of techniques applied to regulate women's sexuality and reproduction, that infinitely vary and incorporate normative and legal regulatory frameworks. Consider, for example, Catriona Macleod and Kevin Durrheim's discussion of adolescent sexual and reproductive health:

> Security operates in adolescent sexual and reproductive health in a number of ways. The management of risk serves as a governmental tactic of security as it represents

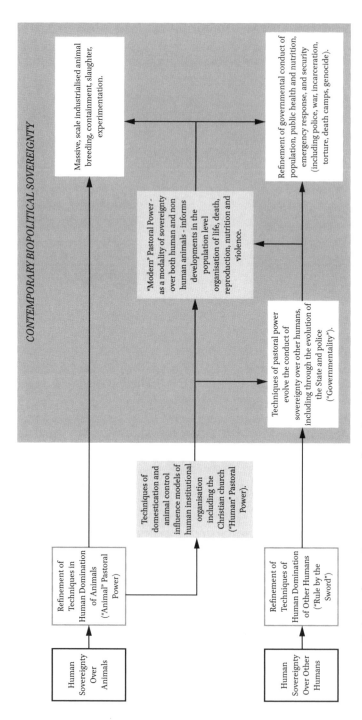

FIGURE 1   *Evolution of pastoral power, governmentality and sovereignty.*

There are distinct differences between contemporary pastoral modes of control of animals and governmentalised forms of sovereignty. Today's pastoral power over animals attains a zenith of efficiency, with high speed operations making quick work of turning living bodies into corpses, in order to feed an unending human desire for flesh. Governmentality, on the other hand, more overtly becomes associated with benign forms of care directed at conducting human populations and fostering life. However, the politics of life and death span across both modes of sovereignty. Increasingly, under governmentalised modes of rule, there are intersections between human sovereignty over humans and that exercised over other animals. All the techniques that science can deploy to make live are enabled to foster the lives of (at least some) animals under human care, even if these same animals are only destined for an early death in line with human utilisation preferences. Similarly, the ways to make humans die begin to look like the ways in which animals are made to die: armies swat away human enemies like pest

---

efforts to deal with the possible and probable events following sexual intercourse, conception and birth. Sexuality education programmes are run to manage the possibility or risk of adolescents either engaging in sex or conceiving. Should a teenager be pregnant, counseling, ante-natal care, adoption services and termination of pregnancy facilities are provided to manage the probability or risk of negative physiological, psychological, emotional and social consequences for the mother and child. These programmes are legitimated through the implicit calculation of the comparative cost of providing services (which represent a tax burden) and not providing them (which would result in a threat to national and social security in terms of demographic difficulties, poor mothering practices, lack of gainful employment on the part of the teenager etc.). The optimal mean (the third trait of security) in terms of adolescent sexuality is abstinence from sex. However, sexual intercourse and even pregnancy lie within the acceptable bandwidth, but carry with them a different set of management tactics than does non-coital behaviour. Put simply, if the teenager is a virgin, there is the danger of the desire for sex, and thus sexuality education programmes recommend "say no". If she is sexually active, there is the possibility of pregnancy, and thus programmes extend their input to the use of contraceptives. If she is pregnant, there are potential physical and emotional complications in the pregnancy, and thus professional medical and psychological assistance is indicated. If she is mothering, the child is probably at risk, and therefore professional assistance and maternal education are required. These traits of security will combine in various ways with pastoral, disciplinary and liberal power relations in the government of the sexual and reproductive lives of adolescents.

See Catriona Macleod and Kevin Durrheim. "Foucauldian Feminism: The Implications of Governmentality." *Journal for the Theory of Social Behaviour.* 32.1, 2002. 41–60. 54. See also Jessica Robyn Cadwallader and Damien W. Riggs. "The State of the Union: Toward a Biopolitics of Marriage." *M/C Journal.* 15.6, 2012.

insects;[63] humans are cut up like cattle in genocides; and rape and death camps begin to appear as if they are industrialised breeding and slaughter facilities.

Perhaps the crowning achievement of governmentality, and the pastoral mode of sovereignty that precedes it, is its ability to cloak violence with care; that is, to hide war under a covering of peace. Pivotal in understanding this intersection of powers is the particular deception that accompanies the logic of pastoral forms of domination: namely, that the techniques employed within a pastoral modality of sovereign power appear to express a "care" for the life of the flock. This attentiveness is so precise, so concentrated, that it overturns the traditional grandeur and overt brutality of other forms of sovereign domination in favour of an opaque, guarded secret form of instrumentalisation, utilisation and accompanying death, that attends to the lives of populations always, even while we sleep.

The Judas Goat

Following through the speculation I have laid out here—namely, that governmentality is really a description for the extension of human forms of domination of animals onto humans themselves—we may wonder what this same process may mean for the evolution of technologies of domination towards animals.[64] As I have suggested, State sovereignty and pastoral power meet and bleed into each other in governmentality. For humans this means that they are increasingly treated like animals: this is in line with Foucault's suggestion that biopolitics represents the "animalization of man" and Agamben's fear of a biopolitics that represents the conflict between "human" and "animal" as categories. However, we have yet to decipher how this same process has redefined human domination of animals. How have human-centric forms of surveillance, domination and death themselves found their way back to violence towards animals, and shaped practices of violence? How has the technology of control altered the practice of the shepherd?

---

63   There are numerous histories to track here. Craig McFarlane is conducting fascinating work on the shared understandings between governmentality and bee keeping. See Craig McFarlane. *Early Modern Speculative Anthropology*. PhD Dissertation. Submitted to York University, August 2014. At: http://yorkspace.library.yorku.ca/xmlui/handle/10315/28256.

64   Indeed, Shukin points out that addressing Foucault's inattentiveness to animals allows for the "the possibility that technologies of human and animal conduct partake in material and metaphorical exchanges, borrow or diverge from one another, traffic in species identifications and equivalences as well as in species exceptions and disavowals." See Shukin. "Tense Animals: On Other Species of Pastoral Power." 152.

In the case of human sovereignty over other humans, there are varying modes of practice of violence, and accompanying these a variety of models for "dehumanisation." Where authoritarian modes of governance remain implicit, albeit veiled within liberal democratic regimes, governmental rationalities are outwardly recognisable in forms of totalitarian political organisation. In such States, violent biopolitical imperatives became openly incorporated within the principles of governmental reason. Dean draws upon Foucault's last chapter of *The History of Sexuality Vol. 1*, suggesting that such regimes explicitly embody the emerging principles of a bloody biopolitics, where the concern for populations, and the power to "foster life and disallow it to the point of death" intersect in the right to regulate biological populations with the sword: crystallising in particular, in racism, propagated forcefully by the State.[65] Dean argues that modes of rule which advance biopolitical objectives through coercive means cannot be separated from governance itself, since authoritarian governmentality remains composed of the same elements that characterise the field of government.[66] However, Dean states that "the notion of sovereignty differs from rationalities of government proper in that the latter are concerned with a fostering of the *living* and augmentation of *life*. In contrast, sovereignty operates by deduction, as a right of death rather than a power over life."[67]

Note that this contrasts with my own argument that I have put forward above: namely, that governmentality is as aligned to life as it is to death. However, *exception*—the capacity for sovereignty to declare who is within and without the law, who is subject to violence and who is a citizen—remains relevant, both to Dean's conceptualisation of authoritarian governmentality and my own thinking about contemporary violence directed towards animals. I have argued, following Agamben, that sovereignty is associated with an ability to constitute the exceptional space. This space is inherently biopolitical, since it aims at the production of the bare life.[68] Exception also operates in a necropolitical guise to decide who lives and who dies. As Meyes points out, the capacity of

---

65 Dean. *Governmentality*. 139–40.

66 Dean. *Governmentality*. 147. To once again render the relation of bureaucracy to government, Dean observes that the existing bureaucratic rationalities must themselves be assessed within the context of governmental rationalities. "It is not simply the logic of the bureaucratic application of the human sciences that is at issue but the reinscription of racial discourse within a biopolitics of the population and its linkage with themes of sovereign identity, autonomy and political community" (144).

67 Dean, *Govermentality*, 202. See also 100.

68 It is the centrality of biopolitics to exception which leads Agamben to contest Foucault's claim that biopolitics is a relatively new phenomenon, arguing, as stated previously, that "Western politics is a bio-politics from the very beginning." See Agamben. *Homo Sacer*. 181.

the shepherd to choose to separate out and individualise the flock is key to the exercise of violence. Drawing attention to *Matthew 25:31–46*, and the judgment prophecy that God would divide between good and bad, "as a shepherd divideth his sheep from the goats," Meyes observes that there is an uncanny resemblance here to the division between "fostering life" and "disallowing until the point of death" which characterises Foucault's biopolitics.[69] Meyes states:

> In the process of caring for the "true flock", of blessing and fostering the life of the sheep, the shepherd excludes the goats, cursing and disallowing their life to the point of death. Thus here Matthew introduces new characteristics to the shepherd: judgement and exclusion. The division between the sheep and the goats, the believer and unbeliever, results in the exclusion of the unbeliever from life and exposure to violence and death.[70]

Foucault's suggestion that contemporary sovereignty may be associated with a power to "foster life" must be read in conjunction with its counterpart, the ominous right to "disallow to the point of death;" in the same fashion as one reads the old power of sovereignty—to kill and let live—as involving the exercise of an interconnected right.[71] The power to kill implies the power to let live, since those who survive the wrath of the sovereign's sword only do so at the mercy of a sovereign power not deployed. The same logical coupling accompanies the biopolitical sovereign right: biopolitics is not merely the "optimisation" of life, but the simultaneous deployment of both facilitative resources to enable life and violence designed to "disallow life." Modern sovereignty commands the resources to enable and foster life, and a connected power to bring life to the threshold of death.

This view of governmentality provides a way to conceptualise the organisation of animal life and death through systems of domination that comprise human sovereignty. Biopolitical organisation of animal life situates violence in a set of discretely coordinated and micro-scale located apparatuses that enable life and death controls. Governmentality is the rationality that underpins these operations. Government allows for the seamless vertical and horizontal integration of elements that deploy technologies, interests, properties and human labour towards an encompassing system of domination. Governmentality, in this context, is therefore really concerned with governing violence: producing

---

69   Meyes. "The Violence of Care." 120.

70   Meyes. "The Violence of Care." 120.

71   See Foucault. *The Will to Knowledge: The History of Sexuality 1*. 138.

modes of violence, technologies and discourses to enable continuing domination. This seems to be a question that is fundamentally linked to how animal welfare is conceptualised. For it is apparent that, when Webster announces that "Man has dominion over the animals whether we like it or not...it is we that determine where and how they will live,"[72] there is a pronouncement of the fact of human sovereignty, which simultaneously declares a governmental objective; namely, to use this right of domination "wisely." This is the effect of sovereignty bending ethical consideration into simply a means for regulating human violence towards animals in order to safeguard continuing utilisation. In other words, understanding governmentality—that is, the rationality of government—is important for making sense of the way in which modes of domination and death are regulated, including on the basis of seeking to maximise the welfare of those who are subject to the instrumentation of sovereign violence.

Judgement and exception combine within governmentality to produce nuanced forms of differentiation in the application of violence. This regulation varies according to species, space and human use. It might include management of native animals and endangered species, urban regulation on the care and restraint of companion animals, laws on the use and disposal of animals in experimentation, hunting laws that determine which animals are to be killed, and which saved, and, of course, complex and interwoven regulation of containment and slaughter practices to limit "unnecessary suffering" within the factory farming "animal industrial complex," with multiple sites of differentiation between species and use to manage the deployment of violence. Yet, there is space within this interplay of techniques and discourses for outright annihilation to take the place of beneficence. In New South Wales (NSW), as in other states in Australia, wild goats are seen as "feral" animals and subject to eradication programs. Amidst a range of intricate guidelines for the "management" of feral goats, there is a State sanctioned technique described which combines both "old" knowledge from herd management with the most contemporary technologies of biopolitical population control and aerial warfare.[73] NSW Department of Primary Industries guideline GOA005 "Use of Judas Goats" outlines these:

> Radio-collared 'Judas' goats are used to locate groups of feral goats that are difficult to find by other methods. This technique involves attaching a radio-collar to a feral goat and releasing it with the expectation that it will

---

72   Webster. *Animal Welfare.* 3.

73   See Anna Williams discussion of the use of decoy animals and decoys in slaughter processes. See Williams. "Disciplining Animals." 50–1.

join up with other goats. Goats are particularly suited to the Judas method as they are a highly social species and will seek the companionship of any other feral goats in the area.

Once the position of the feral herd is established, the goats accompanying the Judas animal are either mustered or destroyed by shooting (refer to GOA003 Mustering of feral goats, GOA001 Ground shooting of feral goats and GOA002 Aerial shooting of feral goats for further details on these methods of control). The Judas goat is usually allowed to escape so that it will search out other groups of feral goats. Once eradication is achieved the Judas goat is located, and then shot and the radio-collar retrieved.[74]

Here we witness a refined application of the shepherd's practice, evolved and weaved with all of the powers of strategy, technologies of violence, and knowledges on the vicissitudes of the flock, all brought to bear with stunning and devastating effect to enable the annihilation of population. No goat is left alive; even the radio collar will be retrieved. Surely this is governmentality perfected. "For the Lamb which is in the midst of the throne shall feed them, and shall lead them unto living fountains of waters: and God shall wipe away all tears from their eyes."[75]

---

74   NSW Department of Primary Industries. Humane pest animal control. Codes of Practice. GOA005 "Use of Judas Goats." Trudy Sharp and Glen Saunders At: www.dpi.nsw.gov.au/agriculture/pests-weeds/vertebrate-pests/codes-of pratice/operating-procedures/humane-pest-animal-control. For an example study of the effectiveness of the use of Judas goats for population eradication, see Karl Campbell, C. Josh Donlan, Felipe Cruz and Victor Carrion. "Eradication of feral goats *Capra hircus* from Pinta Island, Galápagos Ecuador." *Oryx.* 38.3, 2004. 1–6. For a discussion of different "Judas" animals, particularly in slaughterhouse practices, see Helena Pedersen. "Follow the Judas Sheep: Materializing Post-Qualitative Methodology in Zooethnographic Space." *International Journal of Qualitative Studies in Education.* 26.6, 2013. 717–31.

75   *King James Edition.* Revelation 7:17.

PART 2

Conquest

∴

CHAPTER 3

Immunity

When a case of TSE has been officially confirmed, the following measures must be applied:

- an inquiry must be launched to identify the possible origin of the disease and all animals and derived products which may be contaminated;
- in case of confirmation of BSE in a bovine animal, killing and complete destruction of the bovine animals identified as being at risk by the inquiry (in particular, animals belonging to the birth or feed cohort of the infected animal). The Member State may decide to defer the killing and destruction of the animals until the end of their productive life in the case of breeding bulls intended for semen collection, provided it can be ensured that they are destroyed after their death;
- in case of confirmation of BSE in an ovine or caprine animal, killing and complete destruction of all ovine and caprine animals in the herd;
- in case of confirmation of TSE in an ovine or caprine animal, BSE being excluded, killing and complete destruction of all ovine and caprine animals in the herd or, and solely in the case of ovine animals, killing and selective destruction of animals with a genotype susceptible to TSEs. If the infected animal has been introduced from another holding, the Member State may decide to apply eradication measures on the holding of origin in addition to, or instead of, the holding where the infection was confirmed.

European Union, *"Transmissible Spongiform Encephalopathies (TSEs)"*[1]

An estimated eight million cows were killed in the United Kingdom as a result of the discovery of "mad cow disease" or Bovine Spongiform Encephalopathy (BSE). The disease is caused by an infectious protein which eats away at the brain: the human variant—Creutzfeldt-Jakob disease—causes a similar degeneration in the human brain, and humans can be infected through consumption of food infected with the spinal cords or brains of diseased animals. Indeed, infection through ingestion of infected spine and brain is the way in which

---

1   European Union. "Transmissible Spongiform Encephalopathies (TSEs)." *Europa*. Summaries of EU Legislation. At: www.europa.eu/legislation_summaries/food_safety/animal_nutrition/f83001_en.htm.

both humans and animals attain this prion disease: in the case of cows, BSE may be contracted through feeding cows rendered tissue, brain and cords, something Nicole Shukin describes as a "kind of 'mimetic excess' created by capital's closed loops."[2]

The mad cow disease event figures as an immune reaction—both a reaction by cows to being fed the rendered tissue of other cows; but also a reaction by humans to the prospect of contamination by diseased meat, through a wholesale slaughter which aims to purify the food supply. In so far as the cows killed were destined for death anyway (that is, to be slaughtered for human food), they figure as a kind of excessive death: a sacrificial "surplus" slaughter aimed at preventing the possibility of a future where mass contamination would bring to a halt the meat production itself. In thinking through the events that precipitated the BSE crisis, the term "excess" would appear apt in this context, and is worthy of exploration. For it is clearly a kind of excess at play that would allow a system, through a circular process of slaughter and meat production, to allow herbivores destined for slaughter to ingest the brains and spinal cords of those who have already been slaughtered. But there was also excess in response to the discovery of human infections. The slightest threat of infection is responded to with death. Death on this scale requires coordination and, in order, to protect food supply lines, an ability for authorities to move killing away from the routinised death in slaughterhouses. Around 1.7 million bovine were incinerated. The task of incinerating carcasses of slaughtered cows required the construction of new facilities: data from the UK Department for Environment, Food and Rural Affairs reported that one plant incinerated close to 315,000 tonnes of body matter in a four year period.[3]

In the previous chapters we examined Foucault, Agamben, and Mbembe, drawing attention to their discussion and inflections of the concept "bio-politics" and the potential applicability of this concept to understanding human domination of non-human animals. I drew attention specifically to the

---

2 Shukin. *Animal Capital.* 228. See also Robert McKay. "BSE, Hysteria, and the Representation of Animal Death: Deborah Levy's *Diary of a Steak.*" The Animal Studies Group. *Killing Animals.* Urbana and Chicago: University of Illinois Press, 2006. 145–69.

3 United Kingdom Department for Environment, Food and Rural Affairs (no date) "BSE Questions." Department for Environment, Food and Rural Affairs. At: www.defra.gov.uk/animalh/bse/general/qa/section7.html#q4. Other operations, although smaller in scale, are no less precise and efficient: an article in *The Sydney Morning Herald* describes the clandestine work of a ranger in Sydney's Centennial park aimed at removing rabbits: "over 13 nights, Mr Glover and a second shooter, Steve Parker, shot all 380 rabbits in the 186-hectare reserve using subsonic .22-calibre rifles without a single Sydneysider raising the alarm." See James Woodford. "Secret Cull Comes to Light." *The Sydney Morning Herald.* 31 May, 2008. At: www.smh.com.au/articles/2008/05/30/1211654312813.html.

potential for understanding the hostile conflict inherent in Foucault's under-standing of biopower as a descriptor for the aggressive schism between humans and animals. This description of biopolitics as a war between human and ani-mal becomes arguably more focused—more pertinent—when we take into account Agamben's understanding of biopolitics as precisely the production of a moving threshold that is the effect of the conflict between humans and animals, a conflict that is governmentalised in a relationship between sover-eignty, security and population. As I have argued, the war on animals carries the echo of what we might think of as an equally fundamental conflict that both captivates and characterises human societies: namely, the distinction between "nature" and "civilisation." As such, Roberto Esposito's conceptualisa-tion of biopolitics within the context of *immunity* is highly relevant. As I shall discuss in this chapter, Esposito not only offers a conception of biopower that registers a problematic in relation to the maintenance of the nature/civilisa-tion split, but also offers a different perspective in understanding a war against animals, and how the human seeks to "immunise" itself from animals through material and symbolic violences.

Immunity and Property

Biopolitics as a concept potentially carries within it a set of assumptions around the nature of *bios* and that of *zoë*, and how they are distinguished from one another. This distinction relies in itself on generating a nature/culture split. A life beyond a bare life is assumed to be in essence non biological—it belongs to the sphere of politics proper, culture and civilisation—while "bio-logical" life, pure *zoë*, should be no place for politics, at least in so far as we might treat biopolitics as a negative, unnecessary and "modern" (as opposed to classical) form of politics. Whenever we assume there is something "unnatu-ral" in the idea of biopolitics, or imagine that some sure form of politics has been lost today that was present in the classical age, then we inevitably assume that politics and nature are in essence opposed, and then provide additional space for an enlightenment presumption of the inevitability of a split between "nature" and "culture."[4] This suggests that the challenge inherent in thinking through the meaning of biopolitics, and its applicability for thinking about violence towards animals, also involves unpicking the inherent assumption of

---

4 See Haraway. *Companion Species Manifesto.* See also Donna Haraway. *The Companion Species Manifesto: Dogs, People and Significant Otherness.* Chicago: Prickly Paradigm Press, 2003. See also Derrida. *The Beast and The Sovereign Vol. 1.* 305–6 [D407-8] and 315–334 [D419-443].

a nature/civilisation split which underpins biopolitics as a concept. It certainly is notable that Esposito identifies this tension within biopolitics as a concept. He observes:

> ...biopolitics refers, if anything, to the dimension of *zoë*, which is to say that life in its simple biological capacity [*tenuta*], more than it does to *bios*, understood as a "qualified life," or "form of life," or at least to the line of conjugation along which *bios* is exposed to *zoë*, naturalizing *bios* as well. But precisely with regard to this terminological exchange, the idea of biopolitics appears to be situated in a zone of double indiscernability, first because it is inhabited by a term that does not belong to it and indeed risks distorting it. And then because it is fixed by a concept, precisely that of *zoë*, which is stripped of every formal connotation. *Zoë* itself can only be defined problematically: what, assuming it is even conceivable, is an absolutely natural life?[5]

As I have argued, the link between human sovereignty and biopolitics is to be found in a discourse that sees a fundamental division between nature and politics; which in turn creates the language of domination over non-human animals. In this sense the language of this tradition is "political" rather than "philosophical" (or "scientific") in so far as this discourse seeks to prefigure, announce and commemorate domination of animals as a socio-political fact and right. It is in this sense that Aristotle's statement ascribing humans the status *zōon politikon*—"that the state is a creation of nature, and that by nature man is a political animal"[6]—must be understood as grounding a political manifesto; it is a declaration of war that seeks, in the terms I have laid out from Clausewitz, to "compel an opponent to conform to our will." There is an element of this war that aims to produce an imagined community through forms

---

5 Roberto Esposito. *Bios: Biopolitics and Philosophy*. Minneapolis: University of Minnesota, 2008. 14–15. This distinction between *bios* and *zoë* is further problematised by Esposito through the introduction of the material intermediary: namely, technology. Esposito states:

> It's even more the case today, when the human body appears to be increasingly challenged and also literally traversed by technology [*tecnica*]. Thus, if a natural life doesn't exist that isn't at the same time technological as well; if the relation between *bios* and *zoë* needs by now (or has always needed) to include in it a third correlated term, *technē*— then how do we hypothesize an exclusive relation between politics and life?

> See Esposito. *Bios*. 15.

6 Aristotle. *Politics*. 448 [1253a].

of exclusion. As such, we might describe this same language as *immunitary*; as precisely a discourse which aims to establish a fundamental separation between humans and animals in order to enclose and protect an imagined community of entities which claim a "humanity" as an immunitary defence. Thus, again to refer to Aristotle's *zōon politikon*, "man" is defined by belonging to the *polis* through a self situating claim to a human community, and an immunitary right to defend this community from those who are not only inhuman/ahuman but, who by their very difference, pose a threat to this community. It is for this reason that Aristotle is at pains to not only deny political community to other animals that may appear to live in a polis like our own—"bees and any other gregarious animals"—but to announce the security threat posed by the outsider to human community. Again, I repeat the section quoted in Chapter 1:

> And he who by nature and not by mere accident is without a state, is either a bad man or above humanity; he is like the
> *Tribeless, lawless, hearthless one,*
> Whom Homer denounces – the natural outcast is forthwith a lover of war; he may be compared to an isolated piece at draughts.[7]

Difference here is not marked by non-hierarchical and peaceful coexistence; rather, it exists as a threat which the polity must secure itself against. Aristotle remarks: "he who is unable to live in society, or who has no need because he is sufficient for himself, must be either a beast or a god: he is no part of a state."[8] The circularity of the logic here is inescapable: those who are excluded from the *polis* are defined as outsiders who have no place in the *polis*; simultaneously the State must secure itself from those who it has excluded: "beasts and gods" who are "no part of a state." Realms of distinction invite securitisation at the borders of constructed difference.

Esposito's understanding of biopolitics is filtered through a logic of immunisation. This is how the philosopher distinguishes himself from the "negative biopolitics" that he attributes to Agamben, and the "affirmative" Spinozian biopolitics which he associates with Negri. For Esposito, the challenge is to clearly articulate the co-functionality of both a negative and positive biopolitics, and understand the links between these forms and sovereignty, property and liberty. Immunisation figures as a *negative* biopolitics: it constrains the potentiality of a community through protecting life:

---

7 Aristotle. *Politics*. 448 [1253a].
8 Aristotle. *Politics*. 448 [1253b].

...we can say that immunization is a negative [form] of the protection of life. It saves, insures, and preserves the organism, either individual or collective, to which it pertains, but it does not do so directly, immediately or frontally; on the contrary, it subjects the organism to a condition that simultaneously negates or reduces its power to expand. Just as in the medical practice of vaccinating the individual body, so the immunization of the political body functions similarly, introducing within it a fragment of the same pathogen from which it wants to protect itself, by blocking and contradicting natural development.[9]

What is of relevance here in relation to non-human animals is the way in which Esposito delineates between immunisation and community. Immunisation works to contain community in the name of security for the individual, an auto-protection function that safeguards the individual from an *excess* of community: "a temporary or definitive exemption on the part of the subject with regard to concrete obligations or responsibilities that under normal circumstances would bind one to others."[10] Community here is abstractly what binds us to other entities, and mitigates the possibility of differentiation. Sovereignty defines itself as a mode of differentiation that places into conflict entities that might otherwise be non differentiated within a common community. (The "human" thus—and this is my interpolation, not Esposito's—is a political project of immunisation from "the animal" that relies upon the creation of a hierarchised difference).

Esposito's perspective clearly aligns with a Hobbesian view of sovereignty as that formation which deploys violence on behalf of all in the name of the community it seeks to protect: "he hath the use of so much power and strength conferred on him, that by terror therof, he is enabled to conform the wills of them all, to peace at home, and mutual aid against their enemies abroad."[11] But we might also note the overlap with Foucault's own definition of biopolitics as the power to foster life and disallow it to the point of death. In both Hobbes and Foucault, sovereign power is protective of community through simultaneous life and death mechanisms. Reading Hobbes closely, Esposito observes that the justification for sovereign power arrives because of the inability of individuals in the "state of nature" to attain their ends due to persistent conflict. Sovereignty is erected to provide security to individual claims:

---

9   Esposito. *Bios.* 46.
10   Esposito. *Bios.* 45.
11   Hobbes. *Leviathan.* 114. See Esposito. *Bios.* 46–7.

It is here that the immunitary mechanism begins to operate. If life is abandoned to its internal powers, to its natural dynamics, human life is destined to self-destruct because it carries within itself something that ineluctably places it in contradiction with itself. Accordingly, and in order to save itself, life needs to step out from itself and constitute a transcendental point from which it receives orders and shelter. It is in this interval or doubling of life with respect to itself that the move from nature to artifice is to be positioned. It has the same end of self-preservation as nature, but in order to actualise it, it needs to tear itself from nature, by following a strategy that is opposed to it. Only be negating itself can nature assert its own will to live.[12]

Sovereignty is a tool of differentiation: it marks the possibility of a transcendence, through distinction and hierarchy, from a community which is otherwise incapable of segregation. Accordingly, Esposito defines sovereign immunisation as:

> ...an immanent transcendence situated outside of the control of those who also produced it as the expression of their own will. This is precisely the contradictory structure that Hobbes assigns to the concept of representation: the one that is representing, that is the sovereign, is simultaneously identical and different with respect to those that he represents. He is identical because he takes their place [*stare al loro posto*], yet different from them because that "place" remains outside of their range.[13]

This might also be another way to describe the *zōon politikon*, that declaration of war that provides the rationale for the [human] animal who might be like any other animal but declares itself beyond and above other animals. The *zōon politikon* is the animal that makes itself through the transcendence of sovereignty, in a grand immunising gesture. Human community is created and, simultaneously, a securitisation of this space occurs in order to maintain a hierarchised distinction (*homo dignitas*). Sovereign immunisation aims at creating a fundamental social division:

> We know that in a natural state men also relate to each other according to a modality of the individual that leads to a generalized conflict. But such conflict is still always a horizontal relation that binds them to a com-

---

12   Esposito. *Bios*. 58.
13   Esposito. *Bios*. 60.

munal dimension. Now, it is exactly this commonality—the damage that derives to each and everyone—that is abolished through that artificial individualization constituted precisely by the sovereign *dispositif*. Moreover, the same echo is to be heard in the term "absolutism," not only in the independence of power from every external limit, but above all in the dissolution projected onto men: their transformation into individuals, equally absolute by subtracting from them the *munus* that keeps them bound communally. Sovereignty is the not being [*il non essere*] in common of individuals, the political form of their desocialisation.[14]

We can thus recognise in sovereignty a force that is established to individuate and enclose, to "desocialise" as Esposito phrases it. Sovereignty enshrines rights upon individual entities within a regime of power, offering security from the dangers of an excess of community through an individual immunity which places a border around each recognised entity. In this model we might perceive an extension of the mode of exception described by Agamben, as discussed in Chapter 1. Yet here Esposito treats exception differently: it is manifest, individualised, it articulates a sovereign power and an individual desire for immunisation.

The individual immunity offered by sovereignty is materialised through the concept of *property*. Esposito argues that what is constructed by the immunisation of sovereignty as belonging to one's self is, by definition, what is *not* common. It is through a decision upon non commonality that the individual is immunised from the demand for a commonality. Drawing on Locke, Esposito suggests that property is the zone that is rightly not interfered with by an external power, as property is connected to an individual's "Being." As such property is the material linkage between an ontology of the self, it establishes an "onto-juridical foundation...between being (a body) and having one's own body."[15]

Here Esposito refers to the link Locke establishes between a natural right to one's own body as property, and the transformative work the individual performs to appropriate the world as property. Locke states: "Man has a *Property* in his own *Person*. This no Body has any Right to but himself. The *Labour* of his Body, and the *Work* of his Hands, we may say, are properly his."[16]

---

14   Esposito. *Bios.* 61. Note here the diametric reading Esposito offers to a somewhat insipid liberal reading of Hobbes which might argue that sovereignty represents the social contract of the "Commonwealth." There is no agreement here; rather, sovereignty emerges as simply a means to secure differentiation.

15   Esposito. *Bios.* 66.

16   John Locke. *Two Treatises of Government.* Cambridge: Cambridge University Press, 2009. 287–8 [§27].

The transformative relation of labour and work is pivotal within this conceptualisation in the ability of individuals to extend the right to one's own body onto external entities. It is through the transformation of work that one appropriates and possesses the other. Esposito notes: "possessing one's own corporeal form [*persona*], he owns all his performances, beginning with the transformation of the material object, which he appropriates as transitive property."[17] Thus the individual expands its being—both what it is and what it possesses—through a gradual transformation of the world around it. Esposito observes that the relation between property and subjectivity established by Locke enables an interdependent relay between the subject and the object of appropriation through the transformation of work: "if the appropriated thing depends on the subject who possesses it such that it becomes one with the body, the owner in turn is rendered as such only by the thing that belongs to him – and therefore he himself depends on it...Without an appropriating subject, no appropriated thing."[18]

This "primordial" connection between subjectivity and property (to be and to own) is *a priori* to the juridical apparatus. We can note here, as Esposito does, that in a Lockean framework, sovereignty follows property right, and not the other way around. Sovereignty is constructed as a means to defend an inherent property right that is linked ontologically to the subject. Sovereignty thus defends "being" in a full sense, at least for those entities that are granted the security of sovereignty. Sovereignty here functions through immunisation. Security is provided against the threat of common ownership through a guarantee of exclusivity; sovereignty in this guise *insures* against "the potential risk of a world given in common—and for this reason exposed to unlimited distinction."[19] The logic of appropriation operates thus in a negative sense, coming to imply that property, what one owns, is what is not owned in common: that is, what one enjoys and is simultaneously denied to others to enjoy.

Labour and work are central here, although sovereignty severs the connection between work and property in a fundamental way by guaranteeing a right

---

17   Esposito. *Bios.* 66.

18   Esposito. *Bios.* 67. We might note in passing the distinctively Hegelian frame for understanding subjectivity here. G.W.F. Hegel states:

Desire has reserved to itself the pure negating of the object and thereby its unalloyed feeling of self. But that is the reason why this satisfaction is only a fleeting one, for it lacks the side of objectivity and permanence. Work, on the other hand, is desire held in check, fleetingness held off; in other words, work forms and shapes the thing.

G.W.F. Hegel. *Phenomenology of Spirit.* Oxford: Oxford University Press, 1977. 118 [197].

19   Esposito. *Bios.* 67.

to ownership that erases or forgets a necessary connection to work. Thus the juridical apparatus can guarantee property rights without regard to necessary connection. Work provides justification for what one acquires in addition to oneself. However, the juridical apparatus, and its capacity to guarantee property rights without a necessary demonstration of possession or connection through work/appropriation, enables an ongoing and limitless accumulation that is "distant from the body."[20] This represents a potential contradiction, since property incorporates the Other as a belonging to the person; however, accumulation risks enlarging the person, through their expanding holdings, to encompass a realm that is separated from the originating self (the source of the property right): "the appropriative procedure, represented by Locke as a personification of the thing—its incorporation in the proprietor's body—lends itself to be interpreted as the reification of the person, disembodied of its subjective substance."[21]

The immunitary logic which follows biopolitical sovereignty and property relationships, it is argued by Esposito, also establishes a framework for understanding the concept of "liberty."[22] Esposito draws attention to the double meaning of liberty as both *positive* and *negative*, in line with political conceptualisations of positive and negative freedom/rights, at least as classically conceptualised by Isaiah Berlin.[23] Esposito outlines a positive sense of liberty as an affirmative force, linking it to love, libido and friendship: "a connective power that grows and develops according to its own internal law, and to an expansion or to a deployment that unites its members in a shared dimension."[24] On the other hand, negative freedom is linked with immunity through security:

---

20   Esposito. *Bios.* 68.

21   Esposito. *Bios.* 69. The capacity to claim a property right *in lieu* of an established connection is of course central to the logic of capitalism, as I believe Esposito is alluding to here, but it is also central to understanding the logic of colonisation (as a right to acquire both property and sovereignty without demonstrating a pre-existing connection). Further, as I shall argue in Chapter 4, it is central to a juridical logic that enables the capture of non human animals as property.

22   The English text of *Bios* translates the Italian *"libertà"* as "liberty" rather than "freedom." The translator, Timothy Campbell, provides a rationale for this: see Esposito. *Bios.* 209 n49.

23   See Isiah Berlin. "Two Concepts of Liberty." Isaiah Berlin. *Four Essays on Liberty.* Oxford: Oxford University Press, 1969.

24   Esposito. *Bios.* 70. This would appear to be similar to Gilles Deleuze and Félix Guattari's treatment of desire in their critique of Freud. See Gilles Deleuze and Félix Guattari. *Anti-Oedipus: Capitalism and Schizophrenia.* Minneapolis: University of Minnesota Press, 1994. See also Deleuze and Guattari. *A Thousand Plateaus.*

in the moment in which liberty is no longer understood as a mode of being, but rather as a right to have something of one's own—more precisely the full predominance of oneself in relation to others—the subtractive or simply the negative sense is already destined to characterise it ever more dominantly.[25]

In this sense modernity may be understood, through the emergence of individualism, with the instalment and proliferation of an immunitary logic, which comes to dominate understandings of liberty as encompassing negative freedoms from intervention:

> From this point of view, we need to be careful in not distorting the real sense of battle against the individual or collective *immunitas* fought on the whole by modernity. It isn't that of reducing but intensifying and generalising the immunitary paradigm. Without losing its typically polyvalent lexicon, immunity progressively transfers its own semantic centre of gravity from the sense of "privilege" to that of "security."[26]

Liberty in this context is concentrated upon the "person," by connection, to the individual's property: "which makes of liberty the biopolitical coincidence between property and preservation, its meaning tends to be stabilized ever nearer the imperative of security, until it coincides with it."[27] Thus immunisation functions as a security for a right to enjoy what is ours to enjoy, against a common right of enjoyment. The juridical apparatus is thus positioned as a form of insurance, through the mechanisms of coercion: "the point of suture between expression of liberty and what negates it from within—one could say between exposition and imposition—is constituted exactly by the demand for insurance [*assicurativa*]: it is what calls forth that apparatus of laws, though not directly producing liberty, constitute nonetheless the necessary reversal."[28]

I highlight this section on liberty precisely to underline the interdependent relationship between human freedom and animal freedom. As I have observed, there is value in thinking through freedom in the context of human and animal relationships, and observing the way in which sovereignty interacts with freedom. Drawing on Foucault, I have suggested that our war on animals is characterised

---

25   Esposito. *Bios.* 72.
26   Esposito. *Bios.* 72.
27   Esposito. *Bios.* 74.
28   Esposito. *Bios.* 74.

by a relation where human freedom is premised upon the unfreedom of non-human animals. Esposito provides a way to describe the precise rationality of this form of domination. This is not simply a matter of utilitarian use for human pleasure; on the contrary, it seems to go deeper than this. Human freedom is constructed as a negative relation that seeks its reassurance, its *insurance*, from the unfreedom of animals. The possibility that animals may enjoy liberties is likely to generate an immune response. This is surely the meaning behind Plato's discomfort in *The Republic*, his protest at the idea that under a "true" democracy animals might enjoy the same liberty as humans:

> You would never believe it—unless you have seen it for yourself—how much more liberty the domestic animals have in democracy. The dog comes to resemble its mistress, as the proverb has it, and the same is true of the horses and donkeys as well. They are in the habit of walking about the streets with a grand freedom, and bump into people they meet if they don't get out of their way. Everything is full of this spirit of liberty.[29]

The liberty that is threatened by the prospect of democracy, in its fullest sense, is the liberty enjoyed by those who are granted the "dignity" of the human. This dignity, a freedom that rests on the unfreedom of the exception, can only be maintained through the security apparatus of immunisation.

Animal Immunity

Esposito creates a number of openings through which we might theorise the role of immunity within the war on animals. While we will return to examine in more depth property itself in Chapter 4, the remainder of this chapter will focus on how it is that Esposito's treatment of immunity might offer some pathways for thinking through the relation between human and non-human animals, and the way in which the human might be thought of as an animal that securitises itself from other animals through killing.

As discussed above, Esposito offers a challenge (and perspective) on the limits of the nature/culture (*zoë/bios*) divide. Here we might begin to sketch a conception of the way in which the artificisation of human sovereignty might be understood as implicitly tied with the construction of the nature/civilisation divide. Sovereignty emerges as the way in which a community might immunise

---

29   Plato. *The Republic.* 300 [563c].

itself from nature, and simultaneously shield itself from the inherent lack of division and imprecise clarity of borders that might accrue with an undifferentiated conception of the "natural order." Here we are reminded again of the power of Hobbes' imagination of the state of nature—as a state of inherent conflict—where, as Hobbes suggests, community is not possible in "nature" due to an inherent instability generated by multifarious interests between infinite competing parties. As Esposito notes, sovereignty emerges as a primary immunisation strategy; as a method by which individuals can insure their security from nature through submission to a unified will which binds a community.

Could we therefore speculate that if sovereignty aims to save and insure culture from nature—that is, that the culture/nature divide is galvanised through an apparatus of legitimised domination—then might we understand immunity as primarily an immunisation of the human from the animal? That is, a mechanism which in its operation, seeks to act as a means to insure the "human species"? Might human sovereignty over other animals be established as a prerogative to divide and, thus, to provide immunity from animalisation (and in turn define humanity)? This would certainly accord with Agamben's reading of biopolitics as essentially a "conflict between human and animal," a constantly moving border that is articulated and rearticulated again and again through mechanisms of violence and coercion that protect and except the human, its normatively defined best "specimens," at the expense of others who are excluded as a potential source of contamination.

As Esposito (and Derrida[30]) observe in relation to the sovereign process of immunisation, this is not merely a logic of safeguarding the biological or social body from a contamination, but of a securitisation that involves incorporating the contaminant—a self imposed infection—as a means to safeguard from a greater threat of total organic dissolution. This would imply partial incorporation of the animal within the human in order to maintain a clear distinction, to secure that border, between the human and its other; thus already suggestive of the odd formulation of the human as a "political animal." This is of course rich ground, and we could stray here to visiting a range of circumstances where the human is continually articulated through an expression of the animal, either through symbolic, discursive or material incorporation (or all these

---

30   See Derrida's discussion of immunity and autoimmunity in the context of sovereignty in
      Jacques Derrida. *Rogues: Two Essays on Reason*. Stanford: Stanford University Press, 2005.
      Derrida's earlier essay "Plato's Pharmacy," would also be relevant: Derrida remarks here
      that the "noxiousness of the pharmakon is indicated at the precise moment the entire
      context seems to authorise its translation by 'remedy' rather than poison." See Jacques
      Derrida. *Dissemination*. Chicago: University of Chicago Press, 1981. 101.

levels at once).[31] Yet we need only consider two key areas of concern within our war on animals—namely, the large scale farming of animal bodies for human food, and the use of animal bodies as experimental sites for pharmacological research—to appreciate that a certain immunitary logic of defence through partial incorporation circulates through our mainstay practices in relation to non-human animals. Humans quite literally devour that which we seek to separate ourselves from. In relation to factory farming, we cannot escape a certain reality that our close, guarded, diabolic machinery for large scale breeding, containment and slaughter of animals for our human incorporation through food supply operates next to a logical, discursive and material system which aims to exclude in a totalitarian fashion any needless contamination between humans and the animals that are consumed. In the case of pharmacological research, animal bodies "stand in" (in a Latourian[32] sense) for human bodies as a means of future human protection from unforeseen side effects. From the perspective of immunisation, incorporating what one is not need not be a paradox: we might say that we ingest flesh as our immunisation against a contamination by a broader community that might include non-human animals as recognised constituents, and more than mere food or bodies to be experimented upon.

However, if we are to pursue this line of investigation, we must acknowledge that our consumption of non-human animals defies an immunitary logic in so far as the *pharmakon* which is consumed, to secure us from a contamination, is arguably not sparingly ingested, but increasingly represents a continual and growing form of *excess*. Our immunatory incorporation occurs on a grand scale. As I have argued in this book, the war on animals is characterised by excess; by a total and continuing victory. This excess becomes ever more excessive; an acceleration in killing, beyond previously imagined levels, reinforced by the increased worldwide per capita meat consumption that has been recorded by some analysts.[33] In some senses, Esposito offers us a way out of this

---

31   Ethical inquiry into the implications for the use of harvested animal organs for human health, or the ability to culture human-intended tissue using animal bodies might be areas for such a discussion.

32   Latour argues that non human delegates exercise agency within a network by "standing in" for human actors, for example, Latour suggests that the speed hump, or "sleeping policeman," is a non human entity which quite literally acts as a delegate for a real policeman to slow traffic. See Bruno Latour. *Pandora's Hope: Essays on the Reality of Science Studies.* Cambridge: Harvard University Press, 1999. 188–9.

33   See, for example, Rachel Tepper. "World's Meat Consumption: Luxembourg Eats the Most per Person, India the Least." *The Huffington Post.* 5 March, 2012. At: www.huffingtonpost. com/2012/05/03/world-meat consumption_n_1475760.html.

unconventional excess of immunisation, by suggesting that the juridical apparatus, in so far as it separates being from what it appropriates, enables both
an excess of property, and simultaneously an excess of security, through an
immunisation that increasingly distances the consumer from the immediacy
of the object of appropriation. The human technical capacity to contain, breed,
foster and slaughter life on a large scale, through apparatuses that distance the
product that is received at the table from the horrors of its production, enables
both an expanded "human being" in an ontological sense, and commensurably
an intense regime of immunisation to safeguard the continual enjoyment of
this exponentially expanding property right. Sterile packaged meat reinforces
our human community, by holding at a distance any possibility of identification between ourselves and the animals we slaughter.

Yet another way we might approach the same question is to explore the
notion of sacrifice and its relation to immunisation, through René Girard's
work on violence and its relationship to sacrifice. There are indeed some striking similarities between Girard's understanding of the relation between sacrifice and the social order, and the conception of immunisation put forward by
Esposito. In *Violence and the Sacred*, Girard argues explicitly that the sacrifice
emerges as an antidote to a community experiencing crisis: "a sort of infection
is in fact being checked."[34] Thus the sacrifice serves an explicitly preventative
function.

Girard's focus is on the mechanisms by which communities use directed
violence as a means to safeguard community cohesion and status differences.[35]
Perhaps like Hobbes, Girard is aware of the potential for any community to
break down due to a cycle of violence. An exchange of violence threatens the
cohesion of a community, where one act of violence is accompanied by a reprisal that sets in train a cycle of conflict: "Vengeance, then, is an interminable,
infinitely repeatable process...it threatens to involve the whole social body."[36]
Judicial violence channels and organises this vengeance through legitimised
force: "the system does not suppress vengeance; rather, it effectively limits it to
a single act of reprisal, enacted by a sovereign authority specializing in this
particular function."[37] However, where the law cannot guarantee security from
reprisal, a cycle of violence ensues. In order to establish stability, a "scapegoat"
is selected to bear the violence of the community. The victim often has no connection with the real cause of antagonism: "the crucial fact is that the choice of

34   René Girard. *Violence and the Sacred*. London: Continuum, 2005. 31.
35   Girard. *Violence and the Sacred*. See particularly 1–40.
36   Girard. *Violence and the Sacred*. 15.
37   Girard. *Violence and the Sacred*. 16.

the victim is arbitrary."[38] This disconnection is vital, since the aim of the sacrifice is to substitute the death of the sacrificial victim in order to resolve crisis. In this sense the sacrificial victim differs from the target of judicial authority, who is deemed "guilty" of a crime. The sacrificial victim is exposed to community violence without any guilt. In this sense the misunderstanding, the substitution of one violence for another, is absolutely necessary. The violence of sacrifice serves a *containing* function, disconnecting the object of violence and the source of conflict: in Girard's words the "aim is to achieve a radically new type of violence, truly decisive and self-contained, a form of violence that will put an end once and for all to violence itself."[39]

The requirement for the victim to be disassociated from the source of violent antagonism means that there is a tendency for the victim of sacrifice to already be marginalised from the social structures of the community. Girard observes that at first glance the choice of sacrificial victim appears to lack a consistent unifying factor:

> ...the list seems heterogeneous, to say the least. It includes prisoners of war, slaves, small children, unmarried adolescents, and the handicapped; it ranges from the very dregs of society, such as the Greek *pharmakos*, to the king himself.[40]

However, the rationale for the choice of victim lies in the security offered in exposing a victim who is otherwise socially ostracised from community to a violence without fear of revenge:

> All our sacrificial victims, whether chosen from one of the human categories...or, a fortiori, from the animal realm, are invariably distinguishable from the nonsacrificeable beings by one essential characteristic; between these victims and the community a crucial social link is missing, so they can be exposed to violence without fear of reprisal. Their death does not automatically entail an act of vengeance.[41]

As such, the victim is already alienated from the social and political structure: they are constituted within a zone of exception which presents them as a suitable sacrificial victim.

---

38   Girard. *Violence and the Sacred.* 271.
39   Girard. *Violence and the Sacred.* 28.
40   Girard. *Violence and the Sacred.* 12.
41   Girard. *Violence and the Sacred.* 13.

What is interesting for our purposes here is that Girard's framework for consideration of the sacrificial victim establishes "the animal" as the pre-eminent victim, since the absolute exclusion of animals from the human community prevents the possibility of affiliation with the subject of violence, and prevents reprisal: "no mistake is possible in the case of animal sacrifice."[42] In this case, the animal stands in for the human as a shield from potential future reprisal. We find this relationship clearly expressed in Girard's rendering of a section of an Old Testament scene, where Jacob through a deception attains a blessing from his blind father Isaac, that had originally been intended for his brother Esau. Nearing death, Isaac instructs Esau to bring him "savoury meat" in order to receive a final blessing from his dying father. Jacob hears the instruction and with the help of his mother, Rebekah, brings his father savoury meats from freshly slaughtered goats. However, Jacob pauses, fearing that he will be recognised as an imposter by his vision impaired father, who is able to differentiate his smooth skinned son Jacob from his "hairy" skinned son Esau. The promised blessing risks transformation into a curse if the deception were to be uncovered. Rebekah suggests Jacob wear the skins of the goats: a deception that works: "the old man runs his hands over his younger son, he is completely taken in by the imposter."[43] To be saved from the violence of his father, Isaac seeks literal refuge in the security of the animal:

> In order to receive his father's blessing rather than his curse, Jacob must present to Isaac the freshly slaughtered kids made into "savoury meat." Then the son must seek refuge, literally, in the skins of the sacrificed animals. The animals thus interpose themselves between father and son. They serve as a sort of insulation, preventing the direct contact that could lead to violence.[44]

The violence directed towards animals shields and contains the human. The differentiation between human and animal—the non admissibility of the entity designated as animal to the human community—immunises the human

---

42   Girard. *Violence and the Sacred.* 12.

43   Girard. *Violence and the Sacred.* 5.

44   Girard. *Violence and the Sacred.* 5. Observe the odd resonance with a history from Tacitus of the Roman general Germanicus spying on his own troops, in a moment that highlights the inherent paranoia of totalitarian power; the general imitates an animal: "So after dark, dressed in an animal-skin, he left the general's tent by an exit unknown to the sentries, with one attendant. As he walked the camp lines and stood near the tents, he basked in his own popularity ..." See Tacitus. *The Annals of Imperial Rome.* London: Penguin, 1994. 83.

through periodic bouts of securitising violence. Here Girard's analysis is surprisingly close to Esposito, at least in so far as violence is internalised and managed by the community against an object or set of entities, and serves an
immunising function against the threat of non differentiation (an excess of
community). This is, as Girard observes, "a *lesser* violence, proffered as a bulk-
ward against a far more virulent violence" (that is, the threat of a community
breakdown through absolute non differentiation).[45] Importantly, the violence
directed towards animals within this immunitary logic stands in for a generalised antagonism that permeates the social order and seeks to be securitised.
In this sense, the differentiations that stratify the social body—along lines of
gender difference, class, ability, sexuality and race—and generate continual
conflicts and antagonisms between entities that would otherwise be non differentiated—is resolved through a unified violence that is directed towards
animals. This might offer a way to cast the "human rights" project in another
critical light, by observing that the project of offering those who face violence
and discrimination security through the identification of rights owing to
"humans" (rather than rights regardless of species status) does so by enabling
the possibility of a generalised violence towards those who are deemed as lacking the dignity of the "human," through their exclusion from the securitised
category. It is this violence that protects and unifies humans from the antagonisms that might threaten from a generalised homogeneity. In Girard's words:
"We are dealing here with an animal *pharmakos*, a calf or cow that assumes,
not some vague and ill-defined sins, but the very real (though often hidden)
hostilities that *all the members of the community feel for one another*."[46] Despite
vast differences between humans, differences that could be the source of
unhealable schisms, community is forged in spite of this difference through a
unified superiority over other animals. At the most basic level then, "human
rights"—those rights which belong to humans for no other reason than their
humanity—are securitised by a common right of interpersonal, systemic and
epistemic violence towards animals, which as such acts as a bedrock for human
community.

Reuniting this perspective on the animal body with the immunitary framework of Esposito offers us a different appreciation for the mass scale, simultaneous, ingestion and expulsion of non-human animals. The technological
instrumentation of modernity has enabled, through rationalisations and discrete containments, the intense violence which we bear witness to, a hyper-
bolic rendering of a model of sacrifice. This is a sacrificial system that distances

---

45   Girard. *Violence and the Sacred*. 108.
46   Girard. *Violence and the Sacred*. 104.

its victims absolutely and delivers its violence ferociously, without apparent contamination. An excess of sacrifice satisfies an intoxicated desire for an increasing form of differentiation between human and non-human, We might certainly re-read Agamben's admittedly challenging definition of *homo sacer* as "the life that may be taken without constituting a sacrifice" within this context. For Agamben, the sovereign right emerges precisely at the point between sacrifice and homicide, where a right to legally kill without either committing murder or constituting a sacrifice is possible. This is the preserve of kings: the right to kill legitimately without reprisal in the secular space. Indeed as Agamben insists with his definition of bare life, Westernised sovereignty constitutes life within its own political sphere only with this intention, to create a life that may be legally terminated: "human life is included in the political order in being exposed to an unconditional capacity to be killed."[47] As in the Girardian model of sacrifice, the victims themselves are quite literally substitutes for the real cause of antagonism. It is important that somebody dies, it is unimportant who. This reveals a focus of power that is not merely founded upon a life captured within a zone of sovereign exception, nor on a life that may be constituted as a sacrifice, but both. That is, a life that it is necessary to *sacrifice without constituting a sacrifice*. Under conditions of industrialised slaughter and large scale experimentation, the human is thus founded upon a perpetual animal sacrifice, which constitutes, immunises and securitises the human, without formal celebration of the fact of sacrifice. This might also help us understand the subtle distinction between human killing of humans and human killing of animals, two categorisations that threaten to overwhelm each other. Karl Steel explains:

> Butchery materially enacts the divinely ordained privilege of being human. Through routine violence against animals, butchers not only produce meat, but also the clearest proof of the human domination over— and therefore distinction from–animals. Yet at the same time, butchers mutilate bodies that, as blood, flesh, viscera, and bones, resemble the bodies of humans...No profession shows more clearly that the human is an effect, not a cause of animal subjugation, that what distinguishes human from animal is that executioners and soldiers kill humans, and butchers animals, that humans are buried and animals eaten or discarded.[48]

---

47 Agamben, *Homo Sacer*. 85.
48 Steel. *How to Make a Human.* 219. I find an interesting resonance here to Agamben:
The troubling contiguity between the sovereign and the police function is expressed in the intangible, sacral character that in ancient societies and political systems linked

This might explain the paradox of the biopolitical violence that is a factor of daily life, not only in the slaughterhouse, but in the colony or occupied territory, where the sovereign will exert an exacting and intimate *care* for the lives of those who are contained by exception, yet will simultaneously exercise an extreme degree of *carelessness* with those lives when death is called upon. The care goes into the making die, either quickly or slowly, the carelessness arrives as an after effect of the sacrifice that is never really considered a sacrifice.

---

the figure of the sovereign to that of the executioner. This proximity was perhaps never revealed so clearly as by the fortuitous meeting on July 14, 1418, on a Paris street between the Duke of Burgundy, who had just entered the city as a conqueror leading his troops, and the executioner Coqueluche, who had been working for him night and day. The blood-splattered executioner approached the sovereign and, taking his hand, cried 'My dear brother!' See Giorgio Agamben. "The Sovereign Police." Brian Massumi Ed. *The Politics of Everyday Fear*. Minneapolis: University of Minnesota Press, 1993. 61–3. 62.

CHAPTER 4

Property and Commodity

But now
Poseidon had gone to visit the Ethiopians Worlds away,
Ethiopians off at the farthest limits of mankind,
a people split in two, one part where the Sungod sets
and part where the Sungod rises. There Poseidon went
to receive an offering, bulls and rams by the hundred—
far away at the feast the Sea-lord sat and took his pleasure.

> HOMER. *The Odyssey.* Book 1, 20–30[1]

As discussed in Chapter 3, Esposito suggests that property operates as a strand of immunisation within contemporary biopolitics: property extends the being of the individual, and the demand for protection of this being through what is owned provides an immunisation from the threat of a common ownership. Property rights themselves, at least within the Western tradition, are founded upon a capacity to convert that which is not connected materially to one's own body to that which is "owned." This power of conversion expresses dominion. Its strikingly biopolitical character is connected to a power to convert not only the inanimate, but also that which has its own life and motion— historically including not only the non-human, but the slave, the woman and the child—to the status of property. Indeed we might do well to understand the very close connection between the appropriation of animate objects to the status of property, and the logic of property itself. For within a Lockean framework, we find that animals are not merely just one example of what might be considered property, but sit at the very centre of the property right itself, and underpin "man's" earthly dominion and securitisation of self as a "superior" being. It is thus no accident, as I argue in this chapter, that as Francione has noted, the word "cattle" is linked etymologically to the word *capital.*[2] The war on animals is located upon a violent form of continual appropriation, and an equally violent form of conversion of the lives of animals into value within a human exchange system; property and commodity cohabit as artefacts of war.

---

1 Homer. *The Odyssey.* New York: Penguin, 1996. Book 1, H20–30. 78.
2 Francione. *Animals, Property and the Law.* 35.

Property

The pivotal place given by Locke to the conversion of animals to property seems to have been missed by a number of commentaries.[3] For example, despite his focus on biopolitics, Esposito fails to take note or issue with Locke's discussion of animals as property; C.B. Macpherson, in his classic *The Political Theory of Possessive Individualism*, neglects to draw attention to this fundamental role of property rights in animals in the *First Treatise*;[4] Teresa Brennan and Carole Pateman, while questioning the "naturalised" patriarchal authority of men over women in Locke's account, do not consider the status of animals within the account;[5] and Robert Nozick, despite his interest in the moral status of animals in *Anarchy, State and Utopia*, does not draw attention to animals within Locke's account in his classic work.[6] As I shall discuss, while Richard H. Cox focuses on Locke's treatment of animals in several sections of *Locke on War and Peace*, he seems to miss what is distinctive about Locke's approach in both defining property, and questioning an assumed ontological human superiority over other animals (that is, the challenge to anthropocentricism inherent in Locke's account).[7] Francione *does* explicitly raise Locke in his classic study of animals as property,[8] but quickly glosses over the process of appropriation of non-human life, which I believe is pivotal to understanding the peculiar relationship between animals and the conceptualisation of property as a concept.

The primary relationship between property and the appropriation of animals lies in the desire for self-preservation that Locke discusses in the *First Treatise*. In what might be regarded as a defining section of the work, Locke describes both the desire for self-preservation, and its link to reason as a divinely ordained "voice":

---

3 An exception here might be Kim Ian Parker, who states in no uncertain terms: "Locke's main point in this section is that people acquire property by their right to use the animals." See Kim Ian Parker. *The Biblical Politics of John Locke*. Waterloo: Wilfrid Laurier University Press, 2004. 117.

4 Indeed, Macpherson barely refers to Locke's *First Treatise* in this work. Macpherson appears to only reference the *First Treatise* once, at 212. See C.B. Macpherson. *The Political Theory of Possessive Individualism*. London: Oxford University Press, 1962. 199–203. I thank both Robert Ballingall and John Keane for both drawing my attention to this text.

5 Teresa Brennan and Carole Pateman. "'Mere Auxiliaries to the Commonwealth': Women and the Origins of Liberalism." *Political Studies*. 27 (1979): 183–200.

6 See Nozick. *Anarchy, State and Utopia*. 35–42.

7 Richard H. Cox. *Locke on War and Peace*. London: Oxford University Press, 1960; see particularly 57, 92–3, 103–4.

8 See Francione. *Animals, Property and the Law*. 33–49.

For the desire, strong desire of Preserving his Life and Being having been Planted in him, a Principle of Action by God himself, Reason, *which was the Voice of God in him*, could not but teach him and assure him, that pursuing that natural Inclination he had to preserve his Being, he followed the Will of his Maker, and therefore had the right to make use of those Creatures, which by Reason or Senses he would discover would be serviceable thereunto. And thus Man's *Property* in Creatures, was founded upon the right he had, to make use of those things, that were necessary or useful to his Being.[9]

We might note that the Lockean transformation of a detached entity into property through work has a curious inflection in relation to non-human animals, through a power to transform that which we might understand as having a right to property in itself into that which is a mere entity for human use. While Esposito uses the above quote to interrogate how it is that the life of being should be connected and transformed by property,[10] he fails to address the problematic of how it is that non-human animals come to be understood squarely as a form of property, indeed as fundamental to understanding a property right that extends beyond one's own body.

If Esposito fails to raise this concern, Francione provides a necessary means for a corrective. The key to Francione's discussion of animals as property is the idea that the property status of animals proscribes the limits of animal rights within a juridical frame. This limit—which Francione describes as "legal welfareism"—effectively constrains concern for animal suffering against a logic of balancing that use value for human owners. Thus, questions of ethics framed by utility—such as those raised by Singer in his *Animal Liberation*—must necessarily be contextualised in relation to property rights which determine the limits of ethical consideration. Francione observes that:

> ...ownership of animal property is, for all intents and purposes, no different from the ownership of other sorts of property...Animals are property, and our current system of animal protection, legal welfareism, requires that animal interests be balanced against human interests. The problem is that the law has not developed any doctrines that require that animal property be treated differently because an animal is different from inanimate property, such as a tool. Rather, the law requires that animal property

---

9   Locke. *Two Treatises of Govermment.* 205, Book 1, §86.
10   See Esposito. *Bios.* 64.

not be "wasted" or that animals not be killed or made to suffer when there is no legitimate economic purpose.[11]

As I have discussed, this is an illustration of how sovereignty frames ethics. In this case, sovereignty distorts ethics so that it can only operate as a governmentalisation of suffering and killing: it regulates human use, but never challenges the human prerogative to use.

We can, however, delve deeper into understanding property. The Lockean transformation of a detached entity into property through work has a curious inflection in relation to non-human animals, through a power to transform that which we might understand as having a right to property in itself into that which is a mere entity for human use. It is important to recognise that, in understanding this property right, Locke is explicitly contesting the idea that property rights in animals are authorised by a divine right delegated from God. As is known, the *First Treatise* of the *Two Treatises of Government* is a refutation of Robert Filmer's conception of government as a divinely sanctioned institution. Against this view, Locke argues that the life and death powers of sovereignty are a construction that cannot be traced in the Bible to a divinely sanctioned form of authority:

> Wherein I think 'tis impossible for any sober Reader, to find any other but the setting of Mankind above other kinds of Creatures, in this habitable Earth of ours. 'Tis nothing but the giving to Man, the whole species of Man, as the chief Inhabitant, who is the Image of his Maker, the Dominion over the other Creatures. This lies so obvious in the plain words, that any one but our A. [Filmer] would have thought it necessary to have shewn, how these words that seem'd to say the quite contrary, gave *Adam Monarchical Absolute Power* over other Men, or the *Sole Property* in all Creatures.[12]

It important to mark the subtle difference Locke creates here between divinely sanctioned monarchical right, and dominion in the "creatures." Private dominion, and sovereignty, do not flow from a divine right. Locke stresses that there is a difference between *"having Dominion,* which a Shepherd may have, and having full Property as an Owner."[13] The difference lies in the right to use the earth, as a kind of perpetual lease, in distinction from a right to claim a divinely

---

11   Francione. *Animals, Property and the Law.* 35.

12   Locke. *Two Treatises of Government.* 168–9, Book 1, §40.

13   Locke. *Two Treatises of Government.* 168, Book 1, §39.

sanction propriety over the earth: "men may be allowed to have propriety in the distinct Portions of the Creatures; yet in respect of God the Maker of Heaven and Earth, who is sole Lord and Proprietor of the whole World, Man's Propriety in the Creatures is nothing but that Liberty to use them, which God has permitted."[14]

Locke here sets in train an economy of freedoms that establishes a particular mode of appropriation, which will transform a right of dominion to an earthly property right, which in turn is shaped around a life and death power of sovereignty. As I have stated above, the property right over entities other than the self emerges from an interaction with the world around, driven by a desire for self-preservation. It is important to note that the tussle for self-preservation in Locke is not one sided. The "victory" that emerges as a property right in animals is precisely the result of the *contest* between the self-preservation desire of humans and the self-preservation desire of other animals:

> God having made Man, and planted in him, as in all other Animals, a strong desire of Self-preservation, and furnished the World with things fit for Food and Raiment and other Necessaries of Life, Subservient to his design, that Man should live and abide for some time upon the Face of the Earth, and not that so curious and wonderful a piece of Workmanship by its own Negligence, or want of Necessaries, should perish again, presently under a few moments continuance: God, I say, having made Man and the World thus, spoke to him, (that is) directed him by Senses and Reason, as he did the inferior Animals by their Sense, and Instinct, which he had placed in them to that purpose, to the use of those things, which were serviceable for his Subsistence, and given him as means of his Preservation. And therefore I doubt not...Man had a right to a use of the Creatures, by the Will and Grant of God.[15]

Humans and animals both possess a desire for self-preservation, something in the Lockean account which is implanted in all animals, human or otherwise, by God. The desire for self-preservation leads to conflict between entities who seek to use each other in order to endure. Humans and animals are differentiated through the name given to this will toward self-preservation: in humans this is "reason," in animals this is "instinct." However, both desires have been placed in all sensible animals, human and otherwise, to achieve preservation.

---

14   Locke. *Two Treatises of Government*. 168, Book 1, §39.
15   Locke. *Two Treatises of Government*. 204, Book 1, §86.

I underline here the importance of this section in Locke's text in providing the basis for a theory of property. It is worth observing, in this regard, that this section in Locke appears as an aberrant interpretation of the Biblical *Genesis* narrative, since it unsettles the assumed superiority of the human. Indeed Cox notes, with some concern, that this threatens an assumed naturalised human superiority over other animals: "thus the very notion of a rank, precedence, and deference established by God in nature yields to an essentially naturalistic description, in which man's status is decisively lowered *vis-à-vis* the other members of the natural order."[16] However, there is an innovation that occurs here, since it is apparent that an equality between the species sits behind and justifies the labour theory of value Locke advances. If all humans were superior to all animals, then the state of nature would be a field already stratified by relations of naturalised dominion; and as such property would be merely about giving "man" his natural due, a thesis Locke explicitly rejects in the *First Treatise*. Rather, a primordial equality is required in order to establish the scene by which work can transform what was common to that which belongs to individuals as property. In this sense the commons must function as a space of non differentiation, including between species. And work represents the result of a conflict over the commons, where property emerges as a result of this conflict through a successful appropriation of what was common to that which is securitised as a belonging. Property only solidifies itself through a work on the commons that transforms what was previously open to claim by any entity to that which is property of those who have laboured. Locke makes this explicit in the *Second Treatise*:

> The Law Man was under, was rather for *appropriating*. God Commanded, and his Wants forced him to *labour*. That was his *Property* which could not be taken from him where-ever he had fixed it. And hence subduing or cultivating the Earth, and having Dominion, we see are joyned together. The one gave Title to the other. So that God, by commanding to subdue, gave Authority so far to *appropriate*. And the Condition of Humane Life, which requires Labour and Materials to work on, necessarily introduces *private Possessions*.[17]

It is for this reason I would emphasise that a conflict between human and animals, a kind of war, is what appears to found the property relation in Locke. For it is certainly clear, and this is apparent in the discussion of property rights in

---

16   Cox. *Locke on War and Peace*. 57.

17   Locke, *Two Treatises of Government*. Second Treatise. §35.292.

the *Second Treatise*, that the appropriation of property is quite precisely treated as, conceptualised as, a tussle by which "Man" seeks to both overcome the animal and secure the animal from a common claim:

> Thus this Law of reason makes the Deer that *Indian's* who hath killed it; it is allowed to be his goods who hath bestowed his labour upon it, though, before, it was the common right of every one. And amongst those who are counted the Civiliz'd part of mankind, who have made and multiplied positive laws to determine property, this original Law of Nature for the *beginning of Property*, in what was before common, still takes place, and by virtue thereof, what Fish any one catches in the Ocean, that great and still remaining Common of Mankind; or what Amber-griese any one takes up here is *by* the *Labour* that removes it out of that common state Nature left it in, *made* his *Property* who takes that pains about it. And even amongst us, the Hare that any one is Hunting is thought his who pursues her during the Chase. For being a Beast that is still looked upon as common, and no Man's private Possession, whoever has imploy'd so much *labour* about any of that kind, as to find and pursue her, has thereby removed her from the state of Nature, wherein she was common, and hath *begun a Property*.[18]

I have emphasised in this reading the apparent equality between humans and animals in Locke's account of the state of nature, since, as is apparent from the above quote, this equality is required to produce the labour that will justify appropriation. It is because the Hare does not simply give themselves to the human, but must be chased and appropriated through labour, in a risky process where the animal may easily evade capture, that a human property right in the captured animal is established.

However, it must be stressed that this does not mean that God abandons "Man" in Locke's account. Locke is still on the side of the human in the narrative he provides for the state of nature. God favours "Man"; not through granting humans outright divinely sanctioned sovereignty and property rights, but in allowing reason—that is "the Voice of God in him"—to guide a naturalised human appropriation of animals (remember animals are confined only to "instinct"):

> ...reason, *which was the Voice of God in him*, could not but teach him and assure him, that pursuing that natural Inclination he had to preserve his

---

18   Locke. *Two Treatises of Government*. 289, Book 2, §29.

Being, he followed the Will of his Maker, and therefore had the right to make use of those Creatures, which by Reason or Senses he would discover would be serviceable thereunto.[19]

The subtle way in which Locke places reason in his account creates a lack of certainty over whether God endorses "Man's" use of the animals, or merely creates a will for self-preservation that legitimates itself through the voice of reason, which Locke then ascribes as *the Voice of God in him.*" Indeed, since God places a desire for self-preservation in all animals, human or otherwise, it can only be inferred that *"therefore"* humans may utilise other animals as a logical extension; this right to utilise is not established as a divinely ordained truth ("therefore had the right to make use of those Creatures, which by Reason or Senses he would discover would be serviceable thereunto"). Indeed, human reason would appear to arise through the capture of those creatures that humans find for their utilisation; almost literally, we have a desire for self-preservation, "therefore" reason would have it that we must have a right to use other Creatures to satisfy this divinely ordained will. Reason here emerges as a form of situated authorisation for action. Reason allows us to speculate and act through practice, rather than know as fact. This reading seems reasonable in so far as we know that Locke indicates in his *Of the Conduct of the Understanding* that reason is something that is learned through a kind of situated practice, rather than found as an innate quality inherent to humanity which endures regardless of social and political arrangements:

Nothing does this better than mathematics; which, therefore, I think should be taught all those who have the time and opportunity; not so much to make them mathematicians, as to make them reasonable creatures; for though we all call ourselves so, because we are born to it, if we please; yet we may truly say, nature gives us but the seeds of it; we are born to be, if we please, rational creatures, but it is use and exercise only that makes us so, and we are, indeed, so no farther than industry and application has carried us. And, therefore, in ways of reasoning, which men have not been used to, he that will observe the conclusions they take up must be satisfied they are not all rational.[20]

---

19   Locke. *Two Treatises of Government.* 204, Book 1, §29.
20   John Locke. *Of the Conduct of the Understanding.* In *The Works of John Locke in Nine Volumes,* London: Rivington, 1824 12th edn. Vol. 2. At: www.oll.libertyfund.org/?option=com_staticxt&staticfile=show.php%3Ftitle=762&chapter=80854&layout=html&Itemid=27. §6. I thank Emma Planinc for drawing my attention to this discussion.

This grounded use of reason, which emerges in the context of human social organisation, and not in spite of it, suggests that reason develops—evolves—through human endeavour. It is through the artifice of human "civilisation"—a civilisation that includes violent forms of utilisation of other creatures—that human reason, what is rational, emerges. This is indeed the conclusion Cox observes in relation to Locke:

> Man's rationality is not, strictly speaking, a 'natural state' of affairs, that it develops painfully and slowly only if and when industry and pains are exerted, and that the central impulse to that development is the desire to be preserved. This means, in turn, that Locke's eventual description of the state of nature as one of the continual fears, dangers, misery and anarchy, in which everyone is reduced to the state of struggle for mere existence, becomes perfectly consistent... They are guided, like the animals, by desires and the senses, to a rude, brutish, dangerous, and extremely uncertain existence.[21]

The solution for Locke, at least as Cox argues, is for "Man" to create out of the state of nature an order in which human activity can secure "Man" against the assault of nature: "to work out the principles by which a political order may be built so as to most effectively conduce gratification of the ineradicable desire for preservation and comforts." In other words the political order requires the conquest of the non-human to sustain a human freedom from the absolute equality of nature; the human social and political order is the victory prize. Cox says as much, summarising that the "entry of man into the promised land is, therefore, so far from being a work of nature or the blessing of God, that it is the promised result only of the successful conquest of nature by man's reason on behalf of those natural impulses which he finds in himself from the very beginning."[22] Humans conquer as a result of a will for self-preservation, a will they share with other animals; but their victory arrives with the mark of rationality, as a logic which emerges through the practice of conquest. Human superiority is not granted by God; rather, the "divine" voice in the ear of the human, which assures the human of the superiority of itself, arrives as an autolegtimating gesture. As we shall discover in Chapter 8, I believe this aligns perfectly with Derrida's own reading of the foundation of sovereignty as lacking content beyond a claimed superiority that accompanies a victory in a war

---

21   Cox. *Locke on War and Peace.* 93.
22   Cox. *Locke on War and Peace.* 94.

between life forms. This is a tussle that lays claim to bodies, that grapples and appropriates bodies in an active scene of conflict or "chase." A life and death struggle for self-preservation. And a double immunity is at stake for the human: not merely an immunity from a common human claim (as discussed by Esposito), but a human immunity claimed in general from the animal.

This is perhaps why the master–slave relation, in an almost Hegelian sense, seems relevant, both in the sense of understanding the relationship between the subject and that which is objectified through appropriation (both objects and living entities including the slave), and for understanding the microdynamics of the process of objectification, or what we might in a different rendering describe as precisely the process of animalisation. The animal here is that animate entity for which a property right can be ascribed.[23] As Francione describes: "property is understood as that which does not have any inherent interests that must be respected. That is, although I may have an interest in owning property, my property is itself not regarded as a carrier of interests."[24] The Lockean process of appropriation involves stripping an entity as a carrier of "interests" (to use the language of liberalism); it is a peculiar desubjectification of a living entity which, through the framework of human and animal relations, reorients the living entity as not bearing a right in itself, of its own. We would do well here to remember the curious way in which Sovereignty arrives as a guarantor of property right: for we witness here in the process of animalisation—that is, of stripping of rights or interests from a living entity—that sovereignty is announced through the simultaneous humanisation of the origin of domination. Just as the animal is created through a process of appropriation as property—as an entity without its own interests—so too is the human created in this process as sovereign, as an entity which possess a radical transformative hold over its possessions. The human claims to possess the voice of God which provides the legitimation for its own acts of dominion in the name of self-preservation.

Commodity

As I have discussed, a striking feature of our current relationship with animals is that it reflects a use without any apparent bounds: slaughter, containment,

23   In this regard, Stephen M. Best's analysis of the fugitive slave and the relationship to contemporary conceptualisations of intellectual property appears relevant for a deeper analysis. See Stephen M. Best. *The Fugitive's Properties: Law and the Poetics of Possession.* Chicago and London: The University of Chicago Press, 2004.

24   Francione. *Animals, Property and the Law.* 35.

experimentation and consumption upon an unimaginable scale. This relies upon a material and epistemic separation between the subject and the object which is possessed. In the context of intense global capitalist systems of exchange and strongly developed and reliable frameworks of sovereignty which guarantee the agreed pervasiveness of property rights, and fixes and authorises "value" in order to enable exchange, an almost surreal disconnection between humans and non-human animal life is created. In this world, excess might be marked by a capacity for subjectivity to enlarge itself in a seemingly hyper-real way through an extraordinary extension of property right. It is possible for individuals to own far more than they could ever really "appropriate" in an intimate sense within their lifetimes; this includes a potential to appropriate through consumption non-human animal life upon an unimaginable scale. Our theorisation of excess here must be careful, for I am not suggesting that excess must be defined against an asceticism that might be considered as a kind of Puritanism. Our problematic relationship with animals is not a result of an excess consumption. Moderation in killing or violence is not a more ethical outcome. On the contrary, the key here is understanding the way in which surplus or excess arrives as a sign of sovereignty. This is why a problematic of excess does not belong to ethics in terms of balancing desire and need, or harm against utility, or governing between regimes of "necessary and unnecessary suffering." Rather, surplus in this case is properly political in so far as the capacity to enjoy excess can be understood as a mode of rule which constructs freedom on the basis of the unfreedom of others. Sovereignty, at least in this guise, is the pleasure of excess. It is perhaps for this reason that in Locke, questions of government come after the right associated with property. Political sovereignty arrives as a means to securitise property rights; government a means to regulate, manage and distribute between competing rights for a common good. As a result, Locke explicitly divides between the "private" rights of "Man" (founded on the right to use animals, no less) and modes of government which secure those rights:

> Property, whose Original is from the Right a Man has to use any of the Inferior Creatures, for the Subsistence and Comfort of his Life, is for the benefit and sole Advantage of the Proprietor so that he may even destroy the thing, that he has Property in by his use of it, where need requires: but Government being for the Preservation of every Man's Right and Property, by preserving him from the Violence or Injury of other, is for the good of the Governed.[25]

---

25   Locke. *Two Treatises of Government.* 209–10, Book 1, §92.

In this formulation, any regulation of excess and surplus through government does not—indeed cannot—interfere with the natural right of "man" to property: it can only temper it towards a common good. As I have discussed above with reference to Francione, human property interests in animals shape welfare concerns and limit questions of suffering in such a way to not interfere with (indeed *insure*) continuing human utility. Animal welfare approaches have not mitigated this extent of use; indeed they have lubricated an expansion in human use, by providing a means by which animal use can be continued and proliferated despite a numerical increase in the number who suffer and die. And thus we are left with the paradoxical concept of "unnecessary suffering," which always stipulates the suffering "necessary" to not interfere substantively in human use. Tellingly, this is also a discourse of excess and waste. The governance of suffering here wards against an excess of suffering that exceeds (or does not contribute to) the continuing use value of animals for humans. Thus suffering in itself is not a problem; rather, unnecessary suffering—that is, a suffering that is a by-product of waste or excess—is constructed as *the* problem. The property right grants an absolute prerogative to make suffer, "so that he may even destroy the thing." Government delineates between necessary and unnecessary suffering, in such a way as to balance a need for a continuing right to use and enjoy property (to make suffer) against the claims of those who would seek to mitigate this suffering (presumably, animal advocates).

But even this governed suffering is beyond all bounds, beyond all limits, because the nature of the production process itself ensures that animals can always be exposed to a form of violence that exceeds mere "use" value, and rather extends to a life and death relation of excess that ruptures a measurable limit: "Property, whose Original is from the Right a Man has to use any of the Inferior Creatures, for the Subsistence and Comfort of his Life, is for the benefit and sole Advantage of the Proprietor so that he may even destroy the thing." In this sense, animals as property do not circulate in the same way as other "things" nor in the same way as other sentient property, such as "slaves."

Marx identified the capitalist process as a refined system for the exploitation (extraction of surplus) from human labour, calculated through the difference between use value and exchange value: "the value of labour-power, and the value which that labour-power valorizes [*verwertet*] in the labour-process, are two different magnitudes; and this difference was what the capitalist had in mind when he was purchasing the labour-power."[26] The method of

---

26   Karl Marx. *Capital* Vol. 1. Harmondsworth: Penguin, 1986. 300.

pricing necessarily alienates the commodity "consumed" in the production process,[27] so that the conditions of the production of that commodity— exploitative, violent or otherwise—are itself veiled. Thus Marx states:

> The taste of porridge does not tell us who grew the oats, and the process we have presented does not reveal the conditions under which it takes place, whether it is happening under the slave-owners brutal lash or the anxious eye of the capitalist, whether Cincinnatus undertakes it in tilling his couple of acres, or a savage, when he lays low a wild beast with a stone.[28]

---

27 Marx states that the capitalist "proceeds to consume the commodity, the labour power he has just bought, i.e. he causes the worker, the bearer of that labour-power, to consume the means of production by his labour." Marx, *Capital* Vol. 1, 291.

28 Marx. *Capital* Vol. 1, 290–1. It is worth noting here the full paragraph, which is contextually situated as an aside within Marx's discussion of the creation of surplus value, to identify the necessary and "given" distinction between human beings and nature:

> The Labour process, as we have presented it in its simple and abstract elements, is purposeful activity aimed at the production of use-values. It is an appropriation of what exists in nature for the requirements of man. It is the universal condition for the metabolic interaction [*Stoffweschel*] between man and nature, the everlasting nature-imposed condition of human existence, or rather it is common to all forms of society in which human beings live. We did not, therefore, have to present the worker in his relationship with other workers; it was enough to present man and his labour on one side, nature and its materials on the other. The taste of porridge does not tell us who grew the oats, and the process we have presented does not reveal the conditions under which it takes place, whether it is happening under the slave-owners brutal lash or the anxious eye of the capitalist, whether Cincinnatus undertakes it in tilling his couple of acres, or a savage, when he lays low a wild beast with a stone."

It is also worth drawing attention to the two footnotes that accompany this section in Marx's text. The first observes that "The Roman patrician Lucius Quinctius Cincinnatus (dictator of Rome from 458 to 439 BC) was reputed to have lived a simple and exemplary life, cultivating his own small farm in person." The second footnote attributes to Robert Torrens the discovery that the "origin of capital" derives from the "stone of the savage," (used to kill the beast). See also, in this relation, Marx's earlier construction of "man" and "his" appropriation of "nature" in *A Contribution to The Critique of Political Economy*: "no production is possible without an instrument of production, even if this instrument is only a hand. No production is possible without past, accumulated labour, even if this labour is only the dexterity gathered and concentrated in the hand of the savage through repeated practice" (see Marx. *Preface and Introduction to A Contribution to The Critique of Political Economy*. 11). Note the unmistakable symmetry between Marx's primordial ascription of the appropriation of property through violence against animals to that we have read in Locke. "Thus this Law of reason makes the Deer that *Indian's* who hath killed it."

Surplus is the driving principle for capitalist economic exchange, and conflict is generated for control over the surplus extracted. However, in the case of animals, this surplus is generated through a primary exploitation that precedes human labour and exchange, through the conversion—the "objectification" (*Vergegenständlichung*)—of the non-human animal as a simple resource for consumption and conversion within the production process. When Marx comments in *Capital* that: "No boots can be made without leather,"[29] we must assume that the processes of violence and subordination that leads to the production of leather pre-exist—indeed discursively and "naturally" pre-empt—the human labour production process. This is forgotten violence that relies upon forgetting to harmonise social relations.[30] Capitalist exchange, no less than other human production systems, rests upon a violent domination of non-human life which is necessarily impossible to recognise, impossible to price, since non-human animals themselves do not share any portion (even an exploitative portion) of the return, nor is the suffering of animals valued. There is no wage for animals.

For Marx, capitalism relies on the ability of the human *worker* to alienate their own labour power[31] as a commodity. Marx will discuss the curious freedom workers under capitalism have to alienate their labour power and subject this to an exchange value in the market; only the worker's labour power is alienated, while the worker's own body and life remain theoretically bound to the worker as property. Workers exchange their labour because they have no other means by which to attain what is needed to survive (workers are alienated

---

29   Marx. *Capital*. Vol. 1, 272.

30   Marx states:

> ...the most modern and the most ancient epochs will have [certain] determinations in common. Production without them is inconceivable; but although the most highly developed languages have laws and characteristics in common with the least developed ones, it is precisely the divergence from these general and common features which determines their development. It is necessary to differentiate those determinations which apply to production in general in order not to forget the essential dissimilarities in view of the unity that follows from the very fact that the subject, mankind, and the object, nature, are the same. For instance, the entire wisdom of those modern economists who demonstrate the eternity and harmony of existing social relations depends on this forgetting.

> See Marx. *Preface and Introduction to A Contribution to The Critique of Political Economy.* 11.

31   Marx states: "We mean by labour-power, or labour-capacity, the aggregate of those mental and physical capabilities existing in the physical form, the living personality, of a human being, capabilities which he sets in motion whenever he produces a use-value of any kind." Marx. *Capital.* Vol. 1. 270.

from the means of production).[32] As such, the *use value* of the free worker's labour is equivalent to the cost of reproducing one's own life (that is, at a bare minimum, the cost of food, clothing and shelter necessary to survive).[33] One of the tensions that capitalism produces—indeed its spectacular innovation—lies in the ability of the owner of the means of production to pay an exchange value for labour that has no connection to the cost of the means of subsistence (the *use value* of labour to workers themselves). Thus, capitalism is free to pay people at rates below subsistence levels, a capacity that today is key to the extortionate profitability of the international system. This would indeed be key to its advantage over formalised slavery as a production system, since the costs of reproducing labour are almost completely displaced and privatised (they are the worker's own concern) in favour of a focus on simply extracting surplus from exchange.[34] Capitalism's only guiding logic, it would seem, is to continue to reduce the exchange value paid for labour (for example, to pay ever lower real wages) and other commodities, and simultaneously to maximise the surplus extracted from labour in this exchange. This benefit is directly measurable as a cost in the poverty of the billions of humans globally who cannot feed or house themselves, who suffer and die from preventable illnesses, which is all apparently necessary for the very survival of the economic system.

---

32   The pivotal section of *Capital* here is Chapter 6, "The Sale and Purchase of Labour Power." See Marx. *Capital*. Vol. 1, 270–80.

33   Marx. *Capital*. Vol. 1, 276.

34   In contrast to "freely" contracted labour under capitalism, slavery creates a set of different tensions. Marx, and Engels, pointed out that slavery was inefficient, and this is why formal slavery gave way to capitalism. One inefficiency within a system of slavery is that the slave owner must feed and house slaves in order to continue to produce. For the slave owner, this will mean a somewhat different economy from that under capitalism; there will be a continuing incentive to reduce the costs associated with keeping slaves by rationing, deprivation etc., and a simultaneous incentive to increase the productivity of labour through the use of coercion (harsh treatment, torture etc.). At the same time, the property value of the slave owner's stock in human slaves will be continually weighed against the relative costs of the value depreciation of human stock (that is the fact that slaves will get older, more damaged and less productive) and the relative replacement costs of human stock (hence the global incentive to keep capturing and supplying new slaves, or use female slaves to reproduce and rear new slaves to join the workforce). In other words, if there is a ready supply of new slaves, then there will be every incentive for slave owners to abuse their existing stock, since it is easily replaceable. In a strict sense, the slave does not enjoy the ability to alienate their labour in a market exchange; on the contrary, the slave's body, life and potentiality has all been alienated as property, and the slave has no property right themselves in this commodity. Slaves are owned by others, they have no means to own themselves.

This situation is different for animals, and not improved. Like under slavery, the property right in the production animal's life, labour and body has been fully alienated, and is held in the hands of humans. As Noske has observed, this leads to a multifaceted form of alienation that differs substantially in character from the alienation of humans—slaves or workers—in the production process.[35] While the property value of the slave rests in the slave's productive potential as a living entity, the property value in the animal's productive potential must be appraised differently, because of the different sites for "labour" and the differential value placed within production processes upon death itself. For experimental animals, the corporeal response of the animal's living body—its metabolic systems, its reactions and behaviours, its growth, flourishing, and diminution, its life and death—are all potentially productive, value accruing, phenomena.[36] For "livestock," value is tied to the animal's death, since

---

This does not, however, mean that the slave exercises no freedom (or possibility of resistance) in the production process, since within this process there is a continuing need to prevent resistance, precisely through forms of violent disciplinarity. We only need to discipline and control a subject who is by definition a resistive agent. Thus whipping and other means of torture is required to incentivise productivity: under human slavery labour is performed as a way to avoid the threat of yet more sufferings. Thus *there is* indeed exchange here, although we know this economy is arbitrary and cruel, and looks nothing like the "free" exchange of labour under capitalism. The human slave offers labour (both productive and reproductive labour) in exchange for the possibility of avoiding more suffering, or avoiding worse pain than the one that the slave is currently enduring through punishment or deprivation. Pain is not the only means to incentivise work, as the threat of death is also operative in this economy. Slavery also rests upon an immanent threat of death, and labour is given to avoid death, usually a painful death. This exchange relies upon an imposed equivalent value between pain and work; life and death.

I leave open the question of whether an animal can be a slave, although I note that there are reasons to understand the differences between slavery and our treatment of animals. Certainly one fact that must be considered is the history of overt racialisation that accompanies slavery in its late practice, which contains the distinct understanding that the slave is a biopolitically differentiated human who has been converted into the "speaking tool" through modes of violence and domination, but a tool that is different from other animals. In this guise, slavery produced and reproduced racialised distinction, in other words; it was productive in ways that went beyond straight economics. It allowed the production of an ongoing set of dominations that enabled a biological caesura between human populations.

35   See Noske. *Beyond Boundaries*. 18–21. Noske observes that animals face alienation from themselves (their own body and their offspring); alienation from the product of their labour; alienation from other animals; alienation from "surrounding nature" and alienation from "species life."

36   In this context, see Clark. "Labourers or Lab Tools?"

value will only be fully realised when the animal has been raised, is killed and is converted into meat. For dairy animals, body morphology is manipulated to maximise the utility of the animal as a milk producing machine, with animals quickly discarded when this capacity is no longer useful. For reproductive animals, life is simultaneously constrained and maximised towards production of new animals for industrial consumption, in endless cycles of birth, rebirth and nurture until the animal's utility for this purpose has expired. Value here is interdependent upon the biopolitical processes of birthing and growing the living organism, harvesting life towards value-creating activity, and scrupulously timing death to maximise surplus.[37]

While all of these facets of production beckon deeper and lengthy analysis, I would like to specifically focus on the death function of slaughter in food production here. As Dutkiewicz observes, within industrialised slaughter animal death is a value-creating act;[38] the death of the animal is timed to maximise the relative exchange value of the meat that will be produced. As such, death is not threatened to the animal as an incentive to labour (as it is under conditions of slavery), since death will be imposed at the time that is deemed to be most profitable, and not a day before or a day later. At this point, value is realised through a forced exchange of life for death, where a value in death is imposed by the human producer upon the living animal. Here we strike a point of exchange in production, which essentially describes the realisation of the value in the commodity, a process which must be understood as absurd. The reason I say this is absurd is that we know, intuitively, that there can be no equivalence in value between life and death. Yet this is what drives the commodity value of animals as meat. As Marx observes, commodity exchange

---

37   See Dutkiewicz. "'Postmodernism,' Politics, and Pigs." It may be worth considering: what are the degrees of freedom available here for the animal caught within this production process? Firstly we might observe that, in a strict sense, pain is imposed within limits necessary to maximise human use value. Suffering deemed necessary to maximise profits will be imposed on animals; while suffering that has a negative effect on the final value will, at least theoretically, be avoided. Welfare has arguably shifted the economy of suffering within industrialised production. The tendency of welfare would appear to be to remove forms of overt suffering aimed at making animals move or respond in particular ways. Thus, under the rationality of welfare, a curved corral replaces the cattle prod. Rather than painfully prodding the animal to go forward into the slaughter chute, a system of corrals is used which blind the animal to the death that is to come—hence unnecessary suffering associated with the pain of the cattle prod, or emotional pain prior to death, is apparently removed. This does not mean for animals that resistance to pain is not possible, rather that it is severely constrained.

38   Dutkiewicz. "'Postmodernism,' Politics, and Pigs." 303.

requires establishing a form of equivalent value between one entity and another, where one qualitatively different entity is exchanged for another. Here, as Marx notes, we find the strange process where in order for an object to attain value, another object must stand in for it as an equivalent. For example, for oranges to be exchanged for apples, we must treat apples as something they are not (that is, oranges), and simultaneously treat oranges as something equivalent to something they are themselves not (that is, apples).[39] An apple has no inherent value. Value arises within a system when we treat the apple as something it is not by imposing an alternative—say an orange—as its equivalent: "the equivalent form of a commodity, accordingly, is the form in which it is directly exchangeable with other commodities."[40] The apple becomes commodified when the orange can stand in for the apple. Thus Marx states:

> Since a commodity cannot be related to itself as an equivalent, and therefore cannot make its own physical shape into the expression of its own value, it must be related to another commodity as equivalent, and therefore must make the physical shape of another commodity into its own value form.[41]

As such, the process of commodification—a process of imposing equivalence upon contextually differentiated entities in order to generate value—is not merely absurd (literally an "abstraction"), but inherently violent in so far as

---

39 I am reframing here the argument that Marx puts forward to conceptualise equivalent value between linen and a coat. The cleverness of his discussion is picking two commodities that are materially linked, but of course, cannot replace each other directly since they are substantively different:

> ...the commodity linen brings to view its own existence as a value through the fact that the coat can be equated with the linen although it has not assumed a form of value distinct from its own physical form. The coat is directly exchangeable with the linen; in this way the linen in fact expresses its own existence as a value [*Wertsein*].

See Marx. *Capital*. Vol. 1. 147. In this context, note Adam Smith's discussion of the linen shirt in Adam Smith. *An Inquiry into the Nature and Causes of the Wealth of Nations*. Library of Economics and Liberty: 2000. At: www.econlib.org/library/Smith/smWN1.html. Book 1 1.11. Note that Marx himself demonstrates awareness that the identification of use value and its conversion to exchange value is far from a neat process (see particularly Marx. *Capital*. Vol. 1. 131). In this regard, see Gayatri Chakravorty Spivak. *An Aesthetic Education in the Era of Globalization*. Cambridge: Harvard University Press, 2012. 193–6.

40 Marx. *Capital*. Vol. 1. 147.

41 Marx. *Capital*. Vol. 1. 148.

valuation requires erasure of the inherent qualities of one entity in order to create a generalised equivalence and identification with another. One entity is made to look like the other: "by means of the value relation, therefore, the natural form of the commodity becomes the value-form of commodity A, in other words the physical body of commodity B becomes a mirror for the value of commodity A."[42]

This combination of absurdity and violence is brought together perhaps most forcefully in the case of industrialised production of animals as food. This occurs through a coerced imposition of death in exchange for life in order to realise value. Regardless of what sort of life the animal may hold, what potential this life may possess, what sort of value the animal's own life may have for itself (that is, the use value of the animal's own life for itself), within industrialised slaughter this life is always subject to death as the only means by which value in this life can be attained (Thus even animals sold live—"livestock"—are only worth something due to their capacity to be made dead in order to attain a final value. Today, under global capitalism, countless land and sea animals are worth no more than the value that will be realised upon their timely deaths). That commodification relies on something to stand in for something it is not, in order to attain value, is already absurd, something I believe Marx is more than suggestive of in *Capital Vol. 1* through his discussion of abstraction.

---

42   Marx. *Capital*. Vol. 1, 148. Earlier Marx states: "In order to inform us that its sublime objectivity as a value differs from its stiff and starchy existence as a body, it says that value has the appearance of a coat, and therefore that in so far as the linen itself is an object of value [*Wertding*], it and the coat are as like as two peas" (144). It is worth paying attention to the footnote that accompanies this section of Marx's chapter in *Capital* ("The Commodity"), which I believe neatly summarises the problem of epistemic value and its link to human "brotherly" community within a Judeo-Christian context:

> In a certain sense, a man is in the same situation as a commodity. As he neither enters into the world in possession of a mirror, nor as a Fichtean philosopher who can say 'I am I,' a man first sees and recognizes himself in another man. Peter only relates to himself as a man through his relation to another man, Paul, in who he recognizes his likeness. With this, however, Paul also becomes from head to toe, in his physical form as Paul, the form of appearance of the species man for Peter. (144 n19).

Aside from an obvious connection to Lacan's mirror stage, in some ways I believe Marx perfectly pre-empts the problem raised by Derrida in *Politics of Friendship* and the The *Beast and the Sovereign* lectures. Note also the deep resonance with Derrida's early work on language and the metaphor: "should one not always have to speak of the ef-*facement* of an originary figure, if it did not by itself efface itself?" See Jacques Derrida. "White Mythology: Metaphor in the Text of Philosophy." *Margins of Philosophy*. Chicago: Chicago University Press, 1982. 207–29. 211.

However, this absurdity reaches an extreme point where death stands in for life, since death is not only the absolute nullification of life (death is what life is not in a very absolute sense), but simultaneously, the subject of life is tied to its life in such a way that its alienation in death forecloses any possibility for the subject of life to attain the realisation of the use or exchange value in that life. At least in the context of industrialised food production, livestock cannot profit or attain value from their own lives through death. We cannot directly profit from the exchange of our death for the life we previously lived and derived use value in.

For human workers, resistance to the imposition of a value upon labour can take many forms, including in the exchange process, where labour, through collective bargaining, negotiate on the agreed value of their work as a commodity.[43] This relies upon a degree of "freedom," even if, within the scope of capitalism, this freedom is always contextual and precarious. "Freedom" for animals in contemporary production processes is modulated through different economies, and thus generates radically different avenues for resistance to the imposition of value. We are aware that the scope for the resistance of animals to their own death remains extraordinarily constrained in contemporary industrialised breeding, containment, slaughter and experimentation, since the modes of domination that characterise these production processes capture the totality of the lives of the animals caught within them and limit perception of any free movement. However, we might perceive resistance as occurring, precisely at the point at which a drive for animal self-preservation contests an economic human imperative for death. In the Introduction to this book, I drew from Foucault's identification of sovereignty as a moment of total victory, which generates power relations that are formed in relation to life and death:

> The vanquished are at the disposal of the victors. In other words the victors can kill them. If they kill them, the problem obviously goes away: the Sovereignty of the State disappears simply because the individuals who make up that State are dead. But what happens if the victors spare the lives of the vanquished? If they spare their lives...are granted the temporary privilege of life...[they]...agree to work for and obey the others, to surrender their land to the victors, to pay them taxes. It is therefore not the defeat that leads to the brutal establishment of a society based upon domination, slavery, and servitude; ...It is fear, the renunciation of fear,

---

43   Note that this process does not free the worker from commodification of labour itself, only allows negotiation over the relative value of labour that has been commodified. In this regard, see Spivak. *An Aesthetic Education on the Era of Globalization.* 192.

and the renunciation of the risk of death. The will to prefer life to death; that is what founds sovereignty ...[44]

It is at this curious moment in Foucault's text that I believe we find the key to understanding animal resistance to biopolitical commodification at its extreme limit. The statement that ends the quote above—"the will to prefer life to death; that is what founds sovereignty"—is perfectly reversible in terms of its meaning. On a primary interpretation, the possibility of death creates the power of sovereignty over life; we allow ourselves to be enslaved since a life of enslavement under a sovereign power is preferable to death. We prefer to live, and accept a constrained life over the choice of death as a replacement. Yet, in asserting our own will to prefer life over death, we exert our own sovereign preference to live rather than die. And we exert this preference against, in resistance to, an all encompassing sovereign power. An animal will for self-preservation works both with and against the will for self-preservation of humans. At each step of the process of turning a living animal into meat, animals resist due to a desire for self-preservation. If commodification imposes upon animals an equivalence between life and death in order to realise value, an equivalent value that relies upon refusing to acknowledge the qualitative difference between life and death (indeed the essential opposition between these two categories), then the resistance of animals, at each step of the way, is directed towards disrupting the establishment of this relationship of equivalence and value. A chicken struggles against a human operator, as it is thrust into the poultry shackle; a hooked tuna fish, gasping, wrests its body violently on the deck of a ship; a cow hesitates before being prodded to enter the kill chute; a hog turns away as the captive bolt pistol misses. Animals intervene to prevent the translation of this forced equivalence into exchange, since *for animals* accepting the imposition of value will end use and exchange value itself. On the other side, the incentive within industrialised food production will be to nullify this resistance in order to realise the full value of death: any acts of creativity or resistance by animals that delay, compromise, or ineffectively congeal value become a threat to system efficiency. Industrial production captures this conflict as a hotspot of competing forces.

The will to prefer life over death is a primary act of resistance to the process of biopolitical commodification, perhaps the only act of resistance available to animals who are subject to extreme forms of control within production systems. As I argue in the Conclusion to this book, one possible site of human resistance to the war against animals is precisely to focus upon this point of

---

44   Foucault. *Society Must Be Defended.* 95.

exchange, in order to prevent the translation of value—prevent the violent process that works across intersubjective, institutional and epistemic systems to impose an equivalence between life and death—and to support the resistance of animals themselves to this process of commodification.

Staying with Marx, and thinking further about value, we might observe that property rights over animals offer a way to draw a line of distinction between an economic imperative within capitalist rationality to eliminate excess and waste, and a sovereign imperative to enjoy surplus, even if this enjoyment is inherently wasteful. For Marx rightly notes that waste is to be avoided in capitalist economies because it deprives the full transfer of the value of expended labour power within the commodity: "all wasteful consumption of raw material or instruments of labour is strictly forbidden, because what is wasted in this way represents a superfluous expenditure of quantities of objectified labour, labour that does not count in the product or enter into its value."[45] However, as I have suggested above, even within the most efficient capitalist production process, capitalism lacks the capacity to accurately limit the wastage of resources that are not priced effectively (this is at least one of the central causes and challenges associated with the environmental crisis that faces the globe). The cost of extraction for animals—the violent tussle of appropriation and commodification between human and animal that produces animals as bodies for exchange—is not priced within the exchange process; it is a true "free gift to capital."

However, a failure to avoid waste through inefficient pricing does not tell the whole story, since unpriced or ineffectively priced commodities may generate forms of value in exchange that are themselves not priced. In part, this is addressed through Marx's concept of "fetishism," where social relations determine exchange values as "the socio-natural properties of these things"[46] rather than the inherent utility value of the commodity in itself. Marx states that:

> ...the commodity-form, and the value relation of the products of labour within which it appears, have absolutely no connection with the physical nature of the commodity and the material [*dinglich*] relations arising out of this. It is nothing but the definite social relation between men themselves which assumes here, for them, the fantastic form of a relation between things.[47]

---

45   Marx. *Capital.* Vol. 1, 303.
46   Marx. *Capital.* Vol. 1, 165.
47   Marx. *Capital.* Vol. 1, 164–5.

Thus the relationship generated by a common system of valuation in exchange already has no essential connection to the original commodity; it relies upon social processes "between men" to generate value (and presumably, the artifice of sovereignty and law then guarantees the validity of contracts and exchange values). This fetishism hides within it a system of rights and entitlements that guarantee that the commodity will arrive with particular naturalised systems of domination already "taken for granted" and effectively non-priced. For example, although there may be no use value distinction between canvas boots and leather boots, social relations between humans will generate the exchange value difference between these two products, based upon perceived qualities of feel, durability etc. associated with leather. And thus, leather boots may always be "worth more" than canvas boots, in spite of no "real" or "intrinsic" use value difference, as a result of the social relations "between men" that generate exchange values. However, regardless of the final price of the boots, and regardless of whether leather boots can be demonstrated to possess an "inherent" use value which exceeds that of canvas, this value can never adequately account for the violence of its production, which, directly in the case of leather, includes loss of life. This violence is built into the price only through an extraction value accrued by "producers" (the cost of killing and skinning animals) and is not based upon the value of the life of the animal to their own selves (a value that is, by definition, impossible to price).

As above, death is exchanged for life through an imposition of value, not through any essential equivalence. Nor is this death exposed to a wider system of exchange, and therefore priced, since this death is not "put to market" (it exists before exchange). The violence of the production process arrives as an entitlement to domination: it is taken for granted and built into the value as an uncharged extra. The peculiar character of the fetish for this commodity—in this case leather—is tied unremittingly to the violence of its extraction. The sensuality of leather, its feel, its qualities, becomes fetishised in a seamless way that makes imperative the violence of its extraction, even if these same qualities already exceed a use value. In a simple sense, we do not *need* to wear leather boots—it is always surplus—and any expression of our need to wear leather already assumes that it is possible to exchange the life of animals for value through death. There is a pleasure and satisfaction in waste and excess that exceeds the limits of the rationalities of capitalist exchange, and this pleasure is not effectively priced because these benefits are "taken for granted" within the production process.

We might make sense of this when we consider the question of the efficiency of human slavery, and the potential costs and benefits associated with this production process. Slavery in a strict sense is less efficient than capitalism in so far as it leads to inefficiencies in the extraction of surplus value: for example, the slave owner must pay the slave a use value for labour (that is feed and house the worker) in order to continue to meaningfully extract value into the future. This ongoing use value is balanced against the market price of slaves (that is, a replacement cost). On the other hand, and as stated above, with respect to the "free worker" the capitalist has no obligation beyond the exchange value, and is thus free to pay a low wage regardless of whether the wage labourer might be able to feed themselves with this wage.[48] This is at least one of the specific efficiencies of capitalism over slavery as a production system: the immediate cost of the reproduction of labour power is displaced to workers themselves. However, the inefficiency in slavery as a mode of production hides the pleasurable forms of distinction, status differentiation and domination that accompany slavery and tie closely to social and political relationships throughout a society. In an important footnote in *Capital*, Marx observes:

> This is one of the circumstances which make production based on slavery more expensive. Under slavery, according to the striking expression employed in antiquity, the worker is distinguishable only as *instrumentum vocale* from an animal, which is *instrumentum semi-vocale*, and from a lifeless implement, which is *instrumentum mutum*. But he himself takes care to let both beast and implement feel that he in none of them, but rather a human being. He gives himself the satisfaction of knowing that he is different by treating the one with brutality and damaging the other *con amore*.[49]

What intrigues me here is that Marx very clearly draws distinctions between the worker, slave and the animal that highlights that we cannot make too easy a comparison between these three categories of productive agent, since their status orientations and benefits are mutually co-productive. Potentially, as Marx observes, one beats the other to maintain a lodging place in the hierarchical roles attributed to entities within productive processes. Species status distinctions are generated and maintained through the use of hierarchically downward forms of disciplinary violence.[50] This downward violence damages

---

48   See Marx. *Capital*. Vol. 1, "Appendix." 1033.

49   Marx, *Capital*. Vol. 1. 303–304, n18.

50   Indeed Marx may as well have been talking here about the dynamics of violence in maintaining regimes of racial superiority and inferiority, and their historical relationship to segmentation of human labour practices. Note the similarity here to Theodore W. Allen's argument that race is invented to divert conflict over inequality from class to race:

stock, compromises productivity, and is therefore, for Marx, a threat to productivity. However benefits accrue from domination itself. Following Foucault, I have understood freedom within the context of the war on animals as precisely the enjoyment of the unfreedom of animals. Capitalism does not price the enjoyment gained from dominating animals; on the contrary, it is discretely passed from appropriation to consumption at full value. This "free gift" is not priced because it prefigures and is taken for granted—silently, as it were, "subsumed"—in the production process. Death is exchanged for life imperceptibly. This free gift is already so abundant that it need not be priced beyond the cost of extraction; yet its enjoyment is fundamental to grounding the exchange value of the commodity. Humans want leather boots not because they need boots to be made out of leather, but because they *can* have them; it is a human "right" to enjoy leather boots, an enjoyment that hinges on a prerogative to remove the skin of the animal from its own back.[51] Turning again to slavery, while it may be true that "slavery is more expensive" as a production process where maximisation of exchange value is the goal, slavery, on the other hand, by enabling forms of domination unimaginable in a system of "contractual exchange" (that is, unpriced utility), generates symbolic and non material value that exceeds capitalist exchange and is passed through as an entitlement

---

...an all-pervasive system of racial privileges was conferred on laboring-class European-Americans, rural and urban, *exploited and insecure though they themselves were.* Its threads, woven into the fabric of every aspect of daily life, of family, church, and state, have constituted the main historical guarantee of the rule of the "Titans," damping down anti-capitalist pressures, by making "race, and not class, the distinction in social life." That, more than any other factor, has shaped the contours of American history—from the Constitutional Convention of 1787 to the Civil War, to the overthrow of Reconstruction, to the Populist Revolt of the 1890s, to the Great Depression, to the civil rights struggle and "white backlash" of our own day.

See Theodore W. Allen. "Summary of the Argument of *The Invention of the White Race* (Part Two)." *Cultural Logic: An Electronic Journal of Marxist Theory and Practice.* 1.2, 1998. At: www.clogic.eserver.org/1-2/allen2.html.

51   Note the final paragraph in Chapter 6 of *Capital*:

When we leave this sphere of simple circulation or the exchange of commodities, which provides the 'free-trader vulgaris' with his views, his concepts and the standard by which he judges the society of capital and wage-labour, a certain change takes place, or so it appears, in the physiognomy of our dramatis personae. He who was previously the money-owner now strides out in front as a capitalist; the possessor of labour-power follows as his worker. The one smirks self-importantly and is intent on business; the other is timid and holds back, like someone who has brought his own hide to market and now has nothing else to expect but—a tanning.

Marx. *Capital.* Vol. 1. 280.

to be enjoyed by all. A total domination allows for the possibility of waste, for a limitless surplus that is expended without a perception of excess, since it belongs to the foundations of social relations "between men" and underpins value almost imperceptibly.[52] I do not suggest, here, as a neoliberal economist might, that the solution lies in effective pricing;[53] rather it is merely important to note that waste and excess are connected to both modes of production and modes of domination, including—as in a civilisation/nature divide—the construction of an economy through a perception of a right to total domination of "nature" that precedes and is taken for granted in the process of exchange. Excess arrives when there is no need to negotiate terms, no need to limit

---

[52]   There is here room for a longer engagement with Marx's concept of surplus value and the way in which the construction of nature and what is "given" play out in exchange. Angela Mitropoulos observes:

> The conservative critique of capitalism is preoccupied...with taking capitalism to task for setting up crises of its own realisation, as in the expansion of debts that cannot—or will not—be repaid. It is concerned not with the question of moving beyond the interrelated dynamics of expansion and crisis, but of restoring the very foundations of capitalism in the retrieval of the conditions of gratuitous labour. This can be accomplished by way of a technological reorganisation of production that increases the intensity of exploitation, or by the extension of labour time—but it is always naturalised by recourse to the apparently archaic, biological or cultural definitions of obligation, debt and origin. The oikonomic nexus of family, nation and race delivers up the gift of free labour in its most forceful senses through the interrelated boundaries of the wage contract and those of citizenship (that is, the social contract). It does so in the forms of unpaid domestic labour; migrant labour that, by way of visa stipulations or outright criminalisation, is compelled to work for as little as possible; the geographic organisation of cheap and below subsistence labour; to mention the most notable. The oikonomics of present-day organisations of the economy is also apparent in what I referred to earlier as the expectation that women, as a consequence of their very identity as women, deliver a labour that has affective purchase, circulating as an extension of (rather than refusal of or indifference toward) care-giving domestic labour that significantly must appear as if it is not work at all, but freely and naturally given. Far from being marginal to the extraction of surplus labour, this expectation of a labour freely given has always been central to capitalist re/production.

> Angela Mitropoulos. *Contract and Contagion: From Biopolitics to Oikonomia.* Brooklyn: Minor Compositions, 2012. 164. I would add here that we have an additional challenge to imagine how the "free labour" (and free flesh) of animals is incorporated, traded and non priced with exchange.

[53]   In this regard, note Webster's statement: "If our wish is to achieve something of direct practical benefit to the animals, we need, in the spirit of Adam Smith, to make improved farm animal welfare consistent with our own self-interest. In short, we need to increase the *value* of the life of each farm animal; to them and to us." See Webster. "Farm Animal Welfare." 230.

violence, because there is no intrinsic value attached to the life of that which is taken for granted in the production process. It is therefore no surprise that Locke clearly states that slavery without contract, without bounds, is warlike:

> This is the perfect condition of *Slavery*, which *is* nothing else but *the State of War continued, between a lawful Conqueror and a Captive.* For if once *Compact* enter between them, and make an agreement for a limited Power on the one side, and Obedience on the other, the State of War and *Slavery* ceases as long as the Compact endures. For, as has been said, no Man can by agreement pass over to another that which he hath not in himself, a Power over his own Life.[54]

It is clear that animals have no contract; no compact that guarantees their protection from the perfect state of war. However, as Locke indicates, even a compact—which we might read as minimal welfare or indeed rights—obeys a logic of exception that merely suspends and holds in the balance the life and death terms of sovereignty. Here, perhaps surprisingly, we find Locke and Foucault in agreement. Again, as Foucault states, "the will to prefer life to death; that is what founds sovereignty." Rights cannot be founded upon the stated terms for capture by sovereignty. As I shall discuss later in this book, in order to disrupt power relations, rights must instead rupture a sovereign right of dominion.

---

54   Locke. *Two Treatises of Government.* 284–5, Book 2, §24.

PART 3

Private Dominion

∴

CHAPTER 5

Privatisation and Containment

...one could, as with an animal, *sympathize* with the colonized, even "love" him or her; thus, one was sad when he/she died because he/she belonged, up to a point, to the familiar world. Affection for the colonized could also be externalized in gestures; the colonized would have to, in return, render the master or mistress the same affection the mastermistress gave. But, beyond gesture, the master's/mistress's affection for the animal presented itself as an inner force that should govern the animal. In the Bergsonian tradition of colonialism, familiarity and domestication thus became the dominant tropes of servitude. Through the relation of domestication, the master or mistress led the beast to an experience such that, at the end of the day, the animal, while remaining what he/she was—that is something other than a human being—nevertheless actually entered the world for h*is/her master/mistress*.

> ACHILLE MBEMBE. *On the Postcolony.*[1]

As discussed in Chapter 4, Locke proposes a definition of property that is bound together with the active process of appropriating and establishing dominion. In other words, directed violence against another (human or otherwise) founds the property right. Locke uses the term "private dominion" to describe property as precisely the process of appropriating what was previously common and transferring it to a privatised form of control:

> The Law Man was under, was rather for *appropriating*. God Commanded, and his Wants forced him to *labour*. That was his *Property* which could not be taken from him where-ever he had fixed it. And hence subduing or cultivating the Earth, and having Dominion, we see are joyned together. The one gave Title to the other.[2]

Property is thus the outcome of a struggle that transfers a petty form of dominion to the subject, which is collectively securitised through sovereignty. This offers a useful way to understand the process by which humans individually assume and maintain a right to dominate animals. Locke here provides a template for comprehending how it is that the large scale conflict of the war against

---

1   Mbembe. *On the Postcolony.* 27.
2   Locke. *Two Treatises of Government.* Second Treatise. 292. §35.

animals can be privatised within individual fields of dominion. How is it that a right is earned for individuals to contain, maintain and regulate animals? To leash dogs, race horses, kill for food, experiment on, shoot for sport? And how does this right link, through a sophisticated interplay, with a large scale institutional and epistemic violence we might call "war"?

In order to make sense of this interplay of violence, one which links sovereignty with the individual human subject and in turn facilitates the ongoing conduct of war within the guise of apparent peace, I turn now to two examples that provide a conceptual basis for how we might understand this dynamic: firstly, the radical feminist[3] examination of rape as a form of warfare; and secondly,

---

3   I have sidestepped in this chapter the politics surrounding the radical feminist accounts and the challenges from more recent feminist interventions. One of the problems raised by more recent scholarship on the radical feminist accounts is the question of how to situate women's autonomy and agency within structures of violence and domination. We can see this problematic in the view put forward by some radical feminists that women learn and are taught to consent to forms of violation, and this process allows for an eroticisation of domination. John Stoltenburg, for example, argues that erotic s/m practices are in essence valorised acts of violence: he describes "sadism"—in his words, the "causing of pain, suffering, or death [that] is experienced by the person who commits those acts as genitally stimulating and orgasmically gratifying"—as the *eroticization of violence;*" and masochism—"a drive toward pain, abuse, degradation, and annihilation"—as the *eroticization of powerlessness."* See John Stoltenburg. "Sadomasochism: Eroticized Violence, Eroticized Powerlessness." *Against Sadomasochism: A Radical Feminist Analysis.* San Francisco: Frog in the Well, 1982. 124–30. 126. In a similar sense, Catharine MacKinnon argues that s/m replicates masculine power: "the relation dynamics of sadomasochism do not even negate the paradigm of male dominance, but conform precisely to it." See MacKinnon. *Toward Feminist Theory of the State.* 142. For Mackinnon, masculine power revolves around the "eroticization of dominance," something which, for her, problematises the of issue of consent:

> The deeper problem is that women that are socialized to passive receptivity; may have or perceive no alternative to acquiescence; may prefer it to the escalated risk of injury and the humiliation of a lost fight; submit to survive. Also, force and desire are not mutually exclusive under male supremacy. So long as dominance is eroticized, they will never be. Some women eroticize dominance and submission; it beats being forced (171).

These views put forward by radical feminists have been subject to more contemporary feminist critique. For example, Wendy Brown has argued that MacKinnon's account has failed to account for the ability of women to transform their own situation, foreclosing:

> one of the transformative possibilities held out by Marxism, by refusing to vest the class of women with the kind of power Marx vested in the proletariat: anxious not to sentimentalize femininity or female sexual power, she eliminates the very dynamic of social change on which Marx counted for in emancipatory praxis, namely that the class that is "in but not of society" harbors all of the productive force but none of the social or political power of society.

Mbembe's analysis of privatised sovereignty as a mechanism of domination within the "post-colony." Both examples *do not* concern non-human subjects directly; they relate, on the contrary, to understanding violence directed against human subjects by other humans. However, the profit that can be attained by exploring this detour is precisely in securing a means by which we might understand how war is normalised as peace, and the way in which an individual, privatised violence operates as norm within veiled forms of combat. Both examples I explore locate privatised dominion through a system of violence and containment. As such, in this chapter, I also explore containment as a strategy of war, and the way in which zones of containment might help define the micropolitical topography of the war against animals.

Violence and Privatised Government

That the systemic violence of rape must be understood as a form of structural combat is manifestly clear in military war, where sexual violence has been, and continues to be, utilised as a legitimised strategy of assault upon both women and men. War, as a period of all-out annihilatory violence, becomes, in this regard, the space for a routinised right to intense and numerously manifest micro-scale violences, where rape is legitimised as a somewhat "unavoidable" consequence of fighting.[4] In the context of war, rape can also be the biopolitical strategy utilised by an aggressing force for not only the capture and conquest of territory, but the creation of new citizenry. In this sense, sexual violence, like any other form of violence, can found sovereignty. The classical example of such violence was that visited upon the women of Sabine, who were captured as a stratagem for the breeding of a new generation of Romans, a strategy which it is said resulted in the "founding of Rome."[5] So mythologises Livy:

See Wendy Brown. *States of Injury: Power and Freedom in Late Modernity.* Princeton: Princeton University Press, 1995. 92.

4   In a recent episode that sparked international outrage, a public figure in Japan, Toru Hashimoto, offered a justification for the World War Two Japanese system of "comfort women" by suggesting that sexual slavery was required in order to maintain military discipline for fighting men. See Hiroko Tabuchi. "Women Forced Into wwii Brothels Served Necessary Role, Osaka Mayor Says." *New York Times.* May 13, 2013. At: www.nytimes .com/2013/05/14/world/asia/mayor-in-japan-says-comfort-women-played-a-necessary-role .html?_r=0.

5   Susan Brownmiller. *Against Our Will: Men, Women and Rape.* Harmondsworth: Penguin Books, 1976. 34. See also Norman Bryson. "Two Narratives of Rape in the Visual Arts: Lucretta

...at a given signal all the able-bodied men burst through the crowd and seized the young women. Most of the girls were the prize of whoever got hold of them first, but a few conspicuously handsome ones had been previously marked down for the leading senators, and these were brought to their houses by special gangs.[6]

The infamous rape/death camps in the former Yugoslavia functioned in a similar way, since the policy of "ethnic cleansing" was achieved not only through wholesale slaughter, but through the forced impregnation of women.[7] The women who had been made pregnant through rape where held "in custody until it... [was]...too late for the victims to get an abortion."[8] This war strategy is overtly biopolitical in nature: it aims to use violence to breed a new citizenry.[9]

However, sexual assault is not a predominately wartime activity. On the contrary, it operates incessantly as a form of violence that sits side by side with law during peacetime. The fact that rape is formally illegal does not mean that the law opposes, and actively campaigns against, sexual violence. Although the law frequently rhetorically opposes the routinised practice of sexual violence, the enforcement of the law in this regard has remained inconsistent. This is reflected in both the relatively low successful prosecution rates, and in the high percentage of rapes which remain unreported. One must also make note of the historical selectiveness exercised by the State in the enforcement of rape: for example, it has been technically possible in the past for a man to rape a non-virgin, or to rape his wife,[10] or to

---

and the Sabine Women." Sylvana Tomasell and Roy Porter Eds. *Rape: An Historical and Social Enquiry*. Oxford and New York: Blackwell, 1989. 152–73, 155–6; and Dimitris Papadopoulos and Vassilis Tsianos. "How to do Sovereignty Without People? The Subjectless Condition of Postliberal Power." *boundary 2*. Spring 2007. 135–172.

6   Livy. *The Early History of Rome*. London: Penguin Books, 2002. 41.

7   See Beverley Allen. *Rape Warfare: The Hidden Genocide in Bosnia-Herzegovina and Croatia*. Minneapolis: University of Minnesota Press, 1996. 62–5; and Catharine A. MacKinnon. "Rape, Genocide, and Human Rights." *Violence Against Women: Philosophical Perspectives*. Stanley G. French, Wanda Teays and Laura M. Purdy Eds. Ithaca: Cornell University Press, Ithaca and London, 1998. 43–54. 51.

8   Excerpt from Bassiouni Report, quoted in Allen. *Rape Warfare*. 77.

9   Agamben suggests that the forced impregnation in the Serbian rape camps were the product of a new biopolitical logic which had freed itself from a nationalistic/territorial anchoring for biological origin. See Agamben. *Homo Sacer*. 176.

10   See Julie A. Allison and Lawrence S. Wrightsman. *Rape: The Misunderstood Crime*. California: Sage, 1993. 195–218; Joceyln Scutt. "Judicial Vision: Rape, Prostitution and the 'Chaste Woman.'" *Without Consent: Confronting Adult Sexual Violence: Proceedings of a Conference Held 27–29, October 1992*. Patricia Weiser Easteal Ed. Canberra: Australian

rape another man[11] without this constituting illegal violence. Thus, although the law formally forbids sexual violence, the record of the State's enforcement of these laws leads to the conclusion that sexual violence remains a largely tolerated violence: something which feminist analysis on sexual violence has emphasised.[12]

As much as sexual violence may be characterised as tolerated by sovereign power, even integral to its bio-political strategy, it would be a mistake to suggest State sovereignty is the sole "beneficiary" of this violence. For sexual violence contributes to a different economy of power: namely, in moulding systemic relationships of sexuality and gender. In this sense sexual violence must be considered within the context of patriarchal power. This does not mean that men cannot be victims of sexual assault, since men can be subject to high rates of sexual assault within particular contexts such as prisons,[13] and young men and boys can experience relatively high rates of sexual assault. The normative binary construction of gender and sex categories is another factor to consider. As Dean Spade and others have argued, institutional and interpersonal violence against trans people is normalised within social apparatuses,[14] with trans people facing extraordinarily high levels of sexual violence.[15] Violence in these cases often works to mould and construct gender, and, as Judith Butler has argued, frames normative role performativity in such a way that the evolving text of performance prefigures, coincides and echoes a similarly evolving violent materiality: "the body which is torn apart, the wars waged among women, are *textual* violences, the deconstruction of constructs that are

Institute of Criminology, 1993. 173–87; and Megan Latham. "An Unreliable Witness? Legal Views of the Sexual Assault Complainant." Jan Breckenridge and Moira Carmody Eds. *Crimes of Violence: Australian Responses to Rape and Child Sexual Assault*. St Leonards: Allen and Unwin, 1992. 60–7.

11   Peter Poropat. "Sexual Assault of Males." *Without Consent: Confronting Adult Sexual Violence: Proceedings of a Conference Held 27–29, October 1992*. Patricia Weiser Easteal Ed. Canberra: Australian Institute of Criminology, 1993. 219–35.

12   See, for example, Donna Stuart. "No Real Harm Done: Sexual Assault and the Criminal Justice System." *Without Consent: Confronting Adult Sexual Violence: Proceedings of a Conference Held 27–29, October 1992*. Patricia Weiser Easteal Ed. Canberra: Australian Institute of Criminology, 1993. 219–35. 95–106.

13   See David. M. Heilpern. *Fear or Favour: Sexual Assault of Young Prisoners*. Lismore: Southern Cross University Press, 1998.

14   See, for example, Dean Spade. *Normal Life: Administrative Violence, Critical Trans Politics and the Limits of Law*. Brooklyn: South End Press, 2011.

15   See, for example, Rebecca L. Stotzer. "Violence Against Transgender People: A Review of United States Data." *Aggression and Violent Behavior*. 14.3 2009. 170–9.

always already a kind of violence against the body's possibilities."[16] Sexual violence territorialises gendered relations and establishes economies of pain and pleasure; in the context of patriarchy, sexual violence enables an economy of relations between men and women reiterating a normalisation of gendered categorisations.

My interest here is the way in which sexual violence as an individual act cooperates with a systematic form of oppression, and as such I explore below radical feminist accounts of sexual violence. These accounts highlight a conceptualisation of violence as serving a fundamental role in both the regulation of women's behaviour, and in the construction of the respective choices that men and women are able to make. As Ann J. Cahill states:

> The threat of rape…is a constitutive and sustained moment in the production of the distinctly feminine body. It is the pervasive danger that renders so much public space off-limits, a danger so omnipresent, in fact, that the "safety zone" women attempt to create rarely exceeds the limits of their own limbs and quite often falls far short of that radius. Women consider their flesh not only weak and breakable, but also violable.[17]

If we acknowledge that this violence is wholesale and enveloping in nature, and that it is perpetual rather than episodic, how might we describe it? How might we describe a violence that aims to hold its object in a state of perpetual fear; a fear that powerfully shapes actions; a fear that is frequently enlarged and maintained by acts of violence and death that organise conduct within gendered networks of power? Brownmiller argues in *Against Our Will* that rape "is nothing more or less than a conscious process of intimidation by which *all* men keep *all* women in a state of fear."[18] Brownmiller emphasises the fact that sexual violence permeates social relations; it replicates the conditions of war, even if official hostilities have ceased:

> A world without rapists would be a world in which women moved freely without fear of men. That some men rape provides a sufficient threat to

---

16   See Judith Butler. *Gender Trouble.* New York and London: Routledge, 2006. 172. In *Bodies That Matter*, Butler notes the circulatory of violence, knowledge and matter: "we may seek recourse to matter in order to ground or to verify a set of injuries or violations only to find that matter itself is founded through a set of violations, ones which are unwittingly repeated in the contemporary invocation." See Butler. *Bodies That Matter.* 5.

17   Ann J. Cahill. *Rethinking Rape.* Ithaca and London: Cornell University Press, 2001.161.

18   Brownmiller. *Against Our Will: Men, Women and Rape.* 15.

keep all women in a constant state of intimidation, forever conscious of the knowledge that the biological tool must be held in awe for it may turn to weapon with sudden swiftness born of harmful intent... Rather than society's aberrance of "spoilers of purity," men who commit rape have served in effect as front-line masculine shock troops, terrorist guerillas in the longest sustained battle the world has ever known.[19]

Other radical feminist theorists have provided a similar conceptualisation of rape as an enveloping form of warfare hidden under a cloak of civil peacability. We find, for example, this narrative present in Donna Stuart's analysis of sexual violence and the criminal justice system, where it is suggested that the violence perpetrated by men against women amounts to a "war against women,"[20] since acts of violence against women occur with high frequency, and form part of the bedrock of masculine power. Catharine MacKinnon argues that rape is "indigenous, not exceptional, to women's social condition" and is "not an isolated event or moral transgression or individual interchange gone wrong but an act of terrorism and torture within a systemic context of group subjection, like lynching."[21] For MacKinnon, State sovereignty becomes complicit with systemic violence against women, and MacKinnon argues that rape is aided and abetted by the State, underpinning the continuing right of men to perpetuate violence against women. Here, the law and norm meet in the construction of the social order:

> I propose that the state is male in the feminist sense. The law sees and treats women the way men see and treat women. The liberal state coercively and authoritatively constitutes the social order in the interest of men as a gender, through its legitimizing norms, relation to society, and substantive policies. It achieves this through embodying and ensuring male control over women's sexuality at every level, occasionally cushioning, qualifying, or de jure prohibiting its excesses when necessary to its

---

19   Brownmiller. *Against Our Will: Men, Women and Rape*. 209.

20   Stuart. "No Real Harm Done: Sexual Assault and the Criminal Justice System." 96. Susan Griffin states that "rape is a form of mass terrorism, for the victims of rape are chosen indiscriminately, but the propagandists for male supremacy broadcast that it is women who cause rape by being unchaste or in the wrong place at the wrong time—in essence, by behaving as though they were free." See Susan Griffin. "Rape: The All American Crime." Duncan Chappell, Robley Geis and Gilbert Geis Eds. *Forcible Rape: the Crime, the Victim, The Offender*. New York: Columbia University Press, New York, 1977. 47–66.

21   Catharine A MacKinnon. *Toward a Feminist Theory of the State*. Cambridge; Harvard University, 1989. 172.

normalization. Substantively, the way the male point of view frames an experience is the way it is framed by state policy.[22]

And thus there is an epistemic dimension to the "war."[23] For MacKinnon, one aspect of this is that the framing of the experience of violence through a male viewpoint means that women are excluded from routine protection from law by failing to qualify as "persons" in a normative sense: "...in the perspective of human rights, what is done to women is either too specific to women to be seen as human or too generic to human beings to be seen as about women."[24] Violence towards women is rendered as non-violence, while violation is rendered and made visible under law when directed against men: men's "suffering has the dignity of politics and is called torture."[25]

Where open military war promises an annihilatory violence accompanied by a seemingly unrestrained outburst of sexual violence—acts of sexual violence which, as suggested above, are treated as "an inevitable by-product"— "peace" on the other hand generates a more judicious and tactical use of sexual violence; a different type of war, no less. The end of open hostilities would draw to a close the open "rights" of violence available to the soldier; civility ushers a more strategic and guarded practice of sexual violence, one which procures effects of power, and maintains particular instances of domination by men over women—violent contestations—spread across the field of power. It is for this reason that some feminist commentators insist on the need to not arbitrarily separate between rape in "war" and rape in "peace," as International Criminal Law has done through high profile prosecutions of rape as a war crime.[26]

---

22   Catharine A. MacKinnon. "Feminism, Marxism, Method, and the State: Toward Feminist Jurisprudence." *Signs*. 8.4, 1983. 635–658. 644. MacKinnon states elsewhere that the "legitimacy of existing law is based on force at women's expense." See MacKinnon. *Toward a Feminist Theory of the State*. 249.

23   See MacKinnon. *Toward a Feminist Theory of the State*. 119–25.

24   Catharine A. MacKinnon. *Are Women Human? And Other International Dialogues*. Cambridge: Harvard University Press, 2006. 181.

25   MacKinnon. *Are Women Human?* 22.

26   See Kiran Grewal. "Rape in Conflict, Rape in Peace: Questioning the Revolutionary Potential of International Criminal Justice for Women's Human Rights." *Australian Feminist Law Journal*. 33, 2010. 57–80. Grewal comments:

    My concern remains that prosecutions for rape in conflict will only represent a truly revolutionary step forward for women's rights if linked to broader questions of violence against women: in war or in "peace". While I am clearly not alone in expressing this concern, my argument is that much of the feminist and human rights activism and scholarship on the ICTs [International Criminal Tribunals] and their prosecution

If sexual violence is a structural factor that means persistent fear and danger for women, in war or in peace, then the difference between war rape and peace rape lies in understanding the way in which heterogeneous institutional forms treat the same form of violence differently within different contexts. If power is a field of contestations consisting of points of open hostilities and other points of smaller resistances, then patriarchal power also describes a field of such contestations which includes a "continuum of violence"[27] directed at women. Some conflicts are represented by open acts of mass violence—hotspots of intense frictionality—such as the rape/death camps; while other conflicts are marked by a seemingly peaceable day to day existence, where violence occurs but is cloaked through epistemic and institutional mechanisms.

It is this very character of sexual violence—as seemingly everyday, as "private," as a "continuum," as detached from the sphere of "sovereign violence"—which provides the foundation for broader understanding of violence towards non-human animals. Both wars bear some similarity in terms of their conceptualisation. Both wars involve a daily struggle, one met by resistances, minor skirmishes, the actions of "terrorist guerillas"; a set of conflicts which we can assume involves no less consideration, analysis and strategy as those wars formally declared by a sovereignty. At any given moment this violence is occurring: an ongoing friction applied to different bodies in a range of contexts. This set of violences is one which epistemologically constructs its victims as offering a passive space or spaces upon which a violence is targeted; receptacles to be plundered.[28]

There are four possible lessons we might draw from this analysis of sexual violence as war for thinking about violence and domination towards non-human animals. Firstly, violence operates under the guise of peace through either official sanction or through the non responsiveness of law. In either case, State sovereignty remains complicit with the exercise of violence, and creates the possibility

---

of sexual violence has done little to displace the binary of "rape in conflict" and "rape in peace". Rather, all too often their efforts at reforming and improving international criminal justice institutions have actually focussed on the "exceptional" nature of the crimes being prosecuted. While this may lead to short-term gains in terms of those particular prosecutions and/or institutions, it then becomes unclear how this "exceptionality" can be overcome to allow for translation of gains into "peacetime." Whether in peace or in war, the recognition of women's fundamental right to sexual autonomy and bodily integrity seems to remain sadly elusive. (79).

27 Brownmiller. *Against Our Will: Men, Women and Rape.* 97.

28 As Sharon Marcus states, "the horror of rape is not that it steals something from us but that it makes us into things to be taken." Sharon Marcus. "Fighting Bodies, Fighting Words: A Theory and Politics of Rape Prevention." *Feminists Theorize the Political.* Judith Butler and Joan W. Scott Eds. London and New York: Routledge, 1992. 385–403.

for ongoing, systemic forms of domination. For women, inadequate legal processes work in concert with hegemonic cultures of violent masculinity, enabling and legitimating the continuing domination of women by men through the instrumentation of rape. For animals, the inadequacy of anti-cruelty and protection laws to prevent violence towards some animals (for example, "livestock" and experimental animals) is an explicit strategy of law to create the space where systemic violence might be enacted under the cloak of welfare and humane killing. Sovereignty here inculcates different forms of tolerated violence within the auspices of civil peaceability and the "rule of law," which aim to preserve and intensify domination through continuously evolving techniques of violence.

Secondly, there is an arbitrary distinction between war and peace that operates through a continuation of violence through heterogenous means. For women, the incidence of sexual violence is frequent, everyday and incessant, whether or not it occurs in a "formal" warzone. The setting and construction of violence may differ—ranging from the bedroom, a friend's party, a date, an abandoned street or park, to the war zone and the rape/death camp—however, the violence remains. Similarly, war does not stop for animals, regardless of the arrangements of civil institutions. Violence and coercion shape relations in a manifold way, again with the object of maintaining forms of domination. Continuing death and torture for many non-human animals are the mainstay feature of relations with humans; indeed peacetime stability in human civil arrangements can act to guarantee the increased efficacy of apparatuses of non-human domination, particularly in enabling humans to maximally enjoy a surplus of animal derived food, bodies to experiment upon, and cruelties to inflict in the name of sport through stabilised relations of containment and control.

Thirdly, the micropolitics of large scale violence requires a "privatisation" of the sovereign right to violence, through authorised, tolerated and taken for granted systems that facilitate precise, strategic and manifold applications of force. For women, this means that men, authorised or not, maintain a prerogative, either formally or informally, to use sexual violence as a continuing instrument of patriarchal domination. For non-human animals, "humans" are the shock troops: they privatise sovereignty over animals in order to maintain a manifold and intense economy of dominion over non-human animal life.

Finally, we might observe the convergence between feminist concerns in relation to violence experienced by women, and the concerns in this book expressed on violence against animals. There is of course a literature that draws links between feminism and animal advocacy,[29] including notably Adams'

---

29   See, for example, Lynda Birke. "Relating Animals: Feminism and Our Connections with Nonhumans." *Humanity and Society*. November 2007 31: 305–18.

groundbreaking contribution on feminism and meat consumption.[30] I draw attention in particular to Adams' own discussion of sexual violence against women, and "the cycle of objectification, fragmentation, and consumption, which links butchering and sexual violence in our culture."[31] Adams highlights the circulatory of an *episteme* that generates women as rape-able and meat as consumable, through a set of transformations between subject and object (Adams' own scheme suggests that this occurs through an "absent referent" where the original entity that might have been owed moral recognition is substituted for object[32]). Drawing from my discussion above, we might also observe that there is an interconnection between violence against women and violence against animals, not through a process where, for example, women are "dehumanised" as animals and this is the cause of their subjugation, but instead through a set of shared resources and technologies that allow modes of warfare to be conducted amidst stabilised and apparently peaceable relations. At least one of these innovations is the way in which violence can be organised and privatised upon a micropolitical level through institutional and cultural forces, so that each man can be constructed and armed as a possible subject wielding sexual violence as a threat; and each human fabricated and armed as a possible butcher.

This privatisation of violence is fundamental to understanding the micropolitics of sovereign dominion. In Chapter 1, I examined Mbembe's concept of necropolitics, as a description for the sovereign right to make suffer until the point of death; an antidote to the usual reading of biopower as involving the fostering of the life of populations. Although Mbembe's concern here is for understanding relationships between people, particularly in the context of communities after decolonisation, there is a strong applicability of these same concepts for understanding the zones of death and suffering which mark out

---

30   See Adams. *The Sexual Politics of Meat.* See also related work including Susanne Kappeler. "Speciesism, Racism, Nationalism...or the Power of Scientific Subjectivity." Carol J. Adams and Josephine Donovan Eds. *Animals and Women: Feminist Theoretical Explorations.* Durham and London: Duke University Press, 1995. 320–52 (particularly 324–7). On the criminological links between sexual violence and the killing of animals, see, for example, Amy J. Fitzgerald, Linda Kalof and Thomas Dietz. "Slaughterhouses and Increased Crime Rates: An Empirical Analysis of Spillover from 'The Jungle' into the Surrounding Community." *Organization and Environment.* 22, 2009. 158–84. On masculinity and violence towards animals see Brian Luke. *Brutal: Manhood and the Exploitation of Animals.* Urbana and Chicago: University of Illinois Press, 2007.

31   Adams. *The Sexual Politics of Meat.* 47. See particularly Chapter 2, "The Rape of Animals, The Butchering of Women." 39–6.

32   See Adams. *The Sexual Politics of Meat.* 41–2.

our relationships with some non-human animals. The precise authoritarian governmentality that inscribes the working of violent sites of interaction, such as the slaughterhouse and the experimental facility, fit closely with Mbembe's conceptualisation of necropolitical zones.

I turn now to consider Mbembe's discussion of privatised government, in his work *On the Postcolony*. We should be aware that consideration of animals, or more particularly the animalisation of persons as a necessary stage of colonial violence, is a significant focus of Mbembe's analysis. Indeed Mbembe notes, right at the outset of this work, that "discourse on Africa is almost always deployed in the framework (or in the fringes) of a meta-text about the *animal*."[33] He goes on to observe that:

> ...although the African possesses a self referring structure that makes him or her close to "being human," he or she belongs, up to a point, to a world we cannot penetrate. At bottom, he/she is familiar to us. We can give account of him/her in the same way we can understand the psychic life of the *beast*. We can even, through a process of domestication and training, bring the African to where he or she can enjoy a fully human life. In this perspective, Africa is essentially, for us, an object of experimentation.[34]

It is clear here that while Mbembe's overt concern is not for animals, we can no doubt recognise a close understanding of the dynamics of animalisation and the forms of sovereign dominion which compose an instrumental part of the relationship between humans and animals. In particular, the way in which Mbembe positions the animal not as an authentic classification based upon a biological or typological distinction, but rather as an entity that defines itself through a separation marked only by a presumption of dominion, corresponds to the analysis I have so far put forward. The animal is defined as such through a self-declared human prerogative to distinguish itself.

Mbembe, like Foucault, and like the feminist theorists of sexual assault described above, regard the distinction between war and peace as open for necessary analysis, observing that "discussion of the phenomenon of war must not ignore that distinction between a state of war and a state of peace is increasingly

---

33   Mbembe. *On the Postcolony*. 1.
34   Mbembe. *On the Postcolony*. 2.

illusory."[35] Reflecting on the effect of neo-liberalism on Africa from the 1980s onwards, where financial imperatives coincided with the violence of sovereignty within postcolonial states, Mbembe argues that a situation is produced where warfare and civility coincide:

> ...through the harshness of the extractions required, the redeployment of constraints, and the new forms of subjection imposed on the most deprived and vulnerable segments of the population, this form of government forces features belonging to the realm of warfare and features proper to the conduct of civil policy to exist in a single dynamic.[36]

Sovereignty reorganises itself; it does not disintegrate. Sovereignty shifts its topography to situate itself into forms that do not resemble the liberal democratic State in the Western tradition: power works by "establishing new forms of legitimate domination and gradually restructuring formulas of authority built on other foundations."[37]

A central dynamic for Mbembe is the "privatisation" of the means of government, including the diffusement of armed conflict into the locales of everyday life. Mbembe observes, in relation to the States he examines, that there is: "an increase in resources and labour devoted to war, a rise in the number of disputes settled by violence, a growth in banditry, and numerous forms of the privatization of lawful violence."[38] Here the State delegates authorities to use violence, which allows for a diffusion or "fractionation"[39] in the agents of coercion, creating a framework of *"indirect private government"*[40] away from a centralised apparatus and towards numerous devolved privatised entities:

> ...functions supposed to be public, and obligations that flow from sovereignty, are increasingly performed by private contractors for private ends. Soldiers and policemen live off the inhabitants; officials supposed

---

35   Mbembe. *On the Postcolony.* 89.

36   Mbembe. *On the Postcolony.* 74.

37   Mbembe. *On the Postcolony.* 76. As such, Mbembe counters the idea that African States represent "indicators of chaos" (76).

38   Mbembe. *On the Postcolony.* 76.

39   Mbembe. *On the Postcolony.* 74.

40   Mbembe. *On the Postcolony.* 80.

to perform administrative tasks sell the public service required and pocket what they get.[41]

Private terror goes unpunished: as Mbembe remarks, "no one is prosecuted for anything."[42] In this sense the diffusement of the right to violence creates justice that is openly identifiable as "corrupt."[43]

Here in Mbembe's outline of a system of privatised sovereignty, we find a reminder, both of the war against women described by some feminist theorists of rape, and the war against animals I have so far described in this book. For Mbembe the right to wage war, that traditional sovereign right, cannot be separated from a privatised form of domination. A private right to wage war informs the history of sovereignty; it is its genealogy:

> The establishment of a centralized apparatus was part of a long shift from the right to wage private war—a right claimed and exercised, down to the Middle Ages, by feudal lords—to the idea that monopoly on the right to wage war belonged to the king as sovereign and responsible for public order.[44]

In this respect, Mbembe aligns closely with Foucault's understanding of politics as war by other means. But we might extend this understanding further. There is here a dual process, which provides both an outline for the conduct of war within civil society and, simultaneously, a genealogical trace in relation to the complicity of political sovereignty, at least as it is imagined in the West, and the experience of domination of non-human animals. As I have discussed, sovereignty creates the capacity to internalise forms of intense violence within the guise of civil peaceability. It performs this function in part through law and exception, but in particular through the privatisation of the right to wage war; a fractionation of its own sovereign power. Thus when women are unable to safely or confidently seek justice in relation to sexual violence; when the local police station receives funding support from a trans-national corporation, or

---

41   Mbembe. *On the Postcolony*. 80.

42   Mbembe. *On the Postcolony*. 82.

43   Corruption here functions in the same way as excess (as discussed in Chapters 3 and 4); indeed there is in all probability no difference between corruption and excess, in so far as they reflect the operation of dominion which sculpts principles of ethics and justice in their favour. In this sense corruption is not a normative category but a descriptor for the operation of an economy and sovereignty that distributes benefits on a discriminatory basis.

44   Mbembe. *On the Postcolony*. 91.

where anti-cruelty laws contain an exception for animals in experimental laboratories, there is in each of these instances a privatisation of sovereignty, which shifts a right for coercive force from a centralised apparatus to a privatised entity (to men, to private corporations, to human experimenters). Privatisation of sovereign power is not necessarily better or worse than a centralised monopolisation. However, this dynamic is important for understanding the nature of interpersonal and "private" dominion over animals, as it is excercised in an everyday sense. It is through a mode of private sovereignty, "private dominion" as Locke might put it, minutely fractionated and disseminated through the populace, that humans gain their life and death powers over non-human animals. This is an individualised power, a personal prerogative exercised with respect to animals across diverse fields, including animals that meet the knife in the slaughterhouse, animals tormented in experimental facilities, or animals at the end of a leash in suburban backyards. The right to wage war may or may not be confirmed through legislation and sovereign exceptions, it may or may not be tempered through ethics and regulation. The important thing to note here is that this right to wage war does not rely on the functioning of a centralised apparatus. Human sovereignty over non-human animals operates through diffusement and transmission.

Indeed it is worth emphasising again that human violence towards animals comes before State authority; the latter which it would appear merely enables and securitises a pre-existing right. For, as I have discussed with reference to Locke, the genealogy of human sovereignty over non-human animals is bound up with the privatised right to violence. A private right to domination of non-human animals precedes State sovereignty in the civil political sense. The law only arrives to confirm and authorise a privatised violence that was taken for granted before the arrival of the State: "thus this law of reason makes the deer that Indian's who hath killed it; it is allowed to be his goods who hath bestowed his labour upon it, though, before, it was the common right of every one."[45] The right to individualised violence over animals, in this sense, is like the individual right to property. It is tempered by State sovereignty, but sovereign power does not stand in the way of this right; on the contrary, its objective is to facilitate it, to securitise it, to ensure that it endures. As described by Locke, property in animals comes through a private struggle of appropriation; the role of the State is to secure a continuing right to this victory. It is for this reason that it makes no sense to think of human sovereignty through a centralised control apparatus like the civil political State. The State offers stability, authorisations, mechanisms of control and regulation, but it also exists to confirm an originary

---

45   Locke. *Two Treatises of Government*. Second Treatise. 289. §30.

"human right:" namely, the right to dominate animals in private, a right that constitutes a continuing spoil of war. State sovereignty merely stabilises the practice of human sovereignty over animals.

Containing War

Harry Harlow's experiments with rhesus monkeys are familiar within animal advocacy discussions.[46] One particular experiment described by Harlow and his collaborators was the "pit" or "well" of despair. Three month old monkeys were separated from their mothers and placed in a confined receptacle for periods of up to nine months. The "vertical chamber apparatus" was designed specifically to induce depression in their captives:

> A radically different approach to the production of depressive behaviour in monkeys, one that did not involve any social attachments, was made possible by a vertical chamber apparatus created by H.F. Harlow. This apparatus...is a stainless steel chamber with sides that slope downward to a wire-mesh platform above a rounded steel bottom. Depression in humans has been characterised as a state of "helplessness and hopelessness, sunken in a well of despair," and the chambers were designed to reproduce such a well for monkey subjects. Although the confined monkeys are free to move about in three dimensions within the chamber, and although they eat and drink normally and maintain proper weight, within a few days they typically assume a huddled, immobilized posture in the corner of the apparatus.[47]

The research, which provided evidence of the deep emotional effects of isolation and failed connectivity with other beings, also highlights the logic of scientific experimentation on non-human animal life: a logic which allows for precise, encompassing and enduring regimes of violence to capture and painfully manipulate the captive body. *Containment* here is a technology of violence. Zoë

---

46   See Singer's discussion in *Animal Liberation*. Also see Charles S. Nicoll, Sharon M. Russell, and Audrey Lau, reply by Peter Singer. "'Animal Liberation:' An Exchange." *The New York Review of Books.* 5 Nov 1992.

47   H.F. Harlow, M.K. Harlow, S.J. Suomi. "From Thought to Therapy: Lessons from a Primate Laboratory." W.G. Van der Kloot, C. Walcott and B. Dane. *Readings in Behaviour.* 529–40. 537. See also Deborah Blum. *The Monkey Wars.* New York: Oxford University Press, 1994. 79–103; and Donna Haraway. *Primate Visions: Gender, Race and Nature in the World of Modern Science.* New York: Routledge, 1989. 242.

Sofia argues that enveloping or containing systems are often overlooked as technologies, and that "holding" need not be regarded as a passive activity; rather as "a complex action."[48] In this sense, containers, including Harlow's "Pit of Despair," may be regarded as intelligent facilitative systems, and the gateway to other containment technologies (as a link in a process of "supply"). We might conventionally think of a containment system as essentially a "nurturing" space, which might allow for care and subsistence. However, Harlow's containers invert the potential nurturing space through a concentrated violence that ruptures a settled association between containment, facilitation and care.[49]

We normally associate war with a lack of containment, as an occasion for unrestrained, and free bloodletting, where the borders of war are only limited by the imagination and daring of its participants. Although international humanitarian law has sought to place limits on what is acceptable in war, as the history of warfare in the twentieth century demonstrates—from the development of incendiaries and land mines to the routine slaughter of civilians—any sense of restraint according to what may be right or just in war is largely nonexistent. Yet containment is often inherent to the tactics of war. In the *Art of War*, for example, Sun Tzu stresses that a good general will adopt a strategy that will force the enemy to respond; and not the other way round.[50] A military tactician will use force to alter the environment around the enemy, thus constraining the choices the enemy can make within combat: in other words, to *contain* their decisions within an increasingly constrained set of options, that appear more closely to approximate a choice between life or death. The choice to con-

---

48   See Zoë Sofia. "Container Technologies." *Hypatia*, 15.2, 2000. 181–201, 191.

49   Note that Elaine Scarry defines this inversion as one of the characteristics of torture, where everyday items of civility are turned into weapons:

> Just as all aspects of the concrete structure are inevitably assimilated into the process of torture, so do the contents of the room, its furnishings, are converted into weapons: the most common instance of this is the bathtub that figures prominently in the reports from numerous countries, but is only one among many. Men and women tortured during the period of martial law in the Philippines for example, described being tied or handcuffed in a constricted position for hours, days, and in some cases months to a chair, to a cot, to a filing cabinet, to a bed: they describe being beaten with "family-sized soft drink bottles" or having a hand crushed with a chair, or having their heads "repeatedly banged on the edges of a refrigerator door" or "repeatedly pounded against the edges of a filing cabinet." The room both in its structure and its content, is converted into a weapon, deconverted, undone.

Scarry. *Body in Pain*. 40–1.

50   Sun Tzu. *The Art of War*. Sonshi.com, 1999–2011.
At: https://www.sonshi.com/original-the-art-of-war-translation-not-giles.html. Chap. 5. "Force."

tinue to enjoy life will guide the actions of the opponent. This does not mean that containment as a strategy aims at simply entrapping its object within a container. Strategy aims instead towards creating a constraining environment that will guide the opponent eventually towards complete capitulation. It is perhaps for this reason that allowing movement reduces the potential costs associated with capturing an aggravated enemy who may strike out in desperation. Better to exhaust an enemy by gradually constraining the choices available. Thus Sun Tzu urges that when surrounding an enemy "leave an outlet; do not press an enemy that is cornered."[51] Perhaps the exception to this principle is the siege, which aims at a complete and inescapable containment of the enemy. Laying siege usually rests on encircling through a circumvallation of the *container* of the enemy, such as the fortress, the encampment or the city. In this sense the siege uses force to contain the container. The siege seeks to disrupt the functioning of the container by breaking its connections to networks outside of its borders. As supplies of food, water, resources and communication dry up, the facilitative space offered by the fortress under siege begins to deteriorate. The siege as a containing strategy offers the inverse of the nurturing containing space that facilitates the living being(s) within; the siege, on the other hand, presents itself as a container of death aimed at draining the networks within of their resources.

While containment may be regarded as an instrumental strategy of war, I am more interested in how violent containment may operate within less spectacular fields of operation, away from the overt forms of annihilation found in the military warzone. Mbembe in some senses has already described this particular form of siege warfare in the case of colonial occupation:

> The state of siege is itself a military institution. It allows a modality of killing that does not distinguish between the external and the internal enemy. Entire populations are the target of the sovereign. The besieged villages and towns are sealed off and cut off from the world. Daily life is militarized. Freedom is given to local military commanders to use their discretion as to when and whom to shoot. Movement between the territorial cells requires formal permits. Local civil institutions are systematically destroyed. The besieged population is deprived of their means of income. Invisible killing is added to outright executions.[52]

---

51   See Sun Tzu. *The Art of War.* Chap 7. At https://www.sonshi.com/original-the-art-of-war-translation-not-giles.html.

52   Mbembe. "Necropolitics." 30.

Within these civilian zones, containment serves the function of not only generating a micropolitical environment of immanent force for those interned within these containers, but *further*, enables the violence within the container to be concealed, and presents from the outside as a space of civil peace-ability, shielding the concentrated violence within its interior. The devious beauty of this container is that its operations are so effective that overt forms of violence are seen as not violent; in other words, the container contains what would otherwise be seen as violence, by renaming it as something else.

One example of a container of violence is the human prison. This apparatus is, after all, a series of containers—that is, cells—themselves contained within a fortified container, sealed hermetically, it would seem, from the operations of civil society. The prison compartmentalises and concentrates the legal violence of the State. It is the close confines of these walls that generate the necessary hopelessness and brutality that, it is hoped, will reform the prisoner. This is a slow violence that uses capture and seemingly infinite duration to exact force on the inmate. This is a violence that does not need to strike the body, but produces effects on the body by absolutely containing possibility. This is a violence that, in perverse way, cares.[53] Importantly, as far as the prison is concerned, this is a secret violence, a concentrated set of forces that is hidden and operates in silence. This is part and parcel of the historical shift from the spectacle of the scaffold to the disciplinary apparatus that Foucault describes in *Discipline and Punish*. Foucault notes that this means that today we are more likely to be interested in the processes that precede punishment—that is, crime, capture, trial and sentence—rather than the punishment itself:

> Punishment...will tend to become the most hidden part of the penal process... As a result justice no longer takes public responsibility for the violence that is bound up in its practice. If it too strikes, if it too kills, it is not as a glorification of its strength, but as an element of itself that it is obliged to tolerate, that it finds difficult to account for.[54]

In other words, the container of the prison not only functions to remove its inmates from civil society, but to remove from sight, and responsibility, the violence that is inherent to its functioning. And this of course accounts for the usual failure to recognise the prison as a site of violence, as an apparatus

---

53   Saying this, I am aware that to call the prison a caring container is to rupture the usual sense of the word "care". This is a care that only facilitates a bare existence, which holds the biological body within a cradle of violent forces.

54   Foucault. *Discipline and Punish*. 9.

designed to assault the body with capture, rather than a benign institution for rehabilitation as it is more often portrayed. Indeed, as Foucault hints at in this section of *Discipline and Punish*, the shift of focus away from the violence of punishment will act to hide from view and remove from responsibility any sort of violence that is attached to the prison as an apparatus—violence in this sense is treated as an aberration, rather than inherent to the system.[55]

Extending upon this, there is arguably a link between the growth of the prison as an institution for punishment, and the evolution in the practice of torture over the last century. The prison is closely related to the logic of modern torture; the power to contain, to secret away bodies, provides modern torture its efficacy. Darius Rejali's work on torture in Iran is an important contribution in this regard.[56] He finds that despite the fact that contemporary instances of torture appear, in practice, to resemble the classical tortures, today torture obeys distinctly modern imperatives. Modern torture has become an institutional practice that takes place within the apparatuses of disciplinary power: in Rejali's words, "modern torture is private and not public. It takes place in the basements of prisons and detention centres."[57] Disciplinary power did not so much remove torture from the penal apparatus, but reinvested it within a new context. Today's torturers have at their fingertips evolving knowledges and technologies to enable the indefinite and painful continuation of life. The institutional apparatuses which administer the torture of bodies require not only the services of official torturers (guards, interrogators etc.), but the concentrated and planned deployment of medical, bureaucratic and psychological expertise. Underlying these developments in the smart space of the torture complex is the capacity for these practices to occur in silence, to be

---

55   Perhaps an obvious example of this is prison sexual violence. Most of the research in this area indicates that somewhere between 20–40% of male prisoners will be raped while in prison, with many prisoners experiencing ongoing sexual assault throughout their incarceration. Yet, though the high incidence of sexual assault is known—even joked about—its existence has not prompted members of the public or government to consider the relationships between sexual assault and incarceration. Indeed, one commentator observes: "so accepted is... [prison sexual]...assault as part of prison life that an outsider might conclude that on some basic, if unarticulated level, we think it an appropriate element of the punishment regimen." See Robert Weisburg and David Mills. "Violence Silence: Why No One Really Cares About Prison Rape." *Slate*. 1st October 2003. At: www .slate.com/id/2089095/.

56   In Rejali's words "Neither Foucault, nor the humanists can advance a satisfactory explanation for the return to torture, much less the features that characterise it." See Rejali. *Torture & Modernity*. 15.

57   Rejali. *Torture & Modernity*. 13.

hidden from view. Where the old tortures on the scaffold were scrupulously public affairs, today torture occurs behind thick walls that muffle screams and denies any recognition of the pain of punishment. People disappear into the night; bodies are disappeared at the end of the process: in between there is a mute silence. The logic of torture is, perhaps more than ever, tied to its necessary containment.

As I discussed in Chapter 1, Pachirat identifies containment and segmentation as instrumental to understanding the topography of industrialised killing of animals. This slaughter machine requires the capacity to shield from vision not only the totality of killing itself, but through the segmentation of each stage of the killing process, human workers and animals become almost obliviously unaware of the horrors—clean or bloody—that inhabit each room adjacent to them: "yet even on the kill floor itself, the site where one might least expect the realities of killing to be sequestered, immediate and visceral confrontation with the work of industrialised killing is neutralized through a division of labor that finds its sensory expression in a meticulous partitioning of space."[58] Bruno Latour argues that the interaction of humans and non-humans in networks or collectives may be described organisationally as a system of "black boxes."[59] Complex organisations are by and large anonymous in their operation: collections of entities usually do not reveal themselves until the moment in which they break down, when the "black box" must be "opened." Open the black box, and a range of entities within a relational network spill out; step back from the black box and one merely has one component, sealed, and apparently unitary in organisation.[60] We can note that the black box is a container for relational networks, but a container that lacks transparency to those that are connected with it. There are of course many relational networks that conform to this definition—bureaucracies being a clear example—but it is possible to see that the prison apparatus in particular relies on black boxing. Its logic of operation is to hide the violence of it internality.[61]

---

58   Pachirat. *Every Twelve Seconds.* 84.

59   Latour. *Pandora's Hope.* 183–5.

60   Latour. *Pandora's Hope,* 183–5. Latour provides the example of an overhead projector. To us, from the outside, this device is simply a unitary box that conceals its inner functionings. We might never question what networks are in operation inside the overhead projector—we turn it on, it works, and we don't need to question further. Perhaps the only time we might ask a question of its internality is when it fails: the technicians are called in and we discover it is full of parts that connect to each other, which in turn are worlds in themselves.

61   The black box is also a socio-politico-juridical zone of exception in the sense in which Agamben describes. We should be able to recognise here the connection between *exception* and the container of violence and its relationship to the civil space. The container of

Returning to Harlow's experiment, we might perceive the "pits of despair" as precisely located mechanisms designed to internalise war upon the body of the contained living entity. Harlow's earlier experiments with rhesus monkeys already illustrate the distinctly carceral nature of the isolation techniques: "during the prescribed sentence in this apparatus, the monkey has no contact with any animal, human or subhuman."[62] However, the later experiments using the more extreme "vertical chamber apparatus" appeared to more fully complete the art of war: they aimed, quite simply, to break their internees. A simple "V" shaped apparatus with a mesh top prevents movement and aims to extinguish any hope of release. The experimenters—William McKinney, Stephen Suomi and Harlow—describe the design of the chambers in "poetic" terms:

> This rather unusual-appearing apparatus was partially designed on an intuitive basis to simulate those features of depression poetically described as "being in the depths of despair," "sunken in a well of loneliness," "helplessness and hopelessness." A monkey can move about in the chamber, but it does him little good. It was postulated that a chambered monkey would soon cease trying to gain contact with the outer world and give up in despair.[63]

Despite clear results for the experimenters in "producing abnormal behaviour" and prompting "psychopathological disturbance in a much shorter period of time" than previously trialled forms of social isolation, the experimenters still suggest caution in interpreting the results, arguing that when there "is a better understanding of the factors producing the abnormal behavior it should be possible to make more explicit human analogies."[64] Whether or not such experiments are capable of yielding anything of value for providing information to humans about themselves is always epistemologically open to question;

---

violence is that space that is both excluded and included, removed at the same time captured. The juridical power of exception finds its physical form in the container of violence: from the prison, to the camp to the detention center. Bare life may be characterised as the emergent entity produced by this smart, albeit violent, space.

62   Harry F. Harlow, Robert O. Dodsworth and Margaret K. Harlow. "Total Social Isolation in Monkeys." *Proceedings of the National Academy of Sciences of the United States of America.* 54.1, 1965. 90–97. 90.

63   William T. McKinney, Stephen J. Suomi and Harry F. Harlow. "Vertical-chamber Confinement of Juvenile-Age Rhesus Monkeys. A Study in Experimental Psychopathology." *Archives of General Psychiatry.* 26.3, 1972. 223–28. 223.

64   McKinney, Suomi and Harlow. "Vertical-Chamber Confinement of Juvenile-Age Rhesus Monkeys." 227.

however, as a means to identify the ideal template for war as a perfectly contained, hermetically sealed assault on the captured body, this summarises, perhaps most efficiently, Clausewitz's pronouncement that war is *"an act of violence to compel our opponent to fulfil our will."* The experimenters aimed at producing absolute despair; the experiment verified the epistemic reality that the procedure sought to attain.

It would be a mistake to separate out Harlow's experiments as an exception to what we might otherwise believe are benign forms of containment. On the contrary, we must topographically understand systems of animal domination as comprising a set of interlinked partitions that constrain and enable nonhuman animals lives with varying degrees of intensity, according to essentially discriminatory and arbitrary distinctions relating to species type and relevant human utility.[65] Concentrated forms of containment that maintain life for the purposes of large scale slaughter—such as concentrated animal feeding operations (CAFOS)—are linked to supply systems that enable the consumption of vast resources to generate animal bodies, and coordinated supply chains to exit animals, through road and rail transportation, conveyor belts and "curved corrals" to the next smart container: the slaughterhouse. Logistical precision and a "just in time" approach to stock management will maximise profits. In experimental labs, thousands and sometimes hundreds of thousands of rats and mice are contained to be fed, machine like, into a variety of experimental procedures. Where animals do not die in experiments, they will be killed when their human use life is over and incinerated: a life spent moving between containers, from birth to death. But the examples of the CAFO and the experimental lab are both detached from everyday urban realities. The containing effects

---

65   Thus Harlow's experiments with the "vertical chamber apparatus" might as easily be placed next to other experiments in topological distribution of life, including the "nuclear family apparatus," designed by Harlow to regulate the movements of male and female monkeys in order to enforce monogamy. See Haraway. *Primate Visions.* 240–1. Note also the role of containment and social segmentation in Foucault's identification of the emergence of an "inside" response to plague. Where lepers were death with through exclusion, Foucault argues that the plague was dealt with through a process of internalisation, enclosure, surveillance and discipline:

> Plague is the moment when the spatial partitioning and subdivision (*quadrillage*) of a population is taken to its extreme point, where dangerous communications, disorderly communities, and forbidden contacts can no longer appear. The moment of the plague is one of an exhaustive sectioning (*quadrillage*) of the population by political power, the capillary ramifications of which constantly reach the grain of individuals themselves, their time, habitat, localization, and bodies.

See Foucault. *Abnormal.* 47.

of war can be felt much closer to home: the suburban household is also a site for privatisation and containment. For example, some 63% of households in Australia own a pet, a nation with reputedly one of the highest rates of pet ownership in the world; in this same nation 35.8% of households own a dog.[66] The same report finds that eight million birds are owned, and over eighteen million ornamental fish were imported into Australia in 2009.[67] The containment devices within homes—backyards, fish tanks, bird cages—must be understood as connected to the other forms of containment that regulate animal location and movement. Life begins in breeding farms which are linked to the property market through pet stores, which are then linked to suburban homes; at each stage one containment device supplies the other in a sealed system of circulation that attempts to minimise any leakage. Feral animal hunters and urban shelters provide the means to mop up any failures in the containment and supply system; the latter offering another form of containment, although more concentrated. Animals that cannot be contained within this apparently neat topographic system are ruthlessly extinguished: streets are patrolled, stray animals quarantined and euthanised if they are not claimed. These clear vectors of control that accompany the segregated urban landscape are perhaps the reason that Jennifer Wolch suggests, in her famous piece "Zoöpolis," a need for a:

> ...critique of urban planning as part of the modernist project of control and domination of others (human as well as non human) through rationalist city building and policing of urban interactions and human/animal proximities in the name of human health and welfare.[68]

The urban spheres of the West represent a "gulag archipelago" (or from Foucault, a "carceral archipelago") of interlinked forms of containment, delegated authorities, everyday violences and surveillances; a system of "grand" apartheid supported by an equally precise system of everyday "petty" apartheid.

As I have discussed, Clausewitz makes the famous pronouncement that "war is policy pursued by other means." Foucault reverses this same phrase in

---

66   Australian Companion Animal Council. *Contribution of the Pet Care Industry to the Australian Economy*, 2006. 17. The rates of dog ownership compares to 40% of households in the United States.

67   Australian Companion Animal Council. *Contribution of the Pet Care Industry to the Australian Economy*. 17.

68   Jennifer Wolch. "Zoöpolis." Jennifer Wolch and Jody Emel Eds. *Animal Geographies: Place, Politics and Identity in the Nature-Culture Borderlands*. London: Verso, 1998. 119–38. 127–8.

his own pronouncement: "politics is war pursued by other means." Civility relies on the capacity to not so much remove from politics the violence of war, but ruthlessly contain violence, in such a way as for it not to rupture the smooth peaceful connectivities found within the civil space that attempt to establish a seamless epistemological terrain. In this sense civil society might be considered as a mutually agreed containment of the violence of war. Perhaps, to rephrase Clausewitz (and Foucault): "politics is war effectively contained."

CHAPTER 6

Companionship

...about halfway through our long captivity, for a few short weeks, before
the sentinels chased him away, a wandering dog entered our lives. One
day he came to meet this rabble as we returned under guard from work.
He survived in some wild patch in the region of the camp. But we called
him Bobby, an exotic name, as one does with a cherished dog. He would
appear at morning assembly and was waiting for us as we returned, jump-
ing up and down and barking in delight. For him, there was no doubt we
were men.

EMMANUEL LEVINAS, *"The Name of a Dog, or Natural Rights."*[1]

In New South Wales, an Eastern border state of Australia, a *Companion Animals
Act 1998* regulates how domestic pets (particularly dogs) are to be kept in order
"to provide for the effective and responsible care and management of companion animals" (Section 3A).[2] The legislation offers a comprehensive framework
for the control of dogs within the bounds of human civil society, including
provisions for the compulsory identification of dogs by microchipping, with
specific instructions on how surveillance devices are to be installed in the body
of dogs.[3] The legal framework also places responsibility on dog owners to
control dogs in public spaces (Section 13), prevent defecation in those public
spaces (Section 20) and prohibit taking dogs into some public spaces
(Section 14). Further responsibilities include for dog owners to not encourage
dogs to attack (Section 16) with relevant powers for seisures of dogs who attack
people (Section 17).[4] The legislation creates the category of "nuisance dog,"
defined amongst other things as a dog that is "habitually at large" (Section 21(1)
(a)),[5] or a dog that "repeatedly defecates on property (other than a public
place) outside the property on which it is ordinarily kept" (Section 21(1)(c)) or

---

1   Emmanuel Levinas. "The Name of a Dog, or Natural Rights." Peter Atterton and Mathew
    Calarco Eds. *Animal Philosophy: Ethics and Identity.* New York: Continuum, 2004. 47–50. 49.
2   New South Wales. *Companion Animals Act 1998.*
3   The legislation states that "the implantation is to be subcutaneous in the dorsum between
    the scapulae in such a way that the microchip lies at an oblique angle to the plane of the
    skin." *Companion Animals Regulation 1999.* Part 2, Clause 6(1).
4   NSW. *Companion Animals Act 1998.*
5   Stephen Best's tracing of the relationship of the fugitive slave with the conceptualisation of
    property appears relevant here. See Best. *The Fugitive's Properties.*

© KONINKLIJKE BRILL NV, LEIDEN, 2015 | DOI 10.1163/9789004300422_008

"repeatedly causes substantial damage to anything outside the property on which it is ordinarily kept" (Section 21 (1) (f)).[6] The legislation allows for the identification of "dangerous dogs," which is defined amongst other things, as a dog which "without provocation, attacked or killed a person or animal (other than vermin)" (Section 33 (1)(a)).[7] Dangerous dogs may be subject to "control orders" (Section 47(1)), with the legislation allowing for the "destruction" of dogs in particular circumstances.[8] The law also creates a category of "restricted dogs", with the sale, importation, and reproduction of some breeds strictly forbidden.[9] Restricted and dangerous dogs are required to be compulsorily desexed.[10]

The range of measures described above are intensive in scope. They involve compulsory body modification, regimes of surveillance, and controls over movement and bodily function. The laws are discriminatory. They allow for the categorisation of certain dogs, with reproductive controls and death for some dogs a certain outcome of this regime. Arguably these apparatuses of control are designed to enable a tolerated "companionship." They facilitate the possibility of dogs sharing space with humans by using coercive restraint methods to control for any unintended effects that might arise from an unregulated friendship between humans and animals, particularly that which might exceed the bounds of human utility. Although these measures of control are unremittingly acute—we might suggest, and without hyperbole, they display a focused hostility towards their object—they are at the same time seemingly everyday. The *Companion Animals Act 1998* is in many ways an unremarkable piece of legislation: its apparent quotidian civility might make us believe that this set of laws is aimed at facilitating friendship between humans and animals. The fact that arbitrary controls and discriminatory provisions are tolerable, and enacted without any means of review, already presupposes that they merely confirm a truth—a right of domination, the freedom to enjoy an other's unfreedom—is self evident and is not open to question. Importantly, within this framework of force relations, humans (as opposed to just the State) are offered *privatised*

---

6   Note that although a nuisance dog may be a dog that endangers the health of another animal, it is not considered a nuisance if it endangers the health or attacks "vermin"...or... "an animal...in the course of droving, tending, working or protecting stock." NSW. *Companion Animals Act 1998.*

7   NSW. *Companion Animals Act 1998.*

8   NSW. *Companion Animals Act 1998.*

9   NSW. *Companion Animals Act 1998.* See Division 4 and 5.

10 NSW. *Companion Animals Act 1998.* See Division 4 and 5. See Clare Palmer's discussion of de-sexing of pets in Clare Palmer. "Killing in Animal Shelters." The Animal Studies Group. *Killing Animals.* Urbana and Chicago: University of Illinois Press, 2006. 182–4.

forms of dominion over animals. It is up to dog owners to restrain their dogs; to prevent them from being a risk to others; to force dogs to comply with relevant regulations, including physically violent interventions such as microchipping and desexing. Thus, sovereignty flows between the State and its delegates through macropolitical and micropolitical control apparatuses representing an interplay between State sovereignty, human subjects, and their non-human "companions." Human sovereignty over animals, and the dominion that flows from this presumption, rests upon an intricately regulated, and closely guarded, privatised right of violence.

How is it possible to imagine friendship with animals within this context? And if, as this book argues, we are essentially at war with animals, then how might this frame construe and constrain the possibility of companionship with entities we might be at war with, or perhaps are at war with at the same time as we seek to extend friendship?

Donna Haraway's *When Species Meet* aims to investigate the interaction of human and non human animals in "the contact zone" as they are shaped and actively shape each other.[11] Haraway's project builds on an "actor network" and science and technology studies tradition (which Haraway is a formative voice within), often highlighting the productive role of a variety of non human agents within networked processes, including non human animals. Actor Network approaches to technology highlight the interdependency that characterises the relationship between human and non human agents as a consequence of their engaged interaction. For example, the computer is often treated as a passive device that will only respond to human direction. Yet computer networks have radically transformed social and political organisation: they direct action, alter living spaces, and generate new communities. Computers have changed humans: their posture and workplace injuries, the way they work, love, communicate, think. For Haraway, the *cyborg* is a fitting representation of such a "hybridised" entity, which both emphasises the enabling aspects of new technologies, and illustrates the almost irreversible aspect of this process: we are, whether we like it or not, imbricated within an environment in which we constantly interact with and are joined with other entities, human and non human.[12] Thus in her "Cyborg Manifesto," Haraway comments that it "is not clear who makes and who is made in the relation between human and machine...There is no fundamental ontological

---

11   Haraway. *When Species Meet.* See also Haraway. *The Companion Species Manifesto.*

12   See Donna J. Haraway. "A Cyborg Manifesto: Science, Technology, and Socialist-Feminism in the Late Twentieth Century." *Simians, Cyborgs and Women: The Reinvention of Nature.* London: Free Association Books, 1991. 149–81.

separation in our formal knowledge of machine and organism, of technical and organic."[13] Similarly, in Haraway's impressive study of the use of primates in scientific experiments, we find a messy inter-relationship between the scientists and the primates "observed," where it is never clear whether primate behaviour demonstrates a truth about the natural order, or merely illustrates the capacity for primates to be written into a normative script: "the primate body is a discursive construct and therefore a literal reality, not the other way around."[14]

What Haraway offers in *When Species Meet* is an analysis that is premised on the reality that humans and animals interact, share spaces and politically communicate, and as such ethical relationships must be negotiated actively from within a set of ongoing interactions. This means questioning an abstracted analysis that occurs at a distance from the reality of human/animal relations. Instead Haraway chooses an analysis that, while acknowledging suffering and

---

13   Haraway. "A Cyborg Manifesto." 177–8. See also John Law's discussion of the development of Portuguese sailing vessels, the training of their human operators, and innovation in navigation as contributors to the success of the coloniser. See John Law. "On the Methods of Long-distance Control: Vessels, Navigation and the Portuguese route to India." *Power, Action and Belief: A New Sociology of Knowledge?* London: Routledge and Kegan Paul, 1986. 234–63.

14   Haraway. *Primate Visions.* 241. Earlier, referring to pre WW2 psychobiology, Haraway observes that "primates became models for the management of human beings as persons with the fruitful capacity to labor, to increase and multiply and fill the earth. This is the power contested as the heart of primatology" (83). Interestingly, particularly with respect to the critique I advance of Haraway in this chapter, *When Species Meets* includes an explicit distancing from *Primate Visions.* Haraway states, of her earlier work:

When I wrote *Primate Visions*, I think I failed the obligation of curiosity in much the same way I suggest Derrida did. I was so intent on the consequences of the Western philosophical, literary, and political heritage for writing about animals—especially other primates in the so called third world in a period of rapid decolonization and gender rearrangements—that I all but missed the radical practice of many of the biologists and anthropologists, women and men both, who helped me with the book, that is, their relentless curiosity about the animals and their tying themselves into knots to find ways to engage with these diverse animals as a rigorous scientific practice and not a romantic fantasy. Many of my informants for *Primate Visions* actually cared most about who the animals are; their radical practice was an eloquent refusal of the premise that the proper study of mankind is man. I, too, often mistook the conventional idioms of the philosophy and history of science spoken by most of "my" scientists for a description of what they did. They tended to mistake my grasp of how narrative practice works in science, how fact and fiction coshape each other, to be a reduction of their hard-won science to subjective storytelling. I think we needed each other but had little idea of how to respond.

See Haraway. *When Species Meet.* 312 n76.

exploitation, also traces the way human and non human agents share in networks and actively co-shape productions. Haraway notes:

> ...we are in a knot of species coshaping one another in layers of reciprocating complexity all the way down. Response and respect are possible only in these knots, with actual animals and people looking back at each other, sticky with all their muddied histories.[15]

Haraway's commitment to this approach is clearly illustrated in a comparison of two fictional characters from the work of J.M. Coetzee, the animal rights activist and scholar Elizabeth Costello, and the animal shelter worker Bev Shaw:

> Elizabeth Costello, the fictional Tanner Lecturer in Coetzee's *The Lives of Animals*, inhabits a radical language of animal rights. Armed with a fierce commitment to sovereign reason, she flinches at none of this discourse's universal claim, and she embraces all of its power to name extreme atrocity. She practices the enlightenment method of comparative history in order to fix the awful equality of slaughter. Meat eating is like the Holocaust; meat eating is the Holocaust. What would Elizabeth Costello do if she were in the place of Bev Shaw, the animal caretaker in *Disgrace*, whose daily service of love is to escort large numbers of abandoned dogs and cats to the solace of death? Maybe there is no solace for those animals, but only dying.[16]

This everyday relationship that Haraway claims for humans directly involved in interactions with non human animals forms the basis of the ethical project

---

15   Haraway. *When Species Meet*. 42.
16   Haraway. *When Species Meet*. 81. See also Haraway. *The Companion Species Manifesto*. 51–2. It is certainly worth noting that Haraway makes several assumptions here, including that it is not possible to "work with animals" and endorse a position of "radical animal rights" without inconsistency. The fact that many animal rights activists actively engage with animals in factory farms, experimental facilities, sanctuaries and shelters—not only in attempting to highlight suffering and abuse, but in rescuing animals from these situations— seems to play against Haraway's assumption here. Animal rights activists surely make tough ethical decisions in relation to their own practice with animals; this "privilege" cannot be reserved for people who are employed to work in animal industries. For an in-depth discussion of Haraway's work and the rejection of a "vegan abolitionisim," see Zipporah Weisberg. "The Broken Promises of Monsters: Haraway, Animals and the Humanist Legacy." *Journal for Critical Animal Studies*. 7.2, 2009.

that is put forward. Haraway goes on to argue "that human beings must learn to kill responsibly," following from the "feminist insight that embraced historically situated, mindful bodies" are the "site not just of first (maternal) birth but also of full life and all its projects, failed and achieved."[17]

A significant section of Haraway's intervention here is in her analysis of human and animal roles in the context of "agility training," a sport that involves humans working with dogs to complete an obstacle course, in competition with other dogs and their owners. This practice is similar to horse agility events, with the exception that the humans interact with their dogs at a distance.[18] Haraway's connection to the sport is personal, as she competes with her own dog—Cayenne—in agility events. The sport is situated by Haraway as a sphere for interconnection and mutual learning and development; she describes agility training as "a historically located, multispecies, subject-changing encounter in a contact zone fraught with power, knowledge and technique, moral questions—and the chance for joint, cross-species invention that is simultaneously work and play."[19] In her analysis of this practice, Haraway challenges a critique of the domestication of animals that relies upon normalised assumptions of the interaction of nature and culture, and how these in turn shape moral and ethical judgements in relation to how humans and animals interact or ought to interact. Haraway argues, for example, that putting forward a view that domestication is "unnatural" or a "disaster" operates as a "kind of original sin separating human beings from nature"[20] and plays into a discourse that automatically assumes that non human animals are in essence tools or the passive recipients of human control; it assumes that animals have nothing to gain or contribute within a reciprocal engagement with humans. This particular critique of domestication that Haraway addresses also reifies an arbitrary nature/culture distinction, by assuming that the proper, natural place for animals to be "themselves" is in a space free from human intervention: "within this frame, only wild animals in the conventional Western sense, as separate as possible from subjugation to human domination, can be themselves."[21]

Instead of seeking recourse to these formulations, Haraway proposes a different investigation of domestication and regimes of training, by trying to understand how disciplinary regimes acculturate new subjects. Because these regimes discipline both humans and animals, and both these entities co-shape

17   Haraway. *When Species Meet*. 80.
18   Haraway. *When Species Meet*. 208–9.
19   Haraway. *When Species Meet*. 205.
20   Haraway. *When Species Meet*. 206.
21   Haraway. *When Species Meet*. 207.

the other, there is, in Haraway's view, a difficulty in advancing a perspective that the relationship between humans and animals is a one sided form of dominion that treats animals as simply an inert tool, and/or as essentially belonging to a "wild" space of nature. Haraway thus rules out "possessive human or animal individuals whose boundaries and natures are set in advance of the entanglements of becoming together."[22] Importantly for her analysis, *instrumentality*—a process of putting another to work in a functional sense towards a particular end (treating another as a means rather than end in a Kantian sense)—is not seen as a problem in itself, but rather is a site for joined productivity, and beckons analysis: "Training together puts the participants inside the complexities of instrumental relations and structures of power."[23]

Haraway thus re-situates training as a practice that remoulds the body and activity of its participants in interesting ways which do not necessarily correspond with a trainer/trainee view of a downwards disciplinarity. The training regimes for agility practice are necessarily intense, particularly in order to achieve competition success. However, Haraway insists that training methods using "positive reinforcement" are standard within the field, and that "anyone training by other methods will be the subject of disapproving gossip, if not dismissed from the course by the judge who is on the lookout for any human's harsh correction of a dog."[24] Against a critique of animal training as "strong evidence of human control and a sign of the degradation of domestic dogs," Haraway suggests that another view is that training "improves the lives of captive animals" and that "engaging in training (education) is interesting for animals, just as it is for people."[25] Against a view that animal training might work against what is "natural" for animals—wild or domestic—Haraway suggests that training can open up a space that is interesting for both human and animals, because it is beyond norm and expectation: "training requires calculation, method, discipline, science, but training is for opening up what is not known to be possible, but might be, for all interacting partners. Training is, or can be about differences not trained by taxonomy."[26] There is, within this analysis, an interesting and challenging conceptualisation of freedom that is put forward. Haraway attempts to de-hinge the concept of freedom from an enlightenment preoccupation with individual autonomy, and simultaneously illustrate that the point of ethical concern in our relationship with animals is

---

22   Haraway. *When Species Meet*. 208.
23   Haraway. *When Species Meet*. 207.
24   Haraway. *When Species Meet*. 210.
25   Haraway. *When Species Meet*. 222.
26   Haraway. *When Species Meet*. 223.

not in relation to the instrumental use of animals, but in making animals objects for use (and death) and therefore removing human responsibility from the equation. Thus, for Haraway, instrumental use with responsibility represents a real site for ethical engagement, rather than a disavowal of use which comes attached with a disavowal of responsibility.

In a striking section of *When Species Meet*, Haraway cites a section of a Nancy Farmer novel, which describes an animal-based experiment:

> ...during their working hours, the guinea pigs were held in tight little baskets while wire cages filled with biting flies were placed over them, their skin shaved and painted with poisons that might sicken the offending insects with their protozoan parasites.[27]

A character in the novel, Baba Joseph, the caretaker of the animals, puts his hand into the cage and allows the insects to also feed on his arm: "It's wicked to cause pain, but if I share it, God may forgive me."[28] What attracts Haraway to this scenario of sharing suffering is that the fictional character, Baba Joseph, is neither self-assured that the pain of the insects does not exist or does not matter, nor repudiates the need for suffering by freeing the guinea pigs. Alternatively, his actions seek a middle ground, where "responsibility" is taken for the suffering inflicted: "Baba Joseph's bitten arm is not the fruit of a heroic fantasy of ending all suffering or not causing suffering, but the result of remaining at risk in instrumental relationships that one does not avow."[29] Part of the meaning of Haraway's move here is to attempt to ascribe to humans a responsibility for animals that, it is argued, is not present in current discourses, where either experimentation is justified on the basis of necessity, or opposed on a wholesale basis as a moral wrong. Thus Haraway asks:

> What happens if we do not regard or treat lab animals as victims, or as other to the human, or relate to their suffering and deaths as sacrifice? What happens if experimental animals are not mechanical substitutes but significantly unfree partners, whose differences and similarities to human beings, to one another, and to other organisms are crucial to the work of the lab, and, indeed, are partly constructed by the work of the lab?[30]

---

27   Haraway. *When Species Meet.* 69.
28   Nancy Farmer in Haraway. *When Species Meet.* 69.
29   Haraway. *When Species Meet.* 70.
30   Haraway. *When Species Meet.* 73. Later Haraway states: "The problem is actually to understand that human beings do not get a pass on the necessity of killing significant others,

It is worth bearing in mind Haraway's orientation here in terms of thinking about animals in the lab, not merely as inert objects that are subject to tests at the hands of experimenters, but as agents that shape the actions of others and produce in an inter-relational network. It is for this reason that Haraway wishes to challenge an absolute conception of "unfreedom," by offering qualifiers such as "significantly unfree"[31] and "degrees of freedom."[32] This perhaps is also the reason that Haraway situates animals as "workers" rather than "victims" within the framework that is proposed. The desire here is to position animals as active agents involved in productive processes that involve manifold instrumental relationships:

> Taking animals seriously as workers without the comforts of humanist frameworks for people or animals is perhaps new and might help stem the killing machines. The posthumanist whispering in my ear reminds me that animals work in labs, but not under conditions of their own design, and that Marxist humanism is no more help for thinking about this for either people or other animals than other kinds of humanist formulae. Best of all, the Marxist feminist in history and community reminds me that freedom cannot be defined as the opposite of necessity if the mindful body in all its thickness is not to be disavowed, with all the vile consequences of such disavowal for those assigned to bodily entrammelment, such as women, the colonized, and the whole list of "others" who cannot live inside the illusion that freedom comes only when work and necessity are shuffled off onto someone else. Instrumental relations have to be revalued, rethought, lived another way.[33]

Here Haraway suggests that freedom makes no sense if it is positioned against necessity; rather, freedom needs to be considered contextually within the sphere of instrumental relationships, the latter which are not necessarily the source of "unfreedom": "To be in relation of use to each other is not the definition of unfreedom and violation. Such relations are almost never symmetrical ('equal' or calculable)."[34] Because agents within this process are not equally positioned, and use each other instrumentally, absolute categories of

---

who are themselves responding, not reacting. In the idiom of labor, animals are working subjects, not just worked objects" (80).

31   Haraway. *When Species Meet*. 72.
32   Haraway. *When Species Meet*. 73.
33   Haraway. *When Species Meet*. 73. See also Clark. "Labourers or Lab Tools?"
34   Haraway. *When Species Meet*. 74.

freedom are illusory: "working" in this sense becomes a necessity for all who play a component role, since production is a combination of a range of agents, rather than characterised as a subject-object relation between an agent and the tool or inert matter that is instrumentalised.

This approach of course poses a challenge to the Lockean view of property that was discussed in Chapter 4. A traditional enlightenment view of the body and its relationship to property would argue that an innate property right in one's own body presents the possibility of our own instrumentalisation of self in order to sell our labour within a market. Capitalism notionally requires, at least in its liberal rhetoric, the idea that we are "free" to sell our own bodies; in capitalist labour production, we "own" our own bodies (in contrast to, say, a relationship of non ownership under slavery). This freedom is then given to us to enable us to engage with relations of production in different ways, which may not in themselves be strictly "free." This is perhaps captured strikingly in *Capital*, where Marx identifies the peculiar "freedom" of the worker:

> For the transformation of money into capital, therefore, the owner of money must find the free worker available on the commodity-market; and this worker must be free in the double sense that as a free individual he can dispose of his labour-power as his own commodity, and that, on the other hand, he has no other commodity for sale, i.e. he is rid of them, he is free of all the objects needed for the realisation of his labour-power.[35]

Freedom, in this guise, is alienation, which in turn, is a form of unfreedom. This perspective suggests that ownership of one's own body, experienced as a freedom from restraint and necessity, is precisely a liberal economic fantasy, that denies the way in which a range of bodies remain tied to productive processes, with little scope for "freeing" themselves from these relationships. Described in another way, we live in a world of inter-relationships and co-dependence, with multiple shared economies (including language and care work) which we can never de-hinge ourselves from. In this context, what do we make of Francione's claim that the lack of property rights enjoyed by animals in their own bodies is an important factor in understanding human domination? Certainly for Haraway, it would appear that the capacity for non human (or human) animals to make a claim to a property right in themselves is not relevant to an analysis of productive processes; indeed it plays into a dualism that reinscribes a particular idea of liberty that is about freedom from constraint, including the

---

35   Marx. *Capital*. 272–3.

constraint of one's own body. This does not mean that Haraway does not think freedom from restraint is not important, but that freedom must be understood within the context of instrumental relations: "when I say 'unfree' I mean that real pain, physical and mental, including a great deal of killing, is often directly caused by the instrumental apparatus, and the pain is not borne symmetrically."[36] This commitment alters the political challenge for achieving something that equates to an increasing degree of freedom (rather than freedom as a normatively defined end), by focusing on reforming instrumental practices to challenge non symmetry, suffering and "freedom" itself:

> The questions that then interest me are, How can the multispecies labor practices of the lab be less deadly, less painful, and freer for all the workers? How can responsibility be practiced among the earthlings? Labor as such, which is always proper to instrumental relations, is not the problem; it is always the pressing question of non symmetrical suffering and death. And nonmimetic well being.[37]

In other words, if we remove a liberal humanist attachment to defining freedom against necessity and constraint, and question a worldview where instrumentality is a problem in itself, then the task of critical awareness of suffering and death is to examine and take responsibility for the reform of existing practices.

While I share Haraway's concern in relation to avoiding enshrining a view of freedom as only opposed to necessity, and similarly agree that instrumental relationships are not in themselves a problem, I feel that there remain some questions that we might ask of the analysis that is presented. Of course, Haraway's project poses a challenge to the framework I have so far advanced in this book. If animals are workers, like human workers, within shared production processes, then it is impossible to speak about a war that seeks to bend our opponent's actions to our own wills. Similarly, and relevant to the analysis I have presented in Chapter 5, Haraway's framework will make it impossible to map delegations and privatisations of violences within a field of domination that we might call human sovereignty, since a top down system of domination does not appear accounted for in *When Species Meet*. Indeed it seems telling that the word "violence" does not figure prominently in Haraway's analysis,[38]

---

36   Haraway. *When Species Meet.* 74.

37   Haraway. *When Species Meet.* 77.

38   It seems intriguing to me that the actual word "violence" barely seems to figure in Haraway's text. I am aware that the word appears twice in relation to her summary of

because, we might assume, violence already speaks of an irretrievably one-sided non-symmetrical relationship; of forms of conflict that work against bodily resistance to bend wills; of gestures which seek to erase "freedom" beyond a point where consideration of "degrees" might be possible. As Haraway implicitly suggests, the concept of violence already constructs freedom in relation to it, and this would prevent the sort of analysis that Haraway attempts to put forward in *When Species Meet*.

However, it seems difficult to sustain a view that animals might be "workers" in scenes of co-productivity, where human domination manifoldly shapes these relationships. The fictitious (albeit all too real) experiment outlined in *When Species Meet*, involving restraining guinea pigs and subjecting them, in spite of resistance, to what would seem an eternity of torment for human-directed scientific investigation, is difficult to imagine as a scene of shared productivity between agents "at work." It may be, as I have argued in the Introduction to this book, that we might understand production processes as drawing from the creative resistance of animals who are captured and subsumed; these processes would adapt modes of violence to draw a "surplus." Indeed, it is true, that the moment of "pay-off" for the experimenter, the moment of value realisation, is the moment when the body of the suffering animal betrays, in spite of resistance, a truth that the experimenter is seeking to confirm. Animals will no doubt resist this process (their will to prefer life to death, their will to avoid pain), and their own bodily interaction in this process— growth, movement, reaction, diminution—will be harvested for human benefit. Perhaps this "labour" might be conceptualised as work. However, this would not prevent us from also understanding this relation as essentially violent. Indeed in order to sustain this analysis meaningfully, we must understand this exchange and "labour" precisely through the prism of violence, and honestly track the dynamics of this violence and what it may mean for "freedom." Resistance too, must be understood; the "worker" in this case must be conceptualised as a resistive agent, and their productivity understood in context with

Derrida on our treatment of animals (Haraway. *When Species Meet*. 78) and once in her summary of the position of Carol Adams (346, n15). The word "violent" seems to appear with slightly more frequency, particularly in relation to discussion of "nonviolent" training practices for dogs (see for example 62). This does not mean that Haraway is uninterested in violence, since clearly *When Species Meet* is a long meditation on how to frame violence in relation to non violence and what this means for ethics. However, it is curious that Haraway's interest in reframing the problem of our relations with animals away from animal rights discourse results in a withdrawal from the use of the term "violence" itself; even though this is rhetorically understandable, since of course, the term "violence" already closes off the possibility of a conception of "significantly unfree relationships."

this resistance against processes of violence. Certainly, in order for the word "violence" to mean anything beyond its usual application between human subjects, it must be fairly applied to examples such as this. We might indeed go further and say that this form of violence constitutes a "torture." And I use the word "torture" here aware that contemporary international law has tested the limits of the meaning of "torture" over the last decade, where the stakes of this game have constituted the right to use some forms of violence as not-torture, and where very clearly the right to define what constitutes torture is aligned with a sovereign project of domination and control.[39] We surely must be cognizant of these definitional issues, if simply because "freedom" must have a relationship to violence in some way. It seems appropriate in this discussion, for example, to draw attention to the infamous Jay S. Bybee 1 August 2002 Memorandum, which discusses the United States Central Intelligence Agency request to place a stinging insect in a confinement box with the Guantanamo detainee Abu Zubaydah as an interrogation technique (amongst other measures).[40] The experience of violence is an experience of an acute unfreedom, at least, in its subjective content, and it does not seem to be a leap of the imagination to suggest that "insects placed in a confinement box" may well fulfil a definition of violence, if not torture, and that this may be applied to

---

39   Note that the *Convention against Torture and Other Cruel, Inhuman or Degrading Treatment or Punishment* contains vague boundaries in relation to the definition of torture. Article 1 defines torture as follows: "For the purposes of this Convention, the term 'torture' means any act by which severe pain or suffering, whether physical or mental, is intentionally inflicted on a person for such purposes as obtaining from him or a third person information or a confession, punishing him for an act he or a third person has committed or is suspected of having committed, or intimidating or coercing him or a third person, or for any reason based on discrimination of any kind, when such pain or suffering is inflicted by or at the instigation of or with the consent or acquiescence of a public official or other person acting in an official capacity. It does not include pain or suffering arising only from, inherent in or incidental to lawful sanctions." The limitations—that torture only includes "severe" suffering, that torture must be carried out by a "public official" and that torture does not include "lawful sanctions"—already places borders around torture in ways that limit its applicability to a range of acts. Of course this is true of "human rights" treaties in a general sense, which always explicitly (rather than merely implicitly) generate the norm that "humans" are worthy of a treatment above non human animals (humans get "rights" because they are human).

40   Office of the Assistant Attorney General. "Memorandum for John Rizzo, Acting General Counsel of the Central Intelligence Agency: Interrogation of al Qaeda Operative." August 1, 2002. For a long discussion of US endorsed torture techniques in the context of biopolitical violence, see Pugliese. *State Violence and the Execution of Law.*

understanding and framing the fictitious example of Baba Joseph.[41] As I have argued in this work, a continuing challenge for our relationship with animals is how we unpick epistemic violence, particularly that violence which is rendered as "not violence" through a pervasive system of truth.

This does not mean that freedom is absolute, or not relational. We might argue, perhaps following a similar framework to Haraway, that it makes no sense to define freedom against necessity, that even those in constrained positions within institutional apparatuses must be considered as agents within a relational network of productivity (as I have argued in the Introduction to this work), and that perhaps the tortured can be said to shape practices of torture, perhaps through their forms of resistance, and that torturers might do better to take responsibility for the suffering they inflict (even if this seems paradoxical). But there would seem to be a limit to how far this sort of analysis can stretch without acknowledging the broader framework of domination and violence which position agents within this schema of practices that situate bodies and suffering.[42] Nor need we buy into a humanist rhetoric about the meaning of these terms—"violence," "torture" etc.—in order to acknowledge that there is already a relationship of domination inscribed in the process of who gets the right to name violence as violence, torture as torture, a process which I suggest operates in the same conceptual terrain as that which defines human against animal, and prescribes the possibilities for harming each. Again, the naming of violence is itself a facet of the epistemic violence of our war against animals. In this sense, I agree wholeheartedly with Haraway that there is a horror in making humans or other animals "killable," and a problem with a belief that freedom from killing is possible. But it doesn't appear altogether straightforward that the only consequence of this is that humans therefore need to kill (or inflict harm) responsibly, since this leaves the presumption of the right of human domination through violence intact. Ultimately, we need to challenge this right of dominion; that right that frames our relationships in advance, and appears as an apparently naturalistic assumption, even where we might want to challenge what is "natural." I have already suggested that a stronger

---

41   See Office of the Assistant Attorney General. "Memorandum for John Rizzo." 2. The [subsequently overturned] memo only conditionally endorsed the use of this technique: the CIA were informed that they would need to tell the prisoner that the insects do not have a sting that would involve serious pain or death (14).

42   Zipporah Weisberg states: "An ethics based on sharing suffering such as Haraway describes, therefore, appears, once again, to be more of a discursive exercise than an attempt to create the conditions for any concrete ethico-political transformation." See Weisberg. "The Broken Promises of Monsters." 40.

framework for understanding human freedom with respect to violence towards animals is to interrogate Foucault's suggestion that sovereignty might be understood as a freedom to enjoy another's unfreedom. This formulation both expresses Clausewitz's suggestion that war is the process of bending an opponent to our will, and the fact that the pleasure and freedom of those who are successful in war is connected and defined by this process. Freedom, as the experience of another's unfreedom, is a useful lens for determining the relational contours of the war we are engaged in: it allows us to re-render and re-understand apparently peaceable relations, and analyse the apparent benefits of instrumental relationships.

In another section of *When Species Meet*, Haraway provides an analysis of human/animal relationships in the context of the (human) prison correctional system, through a reading of the television show *Cell Dogs*. Here Haraway considers a United States prisoner program which places dogs in training with prisoners as a means of therapy and reform:

> Dog trainers teach the prisoners to teach the dogs basic obedience for placement as family member house pets and sometimes higher-order skills for placement as assistance dogs or therapy dogs. The screen shows the incarcerated dogs preparing for life outside by becoming willing, active, achieving obedience subjects. The pooches are obviously surrogates and models for the prisoners in the very act of becoming the prisoners' students and cell mates.[43]

Haraway acknowledges that coercion frames the training program for the dogs. The dogs must conform to the training regimes or face a life and death decision: "that death awaits the failed dog is a leitmotif in many of the programs, and the lesson for their teachers is not subtle."[44] And this violence frames the context for both human and canine prisoners: "life and death are the stakes in the prison-industrial complex. Prison reform discourse has never been more transparent."[45] Here, we can acknowledge that freedom is absolutely relational. There is no clear freedom from necessity; or freedom as an absolute loss of restraint. Freedom here is caught up within the dense atmosphere of a violent disciplinarity and inter-relationality for both human and animal prisoners. However, there is a tangible difference between the freedom that might be enjoyed by the "cell dogs" and that which might be enjoyed by the prisoners.

---

43   Haraway. *When Species Meet*. 63–4.
44   Haraway. *When Species Meet*. 64.
45   Haraway. *When Species Meet*. 64.

For the dogs, any experience of freedom can only be experienced within the close confines of the continuing duration of human domination. Thus the freedom of being delivered from the threat of death in an animal shelter to a training program in a prison, or the freedom of "graduating" and being transferred from the dominion of prisoners to the control of a "free individual" in a family home, is a freedom that is always conditioned by a human prerogative to enjoy a freedom bound to the continuing unfreedom and death of the animal. In this sense, the kind of understanding that Loïc Wacquant advances of the United States prison system, as a means of social control that replaces the ghetto,[46] might be usefully deployed here to understand the "cell dog" (or the dog analogously in an animal shelter): in both cases the prison merely replaces a different modality of social control; one container is swapped for another.[47] It is

---

46   See Loïc Wacquant. "Deadly Symbiosis: When Ghetto and Prison Meet and Mesh." *Punishment and Society*. Vol. 3(1); 95–134.

47   I note here in this context the recent interest in popular non fiction examining the plight of companion animals in zones of military conflict, and the efforts of service personnel to "rescue" animals from conflict zones. One example is Christine Sullivan's *Saving Cinnamon*, a description of "the amazing true story of a missing military puppy and the desperate mission to bring her home" (see Christine Sullivan. *Saving Cinnamon: The Amazing True Story of a Missing Military Puppy and the Desperate Mission to Bring Her Home*. Sydney: Hachette, 2009). Here, surely, we find the narrative of benevolent human domination of animals find perfect symmetry with a militarist discourse and an attendant propaganda effort designed to support violence against human populations. Like Levinas' dog "Bobby," Cinnamon befriends Navy Reservist Mark Feffer, and "made him feel human amidst the hardness required of a soldier at war" (28). Cinnamon is explicitly positioned as living within a hostile world, conveniently racially constructed to obey the geopolitical contours of the war around: "many of the Afghan nationals, army and civilian alike, did not like Cinnamon being on the base, and they often threw rocks at her or kicked her as she walked by"(26; see also 39, 144). Some dogs—who we might assume lack the trappings of a life in the West—are born into inequality: "as he considered the life that Cinnamon led, Dave wondered why dogs were less fortunate because of where they were born. It wasn't fair" (54). (I am immediately curious if this concern for the inequality in opportunity for dogs extends to other creatures who are born into intense and arbitrary locational disadvantage; not only other animal species, bred to die in factory farms, or suffer at the hands of experimenters; but other human animals who, at least partly through the global economic and military complicity of the West, are born into situations of severe economic deprivation, a reality of extraordinarily poor health outcomes, and constant insecurity through war and State terror). The scene is thus set for Cinnamon's "escape" from Afghanistan, for a "rescue" to be mounted, and for Cinnamon to be given a "second chance" (44) in the United States: "she was adorable, and needed a real home" (44). And thus, a human desire for a new use object meets with a declared interest in welfare to produce the effort to "save Cinnamon": "It would be neat to bring her home.

notable that the dogs will never be free from the life and death threat of arbitrary "euthanasia"; never free from human controls over sexuality, reproduction and sociality; nor will they ever be "free" from a daily control by human operators or persistent enclosure, either by barrier or lead, either in prison or in a family home. On the other hand, the human prisoners are offered a freedom with respect to the animals under their control. It is true, that freedom for these prisoners is always relational: even being free of the prison cell may only be the freedom to be bound to wage labour or the precarity of unwaged poverty; and all these freedoms are framed by the continuing constraints enacted by the authoritarian State, and modes of displinarity and normalisation which will continue to shape action and punish deviance. However, whether or not the prisoners attain reform and freedom from the animal training program, a right to enjoy the unfreedom of animals remains open to them. This is a right to appropriate and to take control of the destiny of the animals in their "care," including a life and death responsibility should their training techniques fail. Even in the heart of the carceral complex, where human bodies are constrained and seemingly "unfree," the right to a freedom to enjoy the unfreedom of other animals remains unchallenged; indeed it is broadly considered "therapeutic."

Instrumentality here does not need to be read as problematic. We are all bound within relations characterised by "dependencies" and mobile forms of inequality and temporality with respect to power. However, instrumentality can be linked to the systemic violence of sovereignty—a right of dominion—that shapes the whole field of these operations and practices of violence. Where this instrumentality is delegated and concentrated into the hands of individual human agents, it operates as a privatised form of sovereignty which, understood in concert across a whole field of power, might enable large scale relational systems of violent domination, including, as discussed in Chapter 5, formations such as patriarchy (as constructed in part on a foundation of systematic individual acts of violence by men towards women) or necropolitical racialised colonisation (as facilitated by a disaggregation of State power into

---

It would be fun to have her, and he knew she'd have a good life in the States" (34). One wonders exactly what Cinnamon was being saved from in this case, and whether her long transport to the West, and eventual incarceration within United States suburbia (a quest to "get her home" [235] no less) might constitute a rescue, or merely a transfer from one hostile property relationship to another? Perhaps *Saving Cinnamon* represents a welfareist response, which—drawing from Jasbir Puar's work on "homonationalism"—might be understood as a type of "critter nationalism": a phenomenon I briefly discuss in the Conclusion to the book. For a broader discussion of the biopolitics of companion animals in the US war effort, see Ryan Hediger. "Dogs of War: The Biopolitics of Loving and Leaving the U.S. Canine Forces in Vietnam." *Animal Studies Journal.* 2.1, 2013. 55–73.

the hands of arbitrary agents—police, military, private militias). How might this same privatised instrumentality surface as domination with respect to animals? Haraway observes:

> Cayenne and I definitely have different native languages, and much as I reject overdoing the analogy of colonization to domestication, I know very well how much control of Cayenne's life and death I hold in my inept hands.[48]

The palpable hesitation in the text here seems to unnecessarily shy away from naming a systematic form of domination that characterises our relations with animals. Naming and understanding this particular mode of violent relation is a way to make sense of a set of exchanges that both exceed and epitomise our day-to-day interconnection with animals; and a way in which we can confidently understand how we are part of this large scale relationality that might be characterised as war. As I have argued, recognising complex co-shaping inter-relationships does not need to be incompatible with recognising a broader frame of organised violence and instrumentalities bound to asymmetrical power. Palmer has described the way in which pet ownership might encompass a spectrum of relations of power, from interactive relationships to absolute forms of domination:

> ...where 'power relationships in general' between humans and animals do not clearly result in the desired disciplining of animals, measures of dominance where animals become "things which cannot resist" are frequently adopted.[49]

Palmer goes further to state: "But such is the nature of the structural inequality between humans and animals that, in most cases, the resort to 'thingification' of animals is likely to be available."[50] Specific modes of instrumentalisation of animal life are characteristic of human sovereignty.[51] Personal actions work in concert with institutional forms of violence that constrain our companions

---

48   Haraway. *When Species Meet.* 216. In this context, see Haraway. *The Companion Species Manifesto.* 51.

49   Palmer. "Taming the Wild Profusion of Existing Things?" 358.

50   Palmer. "Taming the Wild Profusion of Existing Things?" 358.

51   As Marx would put it: "The use and construction of instruments of labour, although present in germ among certain species of animals, is characteristic of the specifically human labour process." See Marx. *Capital.* 286.

in particular ways to meet human utility. Epistemic violence allows us to name these relations, almost without a moment of self reflection, under the guise of "friendship." However, this violent relationality that is founded upon a sovereign prerogative certainly does not preclude innovations in friendship or developing intimacy and connection in resistance to enveloping systems of domination. The reality of these interactions is that humans enjoy emotionally close, interdependent and co-shaping relationships with animals; relationships that no doubt both humans and animals experience as constraining and enabling, frustrating and joyous. The war against animals does, however, frame the terms for this friendship, and forces us to place our relations with non human companions in question. In the next chapter we shall turn to focus on sovereignty itself; how it is defined, and what it might mean for thinking about our relationship with animals.

PART 4

Sovereignty

∴

CHAPTER 7

Capability

> Sovereignty has no essence, since it is what makes different spheres of
> politics empirically representable and intelligible; as soon as we start to
> demand that the concept of sovereignty should refer to something pres-
> ent in the world of empirical beings, our understanding of the concept
> itself must presuppose the same line in water which is drawn in and
> through its meaningful use in potential discourse.
>
> JENS BARTELSON. *A Genealogy of Sovereignty.*[1]

I have so far put forward a view that our relationship with animals reflects a
combative relationship that aims at preserving a form of sovereign dominion
over other creatures. The book has sought to describe features of this dominion: its distinctly biopolitical nature, the forms of governmentality that attend
the conduct of war; the systems of immunity, property and commodity
exchange that underpin our distinctive relations; and the practice of our sovereignty through modes of privatised dominion. I have argued that human sovereignty over other animals is in essence arbitrary. Our self-declared sovereignty
is not gained through our rationality; nor through our cleverness; nor through
our extraordinary moral worth. On the contrary, as discussed when I examined
Locke in Chapter 4, our capability results from our use of violence to appropriate other animals, a process by which we come, after the fact, to claim a supposed "superiority" over other living beings. Importantly, in this view, animals
might equally claim sovereign "rights," were it not for the systems of intersubjective, institutional and epistemic violence that hold out of contention any
such claim. We shall extend on this view further in Chapter 8, when we examine Derrida's view on the meaning of sovereignty, which, as I argue, happens to
conform with the reading of Locke provided in this book.

Acknowledging that humans might not be the only species who might be able
to make a claim on sovereignty appears to open the question of how we might
conceptualise animal sovereignties. In this chapter, I focus on recent scholarship
in liberal political theory—the account of Robert E. Goodin, Carole Pateman
and Roy Pateman, and the account of Donaldson and Kymlicka—which has
attempted to put forward a view that animals are owed sovereignty rights. As
we shall see, a conceptualisation of animal capability, and its relationship to

---

1 Bartelson. *A Genealogy of Sovereignty.* 51.

territory, underpins the justifications made by these authors for awarding sovereign rights to some animals. In my view these accounts rely on an unnecessarily restrictive view of sovereignty, one that does not seem capable itself of challenging the sovereignty that is the focus of this book: namely, our domination of animals. This chapter will explore the promise and shortcomings of these approaches.

Simian Sovereignty

In 1997 a paper entitled "Simian Sovereignty," Robert E. Goodin, Carole Pateman and Roy Pateman offer a provocative imagining of what an animal sovereignty might look like.[2] The paper extends upon the "Declaration on Great Apes" issued in 1993 as part of the Great Ape Project, seeking to extend a "community of equals" to chimpanzees, gorillas and orangutans, and basic rights to life, liberty and freedom from torture. Goodin, Pateman and Pateman argue that the forms of community self determination that follow from human declarations of rights—such as those contained in Article 1 of the *International Covenant on Civil and Political Rights* and the *International Covenant on Economic, Social and Cultural Rights*—extend into forms of sovereignty for collective groups. The modern evolution of sovereignty is closely connected to the emergence of individual rights to freedom and property. From these rights flowed forms of self determination: "the 'rights of man' gave peoples—nations—the right of self-determination."[3] Individual rights rely on principles of mutual non interference ("the right I enjoy should not be interfered with by another" and vice versa). Goodin, Pateman and Pateman tie this principle to the emergence of modern nation States through the Westphalian regime, which externally granted to States rights of self determination and non interference in order to regulate peace and stability between nation States.[4]

However, Goodin, Pateman and Pateman do not treat sovereignty as a static formation; they observe that nation State sovereignty is evolving; globalising economies are reorienting understandings of the nation States, and forms of

---

2   Robert E. Goodin, Carole Pateman and Roy Pateman. "Simian Sovereignty." *Political Theory*. 25. 6, 1997. 821–49.

3   Goodin, Pateman and Pateman. "Simian Sovereignty." 826.

4   As the authors note, this same principle of self determination and mutual non interference underpins the peace and security mandate which forms the foundation of the Charter of the United Nations. Goodin, Pateman and Pateman. "Simian Sovereignty." 827.

democratization have challenged the nature of sovereignty.[5] The question of who gets rights has also altered in line with this democratisation. Individual "human rights" were historically always awarded only on a partial basis, constructed along lines of social distinction, including notably gender and race: women, for example, were initially excluded from these rights; as were colonised subjects who were deemed too "primitive" to access these rights. However, the evolution in the nature of sovereignty, the nation and citizenship have expanded to include groups who were previously excluded. Goodin, Pateman and Pateman suggest that recent questions over the border between human and non human coincide with the shift in the meaning of sovereignty, and the expansiveness of citizenship categories, creating an opening for consideration of non human (ape) recognition:

> Who can now claim sovereign prerogatives, then, and what they can credibly claim under that heading are no longer nearly so clear as they used to be. "Sovereignty" is being deconstructed at the same time that the number of states is increasing and state boundaries eroded. In addition, the controversy over the relation between and the meaning of "human" and "ape" has been rejoined. This allows a new opening for other, different kinds of claims and claimants to the status of "sovereigns" in international society.[6]

The reasons advanced by Goodin, Pateman and Pateman for recognition of great ape capacity for basic rights relate to arguments for equivalent capability: firstly, increasingly recent theoretical questions have been drawn around the distinctions between human/animal, civilised/uncivilised, nature/culture, which trouble the easy separation between human and non human apes; secondly, it can be demonstrated that great apes have a complex social order not unlike human apes; and thirdly, scientific evidence suggests that non human great apes and human great apes topologically and genetically are largely non differentiated, and that claims about the exceptional rational ability of humans (that is, human great apes) cannot be sustained.[7]

---

5   Goodin, Pateman and Pateman. "Simian Sovereignty." 829.

6   Goodin, Pateman and Pateman. "Simian Sovereignty." 830.

7   For an ethical argument for non human animal recognition that does not rely upon differentiation on the basis of capability, see Ralph R. Acampora. *Corporal Compassion: Animal Ethics and Philosophy of Body.* Pittsburgh: University of Pittsburgh Press, 2006. See also Tyler. *CIFERAE.*

Moral equivalence leads to a right of sovereignty. Goodin, Pateman and Pateman place this claim squarely within the rationality that appears to be inherent in the formation of the contemporary State sovereign system. The authors note that had the logic of the Westphalian system been consistent, then great apes would have been recognised as sovereignty holders:

> Ironically, if the logic of sovereignty in the Westphalian order was taken at face value, many of the great apes would already have met the traditional test of *de facto* sovereignty—namely, an authority structure in place over some particular territory. What exactly its details might be, or whether we understand it fully, are irrelevant to the fact that the authority structure exists. Whether we morally approve of the way they go about their own affairs is likewise irrelevant. The whole point of the Westphalian order was simply to protect existing loci of authority, existing sovereigns, against external aggression.[8]

Recognising this historical and logical oversight within the Westphalian system, the authors seek to correct this by arguing for "an internationally protected, autonomous territory for the great apes."[9] Goodin, Pateman and Pateman then outline feasible alternatives for a "great ape homeland," including trusteeship arrangements which would allow great apes to live their life unfettered within a protected State, while other nations took responsibility for maintaining external security:

> ...to accord territorially based communities of other great apes at least the same sort of rights of internal self-determination and the same sort of guarantees against external aggression as we accord any other distinct, territorially based community in the world today.[10]

---

8   Goodin, Pateman and Pateman. "Simian Sovereignty." 833. Of course this point probably suggests an extreme optimism that the Westphalian system was the product of a rational legal division of power, with genuine interests in parcelling power to distinct "homogenous" peoples.

9   Goodin, Pateman and Pateman. "Simian Sovereignty." 840.

10   Goodin, Pateman and Pateman. "Simian Sovereignty." 843. It is not clear what guarantees there actually are in the international system when it comes to protections that are offered, even to recognised "peoples." Despite the protections in the *Charter of the United Nations*, and more recent developments after the Rome Statute, including in the development of the "crime of aggression," surely there is ample evidence that powerful States may violate the self determination rights of a people with relative impunity, or at least support (either actively or through non action) the violation of self determination rights, where

In some respects Goodin, Pateman and Pateman's proposal is remarkable as an experiment in how we might shift and trouble traditional connections between self determination, human moral recognition and sovereignty and offer alternatives for consideration of non human animal status and entitlement. However, the vision prescribed by the authors is limited. One problem is that Goodin, Pateman and Pateman lean on a particular conception of sovereignty that evolves directly from the Westphalian experience. Political theorists of international relations often regard the Peace of Westphalia, established through a set of treaties in the mid 17th century, as helping to fundamentally shape the nation State system and the role of sovereignty within it. This set of treaties established a system of interconnected territories linking population with national borders, and established a set of inside and outside relationships, paving the way for the solidification of Britain, France, Germany, Spain, the Netherlands and Switzerland as nation States. The aim of the treaties was to establish stability in the wake of the 30 years war, and to do so through granting legitimation to autonomous States (as opposed to the Holy Roman Empire). There are a number of features worth noting in relation to this apparent stability. Firstly, "peace" in the Westphalian system was certainly not characterised by the absence of war. On the contrary, war would continue (notably in Sweden and Denmark). However, rather than war being waged by a prince or Pope with access to a private militia, war is instead waged by sovereign States, in the name of the nation and its security. Secondly, the Westphalian system did not generate sovereignty rights for all "peoples." The "peace" generated by the Westphalian model of sovereignty was differential in nature, since while European states claimed this equality in self determination rights and freedom from non interference, "non European states lacked this sovereignty."[11] The stability generated by this order—sovereign states in Europe, sovereign-less

---

this violation works in the interests of powerful States. This, however, does negate Goodin, Pateman and Pateman's suggestion that if there is indeed a consistently applied rationality which applies to international system recognition of self determination rights, that then great apes should be owed these rights.

11 Antony Anghie. "The Evolution of International Law: Colonial and Postcolonial Realities." *Third World Quarterly.* 27:5, 2006. 739–753. 740. Anghie states further:

My argument is that colonialism had shaped not only those doctrines of international law explicitly devised for the very purpose of suppressing the Third World, but had also profoundly shaped the very foundations of international law, including the ostensibly neutral doctrine of sovereignty. The end of formal colonialism, while extremely significant, did not result in the end of colonial relations. Rather, in the view of Third World societies, colonialism was replaced by neo-colonialism; Third World states continued to play a subordinate role in the international system because they were

people elsewhere—externalised the mission of conquest; it set in train a logic that would allow, for example, the Dutch to legitimate their continuing colonial expansion into Asia. Thirdly, the Westphalian system linked a conception of "peace" with security over territory. Peace and stability are associated with the idea of a population finding a home and legitimised rule within a territory, contained within an international system of agreed upon borders.[12]

Because Goodin, Pateman and Pateman situate their model for simian sovereignty squarely within a Westphalian understanding, it is apparent that sovereignty is equated with finding a territorial homeland, and as a result peace, security and territorial stability become interlinked concepts. It is, however, not clear why, when imagining animal sovereignty, territorial rights and sovereignty need to be linked in line with the Westphalian system. One obvious objection to this is that sovereign rights may not clearly link to a single "homeland" for some animals; for example migratory birds. Admittedly, Goodman, Pateman and Pateman's rhetorical strategy is—perhaps like Singer—to point out the logical inconsistency between the requirements for rights within human political affairs and the non inclusion of *some* animals, and argue that as a result it is logically inconsistent to continue to exclude those animals. Apes look like humans in the way in which they occupy territory; therefore they have met a capability test for sovereignty recognition: "many of the great apes would already have met the traditional test of *de facto* sovereignty— namely, an authority structure in place over some particular territory." The approach is logically consistent, but does nothing to challenge how sovereignty is understood. Sovereignty here is only understood within the limited terms of the nation State, which contains a correlate set of ties to population, territory and security. This approach does not allow us to question who gets recognised as having a capability for sovereignty. Certainly it is not clear why it is that other animals—those animals we deem as not having "an authority structure in place over some particular territory"—should be excluded from a right to sovereignty, particularly given that we are likely to quite reasonably suspect that recognising that an entity that has "an authority structure in place over some particular territory" is really code for saying that that entity has a

---

economically dependent on the West, and the rules of international economic law continued to ensure that this would be the case (748–9).

12   The Westphalian model, in combination with Kant's cosmopolitanism, would appear to be a significant element contributing to the design of the *Charter of the United Nations*— combining principles of sovereign equality, a right to territory, non interference and self defence, and an obligation to maintain international peace and security through maintenance of the stability of this system.

distinctly human way of existing with land and with their "fellows." If we argue, as I shall in Chapter 8, that sovereignty is always an assertion of a right without regard to capability—that is, it is a force that arrives without justification, indeed it is self justifying in the way in which it "prevails"—then discussion and distinction between who gets sovereign rights and who does not is already an exercise in sovereignty by those who have claimed this right without prior justification.

It is at this point, and before we turn to Donaldson and Kymlicka, that I would like to think about capability more closely. Capability approaches have been an important recent addition to social justice discussions, particularly through Amartya Sen's original discussion of a capability approach,[13] and then in Martha C. Nussbaum's development of the concept.[14] The main innovation in the capabilities approach is moving beyond liberal based contract theories, utilitarianism, and libertarian views, by arguing for the application of justice on the basis of the flourishing potentiality of individuals within a social and political context. The capabilities approach achieves this by recognising that there are claims to basic forms of potential in each individual that exceed a vision of justice constrained to altering the pattern of the redistribution of goods (as per a contract approach), or redistributing pleasure and suffering (as per a utilitarian approach), or safeguarding basic "rights" (as per human rights and libertarian approaches). In Sen's view, capabilities are:

> ...not fully captured by either utility or primary goods, or any combination of the two. Primary goods suffers from fetishist handicap in being concerned with goods, and even though the list of goods is specified in a broad and inclusive way, encompassing rights, liberties, opportunities, income, wealth, and the social basis of self-respect, it still is concerned with good things rather than with what these good things do to human beings. Utility, on the other hand, is concerned with what these things do to human beings, but uses a metric that focusses not on the person's capabilities but on his mental reaction. There is something still missing in the combined list of primary goods and utilities... I believe what is at issue is the interpretation of needs in the form of basic capabilities.

---

13   See Amartya Sen. "Equality of What?" *The Tanner Lecture on Human Values*. Delivered at Stanford University, 1979. And Amartya Sen. *Commodities and Capabilities*. New Dehli: Oxford University Press, 1999.

14   See, for example, Martha C. Nussbaum. *Women and Human Development: The Capabilities Approach*. Cambridge: Cambridge University Press, 2001.

This interpretation of needs and interests is often implicit in the demand for equality. This type of equality I shall call "basic capability equality."[15]

Nussbaum has extended the capabilities approach to non human animals, as a way to situate a claim for justice.[16] Similarly, rejecting contractarian views—which are limited by their presumption of a rational agent who can enter the social contract—and utilitarian views of justice—which are constrained by a limited view of the good in pleasure or avoidance of pain, or face difficulty in evaluating and aggregating preferences that must be flattened and de-individualised—Nussbaum argues that a capabilities approach has the capacity to take into consideration the conditions of flourishing for all living beings. The capabilities approach "wants to see each thing flourish as the sort of thing it is."[17]

Things get more slippery, however, when we must come to understand and judge what sort of a thing each animal is, and what it may need to flourish. As Nussbaum notes, an imaginative step is required, since we cannot necessarily gain access to the inner worlds of those we may wish to allow to flourish: "the capabilities approach uses sympathetic imagining, despite its fallibility, to extend and refine our moral judgements in this area."[18] The imaginative step however, perhaps predictably, leads us to a set of moral judgements which merely infers and tacitly approves a human "superiority" and prerogative to decide about others, even while Nussbaum attempts to imagine a community of humbled human decision makers, who in making principles for others "do not pride themselves on an alleged unique characteristic," instead aiming to recognise "an interlocking world that contains many types of animal life, each with its own needs, each with its own dignity."[19] Returning to that now familiar

---

15   Sen. "Equality of What?" I have omitted a section of the lecture here:

> If it is argued that resources should be devoted to remove or substantially reduce the handicap of the cripple despite there being no marginal utility argument (because it is expensive), despite there being no total utility argument (because he is so contented), and despite there being no primary goods deprivation (because he has the goods that others have), the case must rest on something else.

Note that the example of the "cripple" is important for Sen in arriving at his approach.

16   See Martha C. Nussbaum. *Frontiers of Justice: Disability, Nationality, Species Membership.* Cambridge: Harvard University Press, 2006. See also Martha C. Nussbaum. "Beyond 'Compassion and Humanity.'" Cass R. Sunstein and Martha C. Nussbaum Eds. *Animal Rights: Current Debates and New Directions.* Oxford: Oxford University Press, 2004. 299–320.

17   Nussbaum. *Frontiers of Justice.* 349.

18   Nussbaum. *Frontiers of Justice.* 355.

19   Nussbaum. *Frontiers of Justice.* 356.

stomping ground of the moral philosophers—that is, the distinction between a person with intellectual disability and a great ape—Nussbaum observes that recognising the dignity in each of these entities prevents us from comparing the child with disability to the chimpanzee, since each entity must have its own form of flourishing, within different contexts. Perhaps unfortunately, this differentiated context happens to be articulated as a "species norm." In a pivotal section of text, Nussbaum states:

> In short, the species norm (duly evaluated) tells us what the appropriate benchmark is for judging whether a given creature has decent opportunities for flourishing. The same thing goes for nonhuman animals: in each case, what is wanted is a species specific account of central capabilities (which may include particular interspecies relationships, such as the traditional relationship between the dog and the human), and then a commitment to bring members of that species up to that norm, even if special obstacles lie in the way of that.[20]

At first blush, Nussbaum's framework suggests the possibility that perhaps it may be possible to recognise the life and world of individual animals without this view being shaped by a human use prerogative: a kind of Aristotelian zoology, without the inherent hierarchy that we identified in Chapter 1. However, on closer inspection, Nussbaum's proposal appears to be simply a more benevolent form of stratification. As I discussed in the Introduction, disability as a category is modulated by the biopolitical conceptualisation of the human species norm; not only a determination of what the "normal" human looks like, but what its other (the non human other) might be imagined as comprising. This categorisation is socially and politically constructed. While it may seem true that a community of humans living with other humans cannot be substituted for the life world of chimpanzees (perhaps a human cannot flourish with chimpanzees, nor can chimpanzees flourish with humans), assuming that each world (the world of the human and the world of the ape) might reflect a "species norm" opens a set of dangerous assumptions, which naturalise particular modes of living and relationality, effectively removing them from the action of politics and hiding systems of domination. For the person with disability, an assumption of the human species norm naturalises a world that is socially and politically constructed to exclude, marginalise and name some people as "disabled." Flourishing for a person with disability doesn't simply require adjusting that person's situation to meet the species norm; the deeper political challenge

---

20   Nussbaum. *Frontiers of Justice.* 365.

is to unseat the species norms that conspire through intersubjective, institutional and epistemic violences to create the "disabled person."

A similar problem relates to the construction of species norms for non human animals. Indeed, the danger I refer to is implicit in the citation above from Nussbaum, which claims that a "species specific account of central capabilities" should include "particular interspecies relationships, such as the traditional relationship between the dog and the human." It would seem unwise to suggest that a capabilities assessment should take into account a relationship produced by a "traditional" system of domination and call this a "species norm." For example, patriarchal relations between men and women, relationships which vary between contexts, are for all intents and purposes "traditional." Yet it would be deeply problematic to suggest that these relationships are informative of a "species norm" for humans. Yet Nussbaum appears to validate this reading of "species norm" here. Nussbaum rejects a view that domestic animals can be "freed," pointing out that domesticated animals often lack the ability to return to the wild since they "have evolved over millennia in symbiosis with human beings."[21] Instead, a paternalistic form of continuing control is justified: "a type of paternalism that is highly sensitive to the different sorts of flourishing that a different species can pursue."[22] This benign form of dominion allows for controls over animals to be justified where entitlements are also guaranteed:

> Such animals should surely not be treated like mere objects for humans' use and control: their own flourishing and their own ends should be held constantly in view. But to say that is not to say that we ought simply to let them run off without human control. The morally sensible alternative is to treat them as companions in need of prudent guardianship, but endowed with entitlements that are theirs, even if exercised through guardianship. In other words, they may be treated as we currently treat children and many people with mental disabilities, who have a large menu of rights and are in that sense far from being "mere property," although those rights must be exercised through human guardianship. (It seems to me that there is nothing evil about exchanging guardianship of animals through buying and selling, provided that their rights are duly protected in this way).[23]

---

21   Nussbaum. *Frontiers of Justice.* 376.
22   Nussbaum. *Frontiers of Justice.* 375.
23   Nussbaum. *Frontiers of Justice.* 376–7. Note that, at the time of writing, Nussbaum's conceptualisation of the rights of people with intellectual disability is thoroughly out of step

Leaving aside the remarkable suggestion that property ownership in animals might have no effect on their own flourishing (are we to assume that property ownership of some humans might also be justified using the same logic?), we might here track an uneasy descent that appears to follow from Nussbaum's logic of capability, which began with the promise of being able to recognise the inherent flourishing needs of individual animals, and ends with a continuing prerogative for humans to decide the fates of animals, through a benevolent form of control that never seems to put human sovereignty over other animals under any deeper sort of critical gaze. Once again, it seems, sovereignty precedes ethics in this case. The problem with using this modulation of the capability approach for animals, it would appear, lies in relying upon assumed capabilities in different creatures, which then proceed to justify hierarchical relations. It is not that creatures do not wish to flourish in their own ways; there would appear to be no essential problem with a capabilities approach on this front. However, if giving animals "their due" requires a judgement on their respective capabilities, the question of who gets to judge, and why they get to judge, seems critically important. In particular, understanding the political process which allows the judge to pass judgement is surely highly significant for analysis. For it seems no surprise that a capability approach would merely enshrine human-established hierarchical relations when humans are given the job of determining capabilities and simultaneously, of patrolling borders to ensure, to paraphrase Regan, that no dog gets more than its due. As we shall discover below in relation to Donaldson and Kymlicka's proposal for a *Zoopolis*, the same potential challenges awaits in their discussion. These are not uncomplicated issues to consider, particularly where we must think how to politically respond to animals that we have maintained dominion over for millennia,

---

with directions in international law, which have increasingly urged for the replacement of guardianship and other substitute decision making arrangements for people with disability with supported decision making regimes. See United Nations Committee on the Rights of Persons with Disabilities. *Draft General Comment on Article 12 of the Convention— Equal Recognition before the Law.* September 2013. Note that the fact that guardianship arrangements for people with disability are undergoing radical change across the globe, indicates that naturalised assumptions about what decisions people can make about their own life are open to continuing political contestation. It should be emphasised that United Nations bodies are hardly radical in these political debates. The fact that guardianship arrangements are currently being challenged at the institutional level by the United Nations and other bodies is indicative of the success of the work done by people with disability themselves over decades to resist and shift the conceptualisation of who gets a right to decide; and perhaps, attendant to this, a political contestation over the species norm itself of what constitutes a normalised "human."

fundamentally shaping animal relations and responsiveness. However, the starting point for this discussion should surely be our own sovereignty; the end point should surely be imagining the possibilities for animal sovereignties, even if this recognition might take away our own sovereign rights.

Citizens, Wild Animal Sovereignty and Denizenship

Donaldson and Kymlicka's *Zoopolis* is in many respects a remarkable work of political theory, that breaks ground in providing a worked out vision for how we might construct human societies without systemic violence towards animals. Donaldson and Kymlicka's starting point is to offer a new framework for considering our relationship with animals, which not only protects the *negative* rights of animals (those which are usually articulated within animal rights approaches, such as freedom from suffering and death, and the right to movement) but supplements these rights with *positive* obligations and recognition of the continued everyday interactions with animals. In this respect, the work represents a breakthrough in political conceptualisation of how we respond to violence against animals.

Sovereignty appears to lie at the heart of the political model proposed in *Zoopolis*. Donaldson and Kymlicka achieve this by offering what appears as effectively a "tripartite" model of sovereignty that comprises *inside*, *outside* and the *border*. Animals *within* and reliant on human communities are conceptualised as being owed *citizenship*; animals that are *outside* of human spheres and belong to their own territorially bounded communities are imagined as possessing *sovereign* rights; while those animals on the *borders* of human communities are imagined as being owed *denizenship* status. Sovereignty might be said to mediate all three of these different modes of living with respect to human political communities—inside, outside and the border—since the political status of any entity within this new global community will be determined by their relationship with a sovereignty (human or other than human). That is, entities either belong or participate in sovereignty through citizenship; alternatively they possess full sovereign rights as part of a community of others; or finally, they do not belong to a territorially bounded political community, but are owed basic rights protections by existing sovereign communities.

With respect to citizenship rights, Donaldson and Kymlicka extend contemporary citizenship theory to thinking about how animals might be granted formal membership of political communities. It is noted that while human rights seek to provide fundamental protections to all humans, citizenship rights provide deeper protections that accrue as a result of membership of a political community: "we typically distinguish between universal human rights, which are not dependent on one's relationship to a particular community, and citizenship rights, which are dependent on membership in a particular community."[24] Donaldson and Kymlicka endorse this division between human and citizenship rights, arguing that while human rights accrue regardless of location, citizenship is connected with community self determination and is inherently linked to territory:

> The commitment to bounded citizenship is not just pragmatic. There are powerful moral values tied up with citizenship, including values of national identity and culture, and of self determination. Many people see themselves as members of collectives that have a right to govern themselves and their bounded territory, and to govern themselves in ways that reflect their national identities, languages and histories. These aspirations to national self government reflect deep attachments to a particular community and a particular territory, and these attachments are legitimate and worthy of respect.[25]

In other words, citizenship in this view is a subset of sovereignty, describing a relationship linking the individual to the sovereign State through a system of membership.

Donaldson and Kymlicka certainly do not think of citizenship in this guise as a passive state of membership or merely as a legal category. On the contrary, they suggest citizenship goes beyond mere national membership, and beyond individual involvement in forms of popular sovereignty that legitimate rule and authority. Instead citizenship encompasses an active space of political agency, where the citizen is understood as "taking on the right and responsibility to shape law."[26] But, as noted by the authors, the latter view of citizenship is

---

24 Donaldson and Kymlicka. *Zoopolis.* 52. In terms of the differentiation between human rights and citizenship rights, see Arendt. *The Origins of Totalitarianism.* Particularly Chapter 9, "The Decline of the Nation-State and the End of the Rights of Man." See also Giorgio Agamben. *Means Without End: Notes on Politics.* Minneapolis/London: University of Minnesota Press, 2000.

25 Donaldson and Kymlicka. *Zoopolis.* 53. Donaldson and Kymlicka go on:
  Indeed part of what it means to respect people is to respect their capacity to develop such morally significant attachments and relationships, including attachments to particular individuals and communities, to territory, to ways of life, and to schemes of cooperation and self government. Bounded citizenship expresses and enables such attachments. (53).

26 Donaldson and Kymlicka. *Zoopolis.* 56.

usually the reason for the exclusion of animals from the category, since active citizenship often implies that citizens will possess particular attributes in order to participate in the *polis*. Indeed, Donaldson and Kymlicka point out that the failure to allow animals to be considered as citizens "rests on a misunderstanding about the nature of citizenship":

> Citizenship has multiple functions, and all of them are, in principle, applicable to animals. Citizenship operates to allocate individuals to territories; to allocate membership in sovereign peoples; and to enable diverse forms of political agency (including assisted and dependent agency). Not only is it conceptually coherent to apply all three citizenship functions to animals, but we argue...it is the only coherent way to make sense of our moral obligations.[27]

Using these three elements of citizenship as a guide (allocation to territory, sovereign membership, political agency), Donaldson and Kymlicka outline several dimensions for how citizenship might function for animal citizens in relation to rights and obligations. They note that the justification and obligation for extending a right of political membership to domesticated animals flows from the long historical injustice associated with mass capture, slavery and death imposed on animals: "having brought such animals into our society, and deprived them of other possible forms of existence (at least for the foreseeable future), we have a duty to include them in our social and political arrangements on fair terms."[28] Donaldson and Kymlicka observe that like human children, animal citizens have a right of basic socialisation to allow them to adapt to a mixed human/animal society[29] Further, citizenship would have implications for freedom of movement, and it is noted that "our current treatment of domestic animals...violates the strong prima facie presumption against confinement and constraint"[30] and human duties for the protection of domestic animals from harm.[31] Donaldson and Kymlicka observe that extending citizenship to domesticated animals would create limits on the use of

---

27   Donaldson and Kymlicka. *Zoopolis*. 61.

28   Donaldson and Kymlicka. *Zoopolis*. 101.

29   Donaldson and Kymlicka. *Zoopolis*. 125. Note that while Donaldson and Kymlicka appear to allow for non humans to play a part in this teaching role ("She will learn not just from other dogs, but also from humans, and possibly the cat too" [124]) there appears to be an unspoken role for humans in directing this socialisation towards adaption of animals to human life.

30   Donaldson and Kymlicka. *Zoopolis*. 129.

31   Donaldson and Kymlicka. *Zoopolis*. 132–134.

animal products, and would regulate the use of animal labour, observing that "much training of domesticated animals is exploitative."[32] Citizenship would extend rights to medical care and intervention, and Donaldson and Kymlicka suggest that this might "be fulfilled through some scheme of animal health insurance."[33] Political representation would be facilitated through advocacy on behalf of animals, requiring "institutional reforms at a number of levels" not only "representation in the legislative process, but it will also require representing animals in, for example, municipal land planning decisions, or on the governance of boards of various professions and public services (police, emergency services, medicine, law, urban planning, social services, etc.)."[34] In the areas of sex, reproduction and nutrition, there would also be increased autonomy for animals under the proposed citizenship model, although with some caveats, including that "humans, at least for the foreseeable future, need to exercise some control over breeding in the interests of domesticated animals"[35] (a viewpoint I shall return to, and ask critical questions of, below) and that vegetable based diets would be preferred for dogs and cats.[36]

Where participatory political inclusion is the focus for domesticated animals, Donaldson and Kymlicka propose recognition of sovereignty for wild animals, developing "a theory of sovereignty which recognizes that the flourishing of wild animals cannot be separated from the flourishing of communities, and which reframes the rights of wild animals in terms of fair interaction between communities."[37] This proposal, I would contend, significantly extends existing theories of sovereignty, which are limited in their ability to recognise non human animals, because there is an expectation of a normatively defined authority structure existing within a community (a "people") in order to recognise a claim of sovereignty.[38] As we have seen, this limitation applies to Goodin,

---

32   Donaldson and Kymlicka. *Zoopolis*. 141.

33   Donaldson and Kymlicka. *Zoopolis*. 143.

34   Donaldson and Kymlicka. *Zoopolis*. 154.

35   Donaldson and Kymlicka. *Zoopolis*. 148.

36   Donaldson and Kymlicka. *Zoopolis*. 152. Although the authors note with respect to cats that "there may be no way for humans to have cat companions without dealing with a certain level of moral complexity regarding their diet and other restrictions necessary for them to be part of human-animal society" (152).

37   Donaldson and Kymlicka. *Zoopolis*. 167.

38   This is one of the challenges faced by Indigenous people in claiming recognition of (pre-existing) sovereign rights. In the case of Australia, for example, rights to land through "native title" claims have required Indigenous people to demonstrate a continuing connection to land, traditional customs and laws. For a discussion of the racialised logic informing recognition of Indigenous rights to land, see Aileen Moreton Robinson.

Pateman and Pateman's model discussed above. In distinction to this approach, Donaldson and Kymlicka argue that there is a strong basis for amending our understanding of sovereignty to reflect the moral purpose in guaranteeing sovereign rights to communities. They suggest a different capability to establish sovereign rights; namely, an "interest in autonomy":

> When evaluating whether and how to accord rights to sovereignty to particular communities, what matters is not the legal institutions they happen to possess, but rather whether they have interests in autonomy, which, in turn, depends on whether their flourishing is tied to their ability to maintain their modes of social organization and self-regulation on their territory.[39]

Donaldson and Kymlicka go on:

> What sort of competence is needed for sovereignty? We would argue that for wild animals—as indeed for humans—what matters for sovereignty is the ability to respond to the challenges the community faces, and to provide a social context in which its individual members can grow and flourish. Sometimes this competence is 'mechanical and spontaneous,' as when animals respond at an instinctual level to their bodily urges, and to opportunities, challenges and changes in their environment. And sometimes this competence is consciously learned (as when the bears in Yellowstone Park learn to open the doors of minivans by bouncing on the roof, and pass on this learning to other bears).[40]

In this model, wild animals are granted sovereign rights due to their competency to manage their own affairs.[41] Granting sovereignty to wild animals does not mean that humans cannot intervene into declared sovereign communities.

"The Possessive Logic of Patriarchal White Sovereignty: The High Court and the Yorta Yorta decision." *Borderlands e-Journal*. 3.2, 2004.

39   Donaldson and Kymlicka. *Zoopolis*. 173.

40   Donaldson and Kymlicka. *Zoopolis*. 175.

41   There are certainly a few facets of this competency that are worth paying attention to. The ability to inculcate community is seen as a necessary capability for sovereignty, and Donaldson and Kymlicka suggest that this may arise as a result of both a "natural" and "social" response ("animals respond at an instinctual level to their bodily urges, and to opportunities, challenges and changes in their environment"). My discussion in Chapter 6 in relation to Haraway's cautions on the way in which a nature/culture divide can function probably apply here. It is worth noting at this point that domestic animals

Donaldson and Kymlicka argue that there are beneficial interventions, such as providing security ("sovereignty is a form of protection against external threats of annihilation, exploitation or assimilation"[42]) whether from an external predatory threat, or internally in terms of guarantees of protection in relation to natural disaster or famine. Nor, even though territory is important to Donaldson and Kymlicka's model (a point we shall return to), does sovereignty entail distinct separated communities:

> ...whether we conceive of a particular territory as a single sovereign multi-species community, or a series of overlapping sovereign communities, the key point is that territory is protected from external alien rule or depredations, and free internally to evolve along its own autonomous course.[43]

However, in Donaldson and Kymlicka's model, political representation for sovereign communities is acknowledged as a potential problem: "wild animals are not in a position to physically defend themselves from interference. They cannot represent themselves in diplomatic negotiations or on international bodies. They cannot make collective decisions about delegating responsibility for the protection of their sovereign interests."[44] The answer proposed is "some form of proxy representation by human beings who are committed to the principle of animal sovereignty."[45]

At least at the level of political representation and security within the Westphalian system of nation states, Donaldson and Kymlicka arrive at a similar position to Goodin, Pateman and Pateman.[46] However, there are some important differences in their approaches. Donaldson and Kymlicka's model represents an advance on Goodin, Pateman and Pateman's model, at least in so

---

presumably lack this competence in Donaldson and Kymlicka's model, since they are in relationships of dependence with humans.

42 Donaldson and Kymlicka. *Zoopolis*. 180. Note the correspondence of this view of sovereignty with Esposito's identification of biopolitics with immunity, and recent moves in defining sovereignty that is closer to contemporary international relations models of a "responsibility to protect." See Gareth Evans. *The Responsibility to Protect: Ending Mass Atrocity Crimes Once and For All*. Washington: Brookings Institution Press, 2008.

43 Donaldson and Kymlicka. *Zoopolis*. 191. See particularly Donaldson and Kymlicka's discussion of migrating right whales (189).

44 Donaldson and Kymlicka. *Zoopolis*. 209.

45 Donaldson and Kymlicka. *Zoopolis*. 209.

46 Seee Donaldson and Kymlicka's reference to Goodin Pateman and Pateman. Donaldson and Kymlicka. *Zoopolis*. 209.

far as it is more inclusive. Goodin, Pateman and Pateman justify the capability of great apes for sovereignty by their lack of differentiation from humans in key areas of functioning and "intelligence," suggesting that great apes satisfy the criteria of a "people" as it currently is understood in international law.[47] As discussed above, it is argued that because humans and great apes are so alike, in particular through possessing a comparable social order, that sovereignty rights are recognisable.[48] In this sense, arguably, Goodin, Pateman and Pateman use a more conservative approach to understanding sovereignty, allowing access to sovereign rights to non human animals who can demonstrate capability that directly resembles that of humans that comprise political communities. This differs from Donaldson and Kymlicka's argument in *Zoopolis*, which recognises the capability for sovereignty in a broader range of entities (beyond just great apes). The innovation here is in focusing on what constitutes a political community as a category, rather than the individual capacities of members of a community of "people." As such, Donaldson and Kymlicka create an alternative set of criteria, which do not strictly rely on any membership similarity to human communities, but rests on a capability of a collectivity to "have interests in autonomy, which, in turn, depends on whether their flourishing is tied to their ability to maintain their modes of social organization and self-regulation on their territory."[49] Because Donaldson and Kymlicka approach sovereignty through a species non-specific level of political community functioning, rather than as status that can only be attained by individuals satisfying a capability test, there is broader scope to include a wider range of animal sovereignties and side step the perhaps inevitable species selectiveness of the model offered by Goodin, Pateman and Pateman. In this sense, as I have said, there is significant innovation in Donaldson and Kymlicka's approach, which results in a vision of sovereignty that is broader than that of Goodin, Pateman and Pateman and potentially includes a wider range of animal sovereignties. It also, at least partially, addresses the concern that under a Westphalian system of sovereignty, humans are granted forms of sovereignty

---

47   The shared Article 1.1 of the United Nations *International Covenant on Civil and Political Rights* and the *International Covenant on Economic, Social and Cultural Rights* states: "All peoples have the right of self-determination. By virtue of that right they freely determine their political status and freely pursue their economic, social and cultural development." Article 1.2 states further: "All peoples may, for their own ends, freely dispose of their natural wealth and resources without prejudice to any obligations arising out of international economic co-operation, based upon the principle of mutual benefit, and international law. In no case may a people be deprived of its own means of subsistence."

48   Goodin, Pateman and Pateman. "Simian Sovereignty." 833.

49   Donaldson and Kymlicka. *Zoopolis.* 173.

on the basis of capabilities that are seen as distinctly human, thus creating an inherent limitation on who can access this right to self determination.

A continuing problem I would raise with Donaldson and Kymlicka's approach relates to the human sovereign prerogative to decide. We saw this above in relation to Nussbaum's capability approach, which when applied to animals required human judgement on a range of animal capabilities, and justified continuing forms of paternalism in the name of animal flourishing. Donaldson and Kymlicka's proposal is not immune from some of these same problems. For example, one question we may ask of Donaldson and Kymlicka is: who gets to decide on citizenship and sovereignty, and who regulates these political statuses? It would appear that the model that is put forward still relies upon humans determining these category differences, and standing at the borders of political status to determine eligibilities and entitlements. In this sense the human prerogative to decide remains in the background of the Donaldson and Kymlicka model: as such we do not find a clear contestation of the idea put forward by Webster that "Man has dominion over the animals whether we like it or not."[50] I acknowledge there is a limit to this sort of objection. Clearly Donaldson and Kymlicka, like Goodin, Pateman and Pateman, are utilizing existing liberal political conceptualisations and attempting to push and reformulate them practically to include non human subjects. And it appears true that the model they propose already pushes the limits of these concepts. However, any attempt to oppose systemic violence towards animals, and include non human animals within the human community, is necessarily radical, and must rupture the usual humanist conceptualisations of the liberal political State. One wonders: why is it that Donaldson and Kymlicka could not go further? Why is it that they reproduce elements of existing political structure (citizenship, the nation State and the Westphalian system) which might be open to critical questioning, and why it is that forms of human continuing domination—with respect to key decision making—remain authorised?

These problems are certainly apparent in Donaldson and Kymlicka's discussion of the regulation of the sexuality and reproduction of domesticated animals. It is to this aspect of their model that I will now turn. Donaldson and Kymlicka acknowledge that humans "exert enormous control over domesticated animals' sex and reproductive lives—whether they *can* do it, whether they *may* do it, and *when, how*, and *with whom* they may do it."[51] However, Donaldson and Kymlicka do not oppose regulation of sex, sexuality and reproduction *per se*, arguing that the regulation of sexuality and

---

50   Webster. *Animal Welfare*. 3.

51   Donaldson and Kymlicka. *Zoopolis*. 144.

reproduction occurs in human societies and in "the wild," and that these controls can be justified. They argue that human societies regulate sexuality for a range of reasons, including the protection of children, protecting individuals from non consensual sex,[52] and through intervention into reproduction and choices, including, for example, "selective abortion to end pregnancies in the case of birth defects."[53] Donaldson and Kymlicka suggest that regulation is driven by individuals in human societies through social practice and norm, although these controls are also bolstered by forms of State intervention: "in general, we expect individuals to be self regulating and responsible when it comes to engaging in sex and accepting its consequences. When they are unable to do so, the state intervenes."[54] These controls, according to Donaldson and Kymlicka, aim at sustainability in population and protection of children: "through self regulation of reproduction, humans can (theoretically) ensure their numbers don't exceed sustainable levels, or their (individual and collective) ability to care for the children they produce."[55] These twin aims, we are told, are effectively mirrored "in nature" for wild animals. Donaldson and Kymlicka, citing the example of wolves, suggest that these animals "strictly regulate sexual and reproductive activity," extending to forms of self regulation,[56] and we are told that certain pious wolves "go their entire lives without having sex."[57] However, in addition to forms of self regulation, external forces also limit population sizes for other animals:

> Amongst some species, almost all adult females mate and produce young. Often, huge numbers of young are produced, and adults invest almost no

---

52   Note that Donaldson and Kymlicka's formulation here of sexuality in relation to consensuality almost mirrors the critique put forward by Mackinnon and others that suggests that patriarchy constructs sexuality as a violation that is consented to. Donaldson and Kymlicka state that "We insist that sex be consensual; one's freedom to have sex isn't absolute, but dependent on a willing partner" (144). This construction implicitly is suggestive that non consensual sex is still sex (rather than violence). A different conceptualisation might suggest that sex is always a process of negotiation with another/others, and collapses into violence when this negotiation fails. This view might treat sex/sexuality not as a drive that must be regulated through prohibition, norm and law, but as a productive and creative process that is opposed to violence itself.

53   Donaldson and Kymlicka. *Zoopolis.* 145.

54   Donaldson and Kymlicka. *Zoopolis.* 145.

55   Donaldson and Kymlicka. *Zoopolis.* 145.

56   Donaldson and Kymlicka. *Zoopolis.* 145.

57   Donaldson and Kymlicka. *Zoopolis.* 145.

energy in caring for them. The population is kept in check by predation, exposure, disease and starvation.[58]

Having established the "inevitability" of the regulation of sexuality and reproduction for both human societies and wild animal societies—through self regulatory norm, law or "nature"—Donaldson and Kymlicka argue on the contrary that the process of domestication strips animals from a context in which sex and reproduction can be effectively regulated. The inability of domesticated animals to control their population, either through self regulation or through external controls such as predation, means that, for Donaldson and Kymlicka, human intervention is required: "this is not an excuse for humans to simply step out of the picture."[59] Thus, humans get to decide; they must decide:

> To the extent that domesticated animals are unable to exercise meaningful agency, humans have a responsibility to act in their interests. As members of the community, domesticated animals are entitled to protection, including where necessary, paternalistic protection. Moreover to the extent they are not internally self regulating, they are subject to the constraints of social life (e.g. to having regulation imposed on them in order to protect the basic rights of others and the sustainability of a scheme of cooperation).[60]

There is much that is risky and potentially problematic in this discussion provided by Donaldson and Kymlicka in relation to the case of sex and reproductive regulation for domesticated animals. The normalisation and/or naturalisation of sex and reproductive controls to ensure "numbers don't exceed sustainable levels" and ensure the "ability to care for the children they produce," seems to sidestep the substantial regulation of sex, sexuality and reproduction that serves a range of purposes other than control of population or security for children. This includes large scale regulations on how sex practices are performed, when, where and with whom, and the normalisation of

---

58   Donaldson and Kymlicka. *Zoopolis*. 145. Note the way in which "care" is situated in relation to reproduction quantity here, and the almost pivotal identification of females as responsible for this process (males are presumably not responsible for the "surplus" production of babies). It is almost as if the female species here, wantonly reproducing without restraint or subsequent care, is constructed in contrast to the pious male wolves discussed previously by Donaldson and Kymlicka, who defer to the "alpha" male wolves, and may "go their entire lives without having sex" for the good of the clan.

59   Donaldson and Kymlicka. *Zoopolis*. 146.

60   Donaldson and Kymlicka. *Zoopolis*. 146.

sex and gender identities through these controls. It is certainly telling that Donaldson and Kymlicka do not attend to the questions that might relate to societal regulation of homosexual or queer sexuality; indeed their conjoined discussion of sexuality and reproduction as if these were the same and interchangeable, either for humans or animals, appears to implicitly normalise heterosexual practice, and aligns sexual pleasure only with the goal of reproduction. Through this all, the challenge of understanding animal pleasures, what constitutes them, what animals desire, genital or otherwise—surely central questions for any future where animals might exert their own individual and collective controls—are put to the side, as if these are not centrally connected to the problem of the regulation of sex and sexuality.[61]

The human prerogative to decide with respect to reproduction begins to resemble a more overt form of biopolitical sovereign regulation when Donaldson and Kymlicka explicitly examine population controls. They acknowledge that humans have intervened in reproductive processes for domesticated animals, and as a result have generated current population numbers: "the only reason they exist in the numbers they do is because we intensively breed them to exploit them."[62] It is argued that in future an end of a relationship of domestication would reduce population sizes (since, for example, chickens would not be bred to be eaten). Donaldson and Kymlicka

---

61   This is perhaps highlighted in Donaldson and Kymlicka's discussion of individual rights, sexuality and reproduction:

> In general, we expect individuals to be self-regulating and responsible when it comes to engaging in sex and accepting its consequences. When they are unable to do so, the state intervenes (e.g., to protect children, to protect unwitting partners from contracting HIV, or unwilling partners from sexual assault). "There is no 'right to have (partnered) sex' as such, but, rather, a right to be free from sexual coercion, or unwarranted sexual regulation. And while most people would insist that we have a 'right to have a family'" (a right which is enshrined in the UN's *Declaration of Human Rights*), this right, too, depends on having a willing partner (or donor, or adoptee). (145).

The suspicion that Donaldson and Kymlicka seem to cast over any claim to a right to sexual pleasure itself seems indicative of a more general problem in how rights and sovereignty are conceptualised with respect to pleasure (see, for example, Françoise Girard. "United Nations—Negotiating Sexual Rights and Sexual Orientation at the UN." Richard Parker, Rosalind Petchesky and Robert Sember Eds. *Sex Politics: Reports From the Front Lines*. Sexuality Policy Watch. 2004. 311–58). I have previously argued, with Deirdre Tedmanson, that the regulation of pleasure must be considered the "fourth pillar" of sovereignty (along with legitimised authority, violence, and race/species distinction). See Deirdre Tedmanson and Dinesh Joseph Wadiwel. "The Governmentality of New Race/ Pleasure Wars?" *Culture and Organisation*. 16.1, 2009. 7–22.

62   Donaldson and Kymlicka. *Zoopolis*. 147.

suggest that population controls in this future scenario would meet different goals:

> Presumably we should head towards population sizes that are (a) ecologically sustainable, and (b) socially sustainable (i.e., reflect some sort of balance between the human duty to care for domesticated animals, and the ways in which animals contribute to joint human-animal society). It is in the interest of domesticated animals that humans regulate their numbers in a sustainable fashion rather than allowing the ravages of ecological or social collapse to do so instead.[63]

Donaldson and Kymlicka point out that population controls need not involve infringements of bodily integrity, and may comprise non-invasive techniques. Donaldson and Kymlicka state:

> ...there are many relatively non-invasive ways in which we can control the reproductive rates of domesticated animals—birth control vaccines, temporary physical separation, non-fertilization of chicken eggs, etc. Moreover, insofar as possible, we can impose birth control measures after animals have had a chance to have a family, if they feel inclined to do so.[64]

Is it really "in the interest of domesticated animals that humans regulate their numbers"?[65] As Palmer points out, justified paternalism might account for reproductive controls where they are genuinely in the "interests" of those being dominated. However, Palmer observes this "is rarely the case with pet de-sexing, where domination combines with instrumentalism, not paternalism."[66]

---

63   Donaldson and Kymlicka. *Zoopolis*. 147.
64   Donaldson and Kymlicka. *Zoopolis*. 147.
65   Donaldson and Kymlicka. *Zoopolis*. 147.
66   Palmer. "Killing in Animal Shelters." 183. Palmer states elsewhere:

> The 'neutering' of pet animals is a process much recommended by animal welfare organisations. It prevents, they argue, the production of "unwanted litters"—that is to say, litters unwanted by humans. This, in itself reveals power-relationships of a kind. But of course, the practices of "neutering" and "spaying" of male and female animals are not just about making them sterile. If that were so, male cats might simply receive vasectomies. These processes are, instead, much more extensive operations designed to desexualise animal bodies, and in addition to produce particular behavioural changes: placidity, docility, less tendency to roam and a slackening in territoriality (and accompanying habits, like peeing on the furniture). Neutering and spaying removes the evidence of animal sexuality from the domestic environment: animal

And the difficulty will always be in separating out between justified paternalism and instrumentality, and determining where human interests trump those
of animals. This issue becomes explicit where questions of animal population
size challenge the sustainability of human populations, and where a human
biopolitical prerogative to decide would predictably act to securitise the sustainability of human populations (over non human populations).[67] Clearly
these are difficult questions for how we might imagine futures with animals
beyond human utilisation. However, the challenge surely must be how to
unseat and question a human right to decide. The measures proposed here
look uncomfortably like a reconfiguration of the human domination, but in an
apparently more benign form, where species difference still justifies differential logics and uses of violence. In this sense, the framework almost explicitly
conforms to a model of biopolitical sovereignty, even if it moves beyond current models in relation to species inclusiveness.

We might make sense of this renewed biopolitical conceptualisation of sovereignty—one that still relies upon species norms and modes of violence to
articulate political statuses—in the relationship created by Donaldson and
Kymlicka between sovereignty, territory and the terms of political membership. As I have discussed, the capabilities for sovereignty in Donaldson and
Kymlicka's model are different from that premised by the Westphalian system
and potentially include a range of non human others. There is further flexibility in Donaldson and Kymlicka's model in the capacity for sovereignty to overlap and recognise mixed utilisation of territory, which demonstrates a
commitment to "abandoning the idea that sovereignty must be univocal and
absolute."[68] However, the biopolitical nature of sovereignty remains intact.
Donaldson and Kymlicka put forward a view of sovereignty that implicitly

---

        sexuality which might be disturbing for any number of reasons (a constant reminder
        of that which is kept hidden in human relationships; a reminder that a pet is an adult
        mammal rather than an infant; the cause of transgressive displays or behaviours).
        See Palmer. "Taming the Wild Profusion of Existing Things?" 357.

67   In the Introduction I discussed Regan's limit case of the lifeboat, where in the extreme
       circumstance of a choice between a human interest in life and that of animals, the sur-
       vival of humans will always, in Regan's model, trump the will to self-preservation of ani-
       mals. It is perhaps frightening that the forms of regulation of reproduction proposed here
       by Donaldson and Kymlicka may begin to look like a variation on the lifeboat case, where
       in an extreme circumstance human population size may be weighed against animal
       population sizes as a matter of survival. This is of course a paradigmatic case of biopoli-
       tics; literally the decision to regulate animal populations in this case will be on the basis
       of the securitisation of human populations.

68   Donaldson and Kymlicka. *Zoopolis*. 190.

articulates a relationship between population and territory, where territory is seen as what fosters and nourishes the life of population. Donaldson and Kymlicka state:

> Sovereignty is importantly tied to territory, since a community, especially most animal communities, cannot be ecologically viable, let alone autonomously self regulating, without a landbase to sustain it. But sovereignty need not be defined in terms of exclusive access of control over a particular territory, but rather in terms of the extent or nature of access and control necessary for a community to be autonomous and self-regulating.[69]

In so far as the biological life of population and territory are explicitly linked, this proposal for sovereignty is expressly biopolitical. Sovereignty in this guise replaces a simple prerogative to rule by the sword (from which stems power over territory and population) with a model of sovereignty that provides access to territory to species communities on the basis of what is required for the autonomy and sufficiency of that species.

A "bare" biopolitical sovereignty need not be problematic. However, as we have discussed, both in relation to the regulation of sexuality and reproduction above, and in previous chapters, there are challenges to how we might escape the hostility between human and animal without challenging the biopolitical determination of politics, particularly if biopolitics is in essence constructed as the contest between human and animal. We might make sense of this in relation to Donaldson and Kymlicka's discussion of citizenship, and the rights that might accrue to those who achieve this form of civil and political inclusion. Citizenship expresses the blood link between the material body and the territory proclaimed as part of the sovereign domain. In this sense, citizenship is the chain that binds the body to the sovereign. We might indeed define citizenship in the same way in which Hobbes imagines civil laws as binding individuals to the king: "artificial chains which they themselves, by mutual covenants, have fastened at one end, to the lips of that man, or assembly, to whom they have given the sovereign power; and at the other end their own ears."[70] Citizenship is an explicitly biopolitical concept in so far as it operates, at least in some guises, as literally a blood link to membership of the *polis* (hence the application of the principles of *jus sanguinis*—blood or family connection—and *jus soli*—territorial connection—to determine eligibility for citizenship rights). Yet even in conceptions of citizenship that rely on active

---

69   Donaldson and Kymlicka. *Zoopolis.* 190.
70   Hobbes. *Leviathan.* 140.

models of political participation, the inside/outside relationship between citizen and non citizen is defining, and illustrates how it is that even a broadly inclusive conceptualisation of citizenship might still be premised on exception. Put simply, we would not need a category of membership to a political community (that is, the citizen) if there wasn't already a hierarchical and exclusory logic in place that seeks to distinguish between citizen and non citizen; that is, to determine a zone of exclusion that defines the rights belonging to citizens in contradistinction to those who do not have these rights. As such, the concept of citizenship is simultaneously a declaration of who is excluded from the *polis*. Arendt observed this with respect to the distinction between human rights and citizenship rights; loss of the latter means a loss of world, even in spite of the minimal guarantees of human rights protections:

> The great danger arising from the existence of people forced to live outside the common world is that they are thrown back, in the midst of civilization, on their natural giveness, on their mere differentiation. They lack that tremendous equalizing of differences which comes from being citizens of some commonwealth and yet, since they are no longer allowed to partake in the human artifice, they then begin to belong to the human race in much the same way as animals belong to a specific animal species.[71]

One response to this schism is to seek to grant citizenship rights to an ever expanding set of entities. Another approach is to abandon citizenship altogether as a means of constituting community. We may recall in Chapter 1 the close linkages we described between sovereignty, biopower and exception. Sovereignty, at least in Agamben's conception, arises precisely at the decision on exception; a decision on who is in and out, a decision which Agamben notes is by definition biopolitical. If, as Agamben describes, biopolitics is an expression of the distinction between humans and animals—a veritable moving zone of conflict—then we might perceive that any model of political membership that prescribes citizenship based upon inside/outside relationships will already be biopolitical, and will already reinscribe the borders between human and animal, even if the terms of that political membership might change. Thus while we may bend citizenship to include other "fellows," the fact that the political community is by definition based on an inside/outside relationship (that is between those who belong to a political community, and those who don't) already recreates the border between human and animal, between those who

---

71   Arendt. *The Origins of Totalitarianism.* 302.

are owed rights and those who are not. This was after all present in the classic Aristotlean conception of the *polis* that I discussed in Chapter 1, that distinction between human, animal and savage which comes about by virtue of creating a border around and terms of membership in relation to the polis: "it is evident that the state is a creation of nature, and that man is by nature a political animal. And he who by nature and not by mere accident is without state, is either a bad man or above humanity."[72] The danger here in relying on citizenship lies in merely in restating/reinstating the conflict between human and animal, and drawing lines based upon potentially arbitrary determinations of capability and species flourishing.

This danger is illustrated in Donaldson and Kymlicka's reliance on the transitory term *denizen*—the third element in their tripartite model of sovereignty and political membership—to describe "liminal animals" who neither owe allegiance or seek dependency from existing nation states (that is, domesticated animals) nor possess sovereignty in their own right (that is, wild animals). According to Donaldson and Kymlicka, these liminal animals rely on humans generally for survival, but do not require specific forms of care or fostering of life:

> Liminal animals occupy a different niche with respect to human communities. By definition, they have adapted to changes in the environment due to human activity, and in this sense they need, or at least benefit from, humans. But, while liminal animals are dependent on human settlement and the resources it offers them, this dependency is more generalized—a reliance on human settlement writ large. Within that context they typically fend for themselves, living independently of individual humans...[73]

Donaldson and Kymlicka divide up liminal animals into "opportunists," "niche specialists," "introduced exotics" and "feral animals." "Opportunists" are species that have adapted to human-built environments, and include "grey squirrels, raccoons, mallard ducks, gulls, crows, bats, deer, foxes, hawkes and many others."[74] The opportunist animal is defined as one who is "dependent on humans in a non specific sense;" Donaldson and Kymlicka argue that these animals "live off human settlement, but do not rely on a relationship with any

---

72   Aristotle. *Politics*. 446 [1253a].
73   Donaldson and Kymlicka. *Zoopolis*. 218.
74   Donaldson and Kymlicka. *Zoopolis*. 219.

specific human(s), and can often adapt to changes in human activity."[75] "Niche specialists" are less flexible animal communities that have adapted to specific human-created environments; Donaldson and Kymlicka cite the example of the hedgerow, which may create a living environment for foxes and mice. Change in the human environment (such as the removal of the hedgerow) threatens the lives of these liminal creatures. "Introduced exotics" are animals brought into an environment which is not their own, and thrown into competition with "native species" in the territory. Examples include rabbits and cane toads, and Donaldson and Kymlicka note that these animals are subject to eradication campaigns as a result of their potential impact on existing ecosystems. The final category of liminal animal described by Donaldson and Kymlicka are "feral animals," which are understood as previously domesticated animals or their descendents who are no longer under human control: "escaped or abandoned cats and dogs come readily to mind. But there are also large populations of feral farm animals, especially in Australia, where feral populations (including pigs, horses, cattle, goats, buffalo and camels) number in the millions."[76]

Why are these animals defined as "liminal" and not offered citizenship rights as "domesticated animals," nor sovereign rights as a "people," in their own right? The answer has to do with their relationship to territory. These "liminal" animals—opportunists, specialists, exotics and feral—are defined through a relationship to territory which looks different from that which might either provide citizenship rights or sovereignty in a full sense. Because these animals do not pay credence to the natural (or human constructed) borders of nation states, because they share human constructed space but do not express connection or allegiance to human communities, because these animals are migratory and do not have clearly demarcated sovereign territories, and because these animals may rely on human constructed habitats, they are only granted provisional membership as perpetual visitors. The effect of ascribing denizenship to these animals is that a right to full membership (either to be members of a pre-existing human community or to possess sovereignty in their own right) is denied because they are not perceived to possess a territory of their own; they are conceptualised effectively as populations without a homeland. In this sense, Donaldson and Kymlicka, despite offering a glimpse of a sovereignty that goes beyond Westphalia, merely reinscribe this model.

A system of bounded nation State communities might work where all can access rights within their respective communities, relative material inequality

---

75   Donaldson and Kymlicka. *Zoopolis*. 220.
76   Donaldson and Kymlicka. *Zoopolis*. 224.

between communities is minimised, and rights of freedom of movement and nationality allow for flexibility and choice. However, we know from our own world that we are far from this cosmopolitan vision of global organisation. Indeed, the stratification of global human labour markets and, the maintenance of massive inequalities in wages, security and opportunities across nation State borders, only emphasises that the nation State system is complicit with the fabrication of distinction which authorises arbitrary differentiation between human population groups, and allows global capitalism to maintain the exploitative forms of circulation that underpin it. The Westphalian conceptualisation of sovereignty is tested as soon as the non-national, the outsider to the territory, the *denizen*, makes a claim to a right of non distinction from those who are granted citizenship rights. As Arendt has observed, those who reside outside of the border always threaten the cohesiveness of the construct of the nation, and put to test the presumption that "even if there were other nationalities within their borders they needed no additional law for them, and that only in the newly established succession states was a temporary enforcement of human rights necessary as a compromise and exception."[77] Arendt goes on to underline that the "arrival of the stateless people brought an end to this illusion."[78]

The problem emerges as soon as sovereignty is founded upon an assumed and self assured naturalised basis: either territory, capability or both. As I have argued, and will expand upon in Chapter 8, sovereignty cannot be considered as founded on anything. It is always an assertion in the dark, a declaration of potentiality, and an act of stupidity. This fact is immediately apparent when we examine our own claim of dominion over other animals, and find no basis for this claim. The injustice of our war on animals is that this presumption of sovereignty is always one-sided: humans are always in the position of declaring their own right to dominion, explicitly and implicitly, upon no established basis, and simultaneously denying any similar claim to those they exclude through this very declaration. As such, determinations of sovereignty exert an epistemic violence that obscures the originary groundlessness of the claim. Rather than asking what makes a being or a collective of beings—human or otherwise—capable to be granted sovereignty, we must instead ask how sovereignty arises as a political claim, and what its effects are in terms of establishing an apparent "truth" of superiority, a myth of superior capability itself. It is to this question we shall turn in the next chapter.

---

77   Arendt. *The Origins of Totalitarianism*. 276.
78   Arendt. *The Origins of Totalitarianism*. 276.

CHAPTER 8

The Violence of Stupidity

The White Whale swam before him as the monomaniac incarnation of all those malicious agencies which some deep men feel eating in them, till they are left living on with half a heart and half a lung. That intangible malignity which has been from the beginning; to whose dominion even the modern Christians ascribe one-half of the worlds; which the ancient Ophites of the east reverenced in their statue devil; – Ahab did not fall down and worship it like them; but deliriously transferring its idea to the abhorred white whale, he pitted himself, all mutilated, against it. All that most maddens and torments; all that stirs up the lees of things; all truth with malice in it; all that cracks the sinews and cakes the brain; all the subtle demonisms of life and thought; all evil, to crazy Ahab, were visibly personified, and made practically assailable in Moby Dick. He piled upon the whale's white hump the sum of all the general rage and hate felt by his whole race from Adam down; and then, as if his chest had been a mortar, he burst his hot heart's shell upon it.

HERMAN MELVILLE. *Moby Dick*[1]

If, as Bartelson contends, "sovereignty has no essence,"[2] if sovereignty cannot be tracked to a set of identifiable naturalised foundations or capabilities in a "people", then how are we to understand it? Through this book I have understood sovereignty as a particular mode of domination that arises through conflict. Following Foucault, I have argued that sovereignty is a means to fix a pattern of domination, through institutions, practices, law and knowledge, which allows for the continuation of war by other means. Taking this broad definition of sovereignty, and linking it clearly with warfare, has allowed for an understanding of sovereignty that goes beyond the territorial and institutional limits of the Westphalian imagination, towards understanding sovereignty as a relation that might extend to our claimed human sovereignty over other animals, a claim that operates across the borders of nation states, and thus is truly cosmopolitan in its scope. Through this analysis, I have argued that we must reverse a prevalent understanding that domination—human or otherwise—is justified by superiority. On the contrary, as we began to see more clearly in

---

1   Herman Melville. *Moby Dick.* Mineola: Dover Publications, 2003. 154.
2   Bartelson. *A Genealogy of Sovereignty.* 51.

© KONINKLIJKE BRILL NV, LEIDEN, 2015 | DOI 10.1163/9789004300422_010

Chapter 4 in relation to Locke, humans are not more intelligent, or more rational, or more just. On the contrary: we dominate and appropriate animals, and through this process of domination, after the fact of appropriation, name ourselves, conveniently, as superior. This chapter completes this analysis through a reading of Jacques Derrida's last lectures, which I believe precisely focus upon this trajectory of analysis of sovereignty that I have laid out here. In this chapter I will examine Derrida's reading of animality and sovereignty, both to understand how we might re-understand human sovereignty over other animals, but also to simultaneously recognise the operation of animal sovereignties as a mode of resistance against human domination.

Derrida's Beasts

Against a continental philosophical tradition that has largely been ambivalent in relation to addressing human violence toward non human animals,[3] Derrida spoke clearly on violence and domination of non human animals in his late work,[4] particularly *The Animal That Therefore I Am* and Derrida's final lectures in 2002–04, published under the English title of *The Beast and the Sovereign* in two volumes (which I will refer to as *Beast 1* and *Beast 2*). The later work, in so far as it deals with animality and sovereignty, is directly connected to this book. In so far as *Beast 1* and *Beast 2* provide slightly different, although interconnected, readings on sovereignty, I will treat both volumes separately in the following analysis.[5]

---

3   See, for example, Peter Singer. "Preface." Peter Atterton and Matthew Calarco Eds. *Animal Philosophy*. and Matthew Calarco. *Zoographies: The Question of the Animal from Heidegger to Derrida*. London: Continuum, 2004. xi–xiii.

4   Two substantive collections so far have been published offering English readers some insight into this work: namely, *The Animal That Therefore I Am* which contained fragments of a ten hour seminar Derrida gave in 1997; and recently, Derrida's final lectures in 2002–04, published under the English title of *The Beast and the Sovereign*.

5   Derrida's work is frequently multilayered and playful; *Beast 1* and *Beast 2* are no exception to this tradition. Derrida approaches his central thematic in *Beast 1* and *Beast 2* in a perhaps typical fashion: that is by teasing out aspects of the problem through a critical textual analysis of apparently disparate pieces of prose and poetry. Many of the texts Derrida analyses in *Beast 1* are representative of the modern Western philosophical canon, including those thinkers that are familiar interlocutors with Derrida's work—Nietzsche, Heidegger, Schmitt and Lacan—as well as less frequent visitors, including Gilles Deleuze and Agamben. Derrida also explores work outside the strict confines of philosophy, including literature and literary theory (for example, Paul Celan, Paul Valéry and D.H. Lawrence). Like much of Derrida's written

The ancient aphorism which describes "man as a wolf amongst men" (*Homo homini lupus est*) is famously drawn upon by Hobbes in his preface to *De Cive*, where he notes wryly:

> all Kings are to be reckon'd amongst ravenous Beasts. But what a Beast of prey was the Roman people, whilst with its conquering Eagles it erected its proud Trophees so far and wide over the world, bringing the Africans, the Asiaticks, the Macedonians, and the Achaeans, with many other despoyled Nations, into a specious bondage, with the pretence of preferring them to be Denizens of Rome?[6]

The predatory relationship between a sovereign and the people is one of the concerns of *Beast 1*, which features an exploration of the way in which sovereignty as a concept is connected to animality, in particular through the analogy of the wolf. The wolf, as Derrida notes in the first seminar, shares with sovereignty a common condition of existing outside the juridical sphere: "sovereign and beast seem to have in common their being-outside-the-law."[7] This point of connection is noted by others, including Agamben in *Homo Sacer*;[8] however, Derrida teases out further the dimensions of this shared relationship, noting for example, the symbolically gendered dimension of the sovereign/beast relationship;[9] the capacity of the wolf/sovereignty for stealth[10] and capture;[11] and the wolf and the sovereign as rogues.[12] It is with respect to the latter observation that we find, early on in *Beast 1*, a frank discussion by Derrida of the spectacles that have become commonplace in the exercise of sovereignty within the contemporary era, including a discussion of global war and terror through Noam Chomsky's *Rogue States*[13] and the role of visual media in establishing the

---

work, there is significant intersection and overlap with themes of his previous writing. Sometimes this is in connection with his more recent ethico-political interventions—for example, on hospitality, giving, friendship and war—and sometimes with earlier work, such as on trace or *différance*.

6   Thomas Hobbes. *De Cive: Philosophicall Rudiments Concerning Government and Society.* London: J.G. for R. Royston, 1651. See "Preface."

7   Derrida. *The Beast and the Sovereign Vol. 1*. 17, D38.

8   See particularly Agamben, *Homo Sacer*. 104–11.

9   Derrida. *The Beast and the Sovereign Vol. 1*. 1, D20; also 9, D28-9.

10   Derrida. *The Beast and the Sovereign Vol. 1*. 10, D30.

11   Derrida. *The Beast and the Sovereign Vol. 1*. 11–2, D31-2.

12   Derrida. *The Beast and the Sovereign Vol. 1*. 22, D45.

13   Derrida. *The Beast and the Sovereign Vol. 1*. 22, 19–20, D41-2 and 88–9, D130. See also in this respect Noam Chomsky. *Rogue States: The Rule of Force in World Affairs*, Cambridge, MA:

operation of "international terrorism."[14] Tied to this is analysis of what might be considered foundational thinkers of sovereignty in the West: Thomas Hobbes, Niccolò Machiavelli, Jean Bodin and Carl Schmitt. Of particular note here is Derrida's commentary on Hobbes, which links with his previously published work on "response" and animality[15] where it is observed that sovereignty shares with the animal a symbolic trait of non response: the sovereign is "above the law [*le droit*] and has the right [*le droit*] to suspend the law, he does not have to respond before a representative chamber or before judges, he grants pardon or not after law has passed... He has a right to a certain irresponsibility."[16]

Derrida's analysis of Jacques Lacan in *Beast 1* provide lots of material for thinking through human violence towards animals. This includes a discussion of cruelty, its attributed connection to human nature, and its apparent disconnection from human treatment of animals: "I am never cruel toward the animal *as such*."[17] In this context, there is commentary on the poverty of ethical consideration that only provides recognition to what is like us ("our fellows") rather than radically other. This clearly links with Derrida's more recent challenges to ethics on questions of hospitality[18] or friendship.[19] However, it is worth noting that *Beast 1* appears to make explicit a call for an ethics that is radical in scope, and uncompromising in a refusal to distinguish human from inhuman:

> A principle of ethics or more radically of justice, in the most difficult sense, which I have attempted to oppose to right, to distinguish from right, is perhaps the obligation that engages my responsibility with respect to

---

South End Press, 2000. It is perhaps worth drawing attention to Derrida's almost cheeky use of Chomsky here: not merely in connection with Chomsky's clear humanist approach, nor the famed debate between Foucault and Chomsky, but also because of Chomsky's public views on poststructuralism which would suggest that both Chomsky and Derrida operate within very different universes. See Noam Chomsky. "Rationality/Science." *Z Magazine: Z Papers Special Issue*. 1995. At: www.chomsky.info/articles/1995----02.htm.

14   Derrida. *The Beast and the Sovereign Vol. 1*. 36–37, D64-5.

15   Derrida. *The Animal That Therefore I Am*. 119–140.

16   Derrida. *The Beast and the Sovereign Vol. 1*. 36–37, 57, D91. Derrida's analysis of Machiavelli on the prince as a "fox" also attributes an irresponsibility to sovereignty, in the ability to use cunning to maintain power and domination, while affecting a visage of respectability: "The prince must be a fox not only in order to be cunning like the fox, but in order to pretend to be what he is not and not what he is" (91, D132-3).

17   Derrida, *The Beast and the Sovereign Vol. 1*. 108, D154.

18   See Jacques Derrida and Anne Dufourmantelle. *Of Hospitality*. Stanford: Stanford University Press, 2000.

19   Jacques Derrida. *Politics of Friendship*. New York: Verso, 1997.

the most dissimilar [*le plus dissemblable*, the least "fellow" like], the entirely other, precisely the monstrously other, the unrecognizable other. The "unrecognizable" [*méconnaissable*], I shall say in a somewhat elliptical way, is the beginning of ethics, of the Law, and not of the human. So long as there is recognizability and fellow, ethics is dormant. It is sleeping a dogmatic slumber. So long as it remains human, among men, ethics remains dogmatic, narcissistic, and not yet thinking. Not even thinking the human that it talks so much about.[20]

Of course this perspective differs radically from a view which would only provide moral recognition to animals on the basis of what they share with humans; I drew into question Goodin, Pateman and Pateman's recognition of great ape sovereignty for this reason in Chapter 7. Where ethics fails through an epistemology that refuses to recognise another, violence follows. Derrida soberly observes here that the inability to meet these conditions is the ethical failure to recognise cruelty "in industrial abattoirs, in the most horrific stockbreeding establishments, in bullfights, in dissections, experimentations, breaking and training, etc., in circuses, menageries, and zoos."[21]

It is in Derrida's analysis of a fragment from Gilles Deleuze's *Difference and Repetition* that we find evidence for a significant reconceptualisation of sovereignty. The title of *The Beast and the Sovereign* seminars ("*la bête…*") is closely connected to a series of word plays which centre around the French word *bête*, a word which contains a rich association of meanings, including not only a function as a noun for "beast," "creature," "dog," "insect," but also as an adjective for "stupid" or "silly."[22] Examining the word "*bêtise*" (or "stupidity"), Derrida observes that "*Bêtise* is not simply error," but represents an unexplainable failure of judgment: "I let myself go, I surprised myself by doing a *bêtise*."[23] Here begins a long rumination on the idea of *bêtise*, and the difficulty of its translation and definition, channelled through a reading of Avital Ronnell, to show that sovereignty implies stupidity in its operation: reason and force follow each other since the prerogative to decide operates as a form of judgment in

---

20   Derrida. *The Beast and the Sovereign Vol. 1.* 108, D155.

21   Derrida. *The Beast and the Sovereign Vol. 1.* 109, D156.

22   The return of the prose to this word "*bête*" and relevant word connections (*bêta, bêtise, bêtement, abêtir* etc.) provides an opportunity for the reader to both experience Derrida's vivid reconceptualisations, and then return afresh to a reappraisal of the core of his subject matter (that is, the "beast" and the "sovereign"). See Derrida. *The Beast and the Sovereign Vol. 1.* 164, D223.

23   Derrida. *The Beast and the Sovereign Vol. 1.* 149, D205.

spite of knowledge, rather than on the basis of conceding a known truth. Derrida notes thus: "*Bêtise* always triumphs, it is always, in the war we are talking about, on the side of the victor."[24] Placing this within the Cartesian tradition, Derrida thus points to both the defining condition of sovereignty—as a right to stupidity—and also the defining aspect of human sovereignty over animals, as a stupidity that simultaneously declares its intellectual superiority over other beasts, and declares *itself*, at this same moment, as not beastly, as above other beasts.[25]

This is an immensely perceptive and useful observation that Derrida makes here. The connection of sovereignty to *bêtise* provides an opportunity for a clever and useful reconceptualisation of sovereignty. Stupidity is an accurate way to describe the obstinacy of sovereignty prerogative: a right to act in spite of a "truth," which in turn constructs superiority as truth; that is, a right to judge poorly (upon no basis) inherent in the right to judge. We need only gaze across the field of human sovereign decision making to verify the accuracy of this description. Everything from the declaration of war as pre-emptive strike to knock out non-existent weapons of mass destruction; the arbitrary creation of "black" zones of juridicial exemption to detain and torture "non combatants" (actions accountable to neither international human rights law nor international humanitarian law); and the systematic denial and erasure of sovereignty claims by colonised people; all these phenomena might aptly be described as examples of wilful stupidity. But outside of, albeit implicated within, these fields of enquiry, it is useful to note that stupidity might also powerfully describe the sovereign prerogative that humans command over non human animals. How else might we describe a claimed superiority by humans over animals (whether based on intelligence, reason, communication, vocalisation, or politics) that has no consistent or verifiable "scientific" or "philosophical" basis? Perhaps the only way to describe this claim of superiority is to imagine it as a kind of stupidity; a "pig-headed" stupidity which in its very exercise confirms a right to stupidity inherent within sovereignty itself.

Beast 2 extends some of these themes further; however, it does so through a more concentrated, focused analysis on the dynamics of sovereign violence. In this series of lectures, Derrida provides a twin reading of Heidegger's *The Fundamental Concepts of Metaphysics* and Daniel Defoe's *Robinson Crusoe*.[26] Derrida draws attention to the "three theses" that Heidegger formulates in the

---

24   Derrida. *The Beast and the Sovereign Vol. 1.* 183, D248-9.

25   Derrida. *The Beast and the Sovereign Vol. 1.* 183, D248.

26   The two books make for what would appear to be an odd comparison; indeed Derrida's remarks in the seminars that Defoe and Heidegger make an "odd couple" (31, D61).

metaphysics lectures—"[1.] the stone (material object) is *worldless*; [2.] the animal is *poor in the world*; [3.] man is *world-forming*"[27]— which stratify the distinctions between entities, granting humans a relation to the world that is not shared by other entities.[28] In Chapter 1, I discussed Agamben's reading of these lectures in relation to the question of boredom. Here, Derrida does not focus specifically on boredom, but asks a series of questions of how Heidegger makes these distinctions between humans, animals and material entities and specifically the force or *Walten* that enables these distinctions to operate. What makes this comparison immediately engaging is the critique that Derrida initiates linking the solitary figure of Crusoe with the solitary figure of Enlightenment "man" in modern philosophy. As such, Derrida links Crusoe with not only with Cartesianism,[29] but also with sovereignty itself:

> The sovereign is alone insofar as he is unique, indivisible and exceptional, he is the being of exception who, as Schmitt says—and this is his defini-tion of the sovereign—decides on the exception and has the exceptional right to suspend right, thus standing, in his own way, as we were saying last year, like the beasts or the werewolf, outside the law, above the law. The sovereign is alone in exercising sovereignty. Sovereignty cannot be shared, it is indivisible. The sovereign is alone (sovereign) or is not.[30]

This sovereignty is immediately involved in a hierarchical separation that removes those who Robinson does not consider his "fellows" from the possibil-ity of moral recognition. Thus Robinson is the sovereign of his island, because he declares himself alone, even if he is simultaneously surrounded by others, including other humans ("savages") and other animals ("Wild Creatures").[31] Sovereignty here is the declaration of non reciprocity; the refusal of alterity through non recognition. Derrida observes:

> ...the book... [*Robinson Crusoe*] ...is a long discussion between Robinson and so many beasts. And the theatre of that discussion is, indissociably,

---

27   Martin Heidegger. *The Fundamental Concepts of Metaphysics*. Bloomington: Indiana UP, 1995. 177.

28   For a detailed analysis of Heidegger's philosophical treatment of animals, see Matthew Calarco. "Heidegger's Zoontology." Peter Atterton and Matthew Calarco Eds. *Animal Philosophy: Animal Philosophy: Ethics and Identity*. New York: Continuum, 2004. 18–30; and Calarco. *Zoographies*.

29   Derrida. *The Beast and the Sovereign Vol. 2*. 53 D89.

30   Derrida. *The Beast and the Sovereign Vol. 2*. 8, D30.

31   See Derrida. *The Beast and the Sovereign Vol. 2*. 4, D24-5.

a theatre of solitary sovereignty, of the assertion of mastery (of self, over slaves, over savages and over beasts, without speaking—because the point is precisely not to talk about them—without speaking of women).[32]

Note here that the absence of animals that constitutes the Robinsonian sovereign loneliness is in life as it is in death. Referring to Heidegger, Derrida reminds us that only *Dasein* (that is, the ontological mode of existence Heidegger reserves for the human) has a specific relationship towards death, which marks out its own relation to itself; in Heidegger's words, "Being-towards-death, as anticipation of possibility, is what first makes this possibility possible, and sets it free as possibility."[33] Thus, in Heidegger's framework, only humans can die; animal life merely comes to an end.[34] At this point it is certainly difficult to not notice the alignment of an assumed inability for animals to die in a human way, with a human political agnosticism to non human animal death on a large scale. That we assume animals cannot die in the way we do; that death does not mean the same for an animal as it does for a human, is a far reaching and continuously repeated, even if essentially untested, assumption. We have already come across this formula in Chapter 3, where I noted that, for animals, there is a right to sacrifice without constituting a sacrifice (which is really another way of saying animals can die without this constituting sacred death in a human sense). This is of course a small step towards justification of the slaughter of billions of animals since, it is assumed, their death does not matter. This is wholesale slaughter that is silenced by non recognition.[35] Certainly, while Derrida does not delve into the practical implications

---

32   Derrida. *The Beast and the Sovereign Vol. 2.* 28, D55-56.

33   Heidegger. *Being and Time.* 307, H262.

34   Derrida. *The Beast and the Sovereign Vol. 2.* 115–16. D174. It is also worth noting a similar distinction is drawn in *Being and Time*:

> When we characterized the transition from *Dasein* to no-longer-*Dasein* as Being-no-longer-in-the-world, we showed further that *Dasein's* going-out-of-the-world in the sense of dying must be distinguished from the going-out-of-the-world of that which merely has life [*des Nur-leben-den*]. In our terminology the ending of anything that is alive, is denoted "perishing" [*Verenden*]. We can see the difference only if the kind of ending which *Dasein* can have is distinguished from the end of a life.

Heidegger. *Being and Time.* 284, H240-1.

35   We might also note, as per Regan's lifeboat case, an assumed human prerogative devalues the death of animals in important ways, which in turn destabilises moral frameworks, even those which aim to specifically provide rights to animals, where none have previously been assumed.

of the non capacity for animals to die, he notes an uneasiness with Heidegger's
formulation:

> I hang onto this curious non-sequitur that consists in defining animality
> by life, life by possibility of death, and yet, and yet, in denying dying prop-
> erly speaking to the animal. But what is more problematic to my eyes is
> the confidence with which Heidegger attributes dying properly speaking
> to human *Dasein*, access or relation to death properly speaking and to
> dying as such. As we shall verify more and more precisely and abundantly,
> what the animal supposedly lacks is indeed the experience of the *as
> such*... What is lacking is not supposedly access to the entity, but access to
> the entity as such, i.e. that slight difference between Being and beings
> that, as we shall see, springs from what can only be called a certain
> *Walten*. A slight difference, because this difference between Beings and
> beings, this difference that depends on the *as such*, is not a being, by defi-
> nition; in a certain sense it is nothing, it is not. But it *waltet*.[36]

This question of *Walten*, which consumes much of Derrida's analysis in *Beast 2*,
provides a different perspective on how we might reconceptualise sovereignty,
and the capacity of non human animals for sovereignty. Here Derrida draws
attention to Heidegger's use of the word *Walten*, defined as to rule or to prevail,
although, as Derrida notes frequently, lacks clear definition.[37] Those words
associated with *Walten* are significant also: *Gewalt* suggests violence but also
"force"; *waltet* and *verwaltete* to do with "management" or government.[38]
Derrida traces these words through Heidegger's text to theorise the apparent,
albeit unclear, connection between *Walten* and sovereignty, noting that the
appearances of the term in "Heidegger's corpus after *Sein und Zeit*" seems to
"without doubt...appeal to a sovereignty of last instance, to a superpower that

---

36   Derrida. *The Beast and the Sovereign Vol.* 2. 116, D175.

37   Derrida asks: "What does this *Walten* (verb and noun) mean, *Walten* which is, as if all at
     once, the event, the origin, the power, the force, the source, the movement, the process,
     the meaning etc.—whatever you like—of the ontological difference, the becoming
     -ontological-difference of the ontological difference, or the supervening of Being and the
     arrival of beings? What *walten*? Why this word which so often goes unnoticed? We shall
     continue asking ourselves this question for a long time?" Derrida. *The Beast and the
     Sovereign Vol.* 2. 256, D355.

38   Derrida's analysis of Benjamin's essay "Critique of Violence" ("*Zur Kritik der Gewalt*") would
     appear to be significant here. See Jacques Derrida. "Force of Law: The Mystical Foundation
     of Authority." *Deconstruction and the Possibility of Justice.* Drucilla Cornell, Michel
     Rosenfeld and David Gray Carlson Eds. New York: Routledge, 1992. 3–67. 36.

THE VIOLENCE OF STUPIDITY

decides everything in the first or last instance, and in particular when it comes to *as such*, the difference between Being and beings"[39]

Here we might discern the importance of Derrida's observation, and its relevance for the interpretation of sovereignty I have put forward in this book: namely, that sovereignty does not refer to a right or capacity to rule, but instead to a form of violence that claims and prevails to govern an arbitrary, indeed "stupid," distinction between those that might otherwise be undifferentiated from us. It is for this reason that sovereignty always arrives as a form of excess; as a kind of absurdity. Derrida asks:

> Is there any possible excess of sovereignty or else is this hypothesis absurd? Absurd like sovereignty itself, which exceeds all responsibility of meaning, before meaning, before the law of language and meaning. Meaning and the law are summoned to appear before the sovereign rather than the other way around.[40]

Clearly Thrasymachus has found a bedfellow. Excess here is important in unpicking the meaning of *Walten*, since sovereign violence always exceeds the moment, and dominates past, presence and future. Sovereignty makes claims to the past (the founding, legitimised, always there authority) which

---

39 Derrida. *The Beast and the Sovereign Vol.* 2. 278, D382. Derrida notes, with reference to Robinson Crusoe, the theo-political sovereign relationship between the protagonist and others:

> …his own human and Robinsonian sovereignty being at one and the same time subject to divine sovereignty, and to its image. And the relation to savages as well as to women and beasts was the condescending, descending, vertical relation of a superior master to his slaves, other sovereign to his submissive subjects—submissive or submissable, mastered or to be mastered, by violence if need be—subjected. (278, D383).

In relation to Heidegger, Derrida observes the:

> …undeniable eminence of *Dasein* compared to the animal poor in the world, deprived of the power of speech, of the power to die, of the power to relating to beings as such… this power of the *Weltbildend* man, capable of the *logos apophantikos* was not explicitly defined, by Heidegger, in the theological political figure of sovereignty, even if this value of *Vermögen*, of *Verhalten* as *Vermögen*, of power and power to configure the world and totality of beings as such could make one think, without a word, of some sovereignty, and even if basically the glance cast by man on the animal resembles in many ways, like an invariant in sum, that of Robinson and so many others, from Descartes to Kant and to Lacan. At bottom, all these people, from Defoe to Lacan via Heidegger, belong to the same world in which the animal is cut from man by a multiple defect in power (speech, dying, signifier, truth and lie, etc.). (278, D381-2).

40 Derrida. *The Beast and the Sovereign Vol.* 2. 279, D383.

establishes its force in the present, and simultaneously looms over the future through a coercive potentiality: I am King, obey me. This is the terror that is peculiar to sovereignty; a threat, an immanence and a history. And thus sovereignty is already more than itself in this moment, it already has an excess of violence. Thus Derrida observes that "the violent, the prepotent, and thus what is superlatively more violent, predominant in violence, is the constitutive essential character of the dominance that is itself predominant potency."[41]

This characteristic of violence is important for understanding how it is that humans should come to assert a sovereign violence that distinguishes between "Being and beings." Derrida notes that all beings exert violence.[42] All beings exert themselves within a field that promises potentiality, potency, force: "it is as if to be beings and *Walten* were the same thing, with this overdetermination of the "over," precisely, this overbidding of the *Über*, of the extra, the excess of trans-potency, the pre-potency in the sense of the prevailing that wins out in a combat."[43] Where the *Walten* of beings differs from the *Walten* of the human is in their respective and specific relationship to this violence. Humans claim this violence as their own; they not only embody (are "gripped" by) it, but are "besieged" by it.[44] This is claimed by Heidegger to be the key to *Dasein's* alienation in the world, its *Unheimlichkeit* ("uncannyness"): namely, that in the process of being taken over by violence, of exerting this violence in its Being, and

---

41   Derrida. *The Beast and the Sovereign Vol.* 2. 286, D391-2. Derrida goes on to state: "In its eruption, *Walten* can retain in itself (*an sich halten*) its prepotent potency (*kann* [underlined] *es seine überwaltigende Macht an sich halten*), but by holding it back it is all the more terrible and distant, and anything but harmless [*inofensif*] (*harmlos*)".

42   Note the connection of this to Derrida's observations on eating: See particularly Jacques Derrida. "Eating Well, or the Calculation of the Subject." Eduardo Cadava, Peter Connor, and Jean Luc Nancy Eds. *Who Comes After the Subject?* London and New York: Routledge, 1991. 96–119. Note also Derrida's comments in an 1990 conversation:

> The biblical commandment "Thou shalt not kill" applies to humans, but leaves out animals. Our culture rests on a structure of sacrifice. We are all mixed up in an eating of flesh—real or symbolic. In the past, I have spoken about the West's phallic "logocentrism." Now I would like to broaden this with the prefix carno- (flesh): "carnophallogocentrism." We are all—vegetarians as well—carnivores in the symbolic sense.

See Jacques Derrida in Daniel Birnbaum and Anders Olsson. "An Interview with Jacques Derrida on the Limits of Digestion." *E-Flux.* 2. 01/2009. At: www.e-flux.com/journal/an-interview-with-jacques-derrida-on-the-limits-of-digestion/.

43   Derrida. *The Beast and the Sovereign Vol.* 2. 287, D392.

44   Derrida. *The Beast and the Sovereign Vol.* 2. 288, D393-4.

claiming it for its own, *Dasein* "forgets" that its essence lies in a shared undifferentiated violence, and not in superiority over other beings:

> Man is seized, gripped, *durchwalten* by the *Gewalt* of this *Walten*, and it is because one forgets this and attributes to this man, as to a subject, the initiative or the invention of language, of comprehension etc.—this is why man has paradoxically become a stranger…to his own essence. Because he believes he is the author, the master and possessor, and the inventor of these powers, he ignores the fact that he is first of all gripped, seized, that he must take them on, and he then becomes basically a foreigner—this is the whole story—to his own *Unheimlichkeit*.[45]

This is all to say that in "essence" there is nothing that separates human and animal beyond a violent force that generates the distinction, and simultaneously positions the human in the position of a knowing authored violent subject, and animal simply as that which is to be mastered. We have thus arrived at a curious point of intersection between Derrida's reading of Heidegger and Locke's view of the property relation in animals. In both cases, human superiority does not underpin human dominion over other animals. There is no superiority, only force. This distinction then is not based on capacity or right; it is instead based upon a blind, excessive sovereign claim:

> All of this does not depend on a *Vermögen*, on a power, on a faculty that man has at his disposal, but consists in taming and joining (*Bändigen und Fügen*) forces or violences (*Gewalten*) that come to grip man and thanks to which beings are discovered *as such*. This *Erschlossenheit* of beings, this patency of beings as such, is a *Gewalt* that man must master (*bewältigen*) so that in this *Gewalt-tätigkeit*, he may be himself, among other beings, historical (*geschichtlich*). For all of this concerns the historicality reserved to *Dasein* and to Being, denied to the animal and to other forms of life. There is historicality of man (and not of animal) only where the *Gewalt* of this *Walten* irrupts to make beings as such appear, in the middle of which man is gripped by violence.[46]

It seems impossible here to miss the strange connection between Derrida's finding on the relationship between the Being of "Man" and the being of "animals" as essentially a conflict with only force as the arbiter, and, in turn,

---

45   Derrida. *The Beast and the Sovereign Vol. 2*. 288, D394.
46   Derrida. *The Beast and the Sovereign Vol. 2*. 289, D395.

Agamben's observation that biopolitics is essentially the conflict between human and animal. While Derrida distances himself from the concept of biopolitics,[47] it is apparent here that in so far as sovereignty is inseparable from

---

47   There is a clear tension in *Beast 1* in relation to how this work is situated within a field of political theory that analyses sovereignty following on from Foucault's notion of biopolitics; a tension that is amplified both by Foucault's simultaneous absence and presence as a foil for Derrida's thinking. Foucault's complete absence from the eleventh session, for example, which features a discussion of the connection between the mental hospital and the zoo, only seems to reinforce that Derrida is in some way secretly answering Foucault's thinking on sovereignty and its relation to power. Foucault's notion of biopolitics receives a more focused analysis, not through a close reading of Foucault *per se*, but through a critique of Agamben's use of the concept in *Homo Sacer: Sovereign Power and Bare Life*. It would not be an over-statement to suggest that Derrida is uncharitable in his views on Agamben's work within the *Beast 1* seminars. Early in the seminar series, Derrida attacks Agamben's style, in particular the latter thinker's somewhat cavalier predilection to seek and name the origin or founda-tion of both politics and sovereignty. Derrida thus accuses Agamben of "acting sovereign":

> He who posits himself as sovereign or intends to take power as sovereign always says or implies; even if I am not the first to do or say so, I am the first and only one to know and recognize who will have been the first. And I would add: the sovereign, if there is such a thing, is the one who manages to get people to believe, at least for a while, that he is the first who knows who came first, when there is every chance that it is almost always false, even if, in certain cases, no one ever suspects so. (92, D135).

These playful, but undoubtedly crisp, remarks on Agamben are not revisited until the twelfth session, where Derrida devotes time to discussing the concept of biopolitics. Here, Derrida draws issue with "Foucault, or more precisely here…Agamben" (326, D433) and the distinction that is drawn in *Homo Sacer* between *zoë* and *bios*, a distinction that is not clear: "I don't believe, for example, that the distinction between bios and zoe is a reliable and effective instrument, sufficiently sharp" (326, D434). To defend this claim, Derrida turns to Aristotle, arguing that because *zoë* and *bios* are by and large indistinguishable concepts within the classical thinker's formulation of the human as *zoon politikon*, there is nothing novel in Agamben's (or Foucault's) claim that politics is biopolitics. Indeed, given that both Foucault and Agamben cite Aristotle's *zoon politikon* in their formulations of biopolitics, they are both aware—at least to an extent—of the non originality of the concept. Derrida extends this further to state:

> In truth, Agamben, giving nothing up, like the unconscious, wants to be twice first, the first to see and announce, and the first to remind: he wants to be the first to announce an unprecedented new thing, what he calls this "decisive event of modernity," and also to be the first to recall that in fact it's always been like that, from time immemorial. (330, D439).

While I think Derrida is correct to point to this contradiction in Agamben—between a biopolitics that is both foundational and also emergent within modernity—I couldn't help but feel that Derrida is too quick to dismiss biopolitics and its relevance to consider-ing sovereignty. While it is true that he frequently pleads with his audience as to his inter-est in biopolitics—"my reservations here…don't mean that I have no interest in anything

biopolitics for Agamben, that both thinkers arrive at a common point of agreement here, at least an agreement of sorts.

Moby Dick

In order to make sense of this particular relationship that Derrida draws between *Walten* and our relationship with animals, I would like to turn to Herman Melville's novel *Moby Dick*, which offers, I believe, a parallel narrative to *Robinson Crusoe* and offers a route by which we might deepen our understanding of Derrida's analysis. *Moby Dick*'s narrative trajectory tells of a Captain Ahab, and his single minded quest to find and face a white sperm whale. The novel is essentially about conflict; in this case quite literally between "man" and "animal." A certain eternal violence permeates the novel, not merely violence wrought by the whalers upon their quarry, but a generalised violence that Melville suggests characterises the sea. Here in the pages of *Moby Dick* we find an expression of the prepotent force of being in general:

> Consider the subtleness of the sea; how its most dreaded creatures glide under the water, unapparent for the most part, treacherously hidden beneath the loveliest tints of azure. Consider also the devilish brilliance and beauty of many of its remorseless tribes, as the dainty embellished shape of many species of sharks. Consider, once more, the universal cannibalism of the sea; all of whose creatures prey upon each other, carrying on eternal war since the world began.[48]

---

that could be called a specificity in the relations between the living being and politics" (326, D434)—Derrida does not really demonstrate this interest in *Beast 1* through any significant analysis of how biological life and politics might coincide within sovereignty. This analysis seems important, not only in unpicking the relation between human and animal, but also in examining how it is that other elements of "biological" difference— such as whiteness and racialisation—should come to infuse political engagement, and inform violent practices. Further to this, it is apparent that the difference between Derrida and Agamben (and by extension Foucault) comes essentially down to method. The genealogical approach of Foucault and Agamben leads to a temporal marking of the event as foundational (as a "threshold"). This is an approach that is at odds with Derrida's aim to "give up the alternative of the synchronic and diachronic...give up the idea of a decisive and founding event" (333, D442): and thus, in the final session, Derrida returns to the question of the translation of the event, arguing that "it is really the whole history of the Western world that is in play in these operations of translation" (339, D450).

48   Melville. *Moby Dick.* 227.

This is an expression of a kind of universal violence that is ascribed to being, of the heat that might arise between competing wills for self-preservation; a violence that lies hidden behind apparent calm. This is also an expression of an excess, "the excess of trans-potency, the pre-potency in the sense of the prevailing that wins out in a combat."

We also find here the moment were the human comes to be possessed by this universal violence, and focused upon domination as a singular form of directed violence. Captain Ahab's obsession arises after an encounter with the white whale, when "Moby Dick had reaped away Ahab's leg, as a mower a blade of grass in the field. No turbaned Turk, no hired Venetian or Malay, could have smote him with more Malice."[49] That the attack is situated immediately as a form of war from an enemy combatant is important, as it charges this scene with the possibility of a contest between a would-be equal who must be mastered. Melville describes what follows as a descent into a kind of "madness," where Ahab becomes possessed by a single minded obsession, which Melville repeatedly describes in the novel with the term "monomaniacal."

> It is not probable that this monomania in him took its instant rise at the precise time of his bodily dismemberment. Then, in darting at the monster, knife in hand, he had but given loose to a sudden, passionate, corporal animosity; and when he received the stroke that tore him, he probably but felt the agonizing bodily laceration, but nothing more. Yet, when by this collision forced to turn towards home, and for long months of days and weeks, Ahab and anguish lay stretched together in one hammock, rounding in mid winter that dreary, howling Patagonian Cape; then it was, that his torn body and gashed soul bled into one another; and so interfusing, made him mad. That it was only then, on the homeward voyage, after the encounter, that the final monomania seized him, seems all but certain from the fact that, at intervals during the passage, he was a raving lunatic; and, though unlimbed of a leg, yet such vital strength yet lurked in his Egyptian chest, and was moreover intensified by his delirium, that his mates were forced to lace him fast, even there, as he sailed, raving in his hammock. In a strait-jacket, he swung to the mad rockings of the gales. And, when running into more sufferable latitudes, the ship, with mild stun' sails spread, floated across the tranquil tropics, and, to all appearances, the old man's delirium seemed left behind him with the Cape Horn swells, and he came forth from his dark den into the blessed light and air; even then, when he bore that firm, collected front, however

---

49   Melville. *Moby Dick.* 154.

pale, and issued his calm orders once again; and his mates thanked God the direful madness was now gone; even then, Ahab, in his hidden self, raved on. Human madness is oftentimes a cunning and most feline thing. When you think it fled, it may have but become transfigured into some still subtler form. Ahab's full lunacy subsided not, but deepeningly contracted; like the unabated Hudson, when that noble Northman flows narrowly, but unfathomably through the Highland gorge. But, as in his narrow-flowing monomania, not one jot of Ahab's broad madness had been left behind; so in that broad madness, not one jot of his great natural intellect had perished. That before living agent, now became the living instrument. If such a furious trope may stand, his special lunacy stormed his general sanity, and carried it, and turned all its concentred cannon upon its own mad mark; so that far from having lost his strength, Ahab, to that one end, did now possess a thousand fold more potency than ever he had sanely brought to bear upon any one reasonable object.[50]

It is difficult to escape the sense in which Ahab's transformation captures the dynamics of the violence that Derrida describes as that which "irrupts to make beings as such appear, in the middle of which man is gripped by violence." Ahab's "monomania" does not strike him immediately; indeed it is merely "corporal animosity" that describes his initial exchange with the white whale, an animosity we might presume is not distinct or separable from the generalised violence all around, "the universal cannibalism of the sea…carrying on eternal war since the world began." What marks the change in Ahab is that this violence courses through him and becomes focused and singular in his desire to dominate. Melville observes that the "monomania" that possesses Ahab is no ordinary madness; that this is not madness without "reason." On the contrary the monomaniacal rage draws adjacent to the intellect of Ahab in order to produce a calculated violence that transforms Ahab himself into a weapon: "that before living agent, now became the living instrument." Here the "potentiality" of Ahab is his possession of a directed instrumentalised violence; a force with "a thousand fold more potency than ever he had sanely brought to bear upon any one reasonable object."

Here, like a ship landing on a rock, we strike the moment where sovereignty emerges from expended force, where a violence that otherwise would be non directed and without specific aim becomes instrumentalised towards a determined focused goal. "Intelligence" is born at this point, an "intelligence" that is bonded to power as potential exercised upon a specific object. The moment of

---

50   Melville. *Moby Dick*. 155.

"intelligence" or "rationality" is not about capability nor inherent capacity. Rather, it is the experience of a force that may prevail, and in prevailing it reveals the instrumental logic—the game plan—of who wields it. Sovereignty auto-legitimises not only its own force but its own rationality. Humans declare themselves exceptionally intelligent, but only through the force of their own law. This would conform absolutely, and accurately, to Schmitt's declaration that "Sovereign is he who decides on the exception." We find here a strong resonance between Derrida (and Melville) and the way in which they understand human violence towards animals, and the thesis advanced by Karl Steel in his study *How to Make a Human*.[51] Reflecting on violence towards animals in the middle ages, Steel tracks the circular logic where violence and knowledge work together to create rational auto-legitimation:

> ...the human tries to distinguish itself from other animals by laying claim to the sole possession of reflective language, reason, culture, and above all an immortal soul and ressurectable body; it lays claim to these qualities for itself, and itself only, through acts of violence against others that, by *routinely* suffering this violence, are designated animal.[52]

However, we might note an important point of emphasis here in the account I am putting forward: namely, that intelligence only comes after violence. It is only after we have prevailed through violence that this violence is authored as "rational." As Steel states: "Domination comes first and the human follows."[53]

Perhaps another way to make sense of this is to notice the unsettled "agency" of the white whale that is mythologised in *Moby Dick*. For it is never clear whether Moby Dick is a rational agent or not, and the text oscillates between treating the whale as merely a "dumb animal" and, simultaneously, as a "leviathan" with a reasoning, calculating mind. Indeed Melville ascribes the whale in various sections of the novel with an intelligence that hangs in question; as possessing an instrumental rationality that must exceed that which could be attributed to an "ordinary" animal:

> Already several fatalities had attended his chase. But though similar disasters, however little bruited ashore, were by no means unusual in fishery; yet, in most instances, such seemed the White Whale's infernal afterthought of ferocity, that every dismembering or death that he caused,

---

51   Karl Steel. *How to Make a Human.*
52   Steel. *How to Make a Human.* 21.
53   Steel. *How to Make a Human.* 89.

was not wholly regarded as having been inflicted by an unintelligent agent.[54]

The double negative Melville uses in this sentence—"not wholly regarded as having been inflicted by an unintelligent agent"—captures perfectly that anxiety at stake here: perhaps the white whale is reasoning like a sovereign. However, sovereignty is not granted. That Moby Dick may have had a transformation like Ahab's, where a monomanical violence transformed the body into instrument, is unclear in the text; indeed this lack of clarity provides precisely the element of terror and impending doom that circulates the novel: "...in its eruption, *Walten* can retain in itself (*an sich halten*) its prepotent potency...but by holding it back it is all the more terrible and distant, and anything but harmless [*inofensif*] (*harmlos*)."[55]

And I refer to this instability aware that the threat of the "rogue" animal—the animal that no longer fears the human; indeed may actively hunt and attack the human—is the subject of a long-standing popular imagination, not only in human responses to the threat of rogue animals, but also in the popular imagination, through so called "creature flicks" where the animal becomes the source of a sustained human terror.[56] "Intelligence" is important here in understanding the threat of the rogue animal, since the potential capacity of the animal to impose a "human like violence"—the capacity to reason, to plan, to strategise, to track, to stalk—is tied to its terror: "every dismembering or death that he caused, was not wholly regarded as having been inflicted by an unintelligent agent." Reason and the force of violence are tied here in the rogue animal, as they are within sovereignty. So it is with Ahab, who we are told, is both mad and rational at the same time: "his torn body and gashed soul bled into one another." What defines the Captain's irrational monomania is its assumed rationality: its potency arrives in tying these two elements together.

We are right to ask here: "Who gets to be king"? "Who gets to bond together force and rationality?" "Who gets to be sovereign?" The terror of the rogue animal surely is that in resisting human violence, in levying a violence that might be interpreted itself as instrumental, this rogue animal would be sovereign. The usual cynical response to the "rogue animal" is to assume it is ridiculous to

54   Melville. *Moby Dick*. 154.

55   Derrida. *The Beast and the Sovereign Vol.* 2. 286, D391-2.

56   We could note also here recent work accounting for animal resistance and acts of vengeance towards humans. See, for example, Hribal, *Fear of the Animal Planet*. See also John Valliant. *The Tiger: A True Story of Vengeance and Survival.* New York: Vintage Departures, 2011. I thank Sue Donaldson for drawing my attention to the latter work.

imagine that a non human animal might be possessed by violence and direct it with instrumental purpose. Rather than be surprised by the rogue animal, I would suggest that we need to be surprised at the near universality of human arrogance here. This is the power of naming after all.[57] To name an animal that may possess sovereign power as a rogue is to declare this animal exceptional, questionable (laughable even) and certainly beyond any norm. It is perhaps no accident that Steel observes that carnivore animals pose a particular threat to narratives of human domination, in so far as they unsettle the sovereign right claimed by humans. Referring to Middle Ages prohibitions on human consumption of carrion, and the anxiety over meat that has not been killed by "men," Steel observes that the:

> ...policing of animal violence in the carrion laws witnesses to, and attempts to counteract, the contingency of the categories of both human and animal, both of which are structural categories of dominance and dominated rather than absolute identities.[58]

The potential reversibility is key here: human sovereignty is contingent upon a continuing violence[59] against a threat of potential animal resistance which might challenge materially exercised and epistemologically enacted "superiority."

Who gets sovereignty? Who gets to name? Derrida asks these questions—namely, who gets the life and death power, and who gets naming rights—at the close of *The Beast and the Sovereign* seminars, framed explicitly in relation to the life and death power of the sovereign:

> The question, that was the question of the seminar, remains entire: Namely that of knowing who can die. To whom is this power given or denied? Who is capable of death, and through death, of imposing failure on the super- or hyper-sovereignty of *Walten*?[60]

---

57   Derrida states:
           ...the question is that of characterization of man; but what in man comes down to
           nomination, language (*Nennen, Sprache*), to comprehension (*Verstehen*), to *Stimmung*,
           to passion or to building (*Bauen*) so many things denied to the animal, all that belongs
           to the *überwältigenden Gewaltigen,* no less than do the sea, the earth and the animal.
           Derrida. *The Beast and the Sovereign Vol. 2.* 287, D393.
58   Steel. *How to Make a Human.* 89.
59   See Steel. *How to Make a Human.* 203.
60   Derrida. *The Beast and the Sovereign Vol. 2.* 290, D397.

We could extend this further to ask explicitly what happens if the animal claims the life and death power over the human: what if the animal is victorious in the war we have been discussing? We perhaps find a clue for this in the final pages of *Moby Dick*. Indeed it is the final death scene where Ahab meets his own fate before the power of the white whale, where the Captain questions what it means to die and surrender sovereignty:

> I turn my body from the sun. What ho, Tashtego! Let me hear thy hammer. Oh! ye three unsurrendered spires of mine; thou uncracked keel; and only god-bullied hull; thou firm deck, and haughty helm, and Pole-pointed prow,—death-glorious ship! must ye then perish, and without me? Am I cut off from the last fond pride of meanest shipwrecked captains? Oh, lonely death on lonely life! Oh, now I feel my topmost greatness lies in my topmost grief. Ho, ho! from all your furthest bounds, pour ye now in, ye bold billows of my whole foregone life, and top this one piled comber of my death! Towards thee I roll, thou all-destroying but unconquering whale; to the last I grapple with thee; from hell's heart I stab at thee; for hate's sake I spit my last breath at thee. Sink all coffins and all hearses to one common pool! And since neither can be mine, let me then tow to pieces, while still chasing thee, though tied to thee, thou damned whale! Thus, I give up the spear![61]

These are the final words of Ahab before he is pulled under by Moby Dick. The final delivery is ambivalent in many respects, since Ahab is facing death, and though he cannot acknowledge it directly, the "all-destroying but unconquering whale" could very well be his equal, since it has equalled him, and is about to best him. Ahab's reluctance to cede before the whale is his death, it has always been his death to come.

This surely is our peculiar obsession with the war we are engaged in: we would rather cling to our monomania, in the face of death, than live without this conflict. We are focused and attached, unwavering, to our war on animals. This is of course why it is that even though there are alternatives—to eating animals, testing on animals, hunting animals—we would rather go on with this war, since clearly life is unimaginable without these pleasures. In this sense, rather than ask the ethical questions "Is it moral to eat meat?" or "Is it moral to experiment on animals?" a perhaps more pressing question, political in nature, demands us to answer "Why is it that when we know we are killing and making animals suffer, do we remain obsessively attached to killing and making

---

61   Melville. *Moby Dick.* 450–1.

animals suffer?" or alternatively "Why is it that we cannot imagine a world where we do not kill and hurt animals?" Ahab's final gasp—"Thus, I give up the spear!"—remains normatively uncommitted. It is on one hand, a final thrust, and final attempt to conquer the whale that he is materially and symbolically bound to. Yet on the other hand the spear is delivered at the edge of a collapse in optimism, when Ahab realises that his fate is bound materially to the whale. The spear is delivered without it wanting to be delivered: it is "let go of" rather than "fired." Can we "let go" of our attachment to violence against animals? What might surrender look like? How would a ceasefire that involves giving up our human rights in favour of the rights of animals transform our own relationship? This signals the other path from a continuing war; namely, a fundamental disarmament.

Conclusion: Truce

> Then, up and down the whole line, Frenchmen, Germans and Englishmen
> spontaneously emerged from their trenches and met in no man's land
> where they exchanged cigarettes, drink, food, photographs and addresses.
> A company of the 2nd Battalion Lancashire Fusiliers even played a game
> of football with a Saxon unit, which they won 3–2.
>
> JOHN ELLIS. *Eye-Deep in Hell.*[1]

The aim of this project has been to use theoretical perspectives to unsettle
and challenge our understanding of our relationship with animals, and offer a
framework to recognise and end the violence that characterises this relationship. In this book I have sought to:

1. *Treat human and animal relationships from the viewpoint of war.* We kill
   and make animals suffer on an unimaginable scale to benefit human
   utility. This ongoing hostility conforms precisely to Clausewitz's formulation of war as "*an act of violence to compel our opponent to fulfil our
   will.*" Drawing from Foucault, we can make sense of this war as a form
   of conflict coded as peace: our institutional arrangements veil the existence of this war; epistemic violence substitutes peace for war so that outright hostility towards beings that resist our domination is systematically
   understood as indistinguishable from "peace."

2. *Understand the war on animals as distinctly biopolitical in character.* Our
   war against animals is biopolitical in at least two guises. Firstly, the political sphere itself is constructed through a continual and violent separation between human and animal. The way in which we construct politics,
   the political subject and consider membership of the political sphere,
   requires a violent division between human and animal. Secondly, the
   mechanisms of human violence towards animals are distinctly biopolitical in character. Systematic human uses of animals—prominently in
   food production and experimentation—require an investment in precise technologies and controls which hold life forms at the threshold of
   life and death in order to maximise human utility. When Agamben suggests that biopolitical sovereignty aims at the production of bare life, we

---

1 John Ellis. *Eye-Deep in Hell: Trench Warfare in World War 1.* Baltimore: The John Hopkins
   University Press, 1989. 172. See also Alan Lloyd. *The War in the Trenches.* London: Book Club
   Associates, 1976. 33.

can say without hesitation that it is the animal that is produced as the constituent subject that embodies this bare life. The production of bare life requires interconnected and intense sites of violent management: the concentrated animal feeding facility; the industrial slaughterhouse; the experimental facility. I have observed that the management of population that Foucault identifies with the evolution of biopolitical rule—governmentality—must be understood in connection with the genealogy of human domination of animals. Rather than treat contemporary government as an evolution in fostering the life of human populations, I have argued that we might treat governmentality as precisely the emergence of a conjoined set of techniques, where human systems for the domination of animals emerge in modernity as a refined set of techniques for governing other humans. At its most extreme, the sites of extraordinary violence towards humans of the twentieth century and beyond—camps, detention centres, torture facilities—begin to look indistinguishable from slaughterhouses.

3. *Recognise the war against animals as involving an ongoing, everyday form of conquest.* Drawing from Esposito I have argued that biopolitics operates as a form of immunity; however, I differ in my reading from Esposito in highlighting the fact that the primary form of sovereign immunisation humans seek is immunity from the animal. In the relation of animals as property, humans find a form of sovereign immunity from contamination from a non human claim on the commons of the political sphere. Humans claim a right to use and consume animals as an exclusive form of property, where this violent relationality literally "insures" a human self appointed differential status: a *sacrifice without constituting a sacrifice.* Property is key here. We can extend Francione's analysis through a close reading of Locke: property represents the everyday form of appropriation by which humans claim dominion over animals. Importantly, this domination is founded not upon any pre-existing form of superiority, rather in a human claim to self-preservation prevailing over that of other animals. This appropriation gives way to a market system that allows for the passing through of the full value of domination: human pleasure in violence towards animals is offered as a "free gift." This everyday form of dominion in property within the war on animals offers us a way to conceptualise our everyday relationships with animals within private spheres. I have argued that, as per the radical feminist analysis of rape, we can understand individual acts of violence towards animals as comprising part of a larger war. I have further suggested, following Mbembe, that we could conceptualise sovereignty here as *privatised:* this is a war

that works through a capacity to individually securitise domination and contain non human animal life. However, this sovereignty is not so much delegated by a centralised authority—as in the Hobbesian conception—but instead is merely a recognised pre-existing "human right." Humans claim a right to dominate animals; a right which pre-exists and is preserved by human sovereignty over other humans. We see this clearly in the life and death powers that humans claim over animals in suburban backyards, so-called "companion animals." Power in this context of war epistemologically organises forms of relationality in ways that replace hostility with apparent friendship. It is from this vantage point that we can appraise human sovereignty as not an accident or as natural or as an act of a benign protectorate, but rather as a calculated form of ongoing hostility.

4. *Conceptualise human sovereignty over animals and work towards animal sovereignties.* Following a Foucauldian perspective, I have argued that our war on animals might be conceptualised as a mode of sovereignty that internalises a continuing combat for the benefit of ongoing human utility. Under this sovereign arrangement, peace covers over hostility in this war; violence is stabilised in such a way to appear peaceable. If we understand human sovereignty over animals as discursively erasing the possibility of animal sovereignties, then it is possible to conceptualise animal sovereignties as a strategic response. I have examined two recent proposals for animal sovereignties: Goodin, Pateman and Pateman's proposal for simian sovereignty and Donaldson and Kymlicka's tripartite proposal for citizenship, sovereignty and denizenship. I found both approaches lacking. In part, this is because of the constraints of the liberal models of sovereignty used (including an attachment to territory and a belief in sovereignty rights only being owed to entities that were "capable"); in part, because of the dangers inherent in the proposals, including the continuing preservation of a human right to decide (for example, in the control of reproduction and sexuality). Taking a different approach, I have examined Derrida's treatment of sovereignty in *The Beast and The Sovereign* lectures, observing that sovereignty is essentially groundless: it lacks content, and is not founded upon any essential capability in those who make this claim. On the contrary, sovereignty operates as a kind of right to stupidity—a right to act in spite of a "truth," which in turn constructs superiority as truth—and that this right is not won on the basis of any capacity to rule, but is only founded upon violence. Humans claim sovereignty over animals because we have prevailed over animals using force, and not because we actually have any "superiority" in capability.

As I have suggested, animal sovereignties must begin from two fronts: recognising a right to "stupidity" in animals (that is, a right to determine themselves in spite of capability or established "truth"), and disarming human sovereignty (that is, removing the violence that founds our claim of dominion).

We are left finally with a set of questions on how to proceed. How might we enact a space of peace? Is a truce possible? In order to provide some resources for how we might move forward, in conclusion I suggest two strands for thinking. First, that we explore the idea of "counter-conduct" in response to the war against animals; secondly, we explore the possibility of *truce*.

In his 1 March 1978 lecture, Foucault turns his attention to the idea of *counter-conduct*. I believe the lecture marks a significant shift in how he understands the problem of resistance, one of many subsequent reformulations of the problem of resistance and its relationship to subjectivity.[2] Here Foucault attempts to understand how it is that individuals resist or revolt against the modes of organisation of their own conduct which are implicit in institutional systems and systems of knowledge. Referring to movements against the pastoral model of power I described in Chapter 2, Foucault states:

> They are movements whose objective is a different form of conduct, that is to say: wanting to be conducted differently, by other leaders (*conducteurs*) and other shepherds, towards other objectives and forms of salvation, and through other procedures and methods. They are movements that also seek, possibly at any rate, to escape direction by others and to define the way for each to conduct himself. In other words, I would like to know whether the specificity of refusal, revolts, and forms of resistance of conduct corresponded to the historical singularity of the pastorate. Just as there have been forms of resistance to power as the exercise of political sovereignty, and just as there have been other, equally intentional forms of resistance or refusal that were directed at power in the form of economic exploitation, have there not been forms of resistance to power as conducting?[3]

---

2   As I shall discuss below, by the 1984 lectures Foucault has reformulated the problem of resistance to power by offering a different conceptualisation of the relationship between knowledge, government and subjectivity.

3   Foucault. *Security, Territory, Population.* 194–5.

The section seems to me to be valuable for considering how it is that we might oppose the war on animals as a system that not only kills animals and makes them suffer, but orders human conduct across intersubjective, institutional and epistemic realms. Ending the war on animals does not merely involve confronting human sovereignty over animals, as if this were a matter of storming the Winter Palace; nor does it mean ending an economic system of power, such as, for example, legislating against animals as property. On the contrary, we are dealing with a set of violences that are deeply embedded into almost every conceivable facet of human organisation, life and knowledge. In other words, resistance must seek to confront conduct: how we are governed, how we govern ourselves, what we know about ourselves, and what we know about others. The importance of this focus is strategically understanding the way in which we might conduct ourselves, or work within communities, might disrupt and enact spheres of peace within the war on animals, not only in intervening in the institutional reproduction of violence, but also in etching a new set of truths that might enable recognition of animal sovereignties.

During the 1 March 1978 lecture, one of the examples of counter-conduct Foucault offers is *desertion*:

> Desertion was an absolutely ordinary practice in all the armies of the seventeenth and eighteenth centuries. But when waging war became not just a profession or even a general law, but an ethic and the behavior of every good citizen of a country, when being a soldier was a form of political and moral conduct, a sacrifice, a devotion to the common cause and common salvation directed by a public conscience and public authority within the framework of a tight discipline; when being a soldier was therefore no longer just a destiny or a profession but a form of conduct, then, in addition to the old desertion-offence, you see a different form of desertion that I will call desertion-insubordination. Refusing to be a soldier and to spend some time in this profession and activity, refusing to bear arms, appears as a form of conduct or as a moral counter-conduct, as a refusal of civic education, of society's values, a refusal of a certain obligatory relationship to the nation and the nation's salvation, of the actual political system of the nation, and as a refusal of the relationship to the death of others and of oneself.[4]

---

4 Foucault. *Security, Territory, Population.* Note the other examples that Foucault offers. The second example Foucault offers that is useful here is that of "secret societies." Foucault observes that societies of religious dissidence that developed in the eighteenth century were increasingly politicised:

Desertion appears as an example of both a current practice of counter-conduct, and one of the possible avenues for refinement as a strategy to resist the war against animals. Certainly, escaping the war on animals by refusing to bear arms is one form of counter-conduct available as a means of resistance. We have seen elements of this practice in veganism, where individuals exempt themselves from the violence of the war against animals by refraining from eating and preparing animal-based foods, and refusing to wear or consume animal-based products. The practice is distinctive in so far as it is not merely reflective of a set of political beliefs, but works across different levels of conduct; vegan practitioners typically modify their ways of living and consumption substantially against prevailing norms; frequently face forms of social isolation due to dietary and other choices; and often confront a barrage of resistance as they come into contact with knowledge systems, as scientists, doctors and well meaning family and friends express concern for the potential dangers vegan practitioners expose themselves to by abstaining from animal products. Indeed, given these factors, I would suggest that veganism—in so far as it seeks to disrupt an institutional system and a system of truth—would figure as a perfect example of a contemporary model of counter-conduct.

However, arguably, the strategy carries with it internal limits. One of these limits, surely, is the fantasy that it is indeed possible to remove oneself from the violence of the war against animals, and that this strategy has efficacy as a

---

...they become increasingly composed of political elements and take on clearer political objectives—plots, political or social revolutions—but always with an aspect of the pursuit of a different form of conduct: to be led differently, by other men, and towards other objectives than those proposed by the apparent and visible official governmentality of society. Its clandestine character is no doubt a necessary dimension of this political action, but at the same time it includes and offers this possibility of an alternative to governmental direction in the form of another form of conduct with its unknown chiefs and specific forms of obedience, etcetera.

The third example Foucault provides is of resistance to medical "truths":

...the refusal of certain medications and certain preventive measures like vaccination, to the refusal of a certain type of medical rationality: the attempt to constitute sorts of medical heresies around practices of medication using electricity, magnetism, herbs, and traditional medicine.

In this last example, I am reminded of contemporary vegan practitioners who work against the advice of medical practitioners and concerned family members to pursue a restrictive diet. They work against prevailing truths of science and traditions which suggest that life is not possible without consumption of animal products. It is almost as if vegan practitioners are continually asked "Are you not aware that you are killing yourself, making yourself sick by not consuming animal products?" And they retort: ""We are not; we contest this truth!" or alternatively, "We don't care!"

means of action. As I have suggested in the Introduction to this book, desertion through the practice of veganism does not remove the subject from the privileges delivered by that war: even if I do not personally consume animal products, I am still a beneficiary of the war against animals. In this sense, veganism alone as a strategy runs the risk of functioning as a self focused personal asceticism—a kind of Puritanism[5]—rather than as a viable means to disrupt the systemic practices that constitute the war against animals.[6] Certainly, we know that despite an increase in knowledge and practice of alternative diets, global per capita meat consumption continues to increase.[7] I don't mean to suggest, however, that this strategy of deserting the war against animals does not have *any* tactical merit. As Foucault points out, desertion becomes a seditious act when it challenges a form of conduct that belongs to an authorised regime of government. The radical possibility that desertion in the war against animals might hold is in challenging human sovereignty and the order of truth and violence it constructs: that is, counter-conduct as a mode of "desertion-insubordination." By necessity, desertion-insubordination not only disrupts intersubjective and institutional violence, but also the epistemological violence of the governing order; it seeks to create a new set of truths that are unimaginable or intolerable within the terms of the prevailing regime. One of the problems that the epistemic violence of the war on animals creates is that life without killing animals is not considered pleasurable, indeed is a life not worth living. Arguably, ascetic modes of veganism—where personal actions to "purify" the self from the consumption of animal products are seen as pivotal to the political project of dismantling animal exploitation—do not necessarily challenge the "truth" that human life requires the killing of animals. Because these ascetic modes of veganism rely upon a model of personal sacrifice, they risk confirming a perception that living without animal killing means having to forsake a set of pleasures for "the cause." They generate fantasies of what Calarco identifies as "ethical purity," where a belief in "good conscience" as a final state is idealised as a goal.[8] Internalised cultures of surveillance and disciplining within alternative communities—so called "vegan policing"—exacerbate this problem, deflecting energies away from a broader goal of ending violence

---

5   I am using the term "Puritan" here in a popular rather than in an historically accurate sense to describe an ascetism that organises itself to resist and contain pleasure.

6   See Foucault's description of personal religious ascetism in the 1 March 1978 lecture in *Security, Territory, Population*.

7   United Nations Food and Agriculture Organisation. *World Agriculture: Towards 2015/2030*. London: Earthscan, 2003. 159.

8   Calaraco. *Zoographies*. 136.

towards animals, instead focusing on provisional goals of constructing apparently perfect "cruelty-free" selves. Perhaps we need to put an end to the idea that desertion involves personal sacrifice or that ending the war against animals must focus on constructing "cruelty-free" subjectivities? Perhaps what we need to explore is how personal practices by individuals and communities to desert the war against animals might seek to invent new unimaginable pleasures;[9] war after all opens up the possibilities for the pleasures of secret, tactical peaces, of divine pleasures enjoyed amidst the trenches, under the noses of the generals.[10] Perhaps we need to explore veganism as set of imperfect practices which are situationally located as forms of resistance to the war on animals, rather than as a mode of identity?

All of this perhaps points to a need to rethink how personal action might alter intersubjective, institutional and epistemic violences. In the Introduction to this book I suggested that in Foucault's late lectures, there is clearer picture provided of a "circulatory" relationship between *subjectivity, knowledge* and *government*. The 1982–83 and the 1983–84 lectures are fascinating in this regard,[11] as Foucault offers an explication for the way in which his analysis had progressively

---

9   See Chloë Taylor's discussion of Foucault, vegetarianism and pleasure in Chloë Taylor. "Foucault and the Ethics of Eating." *Foucault Studies*. 9. 2010. Taylor states: "the Animal Liberation Movement would be well-advised to follow Foucault's suggestion that liberation movements in general should take on ethico-aesthetic tactics, rather than relying solely on utilitarian or deontological moral argumentation" (83).

10   In a 1981 interview for the magazine *Gay Pied*, Michel Foucault speculates that the "development toward which the problem of homosexuality tends is the one of friendship" (Michel Foucault. "Friendship as a Way of Life." *The Essential Works of Foucault 1954–1984, Volume One—Ethics: Subjectivity and Truth*. Paul Rabinow Ed. New York: The New Press, 1997. 135–40). Here, Foucault identifies the difficulty of imagining relations which lack institutional norms, suggesting here that friendship is an ethical relationship that develops as a process of creation between codified behaviours: "they face each other without terms or convenient words... They have to invent from A to Z, a relationship that is still formless, which is friendship: that is to say, the sum of everything through which they can give each other pleasure" (136). In the same interview Foucault notes that the institutional opportunity within heteronormative relations for a more open relationship of men living with other men is rare: "it's only in certain periods and since the nineteenth century that life between men was not only tolerated but rigorously necessary: very simply during war" (139). I would suggest that Foucault's observations on friendship provide a framework for thinking about friendship with non human animals beyond existing institutional norms.

11   See, particularly, Michel Foucault. *The Government of Self and Others: Lectures at the Collège de France 1982–1983*. New York: Palgrave Macmillan, 2010. 4–6; and Michel Foucault. *The Courage of Truth: Lectures at the Collège de France 1983–1984*. New York: Palgrave MacMillan, 2011. 8–9.

shifted, from the operation of domination to modes of government, from the constitution of subjectivity to how one constitutes one's self and, from the question of how truth and knowledge is constructed to tracking the process of veridiction (or "truth-telling"). The temptation within a Foucauldian discourse of power is to erase subjectivity, thus removing the possibility for thinking through how we might resist systems of violence. This challenge appears particularly pertinent when considering how we might resist epistemic violence: if "truth" constructs subject positions and the terms of "resistance," then it would seem impossible to conceptualise resistance "outside" of the terms of a system of truth. Simply put, if everyone believes we are at peace with animals, how might we signal the presence of the war around us? In the 1 February 1984 lecture, Foucault straightforwardly rejects the idea that subjectivity need disappear. On the contrary, in order to understand subjectivity, particularly the intersubjective "experience" of power, he shifts the terms of his analysis:

> What is involved, rather, is the analysis of complex relations between three distinct elements none of which can be reduced to or absorbed by the others, but whose relations are constitutive of each other. These three elements are: forms of knowledge (*savoirs*), studied in terms of their specific modes of veridiction; relations of power, not studied as an emanation of a substantial and invasive power, but in the procedures by which people's conduct is governed; and finally the modes of formation of the subject through practices of self. It seems to me that by carrying out this triple theoretical shift—from the theme of acquired knowledge to that of veridiction, from the theme of domination to that of governmentality, and from the theme of the individual to that of the practices of self–we can study the relations between truth, power, and subject without ever reducing each of them to the others.[12]

The inflection Foucault offers here—the "triple theoretical shift"—offers a way to confront the three forms of violence I have argued constitute the war against

---

[12]   Foucault. *The Courage of Truth*. 9. Foucault begins this section with the following important clarification:

> Connecting together modes of veridiction, techniques of governmentality, and practices of the self basically what I have always been trying to do... And to the extent that this involves the analysis of relations between modes of veridiction, techniques of governmentality, and forms of practice of self, you can see that to depict this kind of research as an attempt to reduce knowledge (*savoir*) to power, to make it the mask of power in structures, where there is no place for a subject, is purely and simply caricature (8).

animals: intersubjective, institutional and epistemic. At the intersubjective or personal level, there is a challenge for how humans constitute themselves as subjects within the war against animals. This is not only in the negative sense of how truth and power construct the self; but also in the positive sense of how practices of the self interact with regimes of truth and modes of government of conduct. In short, even if the war on animals offers us uniforms, weapons and training, there remains the question of how we might conduct ourselves with respect to these resources of violence. At the institutional level, the systems of authority—sovereignty—that legitimate and continue killing and suffering for human benefit order the conduct of both humans and animals and reproduce truths of apparent human superiority. However, there remains a challenge to understand how forms of collective and individual conduct disrupt this authority structure, how regimes of truth both support and undermine this authority, and tactically what might be done to shift institutional relations in order to delegitimate the apparent systemic need to kill and make animals suffer. Finally, at the level of epistemic violence, there is a challenge to not only understand how regimes of truth continue to provide resources that aid and proliferate the war on animals, but how resources might be produced for resistance, and where and how it becomes possible to speak out to create new truths—that is, how it is that veridiction is possible in these cases—against a prevailing set of truths. The last challenge—that is confronting epistemic violence—seems pivotal to me. As Wolfe has noted with respect to the Great Ape Project, providing provisional rights to apparently "higher order" beings only continues a project of reifying the "human" as a superior being;[13] what is needed on the contrary is to challenge the order of truth that always posits the human as superior. If sovereignty enables stupidity—a superiority claimed where there is no particular basis for this superiority claim—then our challenge is to focus upon the mechanisms that reproduce and proliferate these claims, and persistently ask why humans can claim a right to stupidity, yet animals cannot. But, we must ask these epistemic questions aware that the three forms of violence I have described interact and move in a circular relation with each other: for this reason, we cannot simply focus on personal practices at the expense of attending to institutional violence or epistemic violence, nor can we focus on epistemic questions without being aware of their material effects.

An example of a recent animal advocacy campaign provides an indication of the complexity of the task ahead. In March 2011, an animal advocacy group investigated slaughterhouses in Indonesia that had received live exported cows from Australia. Footage was released to the general public showing cows

---

13   Wolfe. *Before the Law.* 11–12.

being subjected "to abuse through eye gouging, kicking, tail twisting and tail breaking" prior to slaughter.[14] The initial reporting led to an unprecedented public response: the story occupied the national press for a long period, inflamed national public street protests, led to an initial ban on live exports to Indonesia, an Australian Government review, and a change in practice and regulation (even though this latter response, predictably, has been weak).[15]

As successful as this campaign was and continues to be, I believe it poses a challenge to the thinking about the political terrain of structural change in the war against animals. This is because the issue of live exports is an example of the way in which truth operates in a circular relationship with power and is interwoven with other sites of political contestation, including, for example, in this case, race and nationhood. The question I am interested in is why it is that there has been so much public focus, at least in an Australian context, on slaughter conditions in live export destinations? Why, in this case, was Indonesia singled out? There is endless evidence from animal advocates of poor treatment of animals prior to death within other industrialised slaughter facilities, including in facilities in Australia. This includes the methods used to restrain and kill animals, the technologies of containment used prior to death, the forms of transportation utilised as part of the slaughter process (themselves productive of death and suffering), and the methods of breeding, nutrition and regulation that accompany the wholesale governmentality of life and death that is part and parcel of animal production and slaughter. However, despite the efforts of advocates, the treatment of animals within *Australian* facilities is rarely understood as representing a systemic problem. Where clear evidence of abject cruelty is demonstrated—such as in a 2012 incident involving sheep being skinned alive in a processing facility—this is usually written off as an anomaly or treated as a result of individual (rather than systematic) criminal culpability.[16]

---

14   Animals Australia and RSPCA. "Live Exports to Indonesia." Factsheet. At: www.banliveexport.com/documents/FactSheet-cases.pdf.

15   The Australian Government created new processes for audit and scrutiny of transport and export destination welfare standards. A ban on live exports has proved difficult politically to sustain.

16   In February 2012 Animal Liberation NSW uncovered a Sydney abattoir with footage demonstrating "sheep being hung up and skinned while apparently still conscious, and a man repeatedly belting live pigs over the head with a metal bar." See Jen Rosenberg and Ben Cubby. "Covert Evidence of Cruelty Halts Abbatoir." *Sydney Morning Herald.* Febuary 10, 2012. The NSW Primary Industries Minister commented that it "may well be a one-off." See Josephine Tovey. "Cruelty Video: 'Rogue' Abattoir Checked Four Times in a Year." *Sydney Morning Herald.* February 10, 2012. In November 2011, Animals Australia revealed footage of pigs being stabbed in the eyes and ears with stunning equipment,

Even official findings of systematic violence in Australian facilities—such as in a 2012 review of red meat slaughterhouses in New South Wales[17]—fail to generate the same level of government and community concern that was evident in relation to live exports to Indonesia. So why should the issue of the treatment of animals in other countries be of concern to the Australian public? The overtly nationalistic language of the public discussion gives us a clue. A recurring element within the live exports campaign has been the deployment of concern that "Australian" cattle have been subject to slaughter at the hands of non Western others. The racialised element of this concern is unavoidable. Spivak coins the phrase "White men saving brown women from brown men"[18] to describe the way in which Western imperialist values can be framed through feminist concern to create an apparently logical and inescapable truth. We might usefully rework Spivak's phrase here: "White people saving white animals from brown people" might be an apt way to describe the outpouring of public concern over animals in non Western abattoirs. "White people saving white animals from brown people" establishes as a "truth" that Australians kill "their" animals in a civilised way, while non Western others do not.

That the cause for unity happens to be a political issue that would otherwise be immensely divisive—that is, animal welfare—demonstrates the remarkable way in which a racialised discourse can galvanise would-be opponents around a common cause. It seems debateable that the "common cause" here is the horror of slaughter itself. The public media attention to live exports to

---

and another animal beaten to death with a sledgehammer. See Animals Australia. "Final Moments." Animals Australia. At: www.animalsaustralia.org/investigations/final-moments/. Individuals were charged, however, substantive charges against the abattoir owners were dropped. See Chris McLennen. "Abattoir Charges Dropped." *Weekly Times Now*. April 16, 2013. In an another (2013) incident, involving footage of turkeys being kicked and stomped on, and other turkeys having their feet ripped off prior to death, the Governmental response was to play down any suggestion that these practices were routine or representative of the industry, with the relevant food authority stating that "it appears the particular situation relates to individuals and not a failure of systems in place to protect animal welfare." See New South Wales Food Authority. NSW Food Authority response to animal cruelty allegations at an Inghams Tahmoor processing facility. NSW Food Authority. 21 March 2012.

17   The review found welfare breaches in all abattoirs surveyed, including in relation to the use of ineffective stunning techniques and poor competency of slaughter staff. See Kelly Burke. "Multiple Deficiencies Uncovered in NSW Abattoirs." *Sydney Morning Herald*. May 18, 2012.

18   Spivak. "Can the Subaltern Speak?".

Indonesia reflects an anxiety over race and nation, rather than a concern for animals *alone*, since a non racialised concern for animal welfare would generate public action both around animal treatment *in* Australia *and equally* overseas. Power here—in this case racialised power—constructs a regime of truth that aims at confirming a particular subjectivity that becomes invested by "concern" for animal welfare over the border of the nation State. Concern for animal welfare is understood as an expression of a white subjectivity, where a kind of "critter-nationalism" is created.[19] This nationalism establishes Australian identity as aligned with a commitment to animal welfare and non cruelty; while non Western export markets are reflective of systemic cruelty, which are in some ways tied to traditional cultural norms and practices. Evidence of cruelty in Australia therefore will always be understood as a mere aberration; evidence of cruelty overseas, on the other hand, will only confirm the "truth" of systemic cruelty.

---

19   I am referring here explicitly to the formulations discussed by Jasbir K. Puar—homonationalism and "pink washing"—in the context of a critique of the way in which gay and lesbian rights are deployed in the name of nation building. See Jasbir K. Puar. *Terrorist Assemblages: Homonationalism in Queer Times.* Durham: Duke University Press, 2007; and Jasbir Puar and Maya Mikdashi. "Pinkwatching and Pinkwashing: Interpenetration and Its Discontents." *Jadaliyya.* August 9, 2012. At: www.jadaliyya.com/pages/index/6774/pinkwatching-and-pinkwashin. In this context, see Amie Breeze Harper. "Race as a 'Feeble Matter' in Veganism: Interrogating Whiteness, Geopolitical Privilege, and Consumption Philosophy of 'Cruelty-Free' Products." *Journal for Critical Animal Studies.* 8.3, 2010. 5–27. Harper discusses some of the disturbing resonances between racialisation and the languages of animals advocacy movements. Observing the prominent white racial dominance of some vegan communities, and the role of veganism in acculturating a particular form of ethical white subjectivity, Harper notes that the "conditions of cruelty" that attend the production of some vegan products "help certain USA vegans practice modern ethics" (14). Aside from Harper's work, there is growing scholarship exploring the interaction of race politics and animal advocacy, including notably the work of Claire Jean Kim: see, for example, Claire Jean Kim. "Multiculturalism Goes Imperial: Immigrants, Animals, and the Suppression of Moral Dialogue." *Du Bois Review.* 4:1 2007. 1–17; and Claire Jean Kim. "Slaying the Beast: Reflections on Race, Culture and Species." *Kalfou: A Journal of Comparative and Relational Ethnic Studies.* 1.1, 2010. 57–74. See also Will Kymlicka and Sue Donaldson. "'Animal Rights Multiculturalism and the Left." *Journal of Social Philosophy.* 45.1, 2014. 116–35; Maneesha Deckha. "Toward A Postcolonial Posthumanist Feminist Theory: Centralizing Race and Culture in Feminist Work on Nonhuman Animals." *Hypatia: Journal of Feminist Philosophy.* 27:3, 2012. 527–45; and Lindgren Johnson. "To 'Admit All Cattle without Distinction': Reconstructing Slaughter in the Slaughterhouse Cases and the New Orleans Crescent City Slaughterhouse." Paula Lee Ed. *Meat, Modernity and the Rise of the Slaughterhouse.* Lebanon: University of New Hampshire Press, 2008. 198–215.

This all poses a challenge for animal advocates who need to take any opportunity to raise the profile of violence against animals. To gain a foothold, advocates must speak to this power–truth relation, since other speech will be unrecognisable. The nature of the power–truth circulatory is that it appears impossible to speak the "truth" from outside of the relationship between subject, existing "knowledge" and modes of government. Advocates who point out that the conditions of animal slaughter at home are substantively no different from those overseas are not "heard," as what they are saying is not racially coded through institutional powers in order to be heard. Animal abuse in Australia will always be constructed as an exception rather than the norm. Similarly, political actors who want to address the racialised nature of the debate, who point out the way in which community concern is constructed along lines of race, are unlikely to be heard, or perhaps worse, will be regarded as in some way unconcerned for the welfare of animals (since the link between being concerned with animals and being concerned with practices in non Western slaughterhouses has been structured by discourse as fundamental). The "incentive" within this economy will remain for advocates to continue to draw attention to the treatment of Australian animals exported to other countries, particularly non Western nations, as the only way to gain traction for reform. Expressing concern for animal welfare will thus be a way of positioning oneself within a geopolitical neo-colonial economy linking globalised industrialised animal slaughter practices with a racialised ethical subjectivity.

The racialised elements of the truth–power circulatory are only one level of this operation. As the discussion of live exports illustrates, the way we construct the "truth" of our relationship to animals is fundamental in constructing our own subject positions in this debate and the subject positions of animals who are the object of human violence. Consider the challenge of discursively unpacking what concepts such as "unnecessary suffering" or "humane killing" might look like. There is no question that the practices subject to media attention in Indonesian abattoirs are challenging to witness and represent forms of intensely visceral violent treatment. However, this is also true of any killing, in any abattoir. Killing happens in all factory farms to produce meat. The idea that there is a "humane form of killing"—a "civilised" way to kill—is already oxymoronic. This is an oxymoron that can only function within a relationship between truth, sovereignty and subjectivity, where an elegant construction is made whereby some forms of killing are seen as "humane," while others are situated as barbaric and uncivilised; a construction that is modulated by a variety of layers, including racialisation. And, as Fiona Probyn-Rapsey points out, the characterisation of "humane" forms of killing, such as captive bolt stunning, only participates in generating an illusion that this process of killing—rather than others—is in essence non violent:

> The emphasis, indeed perhaps anxious over-insistence on stunning… indicates the shock not only of being confronted with violence to animals, but the desire to be kept in a state of numbed indifference and ignorance to that which *we know not to know*. And what we know not to know is that unstunned cattle struggle against death, express interests and a desire to live.[20]

In considering the war on animals that I believe we need to name as such, navigating around these apparently logical circulatories of truth-power is difficult work. That, the West happens to claim, in the case of live export slaughter, or the mechanised death of industrialised killing, including the live hang I have described in the Introduction to this book, a monopoly on "humane forms of killing"—defining its terms and constructing subjectivites as a result—is another feature of this form of power that we must keep in our mind through our contestation of truths. Action in the war against animals must be thought carefully to avoid enacting other forms of epistemic violence.

Across all these fields—intersubjective, institutional, epistemic—there is a political challenge for how to effect a fundamental disarmament. What would a ceasefire look like? In 1983, Andrea Dworkin provided an address to the Midwest Regional Conference of the National Organization for Changing Men in Minnesota, to "an audience of about 500 men, and scattered women."[21] In Dworkin's notes, she observes that she was presented with an opportunity to speak her truth to the audience: "this was a feminist dream-come-true. What would you say to 500 men if you could?"[22] Here, in this context, Dworkin made a remarkable plea to her audience:

> And I want one day of respite, one day off, one day in which no new bodies are piled up, one day in which no new agony is added to the old, and I am asking you to give it to me. And how could I ask you for less—it is so little. And how could you offer me less: it is so little. Even in wars, there are days of truce. Go and organize a truce. Stop your side for one day. I want a twenty-four-hour truce during which there is no rape.[23]

---

20   Fiona Probyn-Rapsey. "Stunning Australia." *Humanimalia*. 4:2, 2013. 84–100. 87.
21   Dworkin. "Take Back the Day."
22   Dworkin. "Take Back the Day."
23   Dworkin. "Take Back the Day."

It appears significant that Dworkin does not call for a "treaty" as an end to war, but a "truce." War ends when opponents stop seeking to injure each other. It is true that after war a formal break in hostilities is sometimes marked with a treaty: a document that agrees on the terms of peace. However, if we follow Foucault's logic on the relationship of war to political power, we need not assume that a treaty suggests a future relationship of equality. Although the treaty provides security and recognition—the terms of peace—the treaty can also be understood in a negative sense as the means for continuing domination, since the agreement frequently confers rights for the victor, and, derived from these rights, accords limited freedoms as "concessions" to the defeated "enemy." Often these concessions are specifically designed not to disrupt the continuing utility—the spoils of war—enjoyed by the victors. The treaty is a document that is premised on the threat of force; more often than not in the ever present threat that should hostilities break out again an annihilatory violence will be unleashed by the stronger party. After the war those who face total defeat are usually compelled to accept limited terms of existence: to pay tithes and reparations, to conform to the laws set down by the victor. This is all a simple choice between life and the uncomforting reality of death. As we have discussed, Foucault states: "the will to prefer life to death; that is what founds sovereignty."[24]

However, *truce* appears as a different form of armistice. The truce might be seen as weaker than a treaty because of its fragility and limited temporality. Ceasefires based upon truce are broken all the time, since they rely on agreements that are founded on mere trust, and are not backed by force. A truce does not signal the final end of hostilities; rather, it creates a space where hostilities are broken, but with no guarantee that war may not be initiated again. Where the treaty might signify the end of war and the beginning of domination by other means—through reparations, continuing exploitation, silent defeat— truce offers a peace that is always conditional, always ready to be broken: fragile and utterly cognisant of the continued reality of war. It is for this reason that a truce contains a potentiality. Truce opens a space for an equality, even if it is not, in itself, capable of fulfilling its promise. Dworkin goes on to state:

> And on that day, that day of truce, that day when not one woman is raped, we will begin the real practice of equality, because we can't begin it before that day. Before that day it means nothing because it is nothing: it is not real; it is not true. But on that day it becomes real. And then, instead of

---

24   Foucault. *Society Must be Defended.* 95.

rape we will for the first time in our lives—both men and women—begin to experience freedom.[25]

It is important to note the care by which Dworkin constructs the promise of the truce. Truce is not an "equality in power," nor the equitable distribution of means of violence. But it might offer the prospect of an opportunity for democratic peaceability between warring parties, even if this is momentary.[26] In this context, I am aware here of the distinction that Derrida draws between fraternity and friendship: the former implying a brotherly bond to a political community or *polis*, the latter the possibility of a proximity without bond or debt, "the one promised or promising without promising anything."[27] In other words, truce might open a space for a debtless friendship, a friendship where there is no apparent reason to be friends, perhaps the only friendship that is likely in war; but a friendship that works through reciprocal and genuine (rather than theoretical) commitment to lay down weapons. And, importantly, the disarmament that may eventuate as a result of truce is the necessary foundation for a set of ongoing relations that might be capable of not merely reproducing existing forms of domination, but ending war, at least upon this particular front of confrontation. In other words, while truce is not the final answer, it is one way to consider a new allegiance, one which operates within the reality of historical and potentially continuing war, and provides the foundation for a different sort of friendship, a different politics. This is a beginning for, as Dworkin phrases it, "the real practice of equality"; a practice, not as a settled state, but a necessarily messy and difficult process of negotiation and renegotiation.

Playing with Dworkin's concept of a temporary truce, I have found myself wondering if there might be a tactical benefit in calling for one day, just one day, where we stop killing animals? If animal advocates were to tactically campaign for a one day truce, one day without killing animals, one day when the slaughterhouses would shut down, what would this look like? What appeals to me about this idea is that, rather than focusing on consumers and the consumption of meat (for example, through a "go vegetarian or vegan for one day"

---

25   Dworkin. "Take Back the Day."

26   This would align with view of democracy as precisely always opportunistic and spontaneous. See, for example, Nicholas Xenos. "Momentary Democracy." Aryeh Botwinick and William E. Connolly Eds. *Democracy and Vision: Sheldon Wolin and the Vicissitudes of the Political*. Princeton and Oxford: Princeton University Press, 2001. And also, Sheldon Wolin. "Fugitive Democracy." *Constellations*. 1.1, 1994. 11–25. 23.

27   Derrida. *Politics of Friendship*. 298.

campaign), a call for a one day truce would actually intervene in the production process of killing animals and, all things holding equal, reduce the number of animals killed. The intervention thus operates explicitly on an institutional level, in so far as it aims to challenge a systemic practice of violence, rather than simply how individuals, on an intersubjective level, ethically respond to institutional violence through their own dietary choices. While institutional violence is the focus, the intervention nevertheless will impact intersubjective practices where they connect to this institutional violence of mass killing, not only in relation to the practices of workers whose labour involves killing, but also in the global impact for markets and consumers of a reduced supply of meat.[28] In addition, the project of achieving a truce has the capacity to directly disrupt an epistemic violence. It is the latter prospect that particularly intrigues me. By focusing on the site of the production of killing, and not the site of consumption, we might be able to shift the normalising truths that underpin systemic violence against animals. If we say we want a one day truce in the war against animals, one day without killing, this allows us to underline the fact that even "humane" killing counts as violence, and that a response to this violence, indeed the barest imaginable "ethical" response, is to offer animals a reprieve: "And how could you offer me less: it is so little." A one day truce could thus disrupt the process which allows for death to be the moment at which value is extracted from the animal; against this commodification, the truce would underline that animals have an interest in the value of their own lives as lived, and thus intervene in a process which imposes an equivalence for the animal between life and death, since this imposed equivalent value assumes that animals have no interest in continuing to live. This strategy allows us to shift the apparent truths of the animal industrial complex, and pry the advocacy gaze away from an obsessive focus on individual ethics, and towards the institutional and epistemic challenge of system violence.

---

28 Naturally, the strategy, even as a thought experiment, seems immensely ambitious to imagine. Even if a group of activists were to achieve a truce in some killing centres in one region of the world, how would these activists prevent another region of the world increasing production to meet this shortfall, through globalised supply links? How might we prevent capitalist production processes and markets from acting to sabotage this movement; for example, by threatening the jobs of workers through the extortionate possibility of capital flight? Again we must be aware of the potential racialised elements in how a campaign might be assembled. How might we prevent forms of Orientalising discourse shaping the intervention, particularly if, for example, the one day truce is taken up by Western activists but not identified as a strategy by non Western activists?

What strategies would be required to achieve a truce? I ask this aware of alternative forms of organising that are occurring elsewhere, which focus on building alliances and avoiding reforms that merely substitute one hierarchy for another by redirecting institutional violence at new targets. In particular I draw attention here to the perspective offered by Dean Spade, who has argued for the need for an alliance politics which links apparently disparate groups through their shared experience of State violence. Referring to the work of the Sylvia Rivera Law Project on the policing of undocumented migrants and the impact this has for trans immigrants, Spade observes:

> Anti-immigrant sentiment was the primary motivation for these policies, though some nonimmigrant vulnerable populations have been harmed as well, and demands change from a place of shared struggle and collective analysis. Working in coalitions of groups affected by immigration enforcement, poverty, criminalization, housing insecurity, and other key sites of the maldistribution of life chances, we can aim to have no one's messaging contribute to scapegoating another vulnerable population.[29]

Spade goes on to point out that the challenge is to always try to situate political demands for change within a wider context that is cognisant of multiple violences:

> At all times, attention to how work is being done, how it interacts with the broader context of neoliberal trends (surveillance, abandonment of the poor, criminalization, cooption), and whether it can impact trans survival is required.[30]

Taking this perspective in mind, can we imagine a different style of politics that might be needed to affect a truce in our war against animals? One strategy must surely be to focus on workers who are directly involved in the process of killing. There has been an increased attention on the conditions of labour faced by human operators within slaughterhouses, including the use of low wage precarious labour and the relatively high rates of injury and trauma that are endemic to the industry: indeed, the non government organisation Human Rights Watch goes as far to claim that there "are systematic human

---

29   Spade. *Normal Life*. 159.

30   Spade. *Normal Life*. 160. Spade goes on: "Such an analysis necessitates contextualizing law reform in a set of broader understandings of power and control and with demands for transformation rather than inclusion and recognition."

rights violations embedded in meat and poultry industry employment."[31] Temporary alliances between animal advocates and slaughterhouse workers have occurred,[32] and of course, much information about blatant cruelty and breach of welfare standards within slaughterhouses has originated from alarmed workers themselves. In order to achieve a truce, one day without killing, might we have to explicitly organise with slaughterhouse staff, including migrant and precarious workers and their communities, who are employed within the heart of the animal industrial complex? Might this campaign need to focus both on the violence of killing, and the violence experienced by workers in the killing process? How might we structure the messaging of this campaign, knowing that the human workers will go back to killing after the truce, as there is no other work we will be able to offer them? What alternative type of political engagement might be needed to sustain this sort of allegiance? No doubt achieving a truce would require us to abandon particular modes of engagement, and call for us to invent new ones. Most likely, we will need to suspend an obsessive focus on individual forms of consumption ethics in favour of looking towards the longer-term strategic problem of how we can realistically intervene in the production process of killing animals and reduce animal death. I certainly do not claim here to have a set of easy answers for how we move forward; however, it seems clear that if we are to seriously challenge the intersubjective, institutional and epistemic violence of the war against animals, if we might seek a truce, a different sort of political strategy is required from the prominent modes of engagement that confront us today.

It is in the peace of truce that we can begin the work of imagining what a world beyond the war against animals might look like. Dworkin's suggestion for a truce that might enable a beginning for a "real practice of equality" seems pivotal. For Dworkin does not claim equality as a form of sameness here; she is not arguing that truce will actually provide a material equality. Rather, truce opens the space for the work towards equality as a practice to begin. This goes beyond alterity, understood in the simple sense of acknowledging and

---

31   Human Rights Watch. *Blood, Sweat and Fear: Worker's Rights in* u.s. *Meat and Poultry Plants*. New York: Human Rights Watch, 2004. 2.

32   For example, the Australian Meat Industry Employees Union has publicly supported, with other organisations such as Animals Australia, the end of live animal exports from Australia, although perhaps predictably the industrial focus of this alliance has been in protecting "Australian jobs" rather than in ending this form of work and animal killing. For more on this history of alliance in Australia, see Gonzalo Villanueva. "Mainstream Crusade: How the Animal Rights Movement Boomed." *The Conversation*. November 7, 2012. At: www.theconversation.com/mainstream-crusade-how-the-animal-rights-movement-boomed-10087.

working with difference between entities. Instead, Dworkin's truce is seeking to generate a space for a different sort of ethical relationship that needs not be predetermined by an existing relation of violence. In *Animal Lessons*, Oliver examines the way in which humans rely upon a difference in animals to construct their humanity: "animals function to teach man how to be human."[33] The challenge Oliver points to is how to construct an ethics between different entities, where a relationship of dependence characterises the difference between those same entities:

> It seems that an ethics of difference or alterity is what we need at this point. My analysis here suggests, however, that even an ethics of difference may not be adequate to considering animals. If the recent history of philosophies of alterity are any indication, we can acknowledge difference without also avowing our dependence on animals or including animals in ethical considerations. We can talk about both identity and difference without examining the relationship between them. Perhaps then, we need to move from an ethics of sameness, through an ethics of difference, toward an ethics of relationality and responsivity. Animal ethics requires rethinking identity and difference, by focusing on relationships and response-ability.[34]

The problem Oliver refers to here is, I believe, a version of the same problem I posed at the beginning of this book: namely, how it is that we might construct an ethics in light of sovereignty, and the dangers of constructing ethics after sovereignty. As Oliver points out, highlighting and building an ethics of difference between humans and animals is fraught where we do not acknowledge our relations of dependence with animals, or, as I have argued, our fundamental relationship of sovereignty over animals. Indeed, it is no accident that Oliver points out that "to acknowledge the dependence of *man* and *humanity* on *animal* and *animality* is to undermine man's sense of himself as autonomous and self-sovereign."[35]

Yet, I would probably differ from Oliver on the question of whether sovereignty remains useful as a political tool in ending the war on animals. In *Animal Lessons*, Oliver asks: "Can we imagine a 'free-range' ethics that breaks out of the self-centered, exclusionary, and domineering notions of individuality, identity

---

33   Oliver. *Animal Lessons.* 21.

34   Oliver. *Animal Lessons.* 21.

35   Oliver. *Animal Lessons.* 21.

and sovereignty?"[36] Certainly, by all means, I have argued in this book that the war against animals constructs human rights and pleasures upon the terrain of continuing unpleasure and systemic forms of violence against animals: in this sense, identity and individuality must be put under the spotlight where they are connected with violence. Sovereignty too, understood as a regime of groundless violence, one that stupidly installs a regime of human superiority, must also be challenged. Disarmament of human sovereignty—that is successively seeking to ameliorate and remove sources of human intersubjective, institutional and epistemic violence against animals—must be a goal. My discussion of counter-conduct and truce above are two (and just two) examples of how to unthink human sovereignty. The second challenge, however, appears to involve recognition and responsivity to the possibility of animal sovereignties. As we have seen, with respect to some liberal visions of animal sovereignty, one temptation is to imagine sovereignty only within the tradition of political liberalism, and therefore think about sovereignty as belonging to a "people," or owed to those who are "capable," or can demonstrate a link to territory. This limited conceptualisation is likely to only provide sovereign rights to those we imagine as similar to ourselves—great apes, for example—and will leave human sovereignty intact, through the right to decide who gets sovereign rights and what that sovereignty looks like. In other words, sovereignty in this guise does not seem different from a set of rights awarded under the terms of a treaty, where a victorious party determines the conditions of surrender. However, there does not seem to be any reason why we cannot reinvent sovereignty, and in this sense I remain interested in the concept. If we are to end a war against animals, a war that has been shaped by how humans view themselves, the institutions and political relationships humans maintain, and the stories humans tell about themselves and others, then we are likely to need a radical reimagination of fundamental political concepts, including of sovereignty.[37] As I pointed out in the Introduction, the reworking of sovereignty is already occurring; for example, in Indigenous challenges to Westernised conceptions of

---

36   Oliver. *Animal Lessons*. 305. Referring to Derrida, Oliver refers earlier to an "unconditionality without sovereignty" (137).

37   One speculation I can offer here is whether it might be possible to treat sovereignty as an assembly; that is, rather than regarding sovereignty as a fixed legitimation or authorisation, to suggest that sovereignty might be a mobile and flexible set of legitimations that are contextually constructed. This might provide an analytic tool for understanding how sovereignty is claimed in the here and now, and simultaneously how it might be re-imagined. Puar's reflection on assemblage theory might be useful here: see Jasbir K. Puar. "'I Would Rather be a Cyborg than a Goddess': Becoming-Intersectional in Assemblage Theory." *philoSOPHIA—A Journal of Continental Feminism*. 2.1, 2012. 49–66.

political sovereignty. It is perhaps for this reason I have proposed an investigation of "truce" as a concept, in creating a space where sovereignty might be reworked. The value of a truce is precisely that it begins a negotiation into how former enemies—who are recognised in truce as having some kind of sovereign presence in themselves—will live together. Because the peace of truce is not secured through the victory of one party, terms remain yet to be contested. Negotiation in this space would not occur on the basis of sameness or knowable difference, but through an unknowability.[38] We do not know our enemy, we do not know what threat they pose, we do not know what friendship might look like; we only face our enemy in the space of truce with the knowledge of each other's claim to sovereignty. This space of an exchange of "stupidity" offers a different starting point; equality will not be based on knowledge of the other, but will only arrive through an assumption that the enemy might very well be an equal, with their own reason and action that may be inaccessible to us; a starting point for a practice of equality indeed.

As Derrida has suggested, sovereignty is only based upon a prevailing violence, which makes a claim of superiority after it has prevailed. An epistemic violence that is internalised within this process is the erasure of the capacity for violence of the other; a simultaneous erasure of the possibility that this other may one day prevail over us. Importantly, the epistemic presumption that grounds our use of animals seems to imply that animals have no particular interest in their lives, no will toward self-preservation, and that animals do not resist our utilisation. Both Shukin and Oliver have pointed out the capacity for the animals we dominate to return violence to the human. Shukin points out the way in which the terror of BSE has in some way returned the violence that humans have wrought and circulated an internally destructive logic of capital.[39] Oliver has described the lion tamer Roy Horn, and his experience of the white tiger who "bit back."[40] There are recent works exploring examples of animals actively resisting human utilisation, such as the history of open animal resistance described by Hribal[41] and detailed studies on animal resistance

---

38   Irigaray asks:

> *Peaceful coexistence?* I don't know just what that means. I don't think peaceful coexistence exists. It is the decoy of an economy of power and war. The question we might want to raise instead is this one: even though everything is in place and operating as if there could be nothing but the desire for "sameness," why would there be no desire for "otherness"?

   See Luce Irigaray. "Questions." *This Sex Which Is Not One.* Ithaca: Cornell University Press, 1985. 119–169. 130.

39   See, particularly, "Postscript" in Shukin. *Animal Capital.* 225–32.

40   Oliver. *Animal Lessons.* 2.

41   Hribal. *Fear of the Animal Planet.*

to captivity, such as Traci Warkentin's examination of whale resistance.[42] However, I believe we can expand the archive further here in working to conceptualise how we understand the "truth" of animal resistance, and how intense production systems work actively to mitigate and silence this political agency. Returning to the scenario that began this book—the account of chickens resisting until death human industrialised killing—we might very well begin a project of undoing the epistemic violence of the war against animals by tracking and narrating animal resistance against human sovereignty across all the intense hotspots of the war against animals: in factory farms, in experimental laboratories, at the racecourse, in the suburban backyard. These are surely all examples of animals returning violence to humans, animals attempting to prevail against the arrogance of human sovereignty, examples indeed of animal sovereignties. Narrating these examples might very well rupture epistemic violences, and beckon the prospect of human disarmament. "Thus, I give up the spear!"

---

42   Traci Warkentin. "Whale agency: Affordances and Acts of Resistance in Captive Environments." Sarah E. McFarland and Ryan Hediger Eds. *Animals and Agency: An Interdisciplinary Exploration.* Leiden: Brill, 2009. 23–44.

Index

Acampora, Ralph R.   225
Adams, Carol J.   13, 34, 187, 213
Agamben, Giorgio   x, 25–26, 28, 33, 59, 65,
    74, 80, 85–86, 88, 90, 92, 96, 98, 121, 129,
    131, 134, 139, 144–145, 180, 197, 235, 237,
    248, 253–254, 258, 263–264, 273, 292
Alastair Hunt   vii
Alberts, Paul   vii
Allen, Beverley   180
Allen, Theodore W.   170–171
Allison, Julie A.   180
Amir, Fahim   vii, 13
Anghie, Antony   227
animal industrial complex   1, 15, 74, 82, 85,
    87, 90, 123
animal rights   38, 41
animal welfare   83, 112, 122, 172, 245, 284, 285,
    18, 21, 33, 36, 37–38
Animals Australia   283, 292
Arendt, Hannah   5, 73–74, 89–90, 235, 248, 251
Aristotle   24, 66–70, 75, 130–131, 249, 264
Arlinghaus, R.   43
Armstrong, Susan J.   56
Arneil, Barbara   50
Atterton, Peter   202, 253, 258
Australian Companion Animal Council   200
Australian Meat Industry Employees
    Union   292

Badiou, Alain   26
Bailey, Christiane   vii
Balbones, Salvatore   31
Ballingall, Robert   148
Bartelson, Jens   62, 223, 252
Bataille, Georges   75
Beijing uprising   72
Benjamin, Walter   71, 260
Bentham, Jeremy   42
Berlin, Isaiah   136
Best, Stephen M.   156
Best, Steve   4
biopolitics   x, 24, 27, 59, 66–89 , 94–96,
    120–122, 128–132, 247–248, 264, 274
Birke, Lynda   186
Blum, Deborah   192

Bodin, Jean   255
Botwinick, Aryeh   289
Botzler, Richard G.   56
Bourke, Deirdre   37
Bovine Spongiform Encephalopathy   40–41,
    128, 295
Breckenridge, Jan   180
Brennan, Teresa   148
Brook, Timothy   73
Brown, Wendy   38, 39, 178
Brownmiller, Susan   60, 179, 182–183, 185
Bryson, Norman   179
Burchell, Graham   101–102
Burke, Kelly   284
Butler, Judith   70, 106, 181–182, 185
Bybee, Jay S.   214

Cadava, Eduardo   262
Cadwallader, Jessica Robyn   vii, 39, 119
Cahill, Ann J.   182
Calarco, Matthew   vii, 32, 80, 202, 253,
    258, 279
Campbell, Fiona Kumari   51, 53
Campbell, Karl   124
capitalism   13–14, 136, 161–173, 212
Carlson, David Gray   260
Carmody, Moira   180
Carrion, Victor   124
Carson, Hampton L.   83
Caulfield, Malcolm   27, 37
Cavalieri, Paola   43
Celan, Paul   253
Chappell, Duncan   183
Charter of the United Nations   224, 226, 228
chicken slaughter   3, 11
Chomsky, Noam   254
Chrulew, Matthew   vii, 18, 111
Clancy, Elizabeth A.   56
Clark, Jonathan L.   10
Clark, Stephen R. L.   22
Clausewitz, Carl von   16–19, 87, 130, 199, 200,
    201, 216, 273
Clifford, Michael   104
Clutton-Brock, Juliet   115
Cochrane, Alasdair   29

Coetzee, J.M.   206
Cole, Matthew   18, 110, 116
commodification   60, 159, 166, 168, 211, 290
    fetishism   172
companion animals   28, 55, 61, 200, 204, 208,
    220, 275
Companion Animals Act 1998   203
Connolly, William E.   289
containment   1, 3, 16, 24, 35, 37, 56, 61, 82, 84,
    90, 94, 99, 110, 116, 122, 140, 142, 156, 166,
    186, 192–201, 283
Cooke, S. J.   43
Coppola, Francis Ford   59
Cornell, Drucilla   260
counter-conduct   x, 59, 62, 276, 278, 294
Cox, Richard H.   148, 152, 155
Cruz, Felipe   124
Cubby, Ben   283
curved corrals   11, 199

Dalziell, Jacqueline   vii
Dane, B.   192
Dean, Mitchell   102, 104–108, 120–121
Deckha, Maneesha   285
Defoe, Daniel   257
Deleuze, Gilles   109, 136, 253–254
Derrida, Jacques   4, 8, 13, 20, 23, 26, 30, 62,
    129, 139, 155, 165, 205, 213, 223, 253–270,
    289, 292, 294
Dietz, Thomas   187
Diggles, B. K.   43
disability   40, 42–55, 56–58, 80, 232–233
disarmament   x, 62, 272, 287, 289, 296
Dodsworth, Robert O.   198
Donaldson, Sue   vii, 29–30, 50, 61–62, 223,
    229, 233, 234–248, 249–250, 275, 285
Donlan, C. Josh   124
Donovan, Josephine   187
Dufourmantelle, Anne   255
Durrheim, Kevin   117
Dutkiewicz, Jan   vii, 82, 163
Dworkin, Andrea   62, 287, 289, 292–293

Easteal, Patricia Weiser   180–181
Ellis, John   273
Emel, Jody   200
Esposito, Roberto   25, 60, 129–141, 144, 147,
    148–149, 156, 239, 274
Etcetera, Meta   vii

European Union   127
Evans, Gareth   239
experimentation   6, 10, 14, 23, 38, 82, 86, 123,
    145, 156, 162, 166, 188, 192, 209, 216, 271, 273

factory farms   1–3, 29, 36, 82, 86, 100, 123, 140,
    162, 165, 199, 273, 286
Farmer, Nancy   209
Filmer, Robert   150
Fitzgerald, Amy J.   187
Foer, Jonathan Safran   4
Food and Agriculture Organization of the
    United Nations   1–2
Foucault, Michel   8, 11, 16, 18, 19, 20, 23–26,
    38, 50–53, 58, 59, 66, 70, 73, 74, 87, 90,
    94, 96, 101–102, 103, 105, 108–113,
    119–122, 132, 137, 167, 173, 195, 196, 199,
    201, 215, 252, 255, 264, 276–277, 279,
    280–282, 288
    biopolitics   24–29, 51, 52, 129, 130–132
    discipline   196, 200
    governmentality   59, 101, 109–119, 122, 124
    pastoral power   18, 59–60, 99, 110, 113,
        115, 119
    sovereignty   24–29, 71, 167
    truth   57
    veridiction   58, 281–282
    war   20, 201
Francione, Gary   11, 22, 37–38, 40–42,
    147–148, 150, 156, 158, 211, 274
French, Stanley G.   180
Freud, Sigmund   35, 136

Galtung, Johan   31–32, 34
Garner, Robert   30, 83
Geis, Gilbert   183
Geis, Robley   183
Giannacopoulos, Maria   vii
Gibbs, David   84
Gilna, Ben   84
Girard, Françoise ,   244
Girard, René   141–145
Giuliani, Gaia   vii
Glenn, Cathy B.   57
Goodin, Robert E.   61, 223–228, 239–241,
    256, 275
Gordon, Colin   18–19, 101–102
Grandin, Temple   11
Grewal, Kiran   vii, 184

Griffin, Susan 183
Groce, Nora Ellen   44
Gruen, Lori   15
Guattari, Félix   109, 136

Haraway, Donna   7, 9, 56, 61, 129, 192, 199,
        204–210, 212, 215–216, 219–220, 238
Hardt, Michael   14, 20–21
Harlow, Harry   192, 198, 199
Harlow, Margaret K.   192, 198
Harper, Amie Breeze   285
Hashimoto, Toru   179
Heath, John   98
Hediger, Ryan   218, 296
Hegel, G.W.F.   75–76, 78, 135, 156
Heidegger, Martin   79, 253, 257–259, 261, 263
        Dasein   78, 263
Heilpern, David. M.   181
Hemmer, Helmut   115
Hindess, Barry   105
Hirschmann, Nancy   50
Hobbes, Thomas   20, 73, 84–85, 102, 132–134,
        138–139, 141, 247, 254–255, 274
Holloway, Lewis   18, 84
Homer   67, 131, 147
Hribal, Jason   12, 116, 295
human rights   144, 184, 225, 229, 234–235,
        237, 251, 257, 271, 291, 294
Human Rights Watch   291–292
hunting   7, 123, 271
Hutchins, Robert M.   66–67, 69

Imhoff, Daniel   65
immunity   60, 129–46, 155, 223, 239, 274
In Defence of Animals   6
Ingold, Tim   10–11, 116
International Covenant on Civil and Political
        Rights   224
International Covenant on Economic, Social
        and Cultural Rights   224
interpersonal ethics   31
Irigaray, Luce   70, 99, 295

Jackson, Zakiyyah Iman   vii
Jacobsen, Trudy   21
Jephcott, Edmund   71
Johnson, Harriet McBryde   44
Johnson, Lindgren   285
Judas goat   124

Kafka, Franz   2, 45
Kalechofsky, Roberta   81
Kalof, Linda   187
Kant, Immanuel   90, 208
Kappeler, Susanne   187
Kauffman, Angelica   117
Keal, Paul   21
Keane, John   148
kill cone   2
Kim, Claire Jean   vii, 285
Kojève, Alexandre   75
Kowalczyk, Agnieszka   13
Kymlicka, Will   vii, 29–30, 50, 61–62, 223,
        229, 233, 234–248–250, 275, 285

Lacan, Jacques   165, 253, 255, 261
Latham, Megan   180
Latour, Bruno   140, 197
Law, John   205
Lawrence, D.H.   253
Lee, Paula   285
Levinas, Emmanuel   202, 217
Linneaus, Carolus   76
live animal exports   287, 292
Livy   179–180
Locke, John   21, 41, 51, 60, 62, 134, 137,
        147–155, 157–159, 173, 177–178, 191–192,
        211, 223, 252, 263, 274
Luke, Brian   187

Machiavelli, Niccolò   255
MacKinnon, Catharine   12, 15, 178, 180,
        183–184
Macleod, Catriona   117
Macpherson, C.B.   148
Marcus, Sharon   185
Marks, Jonathan   44
Marvin, Garry   6
Marx, Karl   97, 158–161, 164, 165, 168, 170–173,
        178, 211, 219, 60
Massumi, Brian   146
Mbembe, Achille   25, 34–35, 46–47, 58, 65,
        87–89, 91, 107, 128, 177, 179, 187–190,
        194, 274
        necropolitics   94
        privatised government   192
McFarland, Sarah E.   296
McFarlane, Craig   119
McKay, Robert   vii, 128

McKinney, William T.   198
McLennen, Chris   284
McWhorter, Ladelle   53
Melville, Herman   252, 265–269, 271
Meyes, Christopher   111, 115, 121–122
Mezzadra, Sandro   13
Mikdashi, Maya   285
Miller, Peter   101–102, 114
Mills, David   196
Mitropoulos, Angela   vii, 172
Mood, Alison   6
Morris, Carol   18, 84
Murray, Samantha   104

Negri, Antonio   14, 20–21, 131
Neilson, Brett   vii
Ness, Immanuel   13
New South Wales Food Authority   284
Nicoll, Charles, S.   192
Nicoll, Fiona   vii, 107
Noske, Barbara   1, 3, 14–15, 27, 35, 82, 100,
      114–116, 162
Nozick, Robert   115, 148
NSW Department of Primary Industries   124
Nussbaum, Martha C.   229–234

Office of the Assistant Attorney General
      (United States)   214
Oliver, Kelly   8, 80, 293–295
O'Malley, Pat   105
Orend, Brian   16
O'Sullivan, Siobhan   29, 33, 82
Osuri, Goldie   vii

Pachirat, Timothy   23–24, 33, 94, 197
Palmer, Clare   7–8, 10–11, 13, 18, 203, 219, 245
Pandian, Anand   110
Papadopoulos, Dimitris   180
Parker, Kim Ian   148
Parker, Richard   244
Pateman, Carole   61, 148, 224–226, 229,
      239–241, 256, 275
Pateman, Roy   61, 224–229, 239–241, 256, 275
Paterson, Charles   80
patriarchy   8, 30, 60, 148, 182, 218, 242
Pedersen, Helena   vii, 124
People for the Ethical Treatment of Animals   4
Perera, Suvendrini   vii, 21
Petchesky, Rosalind   244

Petrinovich, Lewis   21
Pew Commission   100
Pick, Anat   vii, 106
Planinc, Emma   154
Plato   69–70, 97–99, 102, 104, 138–139
      Thrasymachus   97–99, 112, 114, 117, 261
Plumwood, Val   22, 28, 30, 34–35
Pogge, Thomas   90
Polombo, Lara   vii
Poropat, Peter   181
Porter, Roy   179
Potts, Annie   1–2, 11
poultry shackles   2
Probyn-Rapsey, Fiona   vii, 286–287
property   x, 60, 129–138, 147–156
Puar, Jasbir K.   vii, 218, 285, 294
Public Justice Centre   2
Pugliese, Joseph   vii, 35, 115, 214
Purdy, Laura M.   180

Rabinow, Paul   280
Radford, Mike   83
Ramsay, Fleur   vii
rationality
      and dominion   156, 263, 269
Regan, Tom   39–40, 47–50, 54, 56, 246, 259
Rejali, Darius   vii, 3, 196
relationality   9
resistance   x, xi, 3, 10–17, 29, 34, 59, 87,
      162–163, 167, 213–216, 220, 253, 270, 276,
      278, 282, 295
Rieske, Thomas Viola   vii
Riggs, Damien W.   119
Robinson, Aileen Moreton   38, 237
Rock, Melanie   vii
Rollin, Bernard E.   56
Rollin, Michael D.H.   56
Ronnell, Avital   256
Rose, J.D.   43
Rose, Nikolas   97, 98, 101, 103, 113–114, 117
Rosenberg, Jen   283
Rosenfeld, Michel   260
Rossiter, Penny   vii
Rowan, Andrew N.   56
Russell, Edmund   80

sacrifice   73, 87, 112, 138–146, 209, 259, 262,
      274, 279
Said, Edward   33–34

Salem, D.J. 56
Sampford, Charles 21
Sanbonmatsu, Jon 41
Sankoff, Peter 37–38
Saunders, Glen 124
Sawynok, W. 43
Scarry, Elaine 2–4, 193
Schmitt, Carl 72–73, 253–254, 258, 267
Scott, Joan W. 185
Scruton, Roger 16
Scutt, Joceyln 180
self-preservation 41, 51, 62, 133, 148–156,
    167–168, 246, 265, 274, 295
Sember, Robert 244
Sen, Amartya 229–230
Serres, Michel 14
sexual violence 8, 60, 119, 179–187, 191, 196,
    274, 289
Sharp, Trudy 124
Shaw, Martin 16
Shukin, Nicole 110, 120, 128, 295
Sinclair, Upton 13
Singer, Peter 44–46, 55–56, 83–84, 149, 192,
    228, 253
slaughterhouse 80–82, 94, 106, 108, 124, 128,
    146, 187, 190, 199, 274, 282, 284, 286, 289,
    291–292, 24, 32
slavery 19, 68, 81, 84, 91, 108, 115, 161, 166, 173,
    179, 211, 236
Smith, Adam 164, 172
Sofia, Zoë 193
Sofoulis, Zoë vii
Sovereignty
    and citizenship 247–251
    and pastoral power 114–124
    and regulation of sex and
        reproduction 243–246
    and stupidity 256–257
    animal xi, 268–272, 292–296
    as preceding ethics 22, 37–55
    conceptions of 21–22
    exception 71–4
    human ix, 23, 26, 62, 68, 94,
        117–120, 216–220, 241–246,
        256–272
    privatised 186–192, 204, 218
    Westphalian 61, 224, 226–229, 239–241,
        246, 251–252
Spade, Dean 181, 291

Spivak, Gayatri Chakravorty 33–36, 164,
    166, 284
Srinivasan, Krithika vii
Stanescu, James 106
Stanescu, Vasile vii
Steel, Karl 9, 145, 270
Stevens, E. D. 43
Stoltenburg, John 178
Stotzer, Rebecca L. 181
Stuart, Donna 181, 183
stupidity 57, 101, 251, 256–257, 275,
    282, 295
Sullivan, Christine 217
Sun Tzu 193–194
Sundström, Per 44
Suomi, S.J. 192, 198

Tabuchi, Hiroko 179
Tacitus 143
Taylor, Chloë vii, 18, 54, 103, 106, 280
Taylor, Nik 10, 14
Taylor, Sunaura 52
Teays, Wanda 180
Tedmanson, Deirdre vii, 52, 244
Tepper, Rachel 140
Thakur, Ramesh 21
Tietz, Jeff 65
Titian 79
Tolstoy, Leo 1
Tomasell, Sylvana 180
torture 2–3, 29, 59, 80, 106, 161, 184, 186, 193,
    196, 214–216, 224, 257, 274
Tovey, Josephine 283
Tremain, Shelley, , 51, 53
truce x, 8, 62, 276, 290, 293
Tsianos, Vassilis 180
Twine, Richard vii, 1, 10, 14, 18, 82
Tyler, Tom vii, 35, 225

Uexküll, Jakob von 77
United Kingdom Department for
    Environment, Food and Rural Affairs 128

Valéry, Paul 253
Van der Kloot, W.G. 192
veganism x, 31, 206, 280, 285
vertical chamber apparatus 192, 199
Veyne, Paul 97
Villanueva, Gonzalo 292

violence
   epistemic   9, 27, 33–36, 52, 54, 144, 178,
      185, 215, 219, 223, 251, 273, 281, 287, 290,
      294–296
   institutional   31–33, 177, 219, 282,
      289–290, 292
   intersubjective   30–31, 278–282, 290

Wacquant, Loïc   216–217
Wadiwel, Dinesh Joseph   vii, 12, 27, 52, 244
Walcott, C.   192
war
   against animals   3–24
   and biopolitics   24–29
   and containment   193–5, 198–201
   and immunity   138–141
   and slavery   173
   and truce   287–289
   definition   16–17
Warkentin, Traci   296

Watson, Irene   21
Webster, John   21–22, 37, 123, 172, 241
Weisberg, Zipporah   206, 215
Weisburg, Robert   196
Weizmann, Eyal   93
White, Steven   37–38
Williams, Anna   15–16, 123
Wolch, Jennifer   200
Wolfe, Cary   26–30, 44, 55, 59, 282
Wolin, Sheldon   289
Woodford, James   128
Wrightsman, Lawrence S.   180
Wynne, C. D. L.   43

Xenos, Nicholas   289

Žižek, Slavoj   26
Zola, Emile   95
Zubaydah, Abu   214